■ Visions and Heat

■ Visions and Heat:

The Making of
the Indonesian Revolution

William H. Frederick

Ohio University Press
Athens

Library of Congress Cataloging-in-Publication Data

Frederick, William H.
  Visions and heat.

  Bibliography: p.
  Includes index.
  1. Surabaya (Indonesia)—History. 2. Surabaya (Indonesia)—
Social conditions. 3. Indonesia—History—Revolution, 1945-
1949—Social aspects. I. Title.
DS646.29.S8F74   1988   959.8′2   88-25339
ISBN 0-8214-0905-0
ISBN 0-8214-0906-9 (pbk.)

Ohio University Press books are printed
on acid-free paper. ∞

For Muriel,
Anita and Jason

Kian jauh aku pergi,
Kian banyak yang kulihat
Kian tinggi kuhargai milik sendiri
Yang tersia-sia tak dirawat.

Ajip Rosidi

■ Contents

■ Preface

How do we seize the past? How do we seize the foreign past? We read, we learn, we ask, we remember, we are humble; and then a casual detail shifts everything.

Julian Barnes, *Flaubert's Parrot*

The Indonesian national revolution (August 1945 to December 1949) is one of the contemporary world's great revolutions, and as such has yet to receive its scholarly due. The diversity of the archipelago and its responses to revolutionary times, the competition for attention between the struggle with the Dutch and the struggle for a new internal order, and the extraordinary political and social intricacies of this revolution have made both access and interpretation difficult. These attributes have also contributed to the revolution's reputation as having been less than successful, despite the fact that freedom from colonial rule was won, and a remarkable degree of national unity achieved, in the comparatively short period of slightly more than four years.

The dominant Western view of the Indonesian revolution may be fairly described as heavily focused on politics at the national and international levels, on the separation between what have been termed the "national" and "social" revolutions nestled within the larger phenomenon, on the events of the first year of the period (the "physical revolution"), and on the rise and role of Indonesian youth—the *pemuda*—in giving birth to the revolution and the spirit of a new age. Understandably, heavy emphasis has been placed on the sharp break which the revolution appears to have represented in Indonesian life, and on the general sense that the nature and pace of an originally pemuda-generated change were killed, or at least curbed, by an opposing older generation, to whom eventually fell the responsibility for guiding the independent Indonesian nation.

When, as a graduate student, I began the research on which this book is based, my intent was to carry this view or something very much like it forward in a study of the revolution as it was played out in a single locale. This was to be the city of Surabaya, which many spoke of as the birthplace of the revolution, and which I had had the opportunity to visit in early 1964. I recall being impressed with the story of Heroes' Day, commemorating the battle of 10 November 1945 which had brought Surabaya and the Indonesian struggle for independence to the attention of the world, and seeing many ways in which that event could support the sort of local history gradually taking shape in my mind. At the time, students of Southeast Asia evinced great interest in what was loosely referred to as "social history." Partly as a result of my meeting with several Surabayans who played significant roles in the revolution, including Ruslan Abdulgani, I came to believe that it might also be possible to emphasize this aspect of the story by tracing the personal histories of some principal characters in such a way as to shed light on the shifting social ideas and relationships of the period. The project grew as I discovered that no study of Surabaya in 1945 in the sort of depth I thought desirable yet existed. The discovery of rich archival and newspaper sources on Surabaya in the Netherlands and Indonesia seemed to confirm the rightness of my choice.

Rather early in my reading I came to understand what perhaps should have been obvious from the start: that Heroes' Day was in many respects an anticlimax to events of late October 1945, not only because of the Indonesian victory over British troops at that time, but because of the dramatic coalescence of Indonesian social and political forces which appeared to produce it. Accordingly, I turned to this turbulent earlier period as the one of greatest interest and clearest potential for illustrating the points I had planned. Only after leafing through a great many Dutch diaries and Indonesian newspapers covering Surabayan affairs from close up did I become aware of what seemed at first a trivial piece of information: the public transportation, electrical, and water supply systems of the city did not cease functioning during even the most critical days before November 10, and stopped only when the British attack and the Indonesian response to it proved so destructive that city life came to a virtual standstill.

This detail brought me to look at my material in a rather different light. My tendency to emphasize change gave way to a search for threads of continuity, my highlighting of upheaval faded as the persistence of order and of sets of ideas stubbornly shone through, and the chronological limits I had set for myself soon broadened considerably. Was it possible that the pemuda could most accurately be seen in some way other than as the products of a sudden transformation, or as the primary authors of the new age of Indonesian independence? Could it be that the convenient periodization schemes which emphasized definitive breaks in Indonesian history at 1942 and 1945 hid significant social and intellectual continuities? Was the tumultuous, even cataclysmic, characterization of the Japanese occupation of Indonesia—found in Indonesian as well as Western works—accurate? And if it was not, then what could be said about the significance of that period as a prelude to the Indonesian revolution? From the perspective of social history, if earlier interpretations were in one way or another unsatisfactory, how might the birth of Indonesia's struggle for independence be more accurately described? Answering these and similar questions became the principal objective of my research and writing, which quickly took on a revisionist point of view.

This book presents for the first time a detailed description of the nature of several levels of Indonesian society in a single urban locale during not only the all-important early months of the revolution, but the extended period from the last decade of Dutch rule to the surrender of Japanese power. Drawing heavily on oral sources, I have attempted to outline the ways relationships among these levels of society changed over twenty years. The particularly careful examination of pemuda leaders and groups in Surabaya is founded upon, among other materials, a unique run of newspapers for the city in October 1945, as well as extensive interviews (one set obtained only by chance many years after the main research was completed) with all three of the principal youth leaders involved. Finally, the important role of the urban masses—not only in the early days of the revolution but in the long period preceding them as well—is drawn as fully as oral sources and the limited number of printed sources allow; to my knowledge this is the first study to offer such a portrait. Out of these perspectives and the information which, I believe, brings them to life, the goal has been to fashion a coherent, local history of the social aspects of the birth of the Indonesian Revolution.

The prevailing historiographical winds suggest that it might also be wise to note briefly what this study is not. It is not an urban history—that is, not a history of the city of Surabaya—even for the brief period of time under examination. Such a history very much needs to be written, but I have not attempted to do so here, as anyone acquainted with the richness of both the precolonial and colonial periods will recognize immediately. It is also not a political history; I have sought from the beginning to see what lay under and behind political activity, which a number of skillful authors have already discussed. An approach of this sort is, in my view, necessary if the social reality of the politics of the early revolution is to be grasped.

It is perhaps especially important to note that I am fully aware that the material presented here does not adequately represent the political left in Surabayan politics. For reasons which surely can be understood by anyone familiar with contemporary Indonesia, interviewees—particularly *kampung* residents—in that country could not be asked to discuss communism or topics connected with politics of the left without arousing suspicion and even hostility. As a result this study admittedly lacks oral material on these subjects. However, neither archival nor published sources appear to me to offer sufficient grounds (for example, detailed examination of ideas and social background of individuals) on which to discuss communists apart from other urban intellectuals and kampung residents in the larger picture of social change. The "social realities" were much the same for all, and they produced—at least at the time and under the conditions covered here—similar ideas, ideologies notwithstanding. Furthermore, discussions (held after the main body of research for this book was completed) with several persons knowledgeable about and sympathetic to the left in Surabaya appeared to me to support the same view. I am persuaded that for this particular kind of study the comparative lack of specific attention to communism and communists does not constitute a serious flaw; I am also convinced, however, that much serious work on the question of the relative importance of communism and communists—however these may be defined—to Indonesian social history of the 1930s and 1940s remains, and needs, to be done.

Finally, this study is not intended as a microcosmic treatment of the Indonesian Revolution as a whole. It began as and remains an example of local history, the wider context of which is deliberately neglected (and is readily available in general works on the revolution), and the application of which to a broader understanding of the revolution will require much further investigation. If reading these pages brings others to examine once more, and perhaps in a slightly different fashion, the tapestry of Indonesia's revolutionary history, they will have achieved their purpose.

In the long course of preparation through which this book has passed, I have been helped by a great many people and institutions; it is no exaggeration to say that without them this study could not have been completed. The brief mention of names here cannot begin to repay such a debt, and merely indicates some of those to whom I will always be grateful.

The late Harry J. Benda, the late Walter F. Vella, and Robert Van Niel were patient, flexible, and devoted mentors during my years at Yale and the University of Hawaii. Later they were also excellent friends, continuing to combine encouragement and practical criticism in a fashion I found inspiring. George Kanahele first introduced me to the primary materials of the Japanese occupation of Indonesia, which I explored further with the late Mohammad Hatta when that distinguished leader was a Visiting Scholar at the East-West Center in Honolulu. During three years of field work (1969–72), and in subsequent visits to Indonesia, Europe, and Japan, I have had the good fortune to learn from many fellow scholars with similar interests. R. William Liddle and John R. W. Smail have been both good colleagues and valued friends, and have listened helpfully to my troubles and enthusiasms. The late S. L. van der Wal, James Peacock, Rodney de Bruin, Nelis Luhulima, Barbara and Leonard Andaya, Barbara and Ronnie Lee Hatley, Benedict R. O'G. Anderson, Masuda Ato, Kurasawa Aiko, Ruslan Abdulgani, the late Sutomo, Sumarsono, Daniel Doeppers, Sartono Kartodirdjo, Soeri Soeroto, Salim Said, Onghokham, John McGlynn, Heather Sutherland, Willem Remmelink, Anthony J. S. Reid, Saya and Takashi Shiraishi, Jean Taylor, R. S. Karni, Anton Lucas, George Larson, Grant Goodman, and many others shared freely their ideas and experiences, and contributed in a variety of other ways to my research. All have tried to save me from errors large and small, of omission and commission, but I need hardly say that not all will feel they have succeeded. The mistakes and wrongheadedness that remain are mine alone.

Lian The-Mulliner, at Ohio University's Southeast Asia Collection, has provided for a number of years the kind of bibliographic help only the most fortunate of academics can hope to receive. In addition, I owe much to the expertise and patience of the staffs at the following institutions: in the United States: the University of Hawaii's Asia Collection, Cornell University's Echols Collection, the Library of Congress in Washington, D.C., the New York City Public Library, and the Yale University Library; in the Netherlands: the Rijksinstituut voor Oorlogsdocumentatie's Indische Collectie, the Algemeen Rijksarchief, the Koninklijk Instituut voor de Tropen, the Koninklijk Instituut voor Taal-, Land- en Volkenkunde, the Koninklijk Bibliotheek, and the Ministerie voor Buitenlandse Zaken; in

Japan: the Foreign Office Archives, the Diet Library, and the Waseda University Library; in England, the Public Record Office, and the Imperial War Museum; and in Indonesia: the Arsip Nasional Republik Indonesia, the Perpustakaan Museum Pusat (now the Perpustakaan Nasional), the Museum Brawijaya, and the Arsip Kantor Gubernur Jawa Timur.

In all of the locations mentioned above I am also deeply indebted to the dozens of individuals who consented to interviews with me and who spoke freely about past events. The people of Surabaya were especially forthright and cordial in their reception of the idea for this study, and of me personally; the many months I spent in their city were among the most pleasant and meaningful of my life. My assistant in most of the Surabaya interviews, Suparman, managed with seeming effortlessness to be both a warm friend and a skillful employee.

Indispensable financial support for this research came from the University of Hawaii; the National Defense Education Act Titles IV and VI programs; the Fulbright Exchange Program; and Ohio University's Southeast Asia Program, Baker Fund Committee, and University Research Council. The late Harriet Sanders, Hal and Evelyn Henderson, Robert and Barbara Greaves, Heleen Verkade, Jay and Ann Parsons, and Toenggoel and Milly Siagian dispensed all kinds of aid, financial and otherwise, at critical junctures. My students, while distracting me from completing this study as rapidly as I would have liked, have nevertheless forced me to keep a foot in the "real world" and put me periodically on what I imagine to be my intellectual toes, exercise for which I am grateful. Finally, my wife and children, to whom this work is dedicated with much love, have managed to find ways to put up with my mostly uncivilized behavior during the more intense stretches of work on this book, yet retain a sense of humor about academics and their pursuits. This is an attitude I treasure all the more for not always being able to share.

■ Spelling and Citation

■ Spelling

Dutch orthography has undergone gradual change since the 1930s, Indonesian spelling has been altered officially twice since the early revolution, and there are at least two common methods of romanizing Japanese. Under such circumstances, achieving a consistent approach to handling materials that must appear in these languages is at best difficult and bound to please some and displease others. The procedures followed in this book are as follows:

1) Indonesian and Dutch personal names in the text have been left in the original spellings (frequently outdated), unless the bearer is known to have preferred and used a newer form. One exception, however, is Sukarno, who customarily rendered his name "Soekarno" but was known to the world by the modern spelling. Since orthographic changes may now leave the pronunciation of many Indonesian personal names in doubt, the index supplies modern renditions of all old-style names as a guide to the proper spoken form. Japanese names, which generally are written by their bearers in ideographs, have been romanized according to the system used by the most recent Kenkyusha dictionary, regardless of the bearer's preference, and rendered in customary Japanese order, with surname first.

2) Titles of newspapers, periodicals, books, and other published or written materials have been left in the original orthography, regardless of what that may be. This seems necessary in order to assure that readers can correctly identify and locate these items without confusion over transcription.

3) Indonesian place names, where they appear independently in the text and notes, have been spelled in the contemporary Indonesian manner. Exceptions to this are the islands of Java and Sumatra, which are widely known in those spellings and not in their current Indonesian forms of Jawa and Sumatera.

4) Plurals in Indonesian and Japanese are not formed in ways familiar to users of English. Singular forms of nouns in those languages have been used here to indicate both singular and plural

forms, rather than attempting the bastardized form of, for example, *pemudas* as a plural of *pemuda*. The intended meaning should be clear from the context in all cases.

5) Japanese titles and names of organizations have been romanized according to the Kenkyusha system and not according to the hybrid Dutch-Indonesian method generally employed in occupied Indonesia. Diacritical marks used in Japanese have been omitted.

■ Citation

1) Foreign terms are defined and *italicized* at their first appearance in the text; thereafter the reader may consult the glossary for clarification. Similarly, abbreviations or acronyms are often used for organizations or bodies discussed repeatedly in the text; the full name and translation is given at the first appearance, and thereafter the reader is asked to consult the list of abbreviations and acronyms for clarification.

2) Considerations of space have made it necessary to cite materials in shortened form wherever possible. Abbreviations and archival numbers are employed throughout the notes, but complete citations, including titles of numbered archival files, are found in the bibliography. The abbreviated newspaper citations list the date of issue referred to in month-day-year order; where several issues in sequence are cited, the form is month-day/day/day-year.

3) Alphabetization of Indonesian names in, for example, bibliographies and indexes, poses difficult problems for the reader who is unfamiliar with the intricacies of Indonesian culture and language. The procedure followed here is to alphabetize according to the last name of the individual when two or more names exist. Thus, works by the historian Sartono Kartodirdjo are to be found under Kartodirdjo, and by the political figure Doel Arnowo under Arnowo. This does violence to practices followed by some Indonesia specialists, but it is more easily intelligible to the general reader, and is in fact the system increasingly being adopted by Indonesian publishers of biographical dictionaries, who's who compendia, and the like. In order to avoid the awkwardness of citing an Indonesian name that does not readily identify the author, I have used the full name in its customary order throughout the notes.

■ Abbreviations and Acronyms Used in the Text and Notes

AAS   Archief Algemene Secretarie
AKGJT   Archief Kantor Gubernor Jawa Timur (Surabaya)
APG   Archief Procureur Generaal
AR   *Asia Raya*
ARA   Algemeen Rijksarchief (The Hague)
BJERS   *Bewaking van den Japansche Expansie, Residentie Soerabaia*
BKI   *Bijdragen van het Koninklijk Instituut voor Taal-, Land- en Volkenkunde*
BKR   Badan Keamanan Rakyat, People's Security Organization
BMHG   *Bijdragen en Mededelingen van het Historisch Genootschap te Utrecht*
BPAR   Barison Pemuda Asia Raya, Greater East Asia Youth Corps
BPRI   Barisan Pemberontakan Rakyat Indonesia, Forces of the Indonesian People's Rebellion
DPJT   Dewan Pertahanan Jawa Timur, East Java Defense Council
DPRI   Dewan Perjuangan Rakyat Indonesia, Indonesián People's Struggle Council
ELS   Europese Lagerschool, Dutch primary school
ESS   *Encyclopedia of the social sciences*
EWvNI   *Economisch Weekblad voor Nederlandsch-Indië*
GNI   Gedung Nasional Indonesia, the National Building (in Surabaya)
HBS   Hogere Burger School. Dutch High School
HIS   Hollandsch-Inlandsche School, Dutch-language primary school for Indonesians
IM   Indonesia Muda, Young Indonesia
IPO   *Overzicht van de Inlandsche en Maleisch-Chineesche Pers*

Ir.	Insinyur—a Dutch-style engineering degree-holder
JAS	*Journal of Asian Studies*
JPO	Javaansche Padvinders Organisatie, Javanese Scouting Organization
JSEAH	*Journal of Southeast Asian History*
JSEAS	*Journal of Southeast Asian Studies*
KKS	Komite Kontak Sosial, Social Contact Committee
KNI	Komite Nasional Indonesia, Indonesian National Commitee
KNID	Komite Nasional Indonesia Daerah, Regional Indonesian National Committee
KNIK	Komite National Indonesia Kota, Municipal Indonesian National Committee
KNIP	Komite Nasional Indonesian Pusat, Central Indonesian National Committee
KT	*Koloniaal Tijdschrift*
LBD	Luchtbeschermingsdienst, Civil Air Defense Corps
MBZ	Ministerie voor Binnenlandse Zaken
Mr	Mailrapport
Mr.	*Meester*, a Dutch-style law degree-holder
MULO	Meer Uitgebreid Lager Onderwijs, Junior High School
MvK	Ministerie van Koloniën
MvO	Memorie van Overgave
NEFIS	Netherlands Forces Intelligence Service
NGS	*Notulen en gemeentebladen . . . Soerabaia*
NICA	Netherlands Indies Civil Administration
NICJ	*Nederlands-Indië Contra Japan*
NIPV	Nederlands-Indische Padvinders Vereniging, Netherlands East Indies Scouting Association
OBNIB	S. L. van der Wal (ed. and comp.) *Officiële bescheiden betreffende de Nederlands-Indonesische betrekkingen*
PA	*Pacific Affairs*
Parindra	Partai Indonesia Raya, Pan-Indonesian Party
PBI	Partai Bangsa Indonesia, Indonesian Party
Pesindo	Pemuda Sosialis Indonesia, Socialist Youth of Indonesia
Peta	Pembela Tanah Air, Fatherland Defense Forces
PHR	*Pacific Historical Review*
PID	Politieke Inlichtingen Dienst, Political Intelligence Service

PNI	Partai Nasional Indonesia, Nationalist Party
PP	*Pewarta Perniagaan*
PPO	Politiek-politionele Overzicht
PRI	Pemuda Republik Indonesia
PRO	Public Record Office (London)
RAPWI	Recovery of Allied Prisoners of War and Internees
Recomba	Regeeringscommisaris voor Bestuurs-aangelegen-heden, Commissioner for Administrative Affairs
RIPDJ	Indonesia, Kementerian Penerangan; *Republik Indonesia: Propinsi Djawa Timur*
RvOIC	Rijksinstituut voor Oorlogsdocumentatie, Indische Collectie (Amsterdam)
SA	*Soeara Asia*
SDAP	Sociaal-Democratisch Arbeiders Partai, Social Democratic Workers' Party
SH	*Soerabajasch Handelsblad*
SO	*Soeara Oemoem*
SP	*Soeara Parindra*
SPBI	*Soeara Partai Bangsa Indonesia*
SR	*Soeara Rakjat*
SSW	*Sinar Soerya Wirawan*
TKR	Tentara Keamanan Rakyat, People's Security Force
TRIP	Tentara Republik Indonesia Pelajar, Students' Army of the Republic of Indonesia
TSSJ	*Toelichting op de 'Stadsvormingordonnantie Stadsgemeenten Java'*
TvNI	*Tijdschrift voor Nederlandsch-Indië*
TvP	*Tijdschrift voor Parapsychologie*
VBG	*Verhandelingen van het Bataviaasch Genootschap*
VOC	Vrijwillige Oefenings Corps, Volunteer Training Corps (also the initials of the Dutch East India Company)

■ Maps

SOUTHEAST ASIA

Scale: 1"=600mi.

INDONESIA

Jakarta

Bandung

JAVA

Semarang

Solo

Yogyakarta

Surabaya

MADURA

Scale: 1"=100mi.

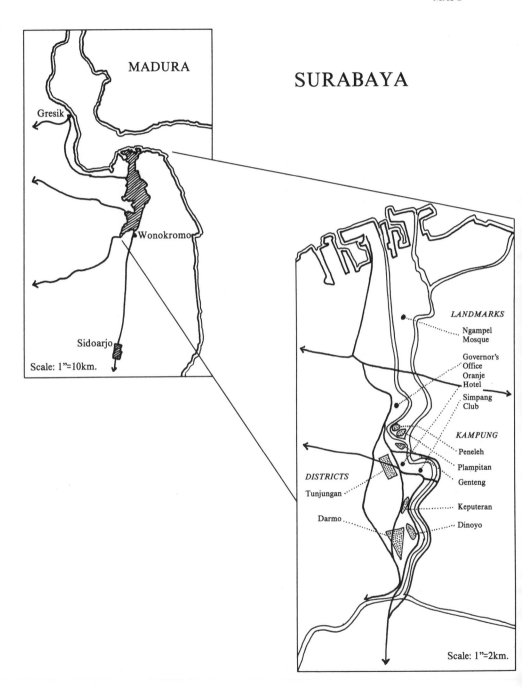

■ Glossary

The language of each term is indicated as follows: (I)=Indonesian, (Jv)=Javanese, (Jp)=Japanese, and (D)=Dutch. Since many Javanese terms have been taken into modern Indonesian, a designation is often rather arbitrary. But the principle followed here has been to mark as Indonesian terms all those of Javanese origin which are commonly used by Indonesian speakers.

aliran (I)	social grouping, usually vertical and dependent on personal relationships
anak bei (Jv)	slang for "anak ngabei," or "child of an aristocrat"; an epithet used of Javanese elite
arek Surabaya (Jv)	the native or "real" Surabayan
asrama (I)	dormitory, live-in training center
azacho (Jp)	lurah, or village head
bapak-anak buah (I)	father-son (relationship)
becak (I)	pedicab
berdiri sendiri (I)	self-help; standing on one's own two feet
bersiap (I)	be at the ready, be on the alert
bersiap-tijd (D)	the tense period of August–November 1945
bokagun (Jp)	fire-fighting corps
bung (I)	colloquial form of address, often with a sense of comradeship and shared revolutionary experience
bupati (I)	regent, administrative head of regency
buruh (I)	labor, worker
buwuhan (Jv)	small gift
cak (Jv)	East Javanese colloquial form of address
camat (I)	sub-district head
carok (Jv)	rural jago, especially one involved in crime

chuo sangi-in (Jp)	Central Advisory Committee
cino (Jv)	a Chinese born in Indonesia, usually of Chinese father and Indonesian mother
den (Jv)	slang form of aristocratic title "raden"
den-bei pentol (Jv)	epithetic form of the two aristocratic titles "raden" and "ngabei," combined with a word referring to the knot on a Javanese headdress for nobles
desa (I)	village
dokar (I)	horse-drawn taxi
durung jowo (Jv)	not (yet) Javanese
fujinkai (Jp)	women's association
fukushuchokan (Jp)	Assistant Resident
gakutotai (Jp)	student defense corps
gamelan (Jv)	traditional Javanese musical ensemble
gang (I)	alleyway
gemeente (D)	literally, "community," but usually given the sense of (Western) municipality
gemeenteraad (D)	municipal council
golongan (I)	common-interest group, social category
gotong-royong (I)	mutual assistance
gua minta (J)	bottomless pit
gun (Jp)	district
guru ngaji (I)	Islamic catechism teacher
gus (Jv)	slang form of aristocratic title "bagus"
haatzaai (D)	sowing of hatred
ideedrager (D)	idea carrier
imam	religious leader
inlandse gemeenten (D)	native or indigenous communities
jago (I)	literally, fighting cock; also used of male neighborhood leaders, bold criminals.
jaman edan (Jv)	time out of joint, era of chaos
jeng (Jv)	honorific form of address
kamajuan (I)	progress
kampung (I)	self-defined Indonesian urban neighborhood
kasar (I)	coarse, direct, outspoken
kaum cukupan (I)	people with somewhat more than enough; middle class
kaum lumayan (I)	moderately well-off people; middle-class
kaum menengah (I)	middle class
kaum menengah atas (I)	upper middle class

kaum terpelajar (I)	educated class; intellectuals
kebupaten (I)	regency
kecamatan (I)	sub-district
kecap (I)	Javanese sweet soy sauce
kedaulatan rakyta (I)	popular sovereignty
keibodan (Jp)	voluntary civilian guard
kekacavan rakyat (I)	mass unrest, disorder
kemajuan (I)	progress
kemenangan akhir (I)	"final victory," used with a variety of meanings, depending on circumstance
kempeiho (Jp)	auxiliary military police
kempeitai (Jp)	military police, often commonly used to indicate police in general
ken (Jp)	regency
kendi (Jv)	clay pitcher for water
kepala sinoman (I)	head of the neighborhood mutual aid association
ketoprak (Jv)	popular dramatic entertainment
kewedanaan (I)	district
kritik (I)	social commentary
kromo (Jv)	the common man
ku (Jp)	village
kutsir (D/I)	word used for dokar drivers
langgar (I)	Moslem prayerhouse
lerok (Jv)	East Javanese entertainment
lingkungan (I)	circle, group
londo (Jv)	Dutch, Dutchman
ludruk (Jv)	urban dramatic form with singing and dancing
lurah (I)	village head
madrasah (I)	Islamic elementary school
maju (I)	modern, progressive
mampu (I)	well-off; potent
man (D)	rough equivalent of British colonial term "boy," used when speaking to ordinary Indonesians
marhaen (I)	the common man (coinage from Sundanese)
massa geest (D)	spirit of the masses
merang (Jv)	paper made of rice-straw
middenstand (D)	middle class
modin (I)	Moslem caller of the faithful to prayer

murba (I)	the common man
ndoro (Jv)	master
nggendong ngindit (J)	equalizing things
ngotakatik (J)	making everything fit
oom (D)	uncle
paman (Jv)	uncle
pangreh praja (Jv)	traditional Javanese administrative corps
pegawai (I)	office worker
pegawai (I)	bureaucrat, administrator, office-worker
pemuda (I)	young man; young activist; freedom fighter
peranakan (I)	a Chinese born in Indonesia, usually of Chinese father and Indonesian mother
pergerakan (I)	the "movement," that is, the prewar movement sympathetic to Indonesian independence
perjuangan (I)	struggle, usually of a physical sort and connected with the revolutionary period
pesantran (I)	Moslem secondary school with a boarding facility
priyayi (Jv)	generally speaking, the elite
puasa (I)	the Moslem fasting month
raad sinoman (I)	neighborhood council
rakyat (I)	the ordinary people; the masses
rakyat jelata (I)	the masses
rampok (I)	pillage, banditry
regentschap (D)	regency
Resident (D)	Dutch colonial official linking Javanese administrative system to the Dutch
romusha (Jp)	literally, "volunteer worker," but often in fact a forced laborer
rukun tetangga (I)	neighborhood association
rust en orde (D)	law and order, peace and order
selamat berjuang (I)	"good luck as you struggle [fight]"
sangi-kai (Jp)	advisory council
saudara (I)	brother; comrade
scholieren (D)	lower-school students
segan (Jv)	combination of aversion and awe, reluctance and attraction
seiji sanyo (Jp)	administrative advising, political participation
seinendan (Jp)	youth association
selamatan (I)	ceremonial, communal meal

selawat (Jv)	small gift
semangat (I)	will; will-power; spirit
sendenbu (Jp)	literally, Department of Information, but perhaps more accurately Propaganda Corps
shiku (Jp)	city precinct
shu (Jp)	residence
shuchokan (Jp)	resident
siap (I)	ready, be prepared; watch out!
sifat (I)	bearing, attitude
singkeh (Jv)	Chinese born in China
sinom (Jv)	youth
sinoman (Jv)	neighborhood mutual aid association
son (Jp)	sub-district
sopir (I)	driver
stadspolitie (D)	municipal police
studenten (D)	better-educated, secondary school pupils
sura ing bhaya (Jv)	"bravery in the face of danger," the motto of the city of Surabaya
teratur (I)	organized; regularized; orderly
tiga jaman (I)	three time periods (colonial, Japanese, and independence)
tokoka (Jp)	special service police, the former PID
tonarigumi (Jp)	neighborhood association
tonarigumicho (Jp)	head of the neighborhood association
tuan (I)	master
tukang (I)	craftsman, specialist in a trade
upas (Jv)	watchman; police
wayang (Jv)	traditional Javanese puppet theater
wedana (I)	district head
wijk (D)	city precinct

■ Chapter One

Surabayans in the Late Colonial Setting

■ Origins and structure of colonial Surabaya

Surabaya as it appeared in the last decades of Dutch colonial rule was the product of a long and complex history. The exact date of the city's establishment is a matter of some dispute, but antecedent settlements may date as early as the tenth century, and a city on the present site is mentioned in inscriptions from the middle of the fourteenth century.[1] The official founding date agreed upon by a group of historians commissioned by the contemporary municipal government is 31 May 1293, with the explanation that an early version of the present name—*sura ing bhaya*, or "bravery in the face of danger"—derives from an episode in which Mongol forces were handed a final defeat by Javanese powers.[2] Whatever the case, the city grew rapidly into a regional capital, rich through its control over rice, manpower, and a variety of trading rights. From the sixteenth to the eighteenth centuries Surabaya, while it struggled stubbornly to retain its independence from Madurese, Central Javanese, and then Dutch forces, continued to play a weighty role in regional affairs of state and to nurture its distinctive artistic styles; it also became associated with rebels of folk-hero stature, such as Trunajaya, Surapati, and Sawunggaling.[3] Over time, the city's reputation for harboring cosmopolitan, headstrong people undoubtedly was embellished, but the characterization of the *arek Surabaya*, the native or "real" Surabayan, as independent-minded and quick to defend himself is an early one that has continued down to the present day.[4]

1

The Dutch, who maintained a presence in Surabaya after the early seventeenth century, did not make a penetrating difference there until the middle of the nineteenth century. In 1835 the city became the site of a major Dutch military installation, causing the old settlement to be razed and forcing its dense population to be resettled.[5] All Javanese, Madurese, Buginese, and other Indonesians were forced to move, while the centrally located parcels of land were reserved for Europeans, Chinese, and some Christianized Indonesians. In place of the earlier, typically Southeast Asian city of wooden buildings arranged in overlapping patterns among trees and streams, arose a new structure of bridges, canals, paved streets, and buildings of brick and stone. Beyond this small area the Indonesians of Surabaya attempted to recreate their former environment and adjust to a flood of newcomers, mostly ordinary laborers from as far away as Rembang, Kediri, and Banyuwangi. Due largely to the opening up of the East Javanese hinterland to the Cultivation System of the Dutch, Surabaya rapidly achieved a position of compelling economic importance. By the end of the century it was the largest city in the Netherlands East Indies, an energetic, if unplanned, tangle of cultural styles and values, in which local tradition jostled for attention with modern technological power and a bustling international trade.[6]

Of the many changes that may be associated with the late nineteenth century, none was clearer or more important than the replacement of an earlier flexibility in ethnic and cultural matters with an increasingly unmistakable—and frequently strident—European rigidity, an ascendancy that bore with it the strains of racism. One potent symbol of this mentality was the Simpang Club, an exclusive Dutch establishment founded in 1887 and later the site of the founding of the Vaderlandse Club, an openly racist and ultranationalist Dutch organization.[7] But it was also reflected in the legal and physical changes Westerners undertook as they redefined the city to suit their purposes and outlook. In 1906, as a result of the so-called decentralization program begun under the Dutch colonial government's Ethical Policy, Surabaya received the designation of *gemeente*, literally "community" but in common parlance "municipality." Despite the Ethical Policy's associationist overtones where indigenous people were concerned, decentralization, and particularly the formation of municipal governments like Surabaya, depended upon the distinct separation of Indonesian and European.[8] The enactments were designed specifically to accommodate and apply to Europeans, giving them control over their local communities[9]; special statutes appeared later to cover what were called "native communities" or *inlandse ge-*

meenten, affirming in some detail the definitive separation between Dutch and Indonesian in the same urban setting. Indonesians were to live within the same municipal boundaries as the Dutch of Surabaya, but were to inhabit different categories of lands from Europeans, were to be taxed differently, judged according to different laws, and administered not by municipal bodies but by the *pangreh praja,* the traditional Javanese administrative corps long ago coopted by the colonial government and directed from a polite distance by a Dutch official known as a Resident.[10] The colonial government, to say nothing of the Dutch in general, did not recognize Indonesians as a genuinely urban people, preferring to think of them as essentially rural folk and leaving them, by the early twentieth century, to be ruled as such though they resided in an obviously urban setting.

Surabaya soon developed physically in ways which neatly expressed this relationship. As the city's population and economic importance grew, the trappings of Western urbanization spread rapidly: a modern harbor, a water purification system, a transportation network of electric tram lines and asphalt roads, and the construction of office buildings for trading companies, banks, agricultural concerns, as well as the colonial government itself.[11] The European population, which by 1926 numbered 24,372 out of a total of 297,495 city residents,[12] acquired large parcels of land for the purpose of building spacious homes and yards in the new colonial style. By the 1930s the city had snaked south along the Kali Mas, a branch of the Brantas River, to the Wonokromo Bridge, where it culminated in the exclusive European quarter of Darmo, known for its ample boulevards, plush homes, airfield, and zoological gardens. Thus, as Europeans placed themselves at a greater figurative and often literal distance from indigenous life, the arek Surabaya were either pushed aside or surrounded. The trend was not entirely new. In the nineteenth century European establishments had occasionally grown around cores of dense Indonesian settlement, though in those days the reverse might just as easily take place.[13] Under the circumstances of greater population pressure and the overwhelming financial power of the European community, however, the balance was altered and urban Indonesians found themselves squeezed into dwindling pockets of land or forced out of central city areas altogether.[14]

While this process lurched forward, partly through the mechanism of municipal purchases of privately owned lands on which Indonesians lived, bringing these residents under direct city administration, the arek Surabaya remained outsiders, or at best hirelings, in the municipal bureaucratic pattern. Surabaya was presided over by a mayor, appointed by the colony's governor-general, and a municipal council, or *gemeenteraad*, of 27 individuals divided unequally along ethnic lines (Europeans retaining a majority) and chosen by an electorate split in the same fashion. In 1940 this electorate amounted to about 21 percent of the Europeans in the city, but no more than 1.5 percent of the Indonesians.[15] The municipal council's actual powers to govern were severely limited. The chamber offered a place for debate and a certain amount of criticism, but these could be muffled when necessary and were of doubtful influence in shaping policy.

The bureaucratic apparatus at the disposal of Surabaya's mayor was large, containing over 20 different departments and employing over 600 workers in 1929; in the same year the city operated on a budget of over f. 18,000,000.[16] Approximately three-quarters of the municipal employees were Indonesian, but in every other respect the city's operations mirrored the degree to which it was dominated by Europeans standards, priorities, and initiatives. The building and repair of roads consumed f. 900,000 in 1929, for example, while in the same year f. 100,000 was devoted to the improvement of city areas inhabited by Indonesians.[17] Many municipal programs, such as those concerned with building centralized openair market places, were initiated to serve European needs and did not, as a rule, exhibit serious concern for the convenience or economic needs of Indonesians. Most municipal laws, and the penalties for breaking them, were intended for the European inhabitants of the city. Codes such as those governing building materials or the vending of food and everyday items were geared to European standards and preferences, and were frequently difficult or impossible for the majority of Indonesians in the city to observe.

In this scheme of things, indeed, Indonesians simply did not count. There was no municipal register or census of Surabaya's indigenous inhabitants, and while a careful headcount of all other ethnic groups was made each year by the city, the number of Indonesians was merely estimated.[18] When, in 1940, this issue was taken up by the municipal council, Indonesians were told that the funds to accomplish the task did not exist. The estimated cost, however, was a mere f. 4,000, a small sum in comparison to the cost of running the municipal council itself, which came to over f. 250,000 annually.[19]

On paper, particularly in the pages of detailed volumes on municipal law and administrative procedure, Surabaya under Dutch rule gave the impression of being a finely tuned bureaucratic engine. In fact, however, it remained an awkward experiment, which had grown without clear models or planning, and which, by the 1930s, had not made appreciable progress toward solving many of the resulting difficulties. The system by which most arek Surabaya lived in the city but were ruled by non-municipal branches of the colonial government was confusing at best, even to the Dutch administrators involved; as we shall see in greater detail later on, it also understandably bewildered and provoked the arek Surabaya. The tensions were felt in every aspect of urban life. Yet there was much about municipal government which was unsatisfactory in the eyes of Dutch residents as well. The municipal bureaucracy was often the target of bitter complaints from all sides that it was both inattentive and inept, and many Dutch residents in the 1930s argued with particular brashness and political divisiveness over whether colonial policy was too protective of Indonesians or not protective enough, especially where political matters were concerned. Even within Surabaya's colonial administration there smoldered controversies on crucial policy issues, many of them involving relations between Europeans and indigenes within the bounds of the city.[20]

A key institution in urban society during the late colonial period, designed to control or at least contain the conflicts within it and to prevent the governmental structure from being weakened by an assortment of pressures, was police power. Beginning in 1919 a regular police force was employed in Surabaya, numbering approximately 1,300 until cutbacks in 1933 reduced it to 950.[21] With the exception of the criminal investigation department, the police were Dutch or Eurasians. Popularly called *stadspolitie* or municipal police, the force was in fact neither paid nor controlled by municipal officials, but by the central colonial government, through its representative the Resident.[22] The mayor of Surabaya was required in theory to obtain permission from the Resident before making use of the police apparatus in any way that departed from normal routine, though in practice police and city officials generally took matters requiring cooperation into their own hands.

Arguably the best known, though least understood, division of the colonial police was the PID (Politieke Inlichtingen Dienst, Political Intelligence Service).[23] This office gathered information for the central government, and was considered to stand somewhat apart from the other branches of the police. Though technically considered to fall within the municipal police hierarchy, the PID had direct access to the colony's attorney general and most of its regular employees did not wear uniforms. By the 1930s, when its work consisted entirely of political surveillance of Dutch, Indonesian, and foreign communities, the PID functioned more as a specialized branch of the pangreh praja than as a police force, especially since it was manned, except at the very highest ranks, entirely by Indonesians, most of whom had pangreh praja training and rank.

The PID enjoyed a formidable, if rather inflated, reputation for knowing everything and being everywhere. This derived in large part from the clandestine aspects of the organization. Although the chief PID officers were easily identified, and the desk-bound investigators and archivists nearly as well known, there existed an extensive network of informants who gathered more detailed and intimate information. In Surabaya there may have been as many as 300 such informants, most of whom were Indonesians of at least moderate education and social standing, making periodic verbal reports to full-time agents[24]; informants' identities were kept secret with remarkable success. Perhaps the most remarkable feature of the PID was the degree to which it was unhampered by legal constraints. No specific statute established the PID or mentioned it by name, and even the central government could not centralize PID operations or bring uniformity to its methods, which often varied greatly from locale to locale.[25] Few clear rules guided PID officers or agents, even in that part of their work which required them to silence and occasionally arrest political activists. Highly subjective criteria were applied according to fluctuating local government opinion, and this left the public with some uncertainty as to what was acceptable and what was not.

Police power was strong enough in the Netherlands East Indies at the end of the 1930s to have elicited the Dutch remark that the colony had become a "police state."[26] The characterization is perhaps overdrawn, especially for Surabaya, which was thought to have a comparatively fair-minded and tolerant police. Most arek Surabaya were not touched directly by the municipal police, who in fact rarely entered Indonesian neighborhoods. But the implicit threat of force and the faint, permeating odor of secrecy were of real significance to the urban setting, conditioning nearly every Indonesian's views of the more immediate and mundane aspects of colonial city life.

■ The arek Surabaya and the gemeente

The arek Surabaya did not comprise a unified social or ethnic group. Newcomers and longtime residents alike were pulled together by an attachment to their particular environment and by a belief that they carried forward a tradition of bravery, realism, and dedication to material advancement.[27] It was said that "real Surabayans" were strong-willed, liked to feel free of social and other obligations, and tended to react violently when pressured; they were also businesslike and hardworking. Vaguely "middle class" in many of their ideals, the arek Surabaya were often "proletarian" by virtue of the types of labor they performed, their lack of economic power in the colonial world, and the vast distance that separated them from both indigenous elites and the favored nonindigenous groups such as Europeans, Chinese, and Arabs. The arek Surabaya might be best characterized as typical of a developing colonial urban proletariat,[28] but at the same time they gained a measure of distinctiveness from local tradition and the special nature of their surroundings.

The average Indonesian in Surabaya inhabited a *kampung*, a sort of self-defined neighborhood. While the same term was used often to designate a small rural settlement, the two were different in a number of important respects. City kampung were larger than their rural counterparts and, even in the eighteenth and nineteenth century, generally far more densely populated. Inhabitants tended to come and go more frequently, and lacked the family ties and close personal relationships which typified the rural settlement. The routine of daily life was also different in the city, as were types of employment, economic ways and means, and much else. Finally, city kampung were often younger and less attached to commonly-held traditions than rural villages, though some customs, such as showing respect for a kampung progenitor, were often retained in one form or another. While there is no satisfactory method for assessing the age of Surabaya's kampung, it seems clear that they were not simple atavisms of pre- or non-urban settlements; they had grown up and developed in a specifically urban context, drawing from it much of their basic character. This evolution began before the nineteenth century, when European influence merely changed but did not create an urban pattern for Indonesians.[29]

Though they may not have entirely understood the changes taking place around them after the mid-nineteenth century, the arek Surabaya recognized their general nature and reacted accordingly. They cannot have missed the implications of the creation of large areas for the exclusive use of Europeans, especially when kampung were encroached upon for this purpose. And when the Dutch founded the gemeente in 1906, popular sentiment connected it with a revolt in the nearby village of Gedangan two years earlier, in which disgruntled villagers from a sugar-growing area declared a holy war on Europeans.[30] The Dutch reaction, it was said, was to establish the municipal government as a tool to separate and protect Europeans from the native population. Strictly speaking this may be called faulty history, but the arek Surabaya's sensitivities did not mislead them regarding the nature of the changing city.

Colonial Surabaya was originally built in large part on illegally acquired kampung lands,[31] a practice which accelerated and was in some senses legalized in the first two decades of the early twentieth century. The result was a growing constriction of Indonesian neighborhoods, and a hardening of kampung boundaries, which then took the form of asphalt roads or concrete buildings or walls. Some kampung found these permanent boundaries protective, but for most they had ill effects. As total kampung area dwindled and population rose, the arek Surabaya came within little more than a generation to live in conditions which were at best crowded and often alarmingly congested.[32] These pressures were responsible for the falling standard of living felt by nearly all of Surabaya's kampung. Although a number of newly established neighborhoods, especially those near the harbor, catered to relatively impoverished newcomers from East Java and Madura, and therefore had low standards to begin with, such was the exception rather than the rule. In kampung of longer standing, fruit trees and gardens made way for additional dwellings; drainage, paving, and repair projects became increasingly difficult to finance; and the intense demand for housing not only raised the cost of building materials but gave landlords little incentive to keep property from deteriorating. Occasionally a kampung was able to resist the worsening conditions with some success, but a downward trend in housing and sanitation standards was noticed throughout Surabaya's Indonesian neighborhoods, and in most a decline in overall welfare accompanied it.[33]

In 1921 the municipal government became aware that increasing numbers of Indonesians were being forced from areas close to Western offices and homes. Concerned that a convenient labor force might dwindle or even disappear, council members decreed that in the future no land development schemes in the city would be permitted unless they provided living space for Indonesians.[34] As a consequence, however, kampung became even more firmly bound by European construction, and even more thickly inhabited than before. Even when the city purchased a particularly overcrowded and troublesome kampung area known as Keputran in 1929, promising to improve it and retain it for Indonesians only, planners could not resist enclosing the parcel with an iron ring of restaurants, shops, hotels, and substantial Dutch and Chinese houses. In addition, the scheme to improve conditions never materialized. Inhabitants were not only required to pay higher taxes under the city than they had under their previous landlord, but many were forcibly displaced.[35] For this the municipal government was never forgiven, and the arek Surabaya of Kampung Keputeran became known for their sullen, recalcitrant attitude and their refusal to obey city laws and officials.[36]

Not all efforts to solve what the Dutch came to call the "kampung question" turned out quite so badly, but much of the kampung improvement program undertaken by the city—not always with great enthusiasm—was disruptive of or insensitive to kampung life, attracting the hostility rather than the gratitude of the arek Surabaya. Although barred by law from involvement in kampung affairs (except in those areas actually purchased by the city), in practice the municipal government interfered whenever it felt like it, generally in matters of health standards and public hygiene, without consulting kampung dwellers. Dutch city officials had difficulty understanding why inoculation against disease or insistence upon particular health and building measures should be resented, but they could not see things from the arek Surabaya's point of view. When municipal officials tried to introduce a piped water supply system to central Surabaya kampung, for example, not only was the new system abused by those who did not know how to use it, but residents objected to paying for water which previously had been obtained free from wells and rivers. Further, the local water-carrying business, which provided income to a number of enterprising Madurese and others, was dealt a severe blow.[37] And when, in an attempt to combat plague and other diseases, the city conducted a notorious rat-killing campaign, kampung dwellers were forced to bear real inconveniences as well as the high cost of repairs according to standards laid down by the city; to make matters worse, Dutch and Eurasian officials carried out the program in the kampung with a condescension so maddening it was remembered clearly more than forty years later.[38]

Nothing, however, made the municipal government as unpopular among kampung dwellers as the tax questions. Indonesians living in areas under the jurisdiction of the central government or private owners (about 70 percent of the arek Surabaya in the late 1920s) paid a percentage of their incomes as tax. In theory and according to the inlandse gemeenten laws, that was the extent of their obligations. In practice, however, the arek Surabaya were subject to a miscellany of exactions from the municipal government, and these were considered unjust impositions made by a foreign, incomprehensible administrative system to which kampung people were subject but did not belong. An annual tag fee for bicycles, for example, and fines levied on

9

riders whose bells and lights did not work properly, were as objectionable as charges for water which previously had been free for the taking. They were also, with some justice, seen as exorbitant, being designed for European rather than kampung pocketbooks. The same thing was true for other municipal fines and levies, such as those collected from salespeople at the marketplace or persons involved in traffic violations. For most kampung dwellers, financial demands of this sort represented an obvious injustice and a serious threat to meager household budgets.

The arek Surabaya thus were increasingly subjected to the forces of a Western colonial order, yet at the same time increasingly prevented from dealing with these forces on anything like equal terms. Predictably, kampung became introverted and their hostility toward the non-Indonesian construction around them solidified. Yet kampung discontent only occasionally found expression in protests or violent outbursts, due perhaps as much to the relative lack of communication among kampung as to the watchfulness of police and pangreh praja. Kampung areas merely simmered, and rightly or wrongly their inhabitants blamed the municipal government for their woes. With their typically bitter humor the arek Surabaya jokingly confused the Dutch word "gemeente" with the Javanese *gua minta*, literally "the cave that begs" but more nearly "the bottomless pit," [39] and reserved for it a rich contempt. It was commonly said that true arek Surabaya would never work for the gemeente, and other Indonesians who did were looked upon as outsiders. Police kept their distance, even the traditionally garbed Javanese *upas* declining to enter kampung except on an emergency. When municipal inspectors came, it was for no more than a short visit.

In the early 1920s general restlessness began to be felt outside kampung boundaries and in the European city. Perhaps because the place of employment, rather than the isolated kampung, was the point at which Dutch and Indonesian worlds came into closest contact, it was there also that a sense of conflict was greatest and the pressure to act most intense. It seems likely, too, that many kampung communities had become so diverse that members had less in common with neighbors than, for example, with workers who shared the same conditions at the workplace or factory. In any case, antagonisms vaguely perceived in the kampung atmosphere tended to acquire clarity and substance in labor disputes outside it. Strikes and protests of importance occurred in 1920, 1921, 1923, and 1925–26. [40] They pitted kampung dwellers, ranging from harbor coolie workers to railroad clerks on the one hand, against Dutch companies and both the municipal and central colonial governments on the other.

The furor and reprisals that followed these actions, all of which failed in their objectives, confirmed the arek Surabaya's place and outlook in the colonial setting. Dutch officials and other residents called for extreme measures and even formed civilian defense groups, while employers dismissed thousands of workers, often for no better reason than that they were suspected of being able to read, and therefore susceptible to "communist" propaganda.[41] The misery at scenes in which police cleared whole kampung of their inhabitants deeply impressed those who saw it, and more than a few young arek Surabaya undoubtedly shared the experience of one kampung boy who was deliberately taken to such a site and instructed on the evils of colonial rule.[42]

In 1931, following a particularly strong outburst of kampung defiance, alarmed city government officials inaugurated a precinct system designed to bring new order to the kampung, within the framework of the gemeente.[43] It was a compromise arrangement which, in fact, continued to keep kampung at arm's length while allowing municipal authorities greater access and control over them than had previously been the case. An attempt was made to choose precinct chiefs from among ordinary kampung residents, but those who took the job (which promised a steady and substantial income) were generally looked upon by neighbors as having betrayed the kampung community. This opinion hardened when kampung residents learned that precinct heads were required to sign oaths of allegiance to the government. In short, the precinct system did not bridge the enormous gap between arek Surabaya and the gemeente. Ironically, and to the consternation of city officials, the system seems not only to have increased kampung dwellers' disdain for the municipality but to have given them the impetus to organize and take action independent of it. In some areas, for example, enterprising arek Surabaya established privately owned or community sponsored kampung defense groups.[44] Activities of this sort were only one facet of the far-reaching changes taking place among the arek Surabaya.

■ The nature of kampung society[45]

By the 1930s the contrast between the kampung and municipal environments reached its peak. Physically the kampung was delineated by the paved street of the European city and was largely sealed off from its traffic and daily routine by walls consisting of the backs of street-facing buildings, connected where necessary with brick or woven bamboo facades. There were several gateways through which bicycles and pedestrians passed in order to reach the narrow, dirt alleyways along which kampung inhabitants lived. Houses, simple and often in poor repair, stood cheek-by-jowl in rows along the alleyways. With the exception of an occasional fruit tree, there was little to soften the harsh exterior presented by these strings of dwellings. The outsider's impression was one of closeness and crowding, of a world built on an entirely different standard from that of the European gemeente: the textures of woven bamboo and whitewashed brickwork contrasted sharply with the concrete, stone, and asphalt surfaces of the city beyond.

Even the calendar of the kampung year proceeded differently from that of the European city. Along the alleyways the year's division into wet and dry seasons was of special significance. Unlike the European city, which was paved and guttered, the kampung was poorly drained; when the rains came, the typical neighborhood was transformed into a sea of mud, and at this time economic differences among the residents were highlighted. The well-off could afford concrete foundations and raised front stoops to prevent rivulets of water from draining off the alleyway into their homes, but families of more modest means had no choice but to put up with months of sodden floors. The kampung year also turned on different holidays. The Moslem fasting month, for example, scarcely altered the daily activities of the larger city, but it was distinctive behind kampung walls. The same was true of other Islamic celebrations, each observed with the particular set of ceremonies by which the arek Surabaya customarily clocked the passing of the seasons. Conversely, the significance of European holidays faded abruptly at the kampung gates. In the case of the Dutch queen's birthday, the gay decorations strung on the street side of the kampung entrance according to colonial custom indicated the limits of the celebration and not, as many Dutch undoubtedly believed, its inclusion in kampung life.

The kampung world, though watched by colonial officials from a distance, was scarcely penetrated, and certainly not guided, by them; the actual hand of government rarely was seen or felt. The most apparent symbols of kampung independence were the individual guardhouses located near the gateways by the main streets. These were manned by volunteers from dusk to dawn, a locally maintained system of protection and traffic control. Even informal links between the kampung business world and the markets of the city, common at the turn of the century, had all but disappeared by the 1930s.[46]

Dutch opinion held the kampung to be stagnant socially and both backward and undifferentiated economically, little more than a misplaced or deteriorating village,[47] a view that was doubtless encouraged by Dutch separation from the kampung. Such notions were mistaken, however. The kampung world of the arek Surabaya was complex and far from static, either socially or economically, and although generalizations may be made about it, there were in fact many such worlds, each more or less distinct from the next. Even the term "kampung," as it figured in everyday use, usually referred not to an entire named area but to a specific alleyway, reflecting the restricted nature of the arek Surabaya's perspective. In the late colonial period, most kampung inhabitants' lives were tied to a narrow, distinctive environment that sometimes measured no more than 10 or 20 by 100 yards.

Individual kampung were identifiable primarily by their age, location, and economic well-being. These aspects were interrelated, and generally speaking kampung with origins in the late eighteenth or early nineteenth century and a location near the city's center tended to house residents of above average education and income. Somewhat ironically, given the arek Surabaya's general outlook on the colonial government, proximity to Dutch employment and modern schooling was a major factor in determining the popularly recognized "better quality" of these neighborhoods. Community spirit and the degree to which inhabitants were reputed to be well-settled and reliable also played a role. Kampung at the edge of the city tended to have more mobile inhabitants, most of whom moved further into the city when they could afford to do so. These kampung suffered materially from being far removed from the income of good jobs, mostly those with Dutch firms and households, or the government. Constructed largely of bamboo and cast-off materials, they had a temporary appearance entirely different from the more substantial architecture of better-situated kampung, though they often had the luxury of space for gardens and a few fruit trees.

But the kampung of Surabaya had personalities that stretched beyond the boundaries imposed by geography and material standards. Frequently these rested upon ethnic identification, and although there was some mixing of ethnic groups, neighborhoods tended to be known by the language or cultural affinities of the majority of their inhabitants. In varying degrees these were viewed as close to or far from the Surabayan norm. Ambonese and Menadonese areas were, like their inhabitants, characterized simply as *londo*, or Dutch, and considered to be somewhat beyond the pale. Madurese kampung, like that people, were thought to be necessarily separate from Javanese Surabayans, but at the same time worthy of respect. Other Indonesian groups posed more subtle problems because they seldom lent a specific character to a given kampung. For example, most Sumatrans, unlike other Outer Islanders, were considered to be "real kampung people" and could blend reasonably well into kampung society. In a similar fashion the Central Javanese, for whom the arek Surabaya frequently reserved a special churlishness, nevertheless found it possible to settle comfortably in mixed kampung. As a rule, neighborhoods at the city's center and on its further edges tended to show the greatest ethnic variety, those in between often being typified as more purely Surabayan.

Religious beliefs and practices also were important in determining a kampung's character. There was not only a difference between, for instance, a Buddhist Javanese kampung (of which several existed in Surabaya) and a Moslem Javanese one, but a series of less obvious gradations of Moslem neighborhoods ranging from extremely devout to relatively open, flexible, and only nominally observant of Islamic practices. Individual kampung retained their religious bearings even when surrounding neighborhoods were quite different. It was not unusual for a kampung identity of this type to be reinforced by a variety of customs practiced exclusively by residents, and some even had burial grounds reserved for their residents only. Nor was it uncommon for a specific alleyway within a kampung area to have its own special identity, frequently connected with religious beliefs or local custom. One well-known example was *gang* (alleyway) number eight in Kampung Plampitan. Though the neighborhood as a whole was widely considered to be progressive and even unorthodox in religious matters, a Gang 8 legend proscribed, in devout Moslem fashion but in this case more for superstitious than religious reasons, the playing of all percussion instruments and *gamelan*, the traditional Javanese musical ensemble.[48] Such customs functioned as strong threads which bound urban minisocieties together.

A number of Indonesian movements seeking in one way or another to link Surabaya's kampung came to the fore in the early 1920s, but they were not especially effective. In addition to attempts at organizing labor, there were efforts on the part of Moslem reformist groups such as Muhammadiyah, Nahdlatul Ulama, and Al-Irsyad to convert whole kampung to their way of thinking and then to link these neighborhoods together under their leadership. The competition took place in the heart of kampung Surabaya, where, for example, interpretations of the Koran were argued and the relative merit of certain kampung burial practices hotly debated. Kampung residents remember the period as one of ferment, but in the long run the arek Surabaya preferred home-grown unorthodoxies to ideas and associations tied to the outside world, whether Dutch or Indonesian.

Though there were exceptions, religious belief in most kampung—even those described as devout—was to one degree or another syncretic. Whatever reputation a kampung might have in religious affairs as far as the outside world was concerned, internally there was an understanding that residents were entitled to their own notions. Harmony was more important than religious conformity, and a realistic religious tolerance usually prevailed. Within kampung walls, those with "different ideas" caused relatively little stir. Even when, as occasionally happened, religious debate crossed kampung bounds, it almost always did so under individual auspices. In such form it was, if not completely acceptable, at least not permanently disruptive. In one such incident, Achmad Djais, a tailor from Kampung Plampitan who had joined the Muhammadiyah, was attending prayers in the neighboring and rather more conservative kampung of Peneleh.[49] Suddenly he pulled out a red handkerchief (the color was a symbol of radicalism, not necessarily communist but of any kind) and, waving it above his head, shouted demands that the sermon not be given in Arabic but in plain Javanese so the congregation might understand it. The outburst caused a momentary uproar, but despite Achmad Djais's association with Muhammadiyah his action was considered individually motivated and taken in stride. Even outside of his own kampung, the arek Surabaya expected and exercised a good deal of freedom of expression.

If a kampung did happen to become identified with any particular religious outlook or organization, it was often because the neighborhood *imam* (religious leader) or *modin* (caller to prayer) was influenced in that direction and gave his sermons or advice a particular twist. The arek Surabaya commonly spoke of "being Nahdlatul Ulama" or "being Muhammadiyah"; what this usually meant in practice was that the neighborhood *langgar* or prayerhouse was associated through its official with the group named, not that a huge conversion had taken place. Less frequently, one or more prominent kampung residents might set the tone for the rest of the neighborhood, and "conversions" might take place on the basis of little more than a desire to follow the prevailing current or put on the appearance of kampung unity. No serious alterations of belief were necessarily involved, and the fundamental nature of the kampung and the ideas of its people remained largely intact.

A similar pattern was followed when, somewhat later, secular political organizations entered Surabaya's kampung seeking support. The majority of residents understood little about the issues raised and held only vague or incomplete notions of what local political elites hoped to get across to them. Even for the moderately educated kampung members, ideological matters and the like were in any case of little significance when alliances were considered. Neighbors' preferences and the general outlook of the kampung community often carried greater weight than any strong individual feelings. Beyond whatever stance one adopted publicly, however, there was always room for personal opinions and actions. Not infrequently, indeed, kampung dwellers who developed an interest in political and organizational activities might belong to two or more parties or groups, competitive with or even opposed to one another, in order to satisfy both neighborhood and individual needs.[50] In this fashion the power of place and community in kampung life continued little diminished, while at the same time the winds of change continued to blow.

Change in the kampung world of the 1930s was a complex and, even to the arek Surabaya themselves, only partially visible process. The Dutch had no meaningful grasp of the kampung's real nature. The Indonesian elite, who even at the height of their interest in the *rakyat* (the ordinary people or, loosely, the masses) seldom rid themselves of the feeling that kampung life lacked refinement, were in this and other ways prevented from understanding the vital forces at work in the city's Indonesian neighborhoods. To these eyes, kampung social contours and internal mutations remained hidden.

Despite their undeniable individuality, most Indonesian neighborhoods in Surabaya shared a number of important characteristics. To begin with, kampung were neither stagnant nor without a certain dynamism. The kampung population always contained a sizable transient population, and even in the most settled neighborhoods houses went up for sale or rent as old residents moved elsewhere and new people entered. Often newcomers found themselves in Surabaya by chance and hoped to improve their fortunes by entering a new line of work there. Sailors for commercial shipping lines, for example, not infrequently quit their jobs and attempted to settle into different, land-bound existences as auto mechanics, clerks, and so forth. They and others like them entered kampung life, sometimes permanently and sometimes not.

In every neighborhood there was also a discernible ebb and flow of residents from more ordinary occupations and from geographic locations closer to hand. A young East Javanese came to the city to join the colonial navy; a school teacher from West Java arrived seeking anonymity and new surroundings after a brief political involvement and scrape with the PID; a Central Javanese, trained as a bookkeeper in a regency office, came to search for the sort of position in a Dutch firm that would give him more freedom and at least some financial security.[51] They all entered kampung life, as often as not shifting and moving from one location to the next as finances and other considerations changed. Alongside this movement of residents, there was also the daily pattern of commercial traffic—bringing hawkers of food, kitchen utensils, religious wares, and much else through the gateways— to lend further energy to the kampung scene.

Kampung society cannot accurately be described as dully egalitarian or undifferentiated, for it exhibited great variations as well as internal tensions. One source of unevenness was the presence of foreigners: Eurasians, Chinese, and very occasionally Arabs or Indians. Hostile feelings toward them were common among the arek Surabaya as well as among Indonesians of other origins, and although displays of prejudice generally were kept in check they nevertheless tingled beneath the surface of daily life. Mothers warned their children of the *singkeh* (old-fashioned Chinese, born in China) or the slippery *cino* (as used then, a *peranakan*, or Chinese born in Indonesia, usually of an Indonesia mother), and frightened them into good behavior with threats about ill-intentioned Dutchmen, from whom Eurasians were seldom differentiated. These attitudes were frequently exacerbated by differences in economic and legal standing between foreigners and arek Surabaya. In general, kampung folk considered the multiracial nature of their communities to be a source of instability and concern, a condition which they would change were it possible for them to do so.

More important, if less immediately apparent to outsiders, was the considerable variance in status among Indonesian kampung residents. Some neighborhoods located close to large Dutch industries showed a rather equal income distribution, but as a general rule every kampung in the city could point to a wide scale of incomes among its inhabitants. A well-paid coolie laborer earned one-third to one-quarter the wages of a skilled craftsman such as a carpenter or metal smith, but the two might live adjacent to each other in similar dwellings; two factory workers with the same level of skills and training might find that their incomes differed as much as 300–400 percent, depending on the firm that employed them.[52] Beyond the simple test of fortune, more subtle criteria of social standing existed: Did the individual possess community spirit? Hold a government job? Have any education? Have first-hand knowledge of the world beyond the kampung, Surabaya, or even Java? Have his own business? These and other factors were part of the manner in which kampung residents judged each other. Despite a strong kampung ethic minimizing the effects such differences might have upon harmonious relations among residents, individual distinctions were everywhere recognized, discussed, and thought to be of significance.

The mechanism which, like a social keel, kept the kampung community on a steady course was known as the *sinoman*. It was neither a leveler of differences nor the core of a self-conscious communalism, but it did bring neighbors together in an organization that was both functional and comforting because it symbolized tradition and a sense of commonality. Though its name is derived from the Javanese *sinom*, or youth, and may have been used to refer to a similar community organization as early as the fourteenth century,[53] the sinoman of Surabaya in the 1930s were not centered upon the younger kampung residents. The organizations were for the most part in the hands of middle-aged, experienced men, and called for participation on a family basis. There was some feeling in kampung society that the sinoman, as the legacy of earlier residents or perhaps even the founder of the kampung, was permanent and unalterable,[54] but it is clear that this kampung institution had been weak and strong, attended to and neglected, according to changing circumstances over a long period of time. The sinoman was a device which served a social purpose, without being either a relic or a simple preservative.

The sinoman operated in a single kampung area, which might include as many as 400 or 500 families living on several alleyways, or as few as 50 or 60 along a single one.[55] Members were those considered to be "true residents" of the kampung, generally limited to Moslem Javanese (and occasionally other Indonesians) of non-elite status. Foreigners and Christians were never included in the sinoman, and upper class Indonesians—persons of aristocratic descent, those with extensive Western education, and the like—were considered marginal at best to the organization and its activity. Rather than creating instability, the exclusiveness inherent in the sinoman probably did much to achieve a kind of balance of power in the kampung and to give the average urban Indonesian some protection from or counterweight against privileged groups in the colonial order.

The sinoman embodied a number of social principles that arek Surabaya held dear: the right of individuals to speak out frankly among

18

peers; the desirability of neighbors, no matter how individualistically inclined, joining together on important occasions; and the fundamental dignity, even equality, of every kampung resident within the social context of the neighborhood community. The head of the group, called the *kepala sinoman*, was chosen popularly, less on the basis of wealth or other prominence than on ability to mix with all types of people and to "understand social matters," or *mengetahui kemasyarakatan*.[56] Neither this leader nor his assistants, who were chosen in similar fashion, served for pay, and they were replaced periodically so that no single person or small coterie carried the burden for long. Like the sinoman itself, leadership within the organization was not permitted to become rigidly institutionalized.

In some kampung, particularly those far from the center of the city and recently established, the sinoman appears to have taken on the duties of a governing body, with the sinoman head often behaving much like a government-appointed official.[57] This, however, was an aberration. The sinoman's proper and usual function was as a mutual assistance (*gotong-royong*) association that focused its attention on providing community assistance on special occasions such as funerals and weddings. The sinoman managed funds built up from small monthly dues collected from all members, and oversaw the use of commonly owned equipment needed in various ceremonies, such as those associated with religious holidays, weddings, funerals, and the like. These events, which otherwise required enormous expenditures from individual families, were thus subsidized by collective effort over a period of time. The sinoman guided this form of group security and assured its continuation along with that of many other customs, such as the exchange of small gifts (*selawat, buwuhan*) among kampung residents.

In most kampung the sinoman was associated closely with religious life. Frequently the organization had its headquarters in the neighborhood prayerhouse and held meetings there before or after evening prayers. Because the sinoman required members to be Moslem, it outwardly gave the appearance of being a religious auxiliary group. But in kampung eyes the business of the sinoman and that of prayerhouse officials were quite separate. While the modin, for example, traditionally collected and redistributed alms on certain holidays, he had nothing whatever to do with the arrangement of the customary communal meal on Mohammed's birthday. The planning of this event required a very fine sense of tact and intimate knowledge of the financial capabilities of every resident; it was a matter of community action, whereas alms-giving was between the individual and

God. Additionally, the communal meal was in the form of a pre-Islamic *selamatan* ritual, and its maintenance by the arek Surabaya is a good example of the way in which the sinoman protected tradition.

On the whole, the power of the sinoman was greater than any other kampung force. Individuals who were not religious and rarely visited the prayerhouse were nevertheless careful about fulfilling their responsibilities to the sinoman. Especially since social status and reputation were involved, few families failed to take seriously the matters of paying sinoman dues and making proper contributions or gestures on special occasions. There were, of course, rare individuals who refused to take part in sinoman activities, but the organization held the allegiance of the vast majority and remained a strong deterrent of aimless heterogeneity and disorder in the kampung. The importance of this function cannot be overstated. As the arek Surabaya's alienation from the municipal government grew in the early twentieth century, the sinoman was able not only to affirm the sense of community and continuity for each kampung world, but to provide a vehicle for the expression of new kampung needs and to offer a structure for kampung survival under changing circumstances. In the 1930s a number of kampung sprouted *raad sinoman* or sinoman councils, designed to compete with the municipal council by replicating it at the kampung level. These sinoman councils were remarkably direct descendants of the common sinoman, and offered strong evidence of the institution's intrinsic suppleness and vitality.[58]

■ Kampung society and its middle class

As their position outside the sinoman made apparent, neither Eurasians nor members of the Indonesian elite exercised any decisive powers in kampung society. The two groups were viewed similarly and were considered to occupy similar stations in life, far removed from those of true kampung people. Relations between the arek Surabaya and Eurasians were uneasy at best. Most kampung Indonesians who worked for Dutch employers compared Eurasians unfavorably to them, commonly complaining that Eurasians were rude to kampung folk and treated them badly, whereas the Dutch merely ignored them.[59] Even in areas where the number of Eurasians was very small, or the Europeans were of some origin other than Dutch, an underlying hostility was often obvious. Serious disagreements and even fistfights between arek Surabaya and Eurasians were fairly common in the kampung.

According to kampung sensibilities, the Indonesian elite—generally called the *priyayi*—were often as "foreign" as Eurasians. Even individuals with some education and contact with the Dutch world found the priyayi a mystery, believing them to be Christians ("because they pay so much reverence to [Holland's Queen] Wilhelmina'[60]) or simply to have their own religion and culture of some unknown sort. As a rule, the priyayi did not mix with the rakyat, and indeed kampung residents seem often to have been under the impression that they were feared and avoided by members of the elite. The arek Surabaya also resented priyayi mannerisms, especially when these took the form of Central Javanese aristocratic and cultural affectations. They disliked, for example, the way social distance was maintained through the use of forms of address: the rakyat felt required to use the honorifics *gus*, *den*, or *jeng*[61] when speaking to the priyayi who showed no respect in return, calling kampung folk *man*, the rough equivalent of the British colonial "boy" and a term employed by Dutch and Chinese factory bosses when speaking to laborers. In private, kampung residents made jokes of priyayi titles and cultural paraphernalia such as distinctive traditional headdresses, mockingly calling priyayi *anak bei* or *den-bei pentol*; or joking that the distinctive knob at the back of the Central Javanese headdress held a rotten egg, causing the wearer to stink unmercifully. The priyayi were often so far removed from kampung realities that, even when they lived in or near such neighborhoods, they appear to have been quite unaware of the ridicule aimed at them.[62]

In kampung eyes the priyayi included a variety of social and economic types, all of whom were seen as more or less the same. Those bearing even minor aristocratic titles were included, as were individuals of obvious standing in the modern, usually Westernized professions, the most important of which were medicine, law, and education. A special emphasis fell on the place of employment, however, and anyone who worked behind a desk or for the colonial government was likely to be considered part of the elite unless he was definitely known to be a "real" kampung person. Office workers (*pegawai*) and priyayi were frequently not distinguished in daily conversation.[63] And since kampung residents had extremely limited knowledge of where pegawai might work besides the municipal government, it was widely assumed that anyone holding an office job was in some way allied with the Western city. Since they did not take part in sinoman activities, priyayi were thought to belong to their own sinoman, sponsored by the gemeente, which seemed only proper and logical.[64] This association removed the elite further still from an opportunity

21

to blend into the kampung social landscape, even had they been so inclined.

As far apart as ordinary kampung folk and the priyayi were, their relationship was nevertheless tempered by a special set of attitudes that did not, for example, influence the way in which the arek Surabaya viewed Eurasians. It is difficult to judge whether the different perspective can be accounted for on the grounds of ethnic feeling alone, but in any case it had real and important consequences. In the kampung setting, priyayi aloofness was often resented but was at the same time not only expected but to a certain extent understood and excused. A common explanation for priyayi unwillingness to mingle with ordinary people or to take part in the sinoman was that their Dutch employers forbade such familiarity and made trouble for those who seemed to enjoy being close to the rakyat.[65] Generally, too, it was the kampung view that the priyayi role in society was to provide a kind of passive leadership by example ("to show the right way"), while that of the rakyat was to follow if they wished. As much as the priyayi were resented as a privileged group, they were also looked upon with a certain awe, and in a very practical way were seen as potential protectors, or even as sources of better social and financial opportunities. The word most frequently used to describe this ambivalent attitude toward the indigenous elite is *segan*, the meaning of which mixes aversion with awe, reluctance with attraction and respect.

One additional factor affected the manner in which the priyayi were treated in kampung society. The populist movement among the Indonesian elite during the 1920s and 1930s influenced larger numbers of that elite to make conscious efforts to soften their frequently disdainful approach to kampung people, and the Depression brought more priyayi and pegawai than before to live in modest kampung quarters. There cannot have been a great deal of real social leveling, but some priyayi attitudes were altered, and the arek Surabaya appear to have acquired a greater appreciation for Indonesians with Western or Western-style educations. They hesitantly began to place their trust in Indonesian doctors rather than in traditional cures, for example, and to evaluate educated Indonesians—generally classed as priyayi—individually rather than as a group. Some, it was said, clung to old habits, while others did not. There were doctors who treated the kampung poor at cost, or sometimes even free, while others, according to popular belief, refused to treat the arek Surabaya and accepted only European and priyayi patients.[66] Some priyayi, though they could not join the sinoman, nevertheless made donations to it and offered both help and sympathy during kampung mourning. It became common for more thoughtful arek Surabaya to speak of the *sifat*, the bearing or attitude, of particular elite families in their midst, and to distinguish between those with a typical priyayi outlook and those who behaved differently. The latter sort still awakened the feeling of segan in kampung folk, but with less hostility. In a few kampung, indeed, it became a matter of some pride to count among neighborhood residents a priyayi who evidenced genuine interest in kampung residents and their affairs. If, as occasionally happened, a kampung boy acquired an education and pegawai status, but remained in his old neighborhood and did not change his behavior toward his neighbors, he often came to be looked upon in a special light, generally proud and approving.

This kampung view, apparently widespread by the mid-1930s, reflects the growing significance at that time of what can only be called the kampung middle class.[67] Distinct from the social levels above it, this group formed its own identifiable stratum among Surabayans in social and functional terms, and was also defined by rough economic criteria. Though consisting largely of entrepreneurs and salaried employees, it included tradespeople, artisans, and some skilled laborers as well. This vague social configuration is not one commonly pointed to as a middle class by scholars and other observers, Dutch or Indonesian.[68] Kampung residents, however, while they did not separate such individuals from the community, habitually viewed those among them with wide experience and strong financial standing as having special status within the kampung. Occasionally the descriptions *kaum lumayan*, the moderately well-off people, or perhaps *kaum cukupan*, people with somewhat more than enough, were used. But the term with greatest currency everywhere in Surabaya's kampung was *kaum menengah*, or people in the middle, a rough equivalent of the Dutch and English terms *middenstand* and "middle class," though obviously not strictly comparable to the Western social phenomena those terms describe.

The kampung middle class occupied a truly intermediate position in Indonesian urban society. In educational background, for example, it enjoyed little or none of the high-level Western schooling available to Indonesians of higher social status or with different aspirations. Middle class children before the 1930s might, if extremely fortunate, attend a local Dutch-language primary school for Indonesians (HIS, Hollandsch-Inlandsche School),[69] but the usual pattern was for youngsters to be sent to an Islamic catechism teacher (*guru ngaji*) in the kampung; or to *madrasah*, a more regularized Islamic elementary school; some male children were afterwards enrolled in a *pesantren* (a Moslem secondary school with a boarding facility) for several years. Then schooling stopped, because the middle class characteristically did not emphasize education as an important part of an individual's development. Like the rest of the kampung population, and markedly unlike the priyayi, middle class parents believed that a job, not schooling, was the most important goal for teenaged sons. Children were expected to find work at a relatively early age, and were subject to strong community censure if they did not.[70] The work ethic was strong, and with it a desire to remain free and independent. A job made it possible for one to avoid relying on others for support or social status, and to bolster one's self pride as a useful individual.

During the 1930s the grip that these ideas held upon the kampung middle class was in many ways relaxed. For what were largely pragmatic reasons, parents began to think seriously of the benefits that modern, non-parochial schooling might hold for their children. Those in a position to see the point, generally men employed in Dutch offices or accustomed to dealing with Dutch businessmen and their representatives, or men who otherwise earned enough to pay for a non-traditional education, departed from the usual attitudes of the arek Surabaya and prescribed heavy doses of book-learning for their sons. A few even sent their daughters to newly founded girls' schools. The intent was clearly to improve the family's lot, as well as the individual's, in both the financial and social senses, and there seems to have been an additional feeling that the new education represented a move in the direction of *kemajuan*, a vaguely perceived but nonetheless attractive "progress."[71]

Seeking education in this way left the kampung middle class in a curious position. On the one hand, it was touched in the process with a certain priyayiness, and even foreignness, since most kampung folk persisted in identifying the priyayi with the world beyond the recognizable patterns of the kampung. Further, whatever success resulted from such education automatically moved middle class families further away from kampung norms in financial standing, interests, and personal relationships. On the other hand, the kampung community was flexible enough to accept much variation and independence of action. The altering sensibilities of the middle class were by no means deep or radical enough to shake the kampung communities in which they arose, and middle class families were seldom pressured or ridiculed by neighbors for adopting new values and habits.[72] The kampung middle class remained firm members of the sinoman and were able to act as full members of the community, provided their attitudes toward neighbors did not appear to change.

In economic standing the middle class also occupied an ill-defined territory between rakyat and elite. Though a small number of entrepreneurs had incomes approximating those of a district head or a doctor, the majority of the middle class enjoyed nothing comparable. Still, their income was appreciably higher than the wages received by most industrial workers and all but the most skilled craftsmen or tradespeople. No absolute range of income was used by the arek Surabaya for identifying the middle class, the usual notion being that those with incomes greater than required for essentials fell into that category. If a family owned more than one house, for example, or invested in other real estate or business, they were certain to be considered above the kampung average in financial capability, and therefore middle class.

Even income differences as apparent as these, however, do not appear to have damaged the social relationships of the kampung and their sinoman. Custom and Islam prohibited the flaunting of wealth, and those who were tempted to make a spectacle of themselves generally found the kampung an uncomfortable place in which to do so. Residents with greater incomes than most were expected to carry a commensurate share of sinoman expenses, to be generous in other ways according to their ability, and to play an appropriate role in the usual charities. There was no social stigma attached to being *mampu* (well-off, but literally capable or potent). It was simply a condition in which some kampung residents found themselves, by virtue of luck or hard work, or both.[73] Young men typically worked for foreign concerns such as shipyards, cigarette factories, garages, and the like only until they could put together enough capital to begin their own modest enterprise; it was every man's dream to be his own boss, and through this sort of independent action become comfortably well-to-do. No one begrudged success to those who were able to follow this difficult road. Perhaps for this reason, kampung residents in the 1930s began to turn to the changing middle class for advice, and to consider its members living examples of what priyayi wrote about in their pamphlets on self-help and personal advancement and, more important, of what most arek Surabaya dreamed about for their future.

Yet the kampung middle class remained unaltered in at least one important respect: its basic orientation against Dutch rule. The long-standing kampung distaste for the municipality, and in an equally .

strong if hazier fashion for the central colonial government, was shared and often fostered by the middle class. Well-to-do entrepreneurs felt keenly the effects of Dutch (and Chinese) competition, as well as innumerable governmental regulations, which they believed limited their business potential severely. Office employees, and other workers who fell into the middle class, were frequently embittered over the obviously favored treatment given to Eurasian colleagues or individuals with an ability to speak Dutch. In some middle class homes hung pictures of Kemal Ataturk, Gandhi, and other foreign leaders of nationalist movements, as well as those of the Indonesians Dr. Soetomo and Sukarno. But a sophisticated understanding of political methods and ideas was only gradually coalescing among members of the kampung middle class, which even in the 1930s was unaccustomed to thinking in terms of an independent Indonesia uniting all indigenous ethnic groups, and which focused instead on an uncomplicated vision of life without Dutch rule.[74]

A particularly good example of a kampung middle class family was that of Ruslan Abdulgani, who grew up in Kampung Plampitan in the heart of Surabaya during the 1920s and 1930s. His father owned a provisions store on the main street just outside the kampung gateway, and earned from it enough to invest in real estate. He owned about thirty houses scattered in various kampung, and a taxi business with seven Fiat cabs, five drivers, and seven apprentices. One of the three wealthiest men in the kampung, the elder Abdulgani was considered by his neighbors to be "upper middle class" (kaum menengah atas). He supported two wives and their children, and was frequently looked to by the community for donations to renovate the prayer-house, distribute alms to the poor, and the like. He did not take his prayers very seriously, but held to a moral code that owed much to Islam and centered upon working hard, living thriftily, avoiding debt, and enjoying only the profit from reinvestments. He had an abiding dislike of the priyayi, with the exception of one or two individuals who seemed sympathetic to the kampung way of life and who, in particular, seemed to understand his own plight as a businessman hampered by Dutch and Dutch-protected Chinese competition. The Abdulgani family had been supporters of the powerful and popular Sarekat Islam, and had known its founder, H. O. S. Tjokroaminoto, who lived in Kampung Plampitan for a while. They also had known Sukarno, who as a young man lived with the Tjokroaminoto family.

Ruslan Abdulgani's mother was a catechism teacher, a guru ngaji, and in characteristic kampung fashion her Moslem beliefs were mixed with others of less orthodox strain. Although her outlook on the world was narrow in its way—her understanding of "nation" being essentially limited to a community of Javanese like herself—she held strong opinions about the Dutch government, which she feared and disliked. Even in the mid-1920s, when like other kampung folk she still found Western-trained doctors mysterious and frightening, Abdulgani's mother hung nationalist leaders' portraits on the wall and, though it was both dangerous and expensive to do so, purchased salt made and sold illegally by village women who plied their trade in the city.[75] She also paid attention to the large number of kampung prophecies and beliefs regarding the future independence of the Javanese people. They were more meaningful, she said, than the generally known Joyoboyo legend[76] and its mention of eventual independence, because they were specific in their assumption that freedom would come in the next generation after a period of bloodshed.

Ruslan's mother's independence of mind and perhaps typical kampung middle class outlook was especially visible in her attitude toward formal institutions, including Islam and the officialdom of the prayerhouse. She joined with her husband, for example, in refusing to follow the traditional custom of giving alms to the kampung modin for distribution as he saw fit. The modin, she said, was rich enough already. The Abdulgani family made its annual donations directly to the kampung neighbors whom they believed most needed and deserved assistance.

Abdulgani's was not an average kampung middle class family. It was better situated than most financially, and the parents were especially keen on seeing that their children received good educations. Ruslan proved to be the most successful academically, attending private schools and eventually the Dutch high school (HBS, Hogere Burger School) in Surabaya. In the eyes of some, he thereby acquired the status of a non-kampung priyayi, though he seems nevertheless to have been respected. The other Abdulgani children did not go far in school, eventually taking jobs in the city administration and in Dutch-owned garages and machine shops. In many other respects, however, the Abdulgani family was much the same as others called kaum menengah by kampung residents. There were cashiers in Dutch firms who sent their sons to HIS and beyond; contractors who could only manage to support one child's schooling for a single year; and garage mechanics who sent their sons first to HIS and then to vocational school. For all the variety of occupations, backgrounds, incomes, and mixtures of schooling given to children, the kampung middle class continued to echo enough of the ideals and values of the arek Surabaya to be counted among them. If they showed an interest in the world beyond the kampung and its ways, this was because it often appeared to offer what the arek Surabaya had for a long time felt a need: incorporation into a more fully modern, yet entirely Indonesian, urban existence.

■ Notes

1. The full range of evidence and appropriate literature is reviewed in works by Heru Soekadri and Sunarto Timoer.

2. The legend of a pre-Mongol battle between a shark (*sura*) and crocodile (*buaya*) is given full play in sources such as von Faber (1931) and Soeroso (1971a), but P. J. Veth (III:816) effectively dismissed it as history.

3. On Surabaya in this period, see de Graaf (1941) and (1958):212–13; de Graaf and Pigeaud:166; P. J. Veth I:368.

4. The reputation of the arek Surabaya as tough and independent-minded, as well as *kasar*, or somewhat coarse, direct, and outspokenly temperamental, is known everywhere in Java and, perhaps, Indonesia as a whole. At the present time, Surabayans still take a certain pride in this popular characterization even when it does not, in fact, fit the individual very well.

5. The classic account is Hageman (1860):267ff.

6. On the frontier flavor see Cabaton:89ff; Chailly-Bert:57; and B. Veth. A splendid panoramic view of Surabayan life and society at the turn of the century is provided by Pramoedya Ananta Toer (1980a) and (1980b).

7. On the Simpang Club see Buitenweg (1966) and von Faber (1931):333ff. On the Vaderlandse Club, see Drooglever.

8. Geschiere:51.

9. Woestoff:37; Cohen:501.

10. Some of the complexities of the legal and land situations are explained in Kerchman:145–58 and Milone:18ff.

11. The account and photographs in von Faber (1936) and Buitenweg (1964) and (1980) portray the changes vividly.

12. VS 1938 I:7.

13. P. J. Veth III:859.

14. The best general treatment of this sort of development is contained in Wertheim et. al., and sources cited there.

15. A far smaller number actually voted. In 1932, when interest in municipal elections was probably at its height, 41 percent of Europeans and about 20 percent of Indonesians permitted to vote actually cast ballots. VS 1932:15.

16. Kerchman:69, 79, and 362.

17. TSSJ:71ff.

18. There was, of course, a count of Indonesians during the 1930 census taken by the central government, but its accuracy is doubtful. TSSJ:19. *Statistische Berichten* notes that the 1925 population figure of 196,825 Indonesians was arrived at through extrapolation, using figures dating from the late nineteenth century and estimated rates of birth and death. Such figures are obviously suspect. In the series of annual reports known as *Verslag van den toestand der stadsgemeente Soerabaja* (VS), population figures began with a rough guess of 150,000 Indonesians in 1920 and increase erratically in even thousands except, unaccountably, for the number of females in 1930, which is given as exactly 136,872.

19. NGS 1940 No. 2:408–409; 1941 No. 1:256; and 1941 No. 2:31–32.

20. In Surabaya the Vaderlandse Club's arch-conservatism was challenged by the different views of De Stuw, which considered itself the champion of a progressive associationism and included many officials of the central government among its members. Disagreeing with both was the Middenstanders Vereniging, a conservative but middle class Dutch organization which could be particularly vociferous in making known its opinions in favor of a "new imperialism." The works by Drooglever, Locher-Scholten (1971), and Jaarsma provide a good introduction to these and related groups.

21. VS 1919:195; ARA MvK Mr 847secret/1933:124.

22. De Jong:39, 43–44, and 90–91.

23. No study of the PID exists, and the frequent mention of it in works on the Netherlands East Indies are brief and vague. Perhaps the lengthiest discussion occurs in Idenburg:143–44. Except where cited otherwise, information provided here is taken from interviews in 1971 and 1972 with three Indonesians who served as PID officers in Surabaya during the 1930s.

24. Contrary to popular belief in both the Indonesian and Dutch communities, the PID did not as a rule employ houseboys, tradesmen, or itinerants as informants. They were considered to be unreliable observers, and agents found communication with them difficult.

25. ARA MvK Mr 3secret/1939.

26. *De Javabode* 12-8-37.

27. P. J. Veth, though he never visited Java, considered from all he had heard and read that Surabayans by the mid-nineteenth century no longer shared "the Javanese national character" and typified, instead, a very different bustling, industrious, and worldly population. (III:859 and 866.) For this characterization I have drawn heavily on material from interviews with Indonesians, many of them Surabayans but some not, in 1971–72.

28. It is exceptionally difficult—and perhaps both a little misleading and ultimately unnecessary—to describe the arek Surabaya as a class, or even in the usual class terms. Ingleson (1981b):492 suggests "semi-proletariat," but does not take into account such things as the genuinely urban character of the arek Surabaya, or their attitudes toward economic and social differences. In suggesting the admittedly complicated "developing colonial urban proletariat," I intend the word "proletariat" to convey the simple, classic sense of a group of people supported largely by wage labor and having at least a vague sense of class consciousness. The remaining terms intend simply to modify that basic idea in such a way as to take into account the special nature of the colonial urban world.

29. Many kampung (the term will be used henceforth to refer exclusively to the urban variety) have founding legends, and some maintain graves of their founders, but neither practice offers firm ground for historical investigation since they are accompanied by no written, and comparatively sketchy oral, materials. The kampung of Peneleh, for example, has at least three stories associated with its origins. The most common is that it was the "chosen place" of the king, with various rulers from the thirteenth to sixteenth centuries mentioned; a second is that it was in the fifteenth century the "chosen place to win" of Sunan Ngampel in his favorite sport of cockfighting; third, it is sometimes suggested that the contemporary name is a corruption of *panean pineleh*, meaning "the place where the exiled king lives" and dating from the days of the thirteenth century King Kertanegara. It seems likely that nearly all of Surabaya's kampung inhabited by Indonesians in the center of the contemporary city (certainly rather far from the ancient center) date from the late eighteenth century or later, with most having their origins in the period 1835–50.

30. The principal materials on the Gedangan revolt are gathered in ARA MvK V. 28 April 1906, No. 33. I have relied also on Sartono Kartodirjo (1973):80–86 and (1972):113–15; and interviews in 1978 with villagers in Gedangan old enough to recall events or stories about them. For the views of Surabayans I have relied on Soeroso (1971) and interviews with this local historian in 1971.

31. Von Faber (1931):26–28, 38; ARA MvK Mr 139/1916; and van Kempen:447.

32. Proper figures are not available for Surabaya, but by 1930 between two and three times the 1906 population of Indonesians inhabited a kampung area of the same size or smaller. This estimate is based on figures in von Faber (1936):2; *Buku kenang-kenangan*:21; VS 1938 I:7; and Wertheim and Giap:233.

33. On kampung impoverishment, see especially *Eerste verslag*; Cobban (1971) and (1974) contain information on Surabaya and several other cities.

34. Von Faber (1936):4–11 and 155.

35. *Rapport . . . Kantor van Arbeid*:58–60.

36. ARA MvK Mr 1004/1935:28.

37. Cobban (1970):189–91.

38. Kampung interviews, 1971.

39. Kampung interview, 1972.

40. On these events see Ingleson (1981a), (1981b), 1983), and (1986).

41. McVey:309–11.

42. Interview in 1972 with Ruslan Abdulgani.

43. ARA MvK Mr 1004/1935:41; interviews in 1971 and 1972 with the former mayor, the former regent of Surabaya, and an Indonesian employee (and later mayor) of the city.

44. SO 3-19-32.

45. This and the following section in this chapter owe much to the description of kampung life, certainly the best available, in Ruslan Abdulgani (1974b). I have not cited information from this source. My knowledge of kampung life in Surabaya during the 1930s depends heavily, too, on a series of more than 125 interviews with arek Surabaya, long-time residents of Peneleh, Plampitan, Dinoyo, Dinoyotangsi, and other kampung, made in 1971 and 1972. These have been cited only when directly relevant and when other sources were lacking.

46. Interview in 1972 with a Surabayan whose father had owned a kampung business before the war.

47. See, for example, the opinions of Resident Cohen in van Kempen:446, of Resident Hillen in Cobban (1970):151, and general opinion in Tillema I:126.

48. Interviews in 1971 and 1972 with residents of Plampitan and Peneleh, adjacent central city kampung areas.

49. Interview in 1972 with a long-time resident of Kampung Plampitan.

50. Interviews in 1971 and 1972 with several persons who did this.

51. Interviews in 1971 and 1972 with kampung residents who actually had these experiences.

52. Based on actual examples provided in kampung interviews in 1971–72.

53. Pigeaud (1964) IV:310.

54. This idea was made particularly forcefully in a 1971 interview with a man who had resided in Kampung Genteng since 1910.

55. In older, more permanently settled, and prosperous kampung such as Plampitan, sinoman existed for nearly every alleyway. In many other neighborhoods, however, of which Dinoyo in 1930 is a good example (it has changed now), the sinoman stretched more vaguely over a larger area.

56. Kampung interviews in 1971 and 1972, especially one in 1971 with a Kampung Dinoyo resident.

57. Interviews in 1971 with residents of both centrally located kampung and those located, now and in the 1930s, closer to the edge of the city.

58. The nature of one such sinoman council is visible in *Raad sinoman*, a document drawn up for use by an enlarged kampung area in Dinoyotangsi.

59. Interviews in 1972 with residents of two different kampung, who lived near Eurasian families.

60. Kampung interview, 1972.

61. Respectively, these are abbreviated, slang forms of the aristocratic titles *bagus, raden,* and *ajeng.*

62. Interview with a pangreh praja son who discovered this only after living in a kampung for a number of years in the 1930s.

63. Kampung interview, 1971.

64. Kampung interviews, 1971 and 1972. In fact, there were funerary associations for municipal employees, and a number of other mutual aid groups as well.

65. Kampung interview, 1971

66. Kampung interview, 1971.

67. The intent is not a precise definition, obviously, but simply the general sense of the standard explanation given in ESS:407. This fits well enough, taking into account the colonial circumstances of the "class"—a word that cannot be used too narrowly, either—of Indonesians described here.

68. Compare Wertheim and Giap:239–41, which follows the usual practice of outlining a middle class of doctors, lawyers, and so forth, a group described in Chapter Two in rather different terms. Interestingly enough, the kampung middle class is also thoroughly ignored by more recent Indonesian authors, as in the articles by Loekman Soetrisno and Yahya A. Muhaimin, both of whom rely heavily on Western constructions. Koentjaraningrat: 282–84 appears to ignore the group I have in mind here altogether, or simply to relegate them to the urban poor.

69. In Kampung Pelemahan Besar, to take an example from an economically moderately well off area, only five children attended Dutch primary school during the 1930s, according to one of them in a 1971 interview.

70. As one young man put it in a 1971 interview, he felt "suspect" when he left a vocational school, apparently for fighting with a Eurasian classmate, and did not immediately seek work.

71. A 1971 interview with a Kampung Dinoyo resident was particularly helpful in putting together this description.

72. Children, however, were sometimes teased by peers for "playing with foreigners" or for going to school and "not wanting to mix with kampung kids anymore." Interview, 1971.

73. Priyayi living in the kampung were viewed rather differently in this regard. Their wealth frequently was thought to be ill-gained, and working for the government was for them considered unacceptable. Middle class people who worked for the municipal government, for example, perhaps because they were not seen as having positions of great authority, and because they were sinoman members to begin with, escaped this sort of disapproval for the most part. Interestingly, however, kampung residents who took jobs as servants in Dutch or other foreign homes frequently were frowned on and sometimes lost standing as kampung members.

74. A generational difference is worth noting. Middle class parents of the 1930s tended to feel as represented here, but they discovered that their children

often were deeply influenced by ideas of unity, organization, and activism gained from exposure at schools, scouting groups, and the like.

75. The colonial government reserved salt manufacture as a monopoly, gaining considerable revenue from this commodity.

76. Joyoboyo, the son of Airlangga who became the first king of the 12th century kingdom of Kediri, was reputed to have made a prophecy regarding the future of Java and its people. Many versions of the forecast existed and one or another of them attracted attention in times of trouble. A particularly strong interest was evinced after 1935, however, when the possibility of war and a Japanese appearance on Java began to loom large in the public consciousness. At least one version of the prophecy's text was interpreted to foreshadow a defeat of the Dutch by the Japanese and, after a period often described as the "life of a corn plant," the disappearance of the Japanese as Java, in some unspecified manner, regained its freedom. On the Joyoboyo prophecy in general, see the works by Zorab, Wiselius, and Tjantrik Mataram.

▪ Chapter Two

New Priyayi and the Question of Change

▪ A new class of leaders

By the mid-1920s in Surabaya the distinct outlines of a new Indonesian social class could be made out even from far away and by Dutch eyes.[1] It was not a middle class, though it filled a vaguely intermediate position between rakyat and pangreh praja. Nor was it simply an extension of the traditional priyayi elite, though it occasionally gave that impression. This new social constellation was, instead, a diverse and complex group of Indonesians which, because it either inherited or adopted some of the cultural attributes of the traditional elite, and because it set out at the same time to challenge the leadership of that elite with new perspectives and values, is most usefully and accurately termed the "new priyayi."[2]

The word "priyayi" requires some explanation. In the classical sense the priyayi were a class of functionaries, usually blood relatives of the king-princes of Java.[3] Strictly speaking, they were not part of the lineage nobility, though they gained acceptance in those circles and imitated the cultural habits they found there.[4] Together with the nobility, the priyayi constituted a traditional cultural and bureaucratic elite, which in everyday usage took its name. This combined elite formed the core of the pangreh praja who served the Dutch colonial government in the nineteenth century and after, but because many newcomers also took part in the transformation by purchasing titles and positions, the cultural attributes of priyayiness were given special emphasis as hallmarks of social quality. Thus the status of

34

pangreh praja and that of priyayi overlapped and, depending on the perspective from which they were viewed, might be distinguished by behavioral nuances acquired through membership in a distinct cultural world.[5] The true priyayi, it was said, possessed inward and outward qualities that were obvious to the initiated at any time or place, and were of far greater importance than occupation, income, or title.[6] In this way the paramountcy of traditional Javanese ideals and standards was for a time maintained in the face of changes brought on by expanding colonial rule.

After the early twentieth century, however, the concept of a priyayi class was increasingly confused as it became obvious that its members were no longer held together by firm social and cultural bonds. One reason for this was that among the pangreh praja there grew a discontent and conviction that the traditional elite were in decline. The future, some held, belonged to more progressive groups, bound by neither the neutrality imposed by the colonial government on the pangreh praja nor the restrictive nature of traditional priyayi society and culture. Young members of pangreh praja families, especially those of comparatively low standing, and of families struggling to advance to priyayi standing through the pangreh praja, were from time to time seized with such notions and rebelled because of them. They began to seek prominence through Western education and work in new fields, extending and altering the priyayi realm. For although these individuals deliberately shed identification with the traditional priyayi class, they nevertheless retained throughout their lives many of its outlooks and sensitivities.

Another reason for uncertainty over the term "priyayi" lay in the colonial government's recruitment, in the first decades of the twentieth century, of a large number of Indonesians to work outside the pangreh praja. This small army of officials, known as pegawai, was hired for the most part on the basis of schooling and ability rather than family background, and while it is true that individuals with priyayi status often were also best educated and therefore qualified for such jobs, this was not always the case. Many of lower social standing gained the required education in one way or another and competed successfully. Furthermore, in times of financial difficulty individuals of modest social standing often took precedence in Dutch hiring practices since they required less pay and frequently gave the impression of being more eager.[7] Despite the influx, the identification of government work with priyayi status held up in a general way, and the newcomers were popularly considered priyayi; in fact, however, acquisition of priyayi traits was uneven, occurring by rough imitation or not at all. This represented another dilution of traditional priyayi culture, and an additional sign that standing in Indonesian society, especially urban society, was coming to depend more on brains than on rank or title.

The colonial government, however, proved unable to absorb all the Indonesians who qualified and trained for service, and these individuals became the foundation of a new class of urbanites. Occasionally they took up the prestigious medical and legal professions, but far greater numbers became teachers, journalists, translators, information brokers, publishers, bookstore owners, and the like. In general, they shared two basic attitudes. The first was a bitterness, or at least discontent, over colonial rule, for few were able to achieve the position or rank they had expected with their schooling. Some even left the government jobs they had acquired, as they felt both unfulfilled and uncomfortable working for the government.[8] The second was a remarkable self-confidence and commitment to the principles of personal independence and self-reliance. They had been forced to fend for themselves in a colonial world which was, beyond the government umbrella, hostile and uncharted territory for educated Indonesians. Successful in their survival tests, they came to believe that education was the key to both freedom and success—defined now not simply in terms of the security of a government job—and that pragmatic self-help could provide solutions not only to personal difficulties but to the problems of Indonesian society as a whole.[9]

From the perspective of many arek Surabaya this new elite remained undifferentiated from others who came under the rubric "priyayi," but in some circles, especially the kampung middle class, a distinction commonly was made between the pangreh praja and the members of the new grouping, who were designated *kaum terpelajar*. This might be translated literally as "the educated," but it is most usefully rendered as "intellectuals," in the broad and uncomplicated sense. The term is preferable to "intelligentsia" because although formal education was an important part of the background of this sort of person, it was not, by their own account, essential to the type. They were a diverse lot, and while for convenience's sake they may be discussed as a group or even a class—again using the latter term in a general, rather than technical, fashion—they did not function as one in the sense that an intelligentsia generally does. Some of these intellectuals were part of the intelligentsia, but many others were not, though they were very much involved in thinking, speaking, and writing about their society and its condition.[10]

In any case, categorization as kaum terpelajar or intellectuals was acceptable to the new priyayi, especially since they made a point of claiming status not on the basis of an inner complex of priyayi ethics and precepts but on the easily identifiable marks of Western education (or its rough equivalent in self-learning or experience) and a pride in non-traditional intellectuality. The terms were frequently used interchangeably, and it was principally as intellectuals that the new priyayi were identified and came to play a leading role in Indonesian urban society.[11]

Not all those viewed as intellectuals in Surabaya of the 1930s had attended a Western-style school, in which the language of instruction was Dutch and the curriculum set or at least based on one approved by the colonial government, but the experience was important to the formation of certain attitudes eventually shared by all members of the new priyayi. Course content probably counted for little in creating these attitudes. For the most part students entered schools with a reasonably clear idea of both the academic tools they could obtain from the courses offered, and the purposes to which they might be put; students also invariably had well-formed ideas about the nature of colonial life. With the possible exception of studies in civics and government at the HBS level, reached by very few Indonesians, there is little evidence that particular academic subjects did anything to alter most students' frame of mind.[12] Other aspects of schooling were more important in this regard.

School was, perhaps before anything else, a social leveler. Dutch education theoretically was restricted to the priyayi class, but by the early 1920s it was perhaps more the rule than the exception for students of different social standing to find ways to enter. Those who attended Dutch "native" primary school (Hollands-Inlandse School, HIS), for example, often did so by circumventing the entrance rules by obtaining recommendation from a Dutch person or posing as a member of a pangreh praja family.[13] Students at the HIS level in Surabaya included the children of farmers, village heads, kampung religious officials, and even practitioners of the mystical arts, as well as those of tradespeople, petty officials, and industrial workers. The families of many may have been to one degree or another opposed to colonial rule, but what students and parents alike seem to have focused on most intently was financial and social improvement; under the existing circumstances, they believed, education in a Western school offered the greatest possibilities. Students attended regardless of their feelings about the colonial government, and whether or not they planned to seek employment with it. Such notions and singlemindedness proved, in the school atmosphere, to be more powerful than social pasts. Even where classrooms were filled with the sons of the traditional elite, the occasional village or kampung youngster was treated with a certain respect and rough acknowledgement as a peer. Particularly at higher levels, egalitarianism was part of a generally understood code of behavior, sometimes reinforced by student traditions. At the Surabaya medical school (Nederlands-Indische Artsen School, NIAS), all graduating students' possessions were taken from them and distributed among lower classmen, making the symbolic point that, however they had entered school, they left it essentially as equals.[14]

School was a world of its own; at the same time as it created a new environment for students, it also tended to alienate them from the society and communities in which they were raised.[15] All children were touched in this way, but the effects probably were strongest on kampung children, who were taunted by friends outside school circles for becoming Europeanized and no longer mingling with ordinary Indonesians. In the classroom, where the overwhelming bias of the Dutch-style education frequently meant that they learned more about the Netherlands than about their native land, students nevertheless were forced to realize that full assimilation into a Dutch world was impossible for them. Unable either to escape their origins or return precisely to them, most students quickly came to share a social outlook which combined resentment of Dutch rule with a sense of responsibility—often abstract, but powerful nonetheless—to the Indonesian populace they were often accused of abandoning.

Restrictive and unifying in some respects, Western-style schooling was broadening in other ways, and can hardly be said to have imposed a stamp of sameness on its students. The effect was more catalytic than formative. Emphasis on individual performance, to say nothing of a tendency to exaggerate the benefits of education in the search for success, forced young minds to think new thoughts, especially about themselves and the future. In addition, of course, reading in one or more European languages opened up broad vistas: works ranging from *Das Kapital* to Dale Carnegie's phenomenally popular *How to Win Friends and Influence People*, from novels to how-to books, were easily available, and daily newspapers also provided access to a variety of ideas. Students generally came away from several years of exposure to this with enormously heightened expectations and widened horizons, an exhilaration born of the new conviction that "man determines events and not the other way around,"[16] and of a new self-confidence. After graduation, students tended to scatter in many directions. Some chose predictable careers in government offices or private professions; at least as many were pushed by either personal traits or circumstance to lead less conventional lives. They often shifted from job to job, location to location, made few real advances and ended up with few lasting goals. The experiences of these individuals—for example the son of a Madurese judge who followed his European schooling with Islamic studies and then worked variously as a clerk in Surabaya's provincial office and as a baker's assistant in a local confectionary[17]—make it clear that Dutch education opened up opportunities in the colonial world, but at the same time introduced Indonesians to a new, individualistic, and uncharted existence in which it was easy to become lost.

Of this point the new priyayi became quickly and keenly aware, and they developed in common—more than any other single characteristic—a drive to create a stable, powerful, and creative existence based on well-defined precepts. They sought, in other words, to make something of their isolation. Intellectuals tended to construct for themselves orderly lives around a core of identifiable goals. What uneducated Indonesians noticed as the regularized or *teratur* quality of new priyayi lives and households, was the outward expression, visible even in such things as precise meal- and bed-times for children, of an internal trust in the powers of reason and self-discipline.[18] This attitude was in part derived from traditional values, and in part the product of a more recent assessment that colonial rule could not be overcome by force of arms, but only by discipline, realism, and self-assurance. For most new priyayi, whether activist or otherwise, thoughts about political attitude and personal behavior were thus closely related, sharing an unmistakably moral tone. A powerful guide in life, the outlook frequently produced in Indonesian urban intellectuals of the day a seriousness and confidence that bordered on the smug.[19]

Although much new priyayi thinking focused on the self, self-help, and personal responsibility, a strong sense of group cohesiveness also made itself felt. One reflection was the large number of social, service, athletic, and political groups intellectuals founded, in which the chief attraction frequently seems to have been the opportunity for a kind of social and intellectual fulfillment, a chance to be with peers.[20] Many of the groups were small, representing a variety of tastes, ideas, and occasionally ideologies; but underlying them all seems to have been a vaguely transcendent sense of community, as well as remarkably similar structures and patterns of behavior deriving from it.

It was this sort of unity, easily overlooked but by no means inconsequential, that tied together what was commonly called the *pergera-*

kan, or "the movement." The term is often translated as "nationalist movement," but this implies a uniform level of activism and politicization, and even a general political unity, which clearly were not a feature of the pergerakan. To one degree or another, all new priyayi in Surabaya were encompassed by the pergerakan because, to one degree or another, all shared an anticolonial vision and hope of eventual independence. Intellectuals expressed and lived out their ideas in a multitude of ways, however. In the 1920s and 1930s Surabaya was the home of a large selection of pergerakan groups ranging from highly political to deliberately apolitical, from "cooperative" (with the colonial government) to "noncooperative," from deeply religious to firmly secular, and from activist to passive. Rivalry, far more than cooperation, colored the lively atmosphere.

Behind the kaleidoscopic exterior, however, were men and women of comparable educational and social backgrounds, roughly similar attitudes toward Indonesian society and their role in it, and the same long-term goal. "We are all headed home," ran a new priyayi saying of the 1930s.[21] It meant simply that, regardless of apparent differences, even political conflict, intellectuals shared certain goals, if not strategies. They worked on similar social levels and operated along fundamentally similar lines. Especially after the early 1930s, meetings and congresses of political parties, as well as religious and social organizations, looked much the same and operated in an almost identical manner; slogans often were nearly interchangeable from group to group, and catchwords like *semangat* (will power, spirit, energy), *perjuangan* (struggle), and *berdiri sendiri* (self-help, standing on one's own two feet) could be found displayed prominently in the rhetoric of all organizations; newsletters, periodicals, and the like appeared with forms and contents notable for their similarity; and virtually all groups exhibited the same attitudes and techniques in approaching the younger generation.[22] At least partly on this account, new priyayi rarely viewed membership in pergerakan associations as mutually exclusive, and they belonged to several at the same time; for their part, the arek Surabaya saw few if any real distinctions among such groups.[23]

While the elaborate pressures placed by the colonial government on the pergerakan after about 1930 limited to some degree the forms which new priyayi activism could take, the structural and other resemblances among pergerakan groups were primarily the result of a universal new priyayi emphasis on the powers of organization. Many new priyayi took for granted that Western organizational models were desirable, but those who had thought through such problems argued that these models had to be followed if colonialism was to be met on its own terms.[24] They provided a clear methodology for accumulating power, and though there were limits to the kinds and amounts of power Indonesians could acquire under Dutch rule, application of the proper organizational techniques could maximize these limits, perhaps even laying the groundwork for their eventual destruction, and could offer considerable protection from attack by the colonial government. Intellectuals also saw that modern organization could be effective in a variety of other, more mundane ways, and to any Indonesians who cared to listen they promoted its application to a host of problems.[25] Leaders of otherwise widely divergent groups issued similar organizational charts and instructions, endless rules for conducting meetings (*Robert's Rules of Order* was popular), and discussions of such items as loyalty to the organization and the importance of carrying out assigned duties, all couched in terms that made them seem like vital chapters in a survival handbook.[26]

Modern, essentially Western, organizational activities also provided the key to intellectuals building a world of their own within the colonial one, a kind of mirror image—modern, yet fully Indonesian— of the Dutch-ruled socioeconomic universe.[27] By the 1930s Surabaya's intellectuals had formed associations financially capable of hiring doctors and lawyers at wages competitive with those offered by the Dutch; banks and other financial institutions aimed at serving the particular needs of Indonesians and investing in their enterprises, including agriculture; and newspapers which, for example, accepted advertising only from Indonesian businesses.[28] The attitude even led intellectuals to challenge the existence of the Dutch presence in simple, direct ways, such as replacing "Netherlands East Indies" with "Indonesia" in print as well as in everyday speech.[29] The significance of organization and organizational activity thus went far beyond intellectuals' thoughts of themselves; it was a vital part of the entire society they wished to bring into being.

■ Varieties of new priyayi

Such an exceptionally diverse collection of individuals was brought together in Surabaya's new priyayi that attempts at generalization are bound to be inadequate. The importance of this group is sufficient, however, to justify a further attempt at illustrating its complex nature. Taken together, capsule biographies of several Surabayan intellectuals—not necessarily those most prominent or best known for political activism—offer a reasonable representation of new priyayi origins and ideas in the late 1930s.

Beginning near the top of the traditional social ladder, Raden Sudirman and his wife, Raden Ajeng Siti Sudari (in public life known by her Westernized married name, Raden Ajeng Sudirman) were pergerakan leaders who had followed their parents in rejecting their aristocratic, pangreh praja heritage.[30] Sudirman's grandfather had been a regent of the traditional type, but his son, Sudirman's father, refused the title Raden Tumenggung and became a doctor, marrying a girl of very ordinary social standing on the way. He apparently had become convinced at an early age that there was no good future in an old-fashioned pangreh praja career, and passed that notion down to his son, who was given a good Dutch education[31] and eventually chose to take a permanent civil service (but still not pangreh praja) position as a customs inspector.

Siti Sudari's grandfather had also been a member of the pangreh praja, though only with the rank of district head, and her father too had opted for medical training rather than follow in the family footsteps. He instilled in his daughter a strong distaste for the pangreh praja and a decidedly anticolonial outlook. In addition, he provided her with a better and more Westernized education than most girls of her day received. Young Siti Sudari attended a Dutch primary school (Europese Lagerschool, ELS), from which she never graduated because of family dislocations, and later continued her education at a private institution. She married the twenty-two year old Sudirman in 1912, when she was fourteen.

The exact nature of Sudirman's involvement in the pergerakan before the 1920s is unclear, but his wife is known to have pursued a number of activities with great vigor. Shortly after her marriage she founded a young ladies' circle with the suggestive name of Puteri Merdeka, or Independence Girls. In 1919 Siti Sudari began in Surabaya the women's group Puteri Budi Sejati, or Women of Pure Intent, the aim of which was partly to socialize but also to build women's self-confidence and foster progressive, modern thought and activity. Both husband and wife became members of the Indonesische Studieclub (Indonesian Study Club) when it was founded in 1924 by Dr. Soetomo, and both went on to play active roles in its successors, the Indonesian Party (Partai Bangsa Indonesia, PBI) and the Pan-Indonesia Party (Partai Indonesia Raya, Parindra). Their personalities differed greatly, however, as did their activities within the same organization. Sudirman, a quiet, retiring, measured man, took high executive positions in the party and rose by 1940 to be the second-ranked officer in the Parindra. He devoted most of his time, especially after Dr. Soetomo's death in 1938 and Sudirman's subsequent retirement from the customs service, to sorting out internal party problems on the one hand and speaking on broad party policy issues on the other. Siti Sudari, by contrast, possessed an extroverted and at times impatient character that bristled with energy. She found her forte in debate, sometimes heated and acrimonious, in the Surabaya municipal council, on which she sat from 1935 to 1942.

So different in many respects, the Sudirmans nevertheless shared the same new priyayi lifestyle and outlook. They emphasized to their children the importance of obtaining a good education, and sent them to the best schools available. At least one daughter, Sudjarmani, attended the same Surabaya HBS to which Sukarno had gone earlier, and which Ruslan Abdulgani attended at about the same time. Commitment to education in general found expression in their support of two student hostels, where students from outside Surabaya could live while attending school in the city. The Sudirmans' circle of friends included Dutch acquaintances, particularly several couples in which one partner was Indonesian, but their closest and most valued friendships were with like-minded Indonesians, many of whom were also loyal Parindra members.

There was money in the family to augment Sudirman's good salary, and these funds supported a large, Western-style house of brick and concrete, and a daily round of activities far removed from that of even the well-off kampung household. Arek Surabaya addressed Sudirman customarily as *ndoro*, or master, a term usually reserved for ranking aristocrats; members of the family used it when addressing Parindra colleagues with noble backgrounds, but tended to feel uncomfortable if peers applied the term to them. The measure of social isolation to which the family was subjected appears to have been considered a condition of its standing in the new priyayi class, and as such was accepted. But no special pride was taken in the obvious social and economic gulf which separated them from the urban population as a whole, and children in the family frequently were reminded that they were "ordinary" people who had absolutely no cause to be socially arrogant.

Many new priyayi possessed, like Sudirman and his wife, high pangreh praja or even noble status against which they had turned, but numerous others did not. This was as visible in the Parindra as in other political parties and social organizations. Sutadji, for example, was born in 1905 to a village family of relatively modest means and faded local prominence.[32] The boy's father, however, had a passion

43

for progress and a habit of educating himself by following courses in agriculture and the Dutch language where he could find them. Believing that farming did not offer his children an adequate future, the father had Sutadji tutored by a school-teacher uncle at home and then sent to Surabaya where, with the help of relatives, a few falsehoods, and a government scholarship for academic ability, he attended Dutch school to the level of MULO (Meer Uitgebreid Lager Onderwijs, junior high school).

A highly individualistic person by nature, Sutadji cut his own somewhat unorthodox path in school and afterwards solved the problem of finding suitable employment by taking secretarial jobs in pangreh praja offices while studying at night school and by mail such subjects as advanced Dutch language, accounting, and colonial financial law. Within a few years he had versed himself well enough to pass the standard examinations in finance and to begin, with those documents in hand, a stable career in fiscal administration for provincial governments. Sutadji joined the Parindra in 1935, shortly after it was established, and helped start the Pontianak (Kalimantan) branch of the party. He liked to mix with other intellectuals and people who, like himself, were self-made, self-possessed, nontraditional (by his reckoning, at least), and capable of making a place for themselves in the colonial environment. He found the idea of Indonesian unity and independence attractive, but was not particularly interested in political activities; he led a quiet, unassuming new priyayi existence equally removed from his village origins and the more energetic and ideological strains of the pergerakan.

A man with a similar modest background, but different temperament, was Sungkono.[33] His father was an uneducated tailor in the town of Purbalingga who had the habit of mixing with people of higher social standing than himself. Sungkono, born in about 1912 with the name Soegiri, was sent to an ordinary government primary school for Indonesians because the social and financial wherewithal to attend anything better was lacking. After graduation he attended night classes for two years to learn Dutch and to prepare for the standard junior official's exam given by the government. Although this informal method of preparing for the test was rarely successful for Indonesians of modest status and means, Sungkono passed; at age sixteen he reached his goal of being accepted into the colonial navy. There he was introduced to political matters and given both chance and cause to read about many of the same issues taken up in pergerakan circles. He felt keenly, for example, the effects of racial discrimination, and at least partly on account of this he nurtured strong anticolonial feelings. In 1933 he became involved in the Zeven Provinciën affair, a Dutch-led mutiny supported by some Indonesian recruits, after which he was forced to leave the navy, change his name, and lead a more uncertain existence in the kampung of Surabaya.

Early in 1938 Sungkono became a Parindra member through involvement in the Surya Wirawan, the party-affiliated youth or scouting group, in which he functioned as a kind of troop leader. He was attracted to the party because it seemed to him the only vital, active Indonesian association of the day. He considered it to be more radical in its deeds (as opposed to words) than rivals such as Sukarno's Nationalist Party (Partai Nasional Indonesia, PNI) or its successors had ever been. Parindra leaders also offered Sungkono paid employment, which certainly played a part in his decision to join.

At any rate, he taught gymnastics and physical fitness at several Parindra-run kampung schools in Surabaya, and was appointed the all-Java Surya Wirawan instructor in the same field. The concept of exercise as an integral part of schooling was not something Sungkono introduced to Parindra circles, for calisthenics were included in party-sponsored schools' curricula several years earlier, but he had experience with fitness training in the navy and believed firmly in its good effects. For many kampung students and parents, however, the idea was still rather revolutionary and Sungkono had to field numerous complaints.[34] In this unusual fashion Sungkono, who remained close to kampung society, was placed in the position of attempting to change it. Though his ways were modest and his social and educational background not very much different from those of many kampung families, Sungkono's experience and ideas, as well of course as some of his intellectual acquaintances, made him part of the new priyayi.

A final figure of interest is Achmad Djais, a man of little or no formal education.[35] His origins and early history are obscure, but he seems to have arrived in Surabaya in his mid-twenties, sometime early in 1918. He married a local girl and settled in the central-city kampung of Plampitan. There he opened a tailor shop that became famous for its excellent work and fashionable styling. It catered to well-off kampung residents, Indonesian officeworkers, intellectuals, and even Dutch clientele.[36] In both occupation and temperament, Achmad Djais fit the arek Surabaya ideal very closely. He was widely admired for his entrepreneurial success, and also considered to be outstanding by virtue of the customers and friends he made among Indonesian intellectuals, who admired his carefully stitched and designed clothing. Perhaps as much pushed by personal inclination as pulled by contacts with new priyayi customers, Achmad Djais became involved in the activities of the PBI and Parindra. In fact, he was appointed a leader of the Surabaya branch of the party, for which he not only gave public talks on the importance of internalizing and spiritualizing the goal of the party, but devised schemes to aid kampung businessmen in their efforts to improve their shops and sales.[37].

Achmad Djais was thoroughly acceptable to the new priyayi with whom he associated, yet remained firmly entrenched in the kampung world. An intellectual "by adoption," he was one of a number of individuals who suggested that there might be some promise in removing the obstacles separating the kampung from the larger urban world. Some idea of his prominence in this regard may be gained from the fact that he is probably the only arek Surabaya or true kampung resident to have a paved, main street—running just beyond the kampung alleyway where he had lived and worked—named in his honor in the contemporary city.

Having looked at a variety of new priyayi who shared, among other things, an association with a single pergerakan group, it is helpful to look at several who had a common profession—journalism—but who chose different political associations. Here again the differences in social background and experiences are, though less striking than in the group above, nevertheless significant; yet it is at the same time clear that the individuals are very much part of an intellectual class, bound together by so many of their visions.

The most successful of the journalists, in terms of popularity as well as finances, was Imam Supardi.[38] Born in 1903 the son of an employee of a Lumajang, East Java, tobacco plantation, Imam Supardi received his education in a rural primary school. With the help of a Dutch family who took a special interest in him, he later attended a series of teacher-training schools. Upon graduation he accepted a position in a rural school even smaller than the one he had first attended, but by this time he was addicted to reading newspapers and periodicals in Javanese and Indonesian. Fascinated with the use of language and the power of the printed word, he began writing for some of the publications he read so avidly, most of them connected with one pergerakan group or another, and thrilled to see his material in print. When he requested that the government school system transfer him to a larger town and was refused, his budding anticolonial feelings blossomed and led him to abandon teaching altogether. Since he had just married, it was fortunate that he was invited by the newspaper pioneer R. P. Sosrokardono, perhaps with Dr. Soetomo's encouragement, to come to Surabaya. There, in 1929, he was given a job on the fledgling PBI-supported *Swara Oemoem.*

Imam Supardi's chief interest lay in expressing ideas in such a way that they could be understood by ordinary Indonesians. He trained himself to write in a style that utilized not only appropriate language but a particularly trenchant humor to get his points across. He borrowed the technique instinctively from the *wayang,* the traditional Javanese puppet drama, and was influenced also by existing publications, notably the popular *Star Weekly,* edited by the Indonesian-Chinese Auw Jong Peng. On the whole, however, the approach was original, as was the notion of blending aspects of traditional, popular culture with modern, progressive ideas for mass consumption.

Imam Supardi wrote for several years on the *Swara Oemoem,* later *Soeara Oemoem,* staff, and in 1933 was able to interest Dr. Soetomo in a new publishing venture, a Javanese-language weekly to be called *Penjebar Semangat,* a title which is difficult to translate gracefully but which conveyed the literal meaning of "Propagator of Enthusiasm, Energy, and Consciousness." This periodical was enormously successful, before long reaching printings of 20,000 copies per issue, more than any other Indonesian publication of the time. Its profits were sufficient to permit the purchase of automatic typesetting and printing equipment, on which both it and *Soeara Oemoem,* as well as a number of Parindra party publications, were produced. Still seeking outlets for his creative energies and entrepreneurial talents, Imam Supardi soon began writing a series of inexpensive pamphlets on a variety of traditional and contemporary subjects. The style was simple and the message direct, uncomplicated by political ingredients; the perspective, however, was that of the pergerakan and the new priyayi, and this National Library, as it was dubbed, was a deliberate competitor with publishing programs sponsored by the colonial government, among them the famous Balai Pustaka.

Imam Supardi had a fierce desire to stand on his own two feet, and he carefully thought out the ways in which this could be accomplished. In this he was typical of a whole community of lesser and greater new priyayi. Only his financial rewards were out of the ordinary: long before all but one or two Indonesians outside of the pangreh praja had even thought of purchasing an automobile, he traveled about Surabaya in a black Mercedes. Still, he wore his success relatively modestly. He was reserved personally, not at all the type of individual his often all-too-obvious written humor might suggest, and he shunned publicity. It was this discretion in particular that made him, soon after his arrival in Surabayan, the confidant of Dr. Soetomo, most of whose publications he ghost-wrote or heavily edited. He retained in what he wrote, as well as in what he believed, a certain cheeky irreverence for everything "official" or "upper class," and a steady confidence in the abilities of the common man.[39] These were qualities that endeared him to the new priyayi whom he had joined, as well as to the arek Surabaya.

A similar penchant for communicating with the ordinary Indonesian, but with an entirely different approach to the task, characterized Imam Supardi's greatest rival in the Surabaya press, Raden Ajat Djojoningrat.[40] This controversial individual was born in about 1903 to a lower pangreh praja family in Central Java and, for the first few decades of his life, he followed a conventional pattern of Western-style education leading to employment in various government offices. Assigned to a position in East Sumatra, however, Ajat grew uncomfortable under the restrictive and arbitrary hand of the colonial bureaucracy. Looking about him he saw other opportunities for making a living and traveled to Surabaya to make the most of them. Propelled by an extraordinary strong-headedness and independence of mind, Ajat began writing pieces for newspapers and then established his own school, the Self Development Institute, which taught a Dale Carnegie-type of course and trained people to be tough, persevering, and bold. It was only such an assertive approach to life, Ajat taught, that could help Indonesians forge ahead and lead truly independent existences; it was the key to success. The school was, of course, a business proposition, but its message was heart-felt and entirely consistent with Ajat's personality. He was merely preaching what he practiced, and attracting considerable interest in the process.

When he first arrived in Surabaya, Ajat had gone directly to the Indonesische Studieclub. Among its members he found kindred spirits and, according to some versions of the story, close friendship with Dr. Soetomo himself. Something soured the relationship, however, and within a year or two Ajat had not only left the group but become its bitter and outspoken enemy. In 1930 Ajat and a certain Isbandi, a teacher in local Taman Siswa schools and also a PNI follower, founded the Javanese-language weekly Djanggala. This paper was written in a journalistic style which depended for its interest on the use of coarse, colloquial language—thoroughly prostituted Javanese, some thought—and sensational attacks on the PBI and other targets. Its rough, often outrageous humor was filled with innuendo and geared precisely to appeal to the arek Surabaya.

The enterprise lasted only a year or two, then foundered on disagreements stemming from Ajat's difficult personality. Undeterred, Ajat soon etablished the Javanese-language daily *Expres* (later *Ekspres* and then *Espres*), which continued in a more professional format and provocative style the example set by its predecessor. With the curious (in view of its sensationalist writing) motto of "the newspaper for people who want to live contentedly," *Espres* reached a circulation of about 3,500. It was joined before long by a number of pamphlets that Ajat authored and distributed. The best-selling example of these bore the title *Tekad*, or Determination, and advised its readers, in a blunt, popular style that self-help is merely a matter of finding the will and courage that are part of every individual's nature but are sometimes hidden. Old patterns, the booklet said, should be broken: no one should be afraid of ghosts, parents, or the pangreh praja if one is in the right. A person can achieve anything, Ajat affirmed, as long as he is determined to reach his goal and willing to be daring in the process.[41]

In the long run Ajat was unable to make a lasting place for himself in Surabaya's lively circle of journalists. His paper was well-known and popular in the city's kampung, where it was appreciated as a scandal sheet, but both the publication and the man himself made many fellow intellectuals uneasy. His unorthodox and angry approach to issues and his apparently erratic behavior, led many to consider him outside pergerakan bounds, an oddity with whom they wished to have as little contact as possible. The opinion did not spring from political partisanship, for individuals from the Parindra, PNI, and other groups were convinced that Ajat was a hireling of the colonial government, perhaps even on the payroll of the PID. In retrospect the charge seems unlikely, but at the time it was serious and left Ajat an outcaste in the small universe of Surabaya's intellectuals. His publishing activity did not long survive the Dutch period.

A third journalist of importance in Surabaya during the 1930s was Doel Arnowo.[42] He was born in 1904 in Kampung Genteng, near the center of Surabaya, across the river from Achmad Djais' neighborhood of Plampitan. His father worked as a clerk for a Dutch sugar export firm and, by investing prudently in kampung real estate, achieved a modest wealth by kampung standards.[43] Uneducated above elementary school himself, Doel Arnowo's father was determined that his son should learn how to progress by attending Dutch school. Against the wishes of both sides of the family, he arranged for his son to enter HIS and forced him to study there. After graduating and spending two additional years in a Dutch technical secondary school, and after his father's death, Doel Arnowo dropped his formal education to take a job at the Surabaya Post Office, where he remained for thirteen years. During this time he read widely in order to educate himself, and joined the PNI, largely for the purpose of being with other young and aspiring intellectuals. Then, in August 1933, he was called before the PID and forced to choose between employment with the government and loyalty to an Indonesian political party; he chose the latter and set after shifting for himself.

For several reasons Doel Arnowo decided upon a journalistic career. The printed page, to begin with, had become the most important outlet for political ideas, replacing speeches and formal gatherings as police rstrictions on these increased.[44] The art of saying more in a sentence or paragraph than met the eye (especially the PID eye) had been developed carefully and become a kind of exciting game with new priyayi writers. Second, writing was not only one of the few occupations that intellectuals outside of government felt themselves suited for, but it also could be moderately rewarding financially. If one combined writing with publishing, it was possible in a large city like Surabaya to eke out a reasonable existence, as long as advertisements and subscriptions held up. Such enterprises were usually not long-lived, but new ones almost always attracted considerable attention for a period of time.

Finally, there were personal circumstances. Doel Arnowo was proud of his largely self-taught verbal ability, and had political ambitions as well. When he found that his friend R. P. Sosrokardono could supply him with a hand press and type, he used his wife's savings to purchase them. Thus began the Indonesian-language biweekly *Berdjoeang* (Struggle). It was written for the most part by Doel himself and contained, besides items of local interest, essays commenting on the state of the colonial government and the nature of various controversies within the pergerakan. Lively smaller notices concentrated on news of PID raids and inquiries, the experiences of Indonesians who had been placed under house arrest or exiled to Boven Digul in New Guinea, and the activities of a large number of pergerakan organizations. Despite the implications of its name, *Berdjoeang* was far from a sensationalist publication. Compared with *Soeara Oemoem* it emphasized opinion more than straight factual reporting, but its standards of language were relatively high and its goal was not so much to excite kampung readers as to influence the thinking of the middle and lower levels of the new priyayi.

Aimed at this group also was Doel Arnowo's *Kamoes Marhaen* (The Common Man's Dictionary),[45] which was intended to teach PNI members and recruits, as well as other pergerakan followers, the proper meanings of foreign terms they often misused and misunderstood. The book contained little that was especially radical or stirring, but it did emphasize words and usages of a political nature and took an intellectual's pergerakan perspective on them. For this reason the PID became interested and, curious that a kampung boy should acquire the sophistication to translate complicated foreign words into Indonesian, interviewed Doel on every entry in the dictionary. He was later jailed for eighteen months. Doel's attempt to reestablish himself in publishing were unsuccessful, and he continued as a job printer and salesman until 1942.

■ New priyayi and arek Surabaya in politics and education

Even in the early years of the twentieth century Surabaya was a center of political activity, and Indonesian leaders (forerunners of the later much enlarged new priyayi class), though heavily occupied with broad "national" issues, did not hesitate to become involved with the problems faced by the arek Surabaya when the opportunity arose. The pattern, however, was clearly one in which grievances hatched in the kampung only later came to the notice of Indonesians outside, who then tried to nurture, aid, and sometimes utilize these spontaneously generated movements.

A good early example is the outbreak of rebelliousness among residents of kampung located on privately owned lands in Surabaya in 1915.[46] Faced with landlords who raised rents dramatically in hopes of clearing the kampung areas so they could be sold for development by Dutch or Chinese capital, arek Surabaya rallied around two kampung residents, one of them a foreman with the government railway system, began to refuse to pay not only their rents but other taxes as well, and even to leave their jobs over the problem. At this point the Sarekat Islam declared itself firmly behind the protestors, inducted the two leaders into the local branch of the party, and offered legal and financial aid. Sarekat Islam lawyers transported kampung representatives to the colonial capital to bring the matter up before the governor-general. In Surabaya leaders organized a huge rally during which 4,000 Indonesians marched to the center of the European city, wearing palm-frond hats inscribed with the initials "SI," to make their point to the colonial authorities.

In the end, however, their accomplishments were limited. The government, though it noted unsatisfactory loopholes in the legal structure, said there was nothing to be done, except to have the municipality purchase the lands, which it was unwilling to do. The mayor applied police and legal pressures, to which neither the arek Surabaya nor Sarekat Islam leaders were able to offer any further resistance, and the disturbances drew to a close. Although it is not altogether clear how it did so, Sarekat Islam tried sporadically to establish itself more formally in many Surabaya kampung, but with little or no success. In 1926 a Sarekat Islam successor group, the Partai Sarekat Islam, attempted to establish kampung branches but these failed out of a general lack of interest and because, in several instances, leaders absconded with membership dues.[47] In the cases of kampung political activity associated with the large strikes and disturbances of the early and mid-1920s, an almost identical pattern is discernible.[48] The arek Surabaya remained separated from the municipal world, and no lasting relationship between kampung society and new priyayi resulted.

Almost certainly with this state of affairs in mind, the Indonesische Studieclub of Dr. Soetomo had focused its attentions from the very beginning on the kampung residents of Surabaya, in hopes that, by acquainting members with their plight, solutions could be found and then applied more broadly to the condition of all Indonesians under colonial rule.[49] Dr. Soetomo himself seems to have first considered the idea of representing kampung interests from within the existing structure, especially the municipal council. But this body, he quickly discovered, was controlled tightly by Dutch members, and he and several colleagues resigned dramatically from the council in 1925.[50] Rather than abandoning their efforts, however, they turned toward the kampung with even greater determination and conceived of creating in Surabaya what amounted to a rival to the Dutch municipal council. This was to be based on the sinoman, and called a Sinoman Raad (Sinoman Council) or, more formally, a Gemeenteraad Bangsa Indonesia (Indonesian Municipal Council).[51]

The experiment was at best only partially successful, and then more as an idea than as the sort of institution the intellectuals of the Studieclub really had in mind. The Sinoman Council itself, after a brief fanfare, soon languished and then ceased to function altogether, and no new leadership or organized program emerged from the experience.[52] Among the arek Surabaya, however, the idea of the sinoman playing a more substantial role in kampung and extra-kampung life was well-received, and the next decade saw a proliferation of sinoman and neighborhood sinoman councils. Cooperative activities, such as multi-kampung, joint-sinoman sponsored circumcision ceremonies were arranged, and occasionally kampung organized themselves in this fashion to pursue a specific complaint with municipal authorities.[53] In a limited and gradual way the barriers between kampung began to break down, the arek Surabaya made their own efforts to influence the course of city government, and a kind of sinoman revival occurred; the notion that such activities expressed anticolonial feelings lingered among kampung dwellers for a number of years.[54] The gap between the municipal government and the kampung was never bridged, however, and the new priyayi ended up looking at kampung developments from arm's length.

In Surabaya's kampung the early 1930s were characterized by an intense struggle for influence among the arek Surabaya by politically active intellectuals. The PBI, several offshoots of the by then banned PNI, and a variety of local splinter parties and individuals all vied for attention. The goal was voter support in an expanded colonial electoral process that promised a greater Indonesian presence on the municipal council. Intellectuals took up the quest with considerable vigor, uniformly professing dedication to the rakyat and reminding their members of the importance of the masses, including those in the city.[55] Surabaya's kampung were plied with egalitarian messages and visions of solidarity against Dutch rule.

The chief difficulty in all of this, however, was that intellectuals sought positions which, in the eyes of even the kampung middle class, gave them at least one foot in the gemeente and made it difficult if not impossible for them to view events from a thoroughly kampung perspective. This dilemma faced intellectuals of all groups, but it can be seen most vividly in the case of the PBI, which defeated its rivals and went on to dominate municipal politics throughout the last decade of Dutch rule. In 1931, for example, the party had solicited funds from kampung folk in order to build a National Building (Gedung National Indonesia, GNI) in downtown Surabaya, the first such structure to be erected by public-spirited Indonesians and therefore a source of great pride.[56] However the value of the gesture was obviated in part by the fact that construction of the GNI required the municipal government to forcibly remove the kampung dwellers who occupied the privately-owned site, leaving them homeless.[57]

Another incident is perhaps even more telling.[58] In late 1932 the kampung area of Dinoyo, located in a portion of the city being gradually cleared for European homes and industrial parcels, was told it must stop all use of the kampung graveyard and bury its dead in a municipal cemetery. Some residents objected, however, and went to PBI leaders for help. A Dinoyo sinoman council was hurriedly put together and a city-wide sinoman council revived, laws were consulted and discussed, and a public meeting on the question was held at the GNI. Soewongso, a sinoman head from Kampung Keputeran, chaired the meeting and asked what right the gemeente had over kampung graveyards, and why the Dinoyo case was being brought up now, though the laws being invoked by the city dated from 1916. How could kampung people afford municipal burial lots, or bear to have themselves declared impoverished in order to receive one free? Dinoyo residents spoke of the long history of the kampung graveyard, its sacred character, and the responsibilities of all arek Surabaya to Islam. At one point an elderly man yelled, "Look, my grandchildren, our sun is rising! Remember your duty and rise up!" When it became clear that the dispute over the graveyard had been occasioned not so much by the violation of municipal law (for in fact such graveyards continued in use in other kampung in the city) but by the gemeente's desire to utilize some of the land for development and asphalted roads, the assembly turned restless and angry.

At this point the difficulty of the PBI position became apparent. Party leaders, including Dr. Soetomo himself, had been deeply involved in helping the Dinoyo residents express their point of view; yet in the course of the meeting they could not help but feel that criticisms of the municipal government were, since PBI members sat on the municipal council, aimed also at them. Furthermore, the new priyayi membership of the PBI were self-consciously "modern," and however great an interest they showed in the arek Surabaya, they nevertheless viewed kampung life as somewhat backward and in need of change. It was not easy for intellectuals to back the forces of "tradition" against those of "progress," even when doing so meant siding with the Dutch-run municipal government. In the end, PBI spokesmen adopted the posture of supporting the Dinoyo residents' right to protest, but at the same time suggesting that a compromise agreement with the gemeente ought to be worked out. The city in fact applied further pressures and began fining persons performing kampung burials, and residents of Dinoyo gave in to a gradual abandonment of their graveyard and the land rights associated with it. The PBI took no further interest in the case, and never again became involved in similar matters. The party's successor, the Parindra, brought to the gemeenteraad various kampung problems—unfair taxes, poor health conditions, unscrupulous landlords[59]—but representation was from a distance. Kampung associations formed independently of political ties and were above all expressions of neighborhood solidarity; the

Parindra, if it played any role at all, was at best an interested observer to these activities.

On the whole Surabaya's new priyayi failed in their efforts to forge a new political relationship with the city's kampung population. The failure is perhaps clearer in the case of the PBI and the Parindra, who were in the spotlight and who have left a more substantial historical record than other intellectual groups in the city, but in fact it was, for a variety of reasons, widely shared. An explanation can be found not in new priyayi insincerity with respect to their devotion to the rakyat, which was always a central theme, but in the naive and often overly romanticized views of society which underlay that devotion. There were few serious attempts to analyze Indonesian society using terms any more complicated than "masses and educated people" or "masses, middle class, and aristocrats." The middle class was outlined by one writer as consisting of "educated persons, government workers, professional people, leather toolers, and cigarette makers."[60] The rakyat, although the subject of endless rhetoric by intellectuals, was similarly ill-defined and reduced to vague terms such as *kromo*, *murba*, and *marhaen* which, despite the ideological associations they acquired, meant essentially the same thing: an undifferentiated mass or "common man," an abstract or even imaginary social construction around which a good deal of romantic fantasy grew up. Consider, for example, a skit written and performed in 1933 by PBI members at a party meeting.[61] The story concerned a poor woman who, abandoned by her husband, managed to have her child adopted by a kind Indonesian doctor. The boy is given a modern education and sent to Holland to be trained as a lawyer. After returning home, he happens to offer legal aid to a woman who has murdered her cruel husband. She is the mother of the young lawyer, who thereafter devotes himself to the rakyat, in which he has discovered his roots.

For a time, especially during the political scramble of the early 1930s, intellectuals saluted and claimed a special understanding of the rakyat, some even going so far in their need to identify with "the masses" that they styled themselves rakyat. Newspapers of all political stripes, all run by intellectuals, demanded that intellectuals drop their patronizing attitudes and leave "us, the rakyat" alone.[62] This posturing was soon abandoned, however. Distinctions began to be drawn between "good" and "bad" intellectuals, and it was noted that only intellectuals who thought of themselves as an exclusivist social group ought to be disapproved of.[63] Doel Arnowo, PNI populist and kampung son that he was, came to emphasize the point that intellectuals, himself included, were an indispensable part of any society; he did not consider, furthermore, that the leveling out of social classes was an attractive possibility for Indonesians to follow.[64]

A graceful solution for these intellectuals who were so hesitant to appear elitist lay in adopting a flexible attitude toward who might be considered an intellectual. The term, it was said, ought not necessarily refer to social background or schooling; what mattered was wide experience, the ability to reason independently, and the kind of natural ability that made individuals responsible leaders.[65] The bias in this approach was, of course, that those judging potential intellectuals held themselves up as models, and if they shunned using formal education as a standard of measurement, they nevertheless insisted that recruits fit the mental contours of the pergerakan. Pangreh praja, who may have met any objective measurements with regard to education or leadership experience, generally were excluded from new priyayi ranks, as were ordinary Indonesians with, perhaps, no lack of intelligence but no positive feeling about the pergerakan and its activities. Not surprisingly, intellectuals' thinking about social change often had a limited, ingrown quality.

This is not to say that new priyayi were not serious about social change, but to indicate that what they had in mind, however frequently the word "revolution" appeared in their writings, was less than revolutionary in the usual sense. They did not visualize a vast or thorough-going change, and they certainly had no intention of triggering some uncontrollable chain reaction throughout Indonesian society. What intellectuals sought was a relatively simple and smooth process by which others might be lifted to their own status and, at the same time, into the gathering momentum of the pergerakan.

One example of how these ideas were translated into action is provided by an episode in the history of the Surabaya branch of Indonesia Muda (Young Indonesia, IM), a PNI-associated organization for better-educated *studenten* (as distinct from lower school pupils, styled *scholieren*).[66] In late 1932 a disagreement blew up over the prerequisites for IM membership. The rakyatist vogue of the day was strong, and some students called for a less elitist approach. IM, they said, ought to adopt a simple standard of age and accept all youths between 14 and 25. It was no accident that a leader of the movement was Ruslan Abdulgani, the kampung boy who went to HBS, who knew first hand about youth beyond the narrow circles of intellectuals that he had joined, and who found it logical to try to interest them in the pergerakan.

For Abdulgani and a few others, materials from the youth affiliate of the Dutch Social-Democratic Labor Party (SDAP) and a Dutch civics text provided the catalytic effect. The necessity of organizing was grasped, along with methods for doing so; a symbol for the new group—which wanted to avoid the PNI-associated term "marhaen" because it "sounded foreign," and also "rakyat" because it "seemed silly"—was borrowed from a textbook photograph of a *kendi*, the clay pitcher traditionally placed at the entrance of Javanese villages to provide travelers with water. The dissenters christened themselves the Kaum Kendi, or Pitcher-ites, and set out to convert the rest of IM to their point of view.

In the 1933 IM congress the age criterion was accepted amid heated debate, and supporters of the measure began to search the kampung of Surabaya for potential members. They discovered that kampung youths understood and cared little about the political purposes of IM, but were eager for basic education. IM members, therefore, started their recruitment efforts by establishing courses in reading and writing. These were extremely popular, and basic education became for a time the core activity of IM. In Surabaya IM members even founded a National Pedagogical Institute, through which principles of teaching, modeled on SDAP literature on the subject, were disseminated. The IM emphasis shifted so completely to the kampung, that the organization's structure was changed so that henceforth branches and sub-branches were to be formed according to kampung and factory, rather than by school as had been the case. Those who took part in the activities considered themselves engaged in "radical" acts, and spoke of how "thrilled and awed" the arek Surabaya were that intellectuals would come to help them. IM members also noted, curiously, that kampung residents in Surabaya "were always ready to be more radical" than they, especially with regard to feelings about the colonial government.

The IM effort in Surabaya met with limited success. Relatively few kampung youth were interested enough in IM to actually join, and when they did there was often discomfort on both sides. Years later Abdulgani himself recalled being unable to conceal his amusement and gentle contempt when, invited to a ceremony inducting kampung youth into a new branch of IM, he heard a recently literate initiate stumble badly over foreign political terms such as *revolusioner* and *anti-kapitalisme*. On the other hand, in 1936 an event took place which seemed to confirm the rightness of the efforts and offer hope for the future. Sukarni, a 20-year-old East Java youth educated to the MULO level, but in Indonesian-run rather than Dutch schools, was elected IM chairman. He was the first chairman who was not educated in government schools to the high-school level or better. The occasion seemed to confirm that social and educational barriers to new priyayi status were being torn down, and the pergerakan expanded before a new and broader audience.

The conclusion that educational snobbery was unacceptable did not, of course, mean that education in general was unimportant—indeed, it might prove the key to future political recruiting—and throughout the pergeraken intellectuals devoted great effort to the education of the arek Surabaya. Nearly all pergerakan associations supported or sponsored schools of one kind or another, which by the late 1930s numbered about 75, employed approximately 200 teachers, and served perhaps as many as 7,500 students.[67] Many, if not most, of these "wild" schools, as they were called by the colonial authorities, were founded after 1933 or 1934; by 1940, Indonesian-run schools were instructing about four times the number of students that attended government institutions in Surabaya. Since the government schools catered in large part to Dutch children, the education of Indonesians in a modern curriculum can be said to have fallen into Indonesian hands.

Although there was considerable variety among Indonesian-run schools in Surabaya, they can be given a reasonably accurate general description.[68] The curriculum was modern, basically Western, and secular in all but reformist Islam schools. Dutch was frequently the language of instruction, and where it was not, the rapidly developing Indonesian language took its place. Even when teachers wished to emphasize their own cultural heritage or perspectives, they chose essentially Western teaching methods and philosophies to help them do so.[69] The intent was not simply to offer a cheap substitute for a Dutch education, but to duplicate it under Indonesian auspices and with Indonesian rather than Dutch biases. Tuition was frequently as high as in government schools, and teachers, usually graduates of government MULO or higher schools, took as much pride in their jobs as their counterparts in the colonial system.

The Indonesian schools did differ from their government rivals, however, in the matter of flexibility. Despite the relatively high tuition rates, for example, entrance was seldom restricted by financial limitations. Most schools offered scholarships, and it was common practice for the financial weakness of some pupils' families to be offset by correspondingly higher contributions from wealthier parents. This was called *nggendong ngindit,* or "equalizing things." Another method of achieving the same effect was to make all or part of the school fee payable in rice, eggs, fowl, or other foodstuffs; this was done in both rural and urban schools. Teachers accepted compara-tively low and fluctuating rates of pay,[70] and frequently operated on their own equalizing principle by simply dividing the school's monthly income equally among the staff. Finally, the curriculum and general approach taken by each school was designed specifically to meet the needs of the community in which it functioned. Some schools produced their own publications, though most teachers de-pended on oral materials. In devout Moslem communities the nor-mally secular and even pointedly non-Moslem Taman Siswa schools adjusted by including the study of Islamic writings in classes; a number of Parindra-supported schools departed from their normal courses to teach vocational subjects where the demand for these dic-tated. On the whole, any course of study was considered worthwhile if it fit the needs of an identifiable clientele and prepared students for taking roles in a modern—and, implicitly, a noncolonial—Indone-sian society.

In Dutch eyes the "wild school movement" was primarily a politi-cal one, and government authorities attempted to control political (that is, anticolonial) teaching. School inspectors regularly visited classrooms in city schools, asked the teacher to leave, and quizzed students about items of nationalist interest, in hopes of determining from the responses how deeply the children had been "politicized." PID officers kept careful watch on many individual teachers, and Dutch officials assumed that the schools were hotbeds of dissent.[71]

Yet these observers missed the point. For them the crucial connec-tion was between an organized political group and a school; their lists of Indonesian-run schools always attempted to identify a party affili-ation in each case. The substance of "politics" in education, however, was broader and more fluid than party affiliations: it amounted to a highly generalized attitude and was not the property of the PBI/Pa-rindra, PNI, Muhammadiyah, Taman Siswa, or similar schools. Even schools that operated primarily as profit-making enterprises built students' self-confidence within an Indonesian context and im-plied a separation from the Dutch sphere of colonial life. The quick-study institutes that had as their chief task the preparation of students for government examinations performed with remarkably little refer-ence to the Dutch world. The exam itself was considered neutral, a tool in an environment perceived as almost totally Indonesian in na-ture. Throughout the "wild schools" it was generally understood that the personal goal of standing on one's own two feet was analogous to the larger one of going without Dutch rule.

The diffusion of the new priyayi message through educational means rather than by agitation or political mobilization made it possible for intellectuals to touch not only those who sought political awareness, which among the arek Surabaya appeared to be relatively few, but a much larger number who aspired to education for a variety of other, generally more mundane, reasons. The pattern so permeated urban life that even strains of Islamic education, normally quite separated from secular varieties, were affected.[72] Here, it seemed, was the basis for a profound social change along the evolutionary lines the new priyayi favored.

■ New priyayi influence on urban society: the kampung view

How deeply did new priyayi ideas and institutions actually penetrate kampung society? This important question is not easily answered, especially since a political gauge is inadequate. As we have seen, most arek Surabaya took indiscriminate, unsophisticated approaches to the pergerakan associations which showed an interest in them. This did not mean, however, that kampung residents were unaffected by the ideas activists espoused and discussed on their kampung rounds. But the nature of the impact was unclear even to the new priyayi involved, and the arek Surabaya frequently were unwilling to admit that their behavior was being influenced by "outside" forces.[73]

Some understanding of the new priyayi impact on the kampung can be gained by examining the arek Surabaya's view of the new educational currents. Modern, progressive schooling was generally considered to be nonkampung or at least extrakampung in nature, associated with life beyond kampung walls. Even in the late 1930s, few kampung could boast a regular school of their own, and nearly all "wild" schools, though commonly called "kampung schools" by intellectuals, were in fact located on paved main streets, where in name and frequently in appearance they could not easily be distinguished from government schools. The reasons for the location were largely practical, but all the same it tended to emphasize the distance separating the new priyayi world from that of the majority of kampung residents.

From the arek Surabaya point of view the "wild" schools existed in an atmosphere of what might be called enlightened priyayiness. There was justification for this outlook, since in many schools one-quarter or more of the teaching staff was of traditional priyayi rank, while the rest had acquired elite standing and behaved accordingly.[74] Teachers tended, for example, to favor the classical Javanese (usually Central Javanese) arts and styles, and to view their pupils as socially different from themselves, frequently referring to them as "the masses" (*rakyat jelata*) and seldom if ever making fine distinctions. The political content which arek Surabaya were quick to notice in the pergerakan schools was also deemed a sign of priyayiness, and although the anticolonial message imbedded in the instruction—most schools, for example, discouraged students from addressing teachers as *tuan* (master), as it implied subservience to a colonial social order, and suggested other terms such as *paman* or *oom* (uncle, in Javanese and Dutch respectively)—was welcome enough, political discussion and recruitment really were not understood or appreciated. Kampung people often called the "wild" schools, as they did government ones, "priyayi schools," and felt equally ill at ease about them.[75]

At the same time, these reservations frequently were counterbalanced by other considerations. Pupils who attended "wild" schools of better quality usually came from families who, on the one hand, found it unacceptable to send their children to government schools but, on the other, considered it backward to have them attend Islamic schools of the traditional sort. Many of these were moderately successful kampung middle class families in which the head of the household took pride in his progressiveness (proven by wealth) and reacted sharply against both the Dutch or Chinese (who limited his success) and Arabs (whom he regarded as an unsavory influence and far too much in control of Moslem schooling.[76] These fathers did not hesitate to pay the high fees of the pergerakan schools,[77] or to brave criticism from the child's grandparents or the neighbors. Well over half the average Indonesian-run school's clientele appears to have come from this stratum of society, the remainder being from intellectual and pegawai families and, in much smaller numbers, comparatively wealthy farming families from outside the city.[78]

Indonesian-run schools posed an uncomfortable dilemma for some ambitious kampung parents. They avoided government schools as a matter of principle, but they also were pragmatically anxious to seize the best possible social and economic advantage for their children. They often supported Indonesian-run schools in spirit, while in fact considering them second-rate compared to government schools, to which they invariably tried to have their children admitted.[79] It was common knowledge that government jobs were closed to graduates of "wild" schools, and a diploma from one of them was therefore worth a great deal less than attendance papers from a government institution. The majority of students attending schools operated by the new priyayi in Surabaya ended up in semimenial jobs or in lower-level white collar positions.[80] For some families these occupations represented an advance, but for others they were less lucrative or prestigious than the one held by the family head. Particularly in this respect kampung residents tended to have ambiguous feelings about new priyayi education.

In addition to regular schools with set curricula, urban intellectuals also sponsored more informal classes in many kampung.[81] These courses were designed to accommodate a variety of ages and learning needs, and were often held at night in order to fit the schedules of working people. It is hard to say precisely what sort of impact these courses had on the arek Surabaya, though horizons must have been opened in many cases, especially when adults were taught the rudiments of reading and writing. Possibly, too, the talks made by pergerakan activists introduced kampung residents to a wider world. Whatever the case, teachers in the courses were closer to kampung residents than colleagues in regular schools, and they often turned over courses to successful kampung students. These were usually young males who, though frequently lacking in even a full primary-level education, were eager to pass on what they knew to others. These individuals were more acceptable to kampung folk than teachers from new priyayi circles, and the material they presented did not give the appearance of being so strange. In a small and tentative way, education beyond the bounds of the new priyayi began to sustain itself.[82]

Surabaya's kampung folk felt the influence of new priyayi activities in other than strictly educational ways. By the early 1930s, various types of communication associated with the modern, Westernized city also had become part of kampung life, and although their form in this different environment was somewhat altered, their effect was nevertheless considerable. Newspapers, for example, had been considered by most kampung people to be essentially foreign things. Publications such as *Soeara Oemoem*, *Sin Tit Po*, and *Espres*, all three of which appeared in Javanese or Indonesian, often were assumed by illiterate arek Surabaya to be written in Dutch or some other language.[83] But when read aloud, newspapers captured the attention of many kampung adults, who often appointed someone as official neighborhood reader and questioned him intently on the items he read.[84] Newspaper subscriptions were expensive enough in kampung terms to be beyond the reach of most residents, but often interest in the news became sufficiently widespread that an illiterate but financially well-off individual provided the funds while someone else was prevailed upon to do the reading every evening.[85] This was a satisfactory arrangement, a modification of kampung tradition that those who can best afford to provide entertainment for the neighborhood are expected to do so, and one that brought the new priyayi world into the everyday kampung consciousness.

Books were also of some importance to kampung life. In a few wealthier neighborhoods bookstores did a modest business, perhaps in the range of 1,000 volumes sold in a year,[86] but in most the cost of a single book was more than the majority of inhabitants could easily afford. A solution to this problem, and an answer to the awakening kampung interest in published materials, was often the establishment of a small lending library limited to neighborhood use.[87] Usually called Taman Bacaan, or "reading gardens," the small library corners often operated out of a kampung resident's front room. For a weekly fee members could read current newspapers, several journals, and a number of books. The initiative in forming these facilities came most often from pergerakan people, but the response was almost always positive. The types of literature offered were frequently considered more satisfactory than the Latinized Javanese reading texts and simplified wayang stories that could be borrowed from some government primary schools.[88] Occasionally readers became so keen that they arranged to take Dutch lessons in order to read publications in that language. In particularly active kampung, the Taman Bacaan became centers of lively debate on all manner of contemporary issues, many of which, of course, concerned the world as it existed well beyond kampung walls.

The trace of ambivalence in the kampung view of the new priyayi's educational activities, slight enough to be overlooked by many new priyayi themselves but significant enough in retrospect to be examined more closely, is more vividly reflected and enlarged in a cultural lens: the contemporary, and typically arek Surabaya, urban dramatic form known as *ludruk*. Numerous theories have been advanced regarding the origins of this local art, the most widely accepted being that it is descended from an indigenous East Javanese entertainment called *lerok*.[89] Receiving its modern name sometime in the early nineteenth century, ludruk according to this view possessed then several of the characteristics for which it is now known, for example, a comic turn and use of transvestite singers.[90] Following World War One, ludruk's two-man show of jokes and songs began, like Surabaya itself, to undergo rapid change. It added characters, acquired more complex stories to act out, and experimented with various types of musical instruments and melodies.[91]

In about 1928, as Studieclub activists were taking a keen interest in kampung affairs, Dr. Soetomo was introduced to the work and ideas of a remarkable innovator in ludruk, Cak Gondo Durasim. This individual was a true arek Surabaya, born and raised in the center of the city in Kampung Genteng Sidomukti. Reportedly illiterate,[92] he nevertheless enjoyed enormous artistic success with his ludruk show. He was particularly well known throughout Surabaya's kampung for his clown role, and through it, his wry criticisms of the municipal government and of Dutch colonial rule in general. These consisted of polished renditions of familiar kampung witticisms, or original jokes based on the kampung style of speech, folded into the ludruk format. In this, Dr. Soetomo saw enormous possibilities. He seems to have lost no time in fostering a closer relationship between Durasim's troupe and the Studieclub, or advancing the idea that their efforts should be joined. Which side in this unlikely partnership was more changed in the process is difficult to say, but in 1930 Cak Durasim announced the formation of an entirely new type of ludruk, performed by his own renovated group before the members of the recently established PBI, and presented not in a kampung setting but on a modern stage at the GNI.[93]

The new style was pithy and progressive. The company, by this time consisting of seven or eight performers, took special pride in its *kritik*, which elevated the earlier sarcastic remark to the level of something approaching social commentary, done with both humor and serious intent. At least partly as a result of suggestions made by Dr. Soetomo, who seems to have pointed out to Durasim the deeper symbolism he saw in ludruk colors and props,[94] criticisms in the performances acquired a sharper edge; still, they were phrased in such a way as to avoid angering the PID (who soon attended most shows) and to emphasize self-help rather than aimless complaint. A typical reminder was "If there aren't enough [government] schools, why don't you go ahead and set them up yourselves?" But there were also more cutting lines, such as the one suggesting that the poverty of Indonesians under Dutch rule must have some reason.

Thus the purposes of ludruk and the pergerakan became intertwined. The GNI was put at the disposal of Durasim's troupe for regular shows, and this innovation brought the PBI both income (the proceeds were split with the troupe), and a different and effective mouthpiece for some of its ideas; ludruk, for its part, received a permanent and modern home, the comparative luxury of a steady income, and greater popularity than it has ever enjoyed.

Ludruk's rise, however, despite the various advantages gained from associating wtih Dr. Soetomo and the PBI, was not without complications. Not all arek Surabaya approved of this form of entertainment, for one thing, especially in kampung where inhabitants took Islam seriously. Other kampung merely frowned upon ludruk as a corrupting influence and allowed only small children to watch, with the idea that they would understand little and soon forget the experience; parents reacted in horror if boys evidenced any desire to become ludruk actors. These kampung residents never supported ludruk, and seemed to look upon its move to the GNI and its association with new priyayi figures as merely further evidence of the art's unsuitability.

There was also the problem of competition from another form of dramatic entertainment, *ketoprak*. This minor stage art's history paralleled that of ludruk in many respects; from recognizable beginnings in the nineteenth century it blossomed in Central Java after about 1926.[95] Ketoprak performances had many of the same components as those of ludruk—singing, dancing, clowns—but they tended to emphasize a splendid, showy atmosphere that ludruk did not possess, especially as it appeared in the GNI.[96] They also acted a wide range of stories, including those from the traditional wayang, much modernized, and from local folklore. The combination proved immediately popular in Surabaya, and amateur troupes sprang up all over the city. Indonesian clerks at the post office, servants at the Simpang Club, and employees at all sorts of companies formed their own groups and produced their own shows. The craze went so far that ketoprak, originally limited to kampung performances, came by popular demand to occupy the GNI stage on nights when ludruk was not scheduled.[97] Though temporary, Cak Gondo Durasim's eclipse by ketoprak was for a time so nearly complete that his group was forced to give a free performance in the Kampung Ngemplak area simply to show that ludruk was still alive.

Ludruk's most significant difficulty, however, lay within itself: it projected a complex image and therefore attracted an audience with mixed attachments to it. The type of performance made famous by Durasim during the 1930s displayed a dual nature. On the one hand it embodied many of the values long held dear by the arek Surabaya: flexibility, spontaneity, and an antielitist, slightly coarse manner,

Rival troupes took pains to achieve in their acts and songs that free, critical approach to life that kampung people admired, and hoped in this way to speak to the arek Surabaya.

On the other hand, ludruk also came to be known for quite a different characteristic: its ability to portray, discuss, and advocate what was *maju,* or progressive and modern. Some kampung inhabitants, especially among the kampung middle class, found this aspect of ludruk especially interesting, as it echoed many of their own notions in a format they could easily understand. But this same characteristic frequently associated ludruk with the world beyond the kampung, and for many arek Surabaya this was uncomfortable or even unacceptable. Criticism in ludruk often focused on matters beyond the kampung horizon, and the crux of ludruk plots usually lay in a situation or with individuals outside the normal kampung context. It is significant that after 1930 nearly all of Surabaya's ludruk troupes followed Durasim's lead and left their kampung habitats to become more permanently established in a building devoted to entertainment of this sort. There they played to audiences drawn from all over the city and from a variety of social levels. Ludruk was no longer a strictly kampung art speaking on a kampung plane.

Ludruk thus presented two faces to its crowds, faces neither mutually opposed nor entirely at ease with each other. It is not surprising that those who attended had mixed feelings about what they saw. The arek Surabaya were both appreciative and resentful of the obvious involvement of the new priyayi in shaping ludruk's message and style. With a mixture of admiration and disappointment, kampung people said in the early 1930s that Cak Gondo Durasim had "become one of those intellectuals,"[98] and they both praised and ridiculed the aspects of the new ludruk which were above them or considered "high class." The attitude mirrored the same hesitations the arek Surabaya had regarding the new priyayi and their pergerakan in general.[99]

■ New priyayi, youth, and social drift

A final view of the state of Indonesian society in Surabaya toward the end of the 1930s can be gained through a brief consideration of the role of youth, especially in relation to the new priyayi initiatives of the day. In kampung life the younger generation was accorded considerable importance; in the sinoman much of the work, though not the decision-making, was done by the young men of the neighborhood, and parents universally counted on youths to forge ahead, be independent, and make a good name for themselves. Since older Indonesian workers in menial or semiskilled positions often were dismissed by Dutch employers because they had "gotten too old,"[100] it fell to young men in their teens and twenties to bolster family income. Those who showed no desire to help their parents in this way frequently were said to be *durung jowo*, or "not Javanese," and one of the most frequent turns of kampung gossip concerned children who took no responsibility for their parents after they had found their way in the world.[101]

For the new priyayi, too, the younger generation was of special interest. Intellectuals hoped for their children the kind of education they themselves had received, or better. They pictured these offspring taking up the same social positions and the same struggle for a new Indonesian society that they themselves had begun. Young intellectuals had in the past given much to the pergerakan in the way of initiative and verve—the founding of Boedi Oetomo in 1908 and the adopting of the Youth Oath in 1928 come most readily to mind—and in the 1930s all activist groups, regardless of their political nature, had the younger generation constantly in their thoughts. The more intellectuals focused their gaze on the future, the more they came to see youth as the foundation on which that future must rest. Special care was taken to recruit and cultivate younger party members. Youth were everywhere among the new priyayi assigned much significance and not a little mystique as the "flower of the nation."

If youth came to be viewed in a special light, the nature of young people was nevertheless appraised realistically and with caution. As in the sinoman, where the younger generation was important but subordinate to the guidance of elders, so was it in pergeraken circles. Intellectuals did not believe that leadership of their movement could, or could be expected to, spring directly out of the untried enthusiasms of the younger generation; they sought to ensure that youths were educated, disciplined, and molded to the job for which they were intended. This approach was taken with all youths, including intellectuals' own children, but it seemed particularly suitable for youngsters from the kampung middle class, whom the new priyayi were anxious to win over—perhaps make over into their own image—but who were also relatively unknown entities.

Besides education in Indonesian-run schools, the chief instrument used by the pergerakan to groom youths was the scouting movement.[102] The uplifting ideas of Baden-Powell's scouting, and more particularly its emphasis on personal development within a framework of discipline, were of great interest to Indonesian intellectuals.

The first Indonesian scouting group, the Javanese Scouting Organization (Javaansche Padvinders Organisatie, JPO), was founded in 1916, one year before the Dutch-approved colonial representative to the world scouting movement, the Netherlands East Indies Scouting Association (Nederlands-Indische Padvinders Vereniging, NIPV). In subsequent years more than a dozen major scouting or scout-like groups were established by activist Indonesians. In addition, a far larger number of small, local youth organizations took root.[103] Though all, with the exception of the NIPV, were forced to develop outside the framework of international scoutdom, and were even prevented by the colonial government from meeting Baden-Powell when he visited the Indies in 1934, they nevertheless retained much of the scouting spirit. The emphasis was on character-building and the growth of individual self-respect, but to a remarkable degree attention also was given to activities which simulated broad and even international vision.

In several respects, however, Indonesian scouting groups of the 1930s differed from their English model. Not themselves political, they were planned and nurtured by pergerakan organizations, some of which were more political than others; all were attuned to the concept of a free and unified Indonesia, and to this goal the individual was both subservient and crucial. In an unspoken fashion, what may loosely be called nationalism permeated the scouting movement wherever it existed. The singing of anthems, wearing of insignia and military-like uniforms, performing of services for the poor or uneducated, and insistence on the use of the Indonesian language in daily affairs all worked toward the concretization of this otherwise abstract national idea. Young scouts, in other words, were new priyayi-in-training, receiving introduction into a world in which their own growth and that of the Indonesian nation or society at large were made indistinguishable.

Especially after 1924, when nearly all Indonesian scouting associations split with the NIPV on the issue of pledging allegiance to the Dutch queen, the movement was openly anticolonial. Bitter rivalry between Dutch and Indonesian scouts, who frequently refused to salute each other as custom suggested and even fought publicly over such matters, was a prominent feature of many new priyayi and kampung middle class children's lives.[104] Indeed, much about Indonesian scouting was designed to pull youths away from Western culture and toward what intellectuals had begun to envision as a modern Indonesian culture; it also cut new priyayi and middle class children away from elite society, especially as a model for behavior. It was widely believed that pangreh praja and other Indonesians holding government jobs would be cashiered if their children joined any group besides the NIPV.

Intellectuals, then, were firmly in positions of leadership, shunning and even ridiculing the old elite. The directors of all scouting groups in Surabaya fit the new priyayi mold. They, and nearly all scoutmasters and other secondary leaders, came from the best-educated strata and frequently believed that their educational background was the prime, though not the only, factor in their being chosen for such scouting roles.[105] They were accepted as leaders by both their own children and by the middle-class youngsters who made up the majority of scouting's adherents.[106] It seemed to many intellectuals that scouting offered an unparalleled link to the future and to the kampung middle class.

Despite such hopes, however, youth and the pergerakan found it difficult to accommodate each other. Among Surabayans the uneasiness had foundations in both generational and social differences, and was plainly visible in the 1930s. PBI leaders, for example, subscribed to the usual platitudes regarding the value of the younger generation, but were at the same time unhappy even with their own children, who after studying at home or abroad came back to criticize the opinions of their elders.[107] As one *Soeara Oemoem* writer editorialized, in all of the emphasis on youth and the pergerakan role, people had begun to lose track of the meaning of the word "pemuda." Literally it mean "young man" or even "young pergerakan activist." As far as the pergerakan was concerned, however, the true meaning of pemuda had less to do with age than spirit. Those who did not see that youth had a responsibility to fulfill and required discipline to do it, did not know the proper meaning of the word, and youths who did not have these things under their belts were not truly pemuda at all.[108] With respect to the popular pergerakan word "semangat," another writer noted many years later, it had never been the intellectuals' intention to indicate anything by it except determination, discipline, and hard work.[109]

Notions of this sort were not limited to the followers of Dr. Soetomo but were widespread throughout pergerakan circles. Doel Arnowo, for example, was sternly critical of the youth of his day, claiming that even those who ought to have known better seemed to lack discipline and a sense of purpose. Worse than making them appear irresponsible, such failings caused the pemuda to be seriously out of touch with the times. Most youth, Doel Arnowo said, had no genuine rakyatist sympathies or understanding, despite their kam-

pung backgrounds; what all responsible intellectuals recognized as
the proper way to think and proceed toward a correct social future was
treated by the pemuda as merely a passing fancy, something not to be
considered seriously. The attitude did not bode well for the future.[110]

The performance of middle class kampung youth was thought especially discouraging. With the exception of a few neighborhoods in
which young men proved effective organizers, middle class youth
showed no great enthusiasm for night courses or pergerakan-
sponsored political and social activities, which were predominantly
supported by persons over thirty years of age.[111] In general kampung
pemuda paid scant attention to organizational loyalties and gained
little understanding of even the nonpolitical aspects of the pergerakan. Kampung youth formed and joined numerous interest groups,
occasionally mingling with new priyayi youths, but on the whole
their thoughts and actions remained limited by kampung horizons.[112]
Many seem to have been attracted by scouting's uniforms, regalia, and
promotion of a kind of rugged individualism. The tame and rather
curious pergerakan-approved portrait of the well-groomed and -be-
haved youth who dutifully went to innumerable youth congresses,
took notes, and fell in love with the girl in the next seat,[113] made little
impression on middle class kampung youths, for whom the surroundings in such a picture must have seemed fanciful and largely
irrelevant.

Surabaya's intellectuals were conscious of their tenuous hold on
youth when the specter of a Pacific war made that realization all the
more disturbing. Approaching conflict forced pergerakan leaders to
look with greater urgency than before at the capacity of youth to lead,
to act as the source of energy and willpower in Indonesian society.[114]
One writer noted insistently that youths had to be prepared to die in
their role as leaders, and implied this might be as much a matter of
holding discipline as facing an enemy head-on.[115]

What the new priyayi saw, however, continued to be disheartening
to them. Why did youth groups continue to increase so rapidly that
no one could keep track of them, and so indiscriminately that defined
goals, articulate leadership, and even genuine memberships were impossible?[116] How could it be that Muhammadiyah youths, for example, let themselves slip so much in discipline and devotion to the
cause that their counterparts in Arab countries called them positively
backward?[117] How could IM members join other groups simultane-
ously and, worse still, hang onto their "youth" status well past their
twenty-third birthdays, refusing to face the world as adults?[118] How
was it possible that the municipal government was able to conjure up

its own, loyalist youth group to compete with those begun by pergerakan leaders, and to have this so-called Pemuda Federation actually
steal away youths who ought to have been supporting genuinely Indonesian groups?

The answer intellectuals had for these and similar questions was
that Indonesian youths were still weak, uneducated, and irresponsible. Furthermore, pemuda themselves were to blame, not their new
priyayi mentors. After about 1938, pergerakan criticism of the
younger generation in Surabaya became increasingly severe, and
leaders of many organizations showed no hesitation in publicly chas-
tising their charges. Pemuda were repeatedly told that they were irresponsible, undisciplined, "wild," and "soft."[119] They were constantly reminded of their duties to the rakyat, of their responsibilities
to themselves and the rest of society, and of the goals of the pergerakan.[120] As one pergerakan magazine for Islamic youth rather harshly
expressed it, there was a general, outspoken concern among intellectuals that unless something was done, the much-vaunted flower of the
nation would turn out in fact to be the trash of society.[121]

On the eve of World War Two it was evident that new priyayi efforts to encourage but at the same time direct pemuda energies, and to
absorb a vitalized younger generation into pergerakan ranks, had for
the most part failed. A relatively small number of individuals had
made the transition from kampung youth to pergerakan member,
from middle class to new priyayi. On the whole, Surabayan youth was
neither as deeply nor as widely affected by intellectuals' leadership as
many had hoped. The younger generation appeared instead to be
aimless and drifting.

Many factors were responsible for this state of affairs, though in the
longer perspective these came down to much the same thing: the inability of the new priyayi to transfer to another social class or generation (even one of its own making) the lessons of the experiences that
bound them together. Larger in numbers and schooled far more di-
versely than the older pergerakan generation, educated and partly educated youths of the late 1930s did not think along similar lines.
Growing up in an era in which the pergerakan's struggle was held in
check by colonial policy and police, pemuda saw little real need for
discipline, planning, or cautious movement forward; these were all
beside the point. Youth sought refuge instead in scouting groups and
a plethora of recreational associations, book clubs, and the like,
which became ends in themselves rather than means. The average
pemuda in Surabaya tended to adopt, under new priyayi tutelage, a
highly individualistic, even self-serving, approach to his surround-

ings. There were no social challenges severe or unique enough to alter this pattern. Surabayan youth experienced no counterpart to the pressures which had molded intellectuals in earlier decades. However much imbued they were with a vague if earnest anticolonial sentiment, these pemuda awaited a galvanizing experience, an event or circumstance with the power to determine the shape and direction of their actions in the future.

■ Notes

1. Colijn:41–42. Colijn pointed specifically to Surabaya, rather than any other city of the colony, as the place where this new class was most clearly in evidence.

2. This term, or the closely related "neo-priyayi," has been used previously, but with a somewhat different content than intended here. Geertz (1965):140, for example, clearly utilizes "new priyayi" to indicate the modern version of the traditional Javanese literati, the intelligentsia. Tichelman (1980):135ff uses a more vague definition for the term "neo-priyayi," but seems to imply a social type bound more strictly by education and, therefore, pseudotraditional priyayi status than is intended here. See the following discussion and, especially, footnote 10.

3. Soemarsaid Moertono:93; Sudjito Sosrodihardjo:18.

4. Sartono Kartodirdjo (1974):154.

5. There is no clear agreement, even among Javanese, as to the precise distinctions between priyayi and pangreh praja, and in any case the definitions have not remained constant over the past half-century or so. A simplified, lower class, and often non-Central Javanese view is that the two groups are simply the same for all intents and purposes, though urban people sometimes, when pressed on the point, acknowledge a difference between "new" and "old," and between the status-bearing nature of modern education on the one hand and the old bloodlines on the other. There are a variety of notions among the upper classes, for example that priyayiness was conferred by the Dutch, whereas the true servants of the people, the aristocratic pangreh praja, may have been connected to but certainly were not beholden to the colonial regime. In recent decades, when the old-style pangreh praja has had greatly

reduced visibility, the word "priyayi" has served very broadly, sometimes indicating the aristocracy, sometimes being used in such a way as to include a host of upwardly mobile types, and even implying something akin to newly moneyed or empowered. On this account, especially, it seems best simply to recognize the overlap and understand that neither term is at all precise. On the problem and the priyayi in general, see Sutherland (1975):55–77. The traditional cultural world of the priyayi is described in Sutherland (1979), Geertz (1959), and Koentjaraningrat.

6. Soetomo (1934):27.

7. Interview in 1971 with Sutadji, who was himself in this category for a time, and who later had considerable experience in hiring personnel for government offices.

8. In interviews in 1971 and 1972 with persons with this sort of background, precisely this feeling comes through with great consistency. What is remarkable is that most individuals do not by preference produce a concrete economic or political reason for their feelings or actions, but speak of something much more emotionally based.

9. Note, for example, the unoriginal but revealing motto, always given in English, of the Pendidikan Oemoen (Public Education) schools, run by PNI supporters: "Knowledge is Power." SPBI May 1943, advertisement inside front cover.

10. The discussion in Syed Hussein Alatas:8ff. on the application of the term in the Southeast Asian setting seems to me convincing and pertinent to its use here. It is perhaps also worth saying that when I use the word "class" in conjunction with this group, I intend it in a general and not a technical sense. In some ways intellectuals or new priyayi did not represent a class at all, and were an amalgam of many economically and socially defined classes in colonial society; but they may be considered to have formed, very loosely, a communicative group and a force in society that was sufficiently different from others to be examined separately. On the whole, this generalized approach to social description seems justified in the absence of precise investigation and terminology in existing academic work, and considering the characteristic ways in which Indonesians seem to view their own social constructions.

11. Kampung interviews, 1971, and interviews in 1971 and 1972 with educated Surabayans, among them Karjono Js., himself a kind of borderline pangreh praja/priyayi product who was especially thoughtful about such matters.

12. Based on interviews with persons attending a variety of schools, 1971–72.

13. Based on interviews with persons having this experience, 1971–72.

14. Interview in 1971 with a former student at the medical school.

15. The description in this paragraph is based on interviews with Dutch-educated students from both kampung and priyayi backgrounds, 1971–72.

16. SO 4-12-41, citing a Taman Siswa aphorism.

17. Interview in 1971 with an individual having this experience.

18. Interview in 1971 with a Surabaya kampung boy who, as a result of schooling and employment, entered the new priyayi world in the 1930s.

19. As evidenced, for example, in the slogan "[we are] courageous because [we are] right" (*berani karena benar*). Soetomo, et. al.:39.

20. The assessment was common in interviews with new priyayi held between 1971 and 1972.

21. Interview in 1971 with Dr. Angka Nitisastro, who in the 1930s was a Taman Siswa teacher and a PNI supporter.

22. The description of the Muhammadiyah congress in SO 1-21/22-40 gives a typical example of that phenomenon. The program, the general message, and many of the trappings—for example, an honor guard of Muhammadiyah scouts—were strikingly similar to those of the Parindra, Nahdlatul Ulama, and a host of other organizations. Even slogans were often almost identical among serious competitors; the cry associated with the PBI and the Parindra, "Hidup!" (literally, "Live!" but meaning "Long live independence!" or "Hidup merdeka!") was used by the group's archrival in Surabaya, the PNI, whose slogan was "Hidup PNI!" *Menjala* 1-21-33. As far as youth is concerned, consider the similarities (even down to the style of uniforms) among, for example, the Parindra's Surya Wirawan, Muhammadiyah's Hizbul Wathon, Nahdlatul Ulama's Ansor, and many other youth branches of pergerakan organizations. Even their magazines were alike. *Soeara Surya Wirawan* and *Soeara Ansor*, for example, wore uncannily similar covers in 1940: both pictured uniformed youths blowing trumpets to awaken a slumbering Javanse countryside to a new day—one of, it may be supposed, progress—against a background of a doubly suggestive rising sun. In all respects the symbolic and rhetorical language of the pergerakan was surprisingly homogeneous. Perhaps this gave the movement a built-in unity that has been much underestimated.

23. SPBI 7-25-35; kampung interviews, 1971.

24. SO 1-2-41.

25. See the example in SO 1-31-41 of a group of local Moslem leaders who formed, in 1939, a Western-style association to save a mosque, and continued it because it proved so effective in dealing with the colonial bureaucracy.

26. See, for example, *Boekoe penoentoen* and, for comparison, the instructions in *Soeara Ansor* June 1941:44 and 59–63. Note there the Nahdlatul Ulama cry that "without organization we would collapse in chaos."

27. Pergerakan followers were frequently at pains to point out that they intended a true synthesis of East and West, a thoroughly Indonesian but also thoroughly modern way of doing things. Sukardjo Wirjopranoto:4–6.

28. Muhammadiyah, for example, paid a young Indonesian doctor f. 250 per month, or twice what the colonial government offered. (Interview in 1971 with a doctor whose experience this was.) As groups such as the Parindra and Taman Siswa grew, they assembled the financial strength to employ Indonesians in a host of jobs similar to those available through the government or

the private Dutch sector, and for similar or better pay. Thus a young account-
ant with experience might find a job with an Indonesian-run bank or cooperative. This was a powerful, basic way of weaning the social and intellectual
elite away from dependence on the colonial power. (Interview in 1971 with a
clerk who had a similar experience.) The newspaper I have in mind here for
Surabaya was *Soeara Oemoem*, which also made a point of publishing
Indonesian-language summaries of all municipal council meetings, emphasizing issues of greatest interest to the arek Surabaya.

29. See the example, and an indication of the government's reaction, in
SO 1-6/7-41.

30. Except where cited otherwise, information on the Sudirmans comes
from interviews in 1971 with their daughter, Sudjarmani, and from the typed
manuscript "Riwayat hidup R. A. Siti Soedari."

31. He is said to have attended school with both Sukarno and the Parindra leader Moh. Husni Thamrin. SO 2-18-41 and 6-13-41.

32. This account is based on interviews in 1971 and 1972 with Sutadji.

33. This account is based on interviews in 1972 with Sungkono.

34. See the example in SPBI 8-12-35.

35. This account is based on interviews with former friends and neighbors of Achmad Djais, 1972.

36. See his advertisement in SO 2-9-33.

37. SPBI 5-15-35 and 6-25-35.

38. This account is based on 1971 and 1972 interviews with Imam Supardi's widow, brother, and several close colleagues; and on *Berita Yudha* 4-3-71.

39. In 1933 Imam Supardi brought his younger brother, Mohammed Ali,
to Surabaya to help handle the additional workload he had acquired. The
young man had only a very basic education, but was told to begin proofing
copy. He was expected to educate himself—quickly—on the job; in less than
ten years he was a principal editor.

40. This account is based on interviews in 1971 and 1972 with Ajat and a
number of his contemporaries; and *Berita Yudha* 4-3-71.

41. Ajat Djojoningrat:n.p.

42. This account is based on interviews with Doel Arnowo in 1971 and
1972.

43. The most common measure of wealth among kampung residents
was the number of houses a person owned. Doel Arnowo's father owned "four
or five" and thus probably had an economic standing not far below that of
Achmad Djais.

44. It was not so easy to place restrictions on the press, though the government certainly tried to do so. By 1933 the PID discovered that it could not
keep up with the volume of reading necessary to monitor the indigenous
press thoroughly, and appears to have focused its attention merely on the
most flagrant abuses or the most radically inclined publications. For this
reason as much as any other intellectuals turned to and emphasized journalism and publishing. SO 10-3-31 and ARA MvK Mr 1004/1935:55.

45. Doel Arnowo:*passism*. Another edition of the *Kamoes marhaen* appeared in 1941 under the title *Kamoes pergerakan. Soeara Ansor* October 1941, advertisement on back cover.

46. This account is based on Korver:113-16 and the sources cited there, especially ARA MvK Mr 139/1916; von Faber (1936):47; and *Rapport . . . Kantoor van Arbeid*:27-28. For a rather different view, see Sartono Kartodirdjo (1973):36-37.

47. *Sawunggaling* 11-1-26.

48. See especially Ingleson (1983) and (1986), which show that in many respects the origins of strikes and labor movements during this period did not lie in the intellectual class, and that even communist intellectuals were far separated from the working, kampung classes.

49. See the statement of purpose in the first issue of the Studieclub newspaper, *Soeloeh Rakjat Indonesia*, cited in IPO 1925, No. 50 (Dec. 5):418-19.

50. *Sin Yit Po* 3-16-25; Ruslan Abdulgani (1974d):19-20; Soetomo (1986):introduction.

51. Von Faber (1936):51.

52. ARA MvK Mr 481secret/1930:5-6.

53. For an example, see SO 1-11-41. For a newly formed multikampung sinoman council, see SO 11-28-32.

54. See the view in SO 2-11-33. The gemeente, it should be noted, was fully aware of this, and the appearance of the Sinoman Council was a major factor in producing efforts by municipal officials to install a precinct system.

55. For example, SO, SPBI 1-15-32.

56. SO 12-17-31.

57. Interview in 1971 with Ruslan Wongsokusumo, associate of Dr. Soetomo and prominent member of the PBI at the time.

58. The following account is based on SO 12-3-32 and 1-12/13/14-33; and interviews in 1971 with Maruwan, a long-time resident of Dinoyo who played a key role in these events.

59. Examples may be found in SO 2-11-41; NGS 1940 No. 1:256-57; 1941 No. 2:13-14 and 31-32.

60. SO 10-12-31.

61. This account drawn from SO 2-18-33 and SPBI 2-17-33.

62. *Menjala* 11-1-32.

63. *Menjala* 12-1-32; SPBI 4-1-33.

64. *Berdjoeang* 5-3-34; the same article is approvingly taken up in *Soeara Ansor* Oct. 1941:86-87.

65. *Soeara Ansor* Oct. 1941:87. The same notion appears repeatedly in interviews in 1971 and 1972 with new priyayi figures active in Surabaya at this time.

66. This account is taken from information provided in the *Abdulgani MS*, as well as Ruslan Abdulgani (1972b) and (1974a).

67. This is an estimate. Official municipal statistics do not record the number of Indonesian-run schools, though a handful appear along with

Dutch institutions in earlier counts. VS 1930, I:333-36. ARA MvK Mr 1004/1935:55 also notes that in Surabaya Residency there were 101 such schools, 21 of which were under special observation in the City; no total is given for the city, however. A later newspaper article reports that there were about 75 of these schools in the city. SO 2-10-41. The numbers of teachers and students given here are based on averages mentioned in the sources above, and the judgment that, compared with rural schools, those in the city would tend to have somewhat larger student bodies and slightly better student-teacher ratios.

68. Information in this and the following two paragraphs is based, except where cited otherwise, on interviews in 1971-72 with teachers and students in such schools during the 1930s.

69. SO 4-2-41.

70. Teachers at the lowest levels earned salaries slightly below those of semiskilled laborers in Surabaya. At higher levels, with the right credentials and experience, the pay was somewhat above the average kampung income. Except in the best Indonesian-run schools, teachers were on the whole paid less than in government schools.

71. ARA MvK Mr 1004/1935:55-57.

72. For example, see *Soeara Ansor* May 1940:18ff.

73. Such was the conclusion drawn by many intellectuals at the time, and echoed in kampung interviews on the subject in 1971-72.

74. Based on interviews with two former teachers, 1971.

75. Interview in 1971 with a kampung resident who attended such schools as a child.

76. Interviews in 1971-72 with former teachers.

77. A good madrasah cost only one-third the amount charged by most private Indonesian-run schools in the mid-1930s. Interview in 1971 with a former teacher acquainted with both systems.

78. According to interviews in 1971 with a former teacher and school director, the ratio seems to have been about the same in "secular" schools as in those run by religious organizations such as Al-Irsyad.

79. Interviews with former students in Kampung Peneleh and Kampung Plampitan, 1971-72.

80. This conclusion is drawn from interviews with a number of former teachers, especially one in 1972 with an individual who made a point of keeping close track of former students from the late 1930s.

81. Much of this account is based on a 1971 interview with a PNI-associated figure much involved in such efforts.

82. According to several former teachers from better-situated kampung, some kampung residents even founded small primary schools for their neighborhoods.

83. Interview in 1971 with a former Kampung Dinoyo resident and son of an illiterate taxi driver.

84. Interviews with residents of several Surabaya kampung, 1971-72.

85. Interview in 1971 with a resident of Kampung Genteng.

86. Based on an interview in 1972 with the former owner of a bookstore in Kampung Peneleh.

87. Based on SO 3-27-41, and interviews in 1971–72 with several persons connected with founding lending libraries of this type.

88. Interviews in 1971 with several long-time residents of Kampung Dinoyo.

89. Some of these theories are discussed in Vanickova:418–19.

90. Pigeaud (1938):322–23.

91. Peacock (1968):30. Wandering ludruk troupes in those days gave performances from kampung to kampung, where inhabitants looked upon them as cheap, light, and enjoyably bawdy entertainment.

92. Here and below, except where cited otherwise, information on Durasim and his troupe comes from interviews in 1971 and 1972 with the last four surviving members of the group as it was constituted in the 1930s.38

93. Interview in 1971 with Ruslan Wongsokusumo, who aided Dr. Soetomo in bringing this about.

94. Dr. Soetomo is said to have asked, when he first met Durasim, whether the ludruk director or any of his fellow actors knew the meaning of the white *sarung* (skirt, cloth) and red *topi* (cap) which were part of the ludruk costume, or of the torch one player carried during the performance. When all replied they did not, Soetomo pointed out that the red and white symbolized the national colors of Indonesia, and the torch stood for the enlightenment of the people. Therefore, he said, ludruk and the pergerakan were one.

95. See *Ensiklopedi umum*:669. Geertz (1959):289 notes that ketoprak experienced a decline between 1923 and 1930. Judging from information supplied in 1971–72 interviews with former ludruk and ketoprak performers, however, this was not the case in Surabaya.

96. Newspaper advertisements and reviews of ketoprak shows in Surabaya during the 1930s speak of contests, judged by the audience, for the most splendid costume, sweetest voice, and so on. SO 10-5-31 offers a good example. Going to these shows became a popular craze for a time.

97. SO 4-21-34.

98. The phrase, which is taken from a 1972 interview with person who remembered it, was *jadi anggota orang pinter-pinter*.

99. It is perhaps worth noting that intellectuals were often ambivalent where ludruk was concerned. Few considered it suitable entertainment for educated people, certainly not to be compared with the "fine" arts, and they seldom attended simply for the enjoyment of it. Based on 1971 interviews with former ludruk players, who paid careful attention to the make-up of each night's audience, as they had to shape dialogue and aim jokes to fit it.

100. At least this was commonly believed to be so, and some kampung residents recalled in 1971–72 interviews that they had been told just that by employers.

101. Based on kampung interviews, 1971–72.

102. Information in this and the following paragraph is taken from *Ensiklopedi umum*:651–52, and Soedarsono.

103. The major ones, with their parent or affiliated organizations were: Nationale Padvinders Organisatie (Algemeene Studieclub); Sarekat Islam Afdeeling Pandu (Sarekat Islam); Hizbul Wathon (Muhammadiyah); Nationale Padvinderij (Boedi Oetomo); Jong Java Padvinderij (Jong Java); Nationale Islamitisch Padvinderij (Jong Islamieten Bond); Jong Indonesische Padvinders Organisatie (Theosophists); Siswo Projo (Taman Siswa); Al Kasjaf wal Fadjrie (Al Irsyad); Surya Wirawan (PBI/Parindra); Indonesische Padvinders Organisatie (Pemoeda Indonesia); Kepanduan Bangsa Indonesia (first under Indonesia Muda, then a conglomerate); and Kepanduan Rakyat Indonesia (a conglomerate of several Islamic scouting groups).

104. Interviews in 1971–72 with several former scouts and scout leaders.

105. Interview in 1971 with a former scoutmaster who had good recollection of colleagues in other groups.

106. There are no figures on this point, of couse. A further complication is that new priyayi who were scouts in the 1930s tend to recall members being all individuals like themselves, while those from the kampung middle class tend to recall that others were mostly "just ordinary [lower class] people [*bawahan saja*] like themselves. The general drift of many discussions with former scouts and leaders about the composition of the groups to which they belonged seems to point in the direction of a largely (slightly above 50 percent) middle class membership.

107. SO 11-21/22-31.

108. SO 12-30-1932.

109. Interview in 1971 with a journalist and follower of pergerakan affairs who did not, however, have attachments to a particular youth group.

110. *Berdjoeang* 7-26-34.

111. Interviews in 1971–72 with several individuals who taught this type of course.

112. A good example is the Persatoean Pemoeda Plampitan. Its members were for the most part Hizbul Wathon (Muhammadiyah) youths, but they met with IM people, of whom Ruslan Abdulgani, a Plampitan boy, was the most prominent. Interview in 1971 with a former kampung resident who belonged to this group.

113. See the anonymously written short story, "Buah kongres yang kedua."

114. SSW Dec 1941/Jan.1942:1–2.

115. SO 1-2-41.

116. See, for example, the complaints in SO 6-3-41 and *Soeara Indonesia Moeda* Sept. 1941:10–11.

117. SO 5-24-41.

118. SO 1-15-41.

119. For examples, see SO 2-21-41 and 4-7-41; and *Soeara Ansor* May 1941:165.

120. A particularly good example is contained in *Soeara Ansor* April 1941:666-68.

121. *Soeara Ansor* Dec. 1941:106ff.

■ Chapter Three

Colonial Transition and the Urban Response

■ The dissolution of Dutch rule

Surabaya was one of the first cities in the Netherlands East Indies to take serious notice of the approaching war, forming a civil air defense corps (Luchtbeschermingsdienst, LBD) as early as 1937, and instituting regular air alerts and blackouts when the Netherlands fell to Germany in May 1940; the city's gleaming white government buildings were everywhere camouflaged with a hastily applied coat of black and gray mottle.[1] In most governmental matters the colonial authorities held fast to existing arrangements, trusting that the usual emphasis on *rust en orde* (law and order) and the usual methods, only slightly more rigorously applied, would see them through. After mid-1938, for example, the PID tightened controls on the pergerakan and invoked existing laws on public expression and assembly with increasing stringency.[2] Proposals were earnestly discussed in Surabaya to establish an Indonesian-language war information bureau and to place public radios in every kampung.[3]

Behind such signs of preparation, however, were indications of uneasiness and an underlying instability, the corrosive effects of which were not long in being felt. In European circles, a faint alteration in the timing of daily life, slower on the one hand and nervously quickened on the other, accompanied the shift in Dutch attentions. Relations between Dutch and Indonesians worsened as Dutch chauvinism grew and fear of spies burgeoned.[4] The attorney general abruptly announced in 1940 that the word "Indonesia," previously considered

81

acceptable for public use, was henceforth banned, and Dutch vigilance even reached the point of outlawing the popular kampung sport of pigeon racing in order "to prevent bad news from being spread."[5] The idea that Indonesians needed to be guarded against, shared by many Dutch in Surabaya, resulted in the formation of a Volunteer Training Corps (Vrijwillige Oefenings Corps, VOC) under the aegis of the Vaderlandse Club.[6] This new group, with its severely anti-Indonesian bent, was quickly adopted as the official municipal defense force and soon spawned a municipally-sponsored program designed to mobilize Dutch youth, who turned their schools into barracks and periodically drilled in full uniform.[7] Intended to show strength and solidarity, these efforts nevertheless were poorly organized internally[8] and created much confusion between civilian and military activities, bringing VOC, LBD, and the colonial army into real disagreement.[9]

Municipal projects to safeguard Surabayans against air attack illustrate another sort of disorder and the disturbing effects it could have on urban society as a whole. During 1940, for example, hundreds of bomb shelters were dug in the sandy, low-lying ground.[10] In the first few weeks of the rainy season, however, they filled with stagnant water, offering a deluxe breeding ground for mosquitoes, and health authorities complained that many of the shelters ought to be filled in. Early in 1941, when the city announced that sufficient shelters were available for only 80,000 to 100,000 persons and that no more were to be constructed, the question immediately arose of whom the government intended to save first.

Even more disturbing to the Indonesians who learned about it was a curious scheme devised by city officials to answer the problem of what to do with non-European residents.[11] This plan proposed to "thin out" several of the most heavily populated sections of the city in order to guard against loss of life in bombings or internal disturbances. (Bomb scares and rumors of uprisings had sent city dwellers into the countryside as early as May 1940.[12] Approximately 65,000 people—40,000 Indonesians, 20,000 Chinese, and 5,000 Arabs, or 10 percent, 45 percent, and nearly 100 percent of these populations respectively—were to be moved about 25 miles to a location on the main road south of the city. They were to receive sufficient food for 3 to 5 days, and rice rations for a short time afterward. Bamboo shelters were to be built for Chinese and Arabs; most of the arek Surabaya were expected to "melt into" the villages outside the city. No provisions were made for health services, child care, or transportation of adults to jobs, though planners made a point of saying that all evacuees would be required to report to work in the city as usual. The plan, which was approved by the governor general for implementation, attracted such strong opposition from Chinese and Indonesians that, after several weeks of heated discussion, it was dropped altogether. But the impression it left was more than a little unsettling.

In this and other ways, Indonesians became aware of the changes taking place around them. Kampung folk, though unaware of details and nuance, sensed tension in the atmosphere from their reading of the indigenous press, the more sensational items from which were spread by word of mouth, and from their own experience with municipal authorities and members of the defense groups and the colonial army. A relatively common conclusion among the arek Surabaya after mid-1940 was that the Dutch were becoming confused and preoccupied with the war.[13] Intellectuals whose daily lives brought them into contact with the Dutch also felt intensified pressures and a certain panic in the air as they worked in their offices.[14] The prospects of a Pacific war had been considered for nearly two decades in pergerakan circles, and some new priyayi had come to view both war and eventual independence as inevitable[15]; journalists went so far as to announce that the fall of Holland to the Germans also marked the beginning of the march to Indonesian independence, and used the phrase "final victory" (kemenangan akhir) to refer not only to an Allied triumph in the war but also to the achievement of Indonesian freedom, whether in war or peace.[16] But behind this confidence lurked concern over the erratic behavior of the colonial government, and a penetrating fear of the Japanese and what their arrival might actually mean. While some leaders counseled that the proper response to growing confusion and disintegration was a calm and more or less detached outlook,[17] even the most sophisticated of Surabaya's new priyayi were severely shaken and many left the city for the rural areas of East and Central Java.[18]

By early 1941 Surabaya had already begun to slip into disarray. The periodic exoduses of the arek Surabaya to rural areas soon were accompanied by movement in the opposite direction, as Dutch and pangreh praja sought refuge in the provincial capital. Population rose in the city, and housing grew scarce.[19] Police reported that law and order was increasingly difficult to maintain, notably among Europeans but among other groups as well. Dislocations associated with military preparations were at the root of much of this instability, but widespread demoralization was also blamed.[20] Despair and hysteria grew like dark crystals until, at the final municipal council meeting held in January 1942, Dutch members no longer even attempted to disguise their hopelessness, while elsewhere in the city municipal officials and prominent residents earnestly discussed shooting the carnivorous and poisonous creatures in the Surabaya zoo, lest they later be released by the Japanese to prey on Europeans.[21]

To a great extent Dutch fears rested on misconceptions about the Japanese and these are worth outlining briefly in view of both the particular role the Japanese played and the relationship which developed between them and the Dutch during the first and last months of occupation. Officially the colonial government's posture toward the 6,000 or more Japanese residing in the Netherlands East Indies was strictly neutral, but beneath this thin disinterest lay an apprehension that a common bond between Asians—Japanese and Indonesians—was being forged as Europeans slept. To guard against this, a special section of the PID was formed in 1937 to gather information on all resident Japanese, and in 1939 strict censorship of all printed materials of Japanese origin was initiated.[22] Yet the Japanese remained a mystery to the colonial government. Japanese language expertise was scarce and Japanese circles were almost impossible to penetrate; since Japanese enjoyed the same legal status as Europeans, they could not be subjected to the same controlling tactics as, say, Indonesian activities, and PID officers were forced to wait patiently outside club meetings and other gatherings.[23] PID officers widely suspected that both Japanese businesses and social organizations were merely covers for extensive clandestine activities, and one 1940 report even suggested that the exemplary record of Japanese in East Java was itself a subtle form of propaganda impossible to combat.[24]

Surabaya's 1,400 or so Japanese in 1940 played an important and visible economic role, owning 14 banks and large commercial ventures, 15 wholesale import outlets, 14 retail stores, 5 scrap iron companies, 4 hotels and restaurants, and a number of other enterprises.[25] In other ways, however, they remained isolated from the daily realities of colonial urban life, and from both Dutch and Indonesian communities. Most Japanese resided in tight clusters, often sharing houses in the better Dutch neighborhoods but, unlike most Europeans, employing few servants, usually Chinese. A tightly knit social life centered on a dozen or so associations for youth, travel, Japanese arts, and the like.[26]. Despite many examples of business failure, the colony was on the whole viewed as a land of economic opportunity, and the example of individuals like Okano Shigezo, who after several failures succeeded in building a successful chain of department stores in Surabaya and several other Javanese cities, seemed to confirm the economic myth and inspire many followers.[27]

Not surprisingly, given these circumstances, Japanese tended to view colonial affairs through European lenses, only slightly tinted to suit their own needs. Few spoke or read either Dutch or Indonesian beyond the most elementary level, and fewer still took an interest in indigenous political life, at least in part because they were aware of how closely they were watched by the PID. A few Japanese took language or art lessons from Indonesians, but relations with politically outspoken individuals were quite rare.[28] For the most part, indeed, Japanese viewed Indonesians as indolent, childlike, and placid, and admired the Dutch colonial system, which was characterized as efficient and productive, vindicating perfectly the policy of rust en orde.[29] What the Dutch feared most—that the Japanese would ingratiate themselves with Indonesian intellectuals and turn them against the colonial government—was highly unlikely, and PID efforts to substantiate such concerns in Surabaya came to little.[30]

The Dutch in Surabaya appear to have imagined that the Japanese in their midst favored a Pacific war and were in fact the vanguard of the "drive to the south." The characterization is almost certainly mistaken. While it is true that Japanese throughout Southeast Asia increasingly were caught up in the rhetoric of expanding Japanese interests, the majority in Surabaya at least saw development taking place through trade, hard work, and peaceful economic networking.[31] There was little feeling that business stood to benefit from military expansion, and when, in June 1941, the Japanese consul in Surabaya urged his countrymen to return home, many refused, hoping to protect their holdings overseas as well as to avoid the draft.[32] Six months later, when Dutch police hastily gathered the remaining Japanese and placed them in a makeshift detention camp in the municipal park, the captives' overwhelming concern was the destruction of their livelihoods, for which they knew they could expect no compensation from the Japanese military regime.[33]

On 3 February 1942 the war, which for so long had seemed remote and only vaguely comprehensible to many of Surabaya's inhabitants,[34] became abruptly and palpably real as Japanese forces carried out the first of more than sixty bombings of the city in little more than a month.[35] Especially for Europeans, normal daily life came to a halt as schools closed, staple goods and money were hoarded, deliveries of food became unreliable, and servants and coolie laborers disappeared from their places of work.[36] As Surabaya became isolated from the rest of the Indies, and on 26 February even lost telephone contact with the capital,[37] a hastily passed municipal law against leaving the city increasingly was ignored. Tens of thousands of evacuees filled the roads south.[38] With the Battle of the Java Sea raging in the waters north of Surabaya, some Dutch spoke hurriedly of killing all European hospital patients in the city if they could not be moved before the "barbarous" Japanese touched shore.[39] By 1 March the defeat of the Dutch navy was common knowledge, and one Dutch housewife observed in her diary,

> The old Surabaya, always full of life and busy with speeding cars, cheerful people, spacious gardens, horse- or ox-drawn carts, bicycles, pedestrians, street vendors, little European children in bright smocks . . . all had disappeared. Everything was drawn in and hidden, and only the singing heat lay over the empty streets.[40]

Many European families attempted to boost their morale by planting corn in their front yards, hoping that the Joyoboyo legend might be true and that the Japanese would leave within 75 days (the maturation period of a corn plant). A popular greeting of the day became "Remember the 16th of June!"[41] but the optimism this expressed was remarkably thin.

In the silence and suspense the Dutch order waned. Immediately following the Battle of the Java Sea, the attorney general ordered all PID records destroyed and personnel dispersed in the countryside, where it was thought they might avoid persecution by urban Indonesians as well as the Japanese. In Surabaya these tasks were carried out between 28 February and 2 March 1942. Five or six loads of paperwork were destroyed in the smelting ovens of a local manufacturer, while PID staff received three months' wages and indefinite leave.[42] Indonesians in other branches of the police force drew the conclusion that Dutch rule was finished, and began to desert. From a municipal police force of about 600, 250 left at the end of February, including more than half of the highly disciplined bicycle brigade.[43] The Dutch themselves provided a dark backdrop for these dramas by implementing, on the afternoon of 1 March, a carefully planned scorched-earth policy designed to destroy every military and civilian installation of any conceivable use to the enemy.[44] Though incompletely carried out, the work of demolition teams exceeded the destruction caused by the recent Japanese bombings, and deeply disturbed Dutch and Indonesian residents alike. With great clouds of black smoke rising over the city from the harbor, the oil refineries, and the airfield, it seemed as if Surabaya had become a witch's cauldron, a sea of fire from which there was no escape.[45]

Equally unnerving was the wave of violence and looting which arose, first in rural areas and then in the city itself. This *rampok* (pillage, banditry) began in mid-February as the countryside emptied of Dutch and the pangreh praja became increasingly paralyzed.[46] Sensing the lifting or suspension of colonial authority, Indonesians in villages and small towns began looting shops, abandoned offices, European homes, and public facilities. To the pangreh praja, who were able to do little but watch or flee, it seemed clear that the main cause of this phenomenon was a hatred of colonial rule, which now had an opportunity to be vented. The Dutch and, later, the Japanese believed the phenomenon to be connected with the pergerakan,[47] but in retrospect there appears to be no indication that this was the case. Intellectuals, indeed, generally were horrified by the outbreak of lawlessness and mob violence, as well as puzzled about its cause.[48] Although in isolated cases local bandits of a more or less traditional nature may have been the instigators, in general the rampok was the unpremeditated response of local people to the unsettled atmosphere and a variety of specific local tensions.[49]

By the first days of March the rampok had spread to the city.[50] Here the situation was somewhat different, in that the concentration of police, military, and armed Dutch residents prevented the more virulent forms of rampok from taking hold. But large-scale looting took place at industrial sites to the south of the city, at the harbor, near military and police posts, and around factories. Police attempts to control matters were largely unsuccessful. For several days the ransacking continued unchecked, fanned by the demolitions (which provided the proper atmosphere and left damaged goods scattered everywhere) and by the frequency with which military and civilian offices were emptied. Equipment from household goods to motorbikes often wound up on the streets, where the rush for these items was at times so frenzied that it encouraged looters to look for more inside public and private buildings. It was this scene, punctuated with continued Japanese bombings, which convinced many Europeans that the end had come.[51]

By 5 March the hopelessness of defending Surabaya against the Japanese was clear. Dutch troops had no recent reconnaissance data and did not even know from what direction the Japanese were advancing.[52] Outside the city the European soldiers quarrelled fiercely, fired their weapons wildly at Indonesians and each other, broke into Chinese stores for food and supplies, and deserted altogether; when these soldiers reached the city, residents complained that they roamed about looking for food and drink but lacked the courage to stand up to the rampok gangs that by this time had begun to plunder Dutch homes in the fashionable sections of town.[53] In the afternoon five Japanese tanks appeared at the Wonokromo Bridge, the southern gateway to Surabaya, but soon withdrew under sporadic fire.[54] This was the city's last act of defense, followed by a day of tense and empty waiting. As Dutch troops evacuated Surabaya on 7 March, leaving only about 1,200 volunteers as a defense force, the city veered momentarily in the direction of panic.[55] The governor of East Java began making preparations for immediate surrender, but when some Dutch residents heard this news they threatened to shoot him if he did not withdraw his instructions.[56] No effort was made to control the exodus of thousands of ordinary Indonesian city folk, or to hold back the tide of rampok that engulfed even LBD and municipal defense posts.[57]

In the evening, however, the situation calmed. Dutch sat dispirited and bitter in their homes or barracks, awaiting an unknown fate. Kampung residents, stirred by the whirling disorder and impressed by what they clearly recognized as the destruction of the Dutch hegemony, were both fearful and hopeful about the future. Among the relatively small number of pergerakan activists remaining in Surabaya, there was continued talk of the opportunities the war offered, not only to weaken Dutch rule but to rejuvenate Indonesian life as well. The self-strengthening already begun under the pergerakan was now absolutely necessary for survival, and for assuring that after the war the foundation for a new society would exist.[58] Yet the precise nature of the future was unclear, and many turned to introspection in order to conquer their apprehensiveness. Parindra leaders, for example, gathered late in the evening of 7 March at the grave of Dr. Soetomo, seeking the courage to continue their struggle against all odds.[59] The next dawn's light revealed a Japanese flag raised high on the Wonokromo Bridge, bringing an era to a close but offering no clues as to precisely what lay ahead.

■ Transition to Japanese rule

In Surabaya power was transferred from Dutch to Japanese hands with comparative ease; the city closed the brief transition period with less difficulty than any other in the Indies.[60] To many residents, the surrender and beginning of occupation seemed to bring the war to a close. There was a momentary lifting of tensions, and when the city lights were turned on for the first time in more than three months they seemed to welcome the return of normal times.[61] Perhaps the chief factor in this smooth passage was the attitude of the Dutch, which strongly favored rust en orde. Especially if, as they tended to believe, the Allies would win the Pacific war quickly, it seemed logical to aid the Japanese in the task of maintaining order, and to insist that Dutch and Indonesian civil servants remain at their posts.[62] Some Dutch went further than this, either frankly admiring Japanese authority or feeling at least sufficiently impressed by it to feel compelled to play a helpful role.[63]

On the morning of 8 March 1942, a small group of Dutch, including the governor of East Java and the mayor of Surabaya, met with the commander of the Japanese Army's 48th Division in Sidoarjo, south of the provincial capital.[64] The Dutch officials saluted the Japanese officers, in order to "make a good impression." Since there were no firm plans for the occupation of Surabaya, one was devised on the spot with the cooperation of the Dutch. Surprised to learn that the city was now defended by about 700 volunteers rather than 7,000 army regulars, the Japanese asked about the situation of the native population. The Dutch replied that they "still had [the Indonesians] under their thumb" but warned that trouble might result from a noisy or disorderly taking of the city. The Japanese agreed not to use shock troops and to accept the help of both the municipal defense force and the Dutch police in keeping order. A large Japanese flag and a supply of Rising Sun armbands were presented to the Dutch officials, who returned to the city impressed with the discipline, propriety, and reasonable outlook of their new rulers.

When the occupying forces began to march into Surabaya, much of the city was quiet. Storefronts were boarded over, offices closed, houses silent.[65] Along Darmo Boulevard, however, where European homes and gardens made an elegant entrance to the colonial urban world, Indonesians gathered to cheer Japanese soldiers as they walked or bicycled past, and to jeer at the few Dutch officials on the scene.[66] The show of anti-Dutch feeling was strong enough to convince the Dutch who saw it that their authority was lost irretrievably in Indonesian eyes.[67] In a few instances the arek Surabaya's hostility took a violent turn. One kampung near the Wonokromo Bridge, embittered over Dutch intrusions and destruction during the previous week, took the opportunity to set upon a Dutch police patrol with knives.[68]

Japan's primary interest during the first few months of occupation in Surabaya lay in achieving and then maintaining stable conditions. If this did not amount to restoring the precise *status quo ante*, it was as close as the Japanese could get as the new—and Asian—masters of the city. In a symbolic gesture, Radjamin Nasution, the only non-Christian Indonesian among four city aldermen, was named mayor almost immediately. The appointment was accorded little publicity, however, and the position given negligible actual significance, as the former Dutch mayor continued for some time to function as a leader in the European community and as Radjamin himself was soon replaced by a Japanese.[69] Far more telling with regard to Japanese intentions were the continuities: both Dutch and Indonesian civil servants, including those in the various branches of police, were instructed to continue in their jobs as usual, and to act as sole liaisons with the Japanese military; government offices which had moved to avoid being bombed were returned to their original locations; military headquarters were established at some distance from the center of civilian administration so as not to be confused with it; and major industries, businesses, and utilities were urged to get things running smoothly again as quickly as possible.[70] Officials in Surabaya early announced that "the normal daily life [of the city] remains subject to all former rules and regulations, under the supervision of the Japanese Army."[71] Two weeks later law courts were handling their customary case loads, and official announcements emphasized that pleas of extraordinary circumstances in cases involving events in February and March were unacceptable.[72]

However, not all was quickly or easily restored. Several months passed before full train service could be offered, since many bridges in East Java had been destroyed by Dutch demolition teams; communication by mail and telegraph was slow in being reestablished.[73] A staggering amount of paperwork also faced the new administration, mostly recompiling statistical and financial data destroyed by the Dutch, but in some cases finding and recording information which had not been available earlier.[74] Finally, there were unexpected difficulties with the city's Indonesian population. The Japanese were quickly frustrated, for example, by the arek Surabaya's unwillingness to take the reinstatement of LBD practices and blackouts seriously, or observe the curfew which had been reimposed.[75] Even the most mundane and seemingly unconnected circumstances sometimes proved beyond the grasp of occupation officials. For instance, Indonesian ox cart drivers' habit of permitting their animals to relieve themselves in the streets was incomprehensible to the Japanese, who were anxious to create order (as they knew it), yet was also quite impossible to control.[76]

Overshadowing difficulties of this sort were two major concerns. The first was unstable economic conditions, particularly as these were reflected in the wildly fluctuating prices of foodstuffs and services. The Japanese expended much effort in attempting to control inflation, largely by establishing ceiling prices for most goods and dealing harshly with hoarders. Success was limited at best.[77] The price control section of the municipal police was strengthened with personnel from the PID and elsewhere, but watchfulness and heavy fines did not prevent stockpiling and price gouging, to say nothing of the growth of a black market.[78] Authorities were so disappointed in the initial response to their attempts to establish economic order that, a month after the transfer of power, the municipal administration itself undertook to sell staple goods at fixed prices.[79]

A second and equally pressing concern for the Japanese was the continuing lawlessness. Rampok and ordinary thievery proved difficult to halt in Surabaya. Newspapers reported major incidents weeks and even months after the Dutch surrender, and news filtering in from the rural areas of Java and Madura indicated that the countryside was far from settled.[80] Military authorities were anxious to bring these activities to a halt, but despite a folklore to the contrary (in Dutch as well as Indonesian circles) their methods do not appear to have been extraordinary. Executions and maimings were rare in the city, and patient investigative police work seems to have had the desired effect before long.[81] Though the incidence of crime eventually dropped to relatively normal levels, the Japanese were deeply impressed by what appeared to them as an innately undisciplined indigenous population. Throughout the occupation the Japanese remained exceptionally sensitive to the potential for disorder among the Indonesians of Surabaya and the surrounding areas.

In some measure on this account, relations between Japanese and Europeans in Surabaya were especially complex. If nothing else, the New Order that the Japanese wished to establish on Java was to be explicitly non- and even anti-Western in nature. Yet practically speaking the immediate internment of all Europeans would have been unwise, since there were no adequate facilities for doing so and since, more important, European experience and expertise in maintaining the colonial order were needed badly. Aided by disagreements among the Japanese themselves on the issue, the Dutch in Surabaya were dealt with in a compromised fashion.[82] Military personnel were quickly placed in camps—generally existing barracks—and government officials followed soon after. Other civilian males were interned gradually, and women and children remained free for nearly eighteen months. In the meantime, the occupation authorities permitted the Dutch considerable freedom to handle their own affairs, and even provided public kitchens and subsidies to the needy.[83]

Many Dutch felt remarkably comfortable in their relationship with the Japanese. Though the seriousness of their intent to remove Western influence from colonial life eventually dawned on Europeans, this was a rather late development. There was little violence between the two groups, and no prolonged attempts at Dutch resistance. One reason for this was that the Dutch, shorn of their power, were suddenly strangers in a newly strange land. The majority preferred the prospect of dealing with the Japanese rather than with Indonesians, whom they considered the greater and more permanent of two evils.[84] The most searing realization of this period was that anti-Dutch sentiment ran deep in the indigenous population. Dutch families who ventured outside of Surabaya during the first weeks of occupation reported very hostile reactions from the inhabitants of small towns and villages; in the city, where conditions were more constrained, many Dutch nevertheless felt engulfed by hostile crowds and spoke of the "traitorous role" of Indonesian intellectuals, especially those associated with the Parindra.[85] One military officer based in Surabaya wrote later,

> We had a general notion about the Javanese people. I quite understood that they didn't exactly worship us [Dutch], but that they harbored such a hatred for us as then appeared came as a great surprise to me. I never thought it was so bad.[86]

Many Dutch, indeed, were inclined to believe what Japanese officers said when they noted offhandedly that Europeans in Surabaya would have been much worse off had Indonesians been in control.[87] And if some thought about returning to their old lives at war's end, they did so only vaguely and with a certain sense of hopelessness. As one Dutch priest wrote about his journey from Surabaya to a prison camp in West Java, it had begun to occur to the Dutch "how unimportant we are, how weary and impotent.[88]

At the same time as they were coming to grips with the "European problem," the Japanese also had to reach an understanding with the Indonesians. Despite the tone of Tokyo's earlier propaganda efforts, the new rulers' approach to the indigenous residents of Surabaya was cool. Some of this diffidence had its origins in the prejudices of Japanese officers and in the bad impression left by weeks of rampok.[89] Equally important, though, was a lack of clear policy, to say nothing of expertise, in dealing with Indonesians.

There is no clear evidence that Indonesians offered or were invited to accompany the Japanese when they entered Surabaya, despite the persistence of beliefs to the contrary. As they marched through the city Japanese troops distributed an ample supply of tiny Japanese and

Indonesian flags, and of canned milk and other foods, in an effort to win over the arek Surabaya.[90] But Indonesian leaders did not step forward to greet the Japanese, and when a small, self-appointed delegation of Parindra directors tried to meet the new military commander they were informed summarily that this was impossible.[91] The Dutch mayor's impression, as he worked with the Japanese authorities, was that they made exceptionally little effort to seek out prominent Indonesians in the city during the first weeks of occupation.[92]

There were obvious reasons for the Japanese to be wary of pergerakan intellectuals, the most important being that their thought and behavior had been shaped in an anticolonial mold, making them potentially troublesome in a Java which, however "new," was not decolonized. On the other hand, Indonesians with modern educations, progressive ideas, and some understanding of political action were the most easily comprehensible segment of indigenous society for the Japanese and as close to natural allies as they were likely to find. Under these circumstances it might be expected that occupation officials might have arrived with a reasonably accurate notion of what sorts of intellectuals resided in Surabaya and perhaps even which of them they wished to speak with first. In spite of the common belief that lists of this sort existed, usually for the purpose of executing or jailing those named, concrete evidence is lacking.[93] The Japanese made a few initial inquiries, often with the wrong persons, about Indonesians working in the press or belonging to one or another political group. Later events revealed that the police were quite capable of making arrests on a grand scale on the basis of entirely mistaken identifications. The few intellectuals who did happen to fall into a working relationship with the Japanese during the first months of occupation did so haphazardly, often as a result of their ability to speak some English.[94] Several months after the surrender, the Japanese recognized their handicap and initiated a registration of educated Indonesians in Surabaya.[95]

Pergerakan intellectuals did have guarded hopes of improvement, but these soon evaporated as it became obvious that the new government was far more interested in convincing office employees to return to work than in seeking the cooperation of activists. The Japanese attitude toward political life, furthermore, appeared anything but promising. Barely two weeks after entering Surabaya, the Japanese decreed an end to the still exhilarating practice of flying the Indonesian flag and to political organizations of any kind.[96] The language of the announcements indicated the measures to be temporary, but they were met with disappointment and disbelief. Parindra leaders simply attempted to ignore the orders, and they even flatly refused a request to disband that came directly from the headquarters of the military government, an action which may have helped to bring about the arrests of Parindrists in Surabaya and Malang several weeks later.[97]

In July there came word that Sukarno, freed from the Sumatran exile imposed by the Dutch, would soon visit Surabaya.[98] This news encouraged many intellectuals to hope that their leadership might be recognized in the New Order after all. A large reception was planned, with a full program of speeches and mass gatherings reminiscent of the leader's visit to the city in 1931. Shortly before the events were to begin, however, the authorities forced changes in Sukarno's schedule. His speaking engagements were limited to one appearance and relocated to a relatively small building rather than an open area as originally planned. In addition, a gala formal party was cancelled and replaced with informal visits to a few private homes. Even with these restrictions, however, the tour managed to have something of an air of triumph about it. Sukarno's speech was not as impressive as some had expected, but it focused on the popular pergerakan topic of freedom from Western colonial rule, and featured Sukarno dressed in a suit modeled on those worn by Indian nationalist leaders. Omnipresent Japanese flags and slogans aside, the occasion seemed to imply that the pergerakan still had considerable promise.

All of this produced enormous crowds of followers and onlookers in Surabaya, which alarmed the Japanese. The day after Sukarno left the city, police announced the prohibition of all meetings and organizations, whether political or not. This order finally forced the Parindra, the last of the prewar parties still functioning, to disband.[99] A month later, complaining that the new warnings had not been heeded, the Japanese attempted a massive drive to gather up all those suspected of anti-Japanese activity.[100] As many as 85 individuals were arrested, and some were later tortured and executed.[101] The arbitrary nature of these arrests, which mixed PNI, Parindra, PKI, and other individuals indiscriminately, stunned the new priyayi. The lesson seemed to be that Japanese rule was highly unpredictable and aimed against all educated Indonesians. The majority of pergerakan activists became frightened, and sought to keep a low profile in any way open to them. The young Ruslan Abdulgani continued in his position at the government office of economic affairs, which he had held under the Dutch. Roeslan Wongsokusumo, one of the highest ranking Parindra officers, dropped out of public view altogether, taking a job as a local newspaper distributor. Others disappeared temporarily, remaining at home or visiting friends and relatives elsewhere.

If the initial Japanese treatment of the new priyayi seemed harsh, that of the pangreh praja was cautiously supportive. From the first days of the occupation the Japanese made it clear that they understood the degree to which they depended on the pangreh praja for the maintenance of rust en orde. The usual pattern in East Java had been for military commanders to seek out higher-ranking pangreh praja in each city or town they passed, deliver a letter of authority (in Japanese) to him, and request that he retain his staff and take over all affairs normally handled by Dutch administrators in the area.[102] In most cases there was no further contact for about six weeks. Many pangreh praja understandably believed that the Japanese placed considerable trust in them.

This happy if vague state of affairs did not continue. The Japanese called the first meeting of the regents of East and Central Java on 22 April 1942, in Surabaya's City Hall.[103] This was the same day on which Dutch administrative personnel and other government officials were summoned to Surabaya and interned. The regents were shielded carefully from that event, and found their conference room guarded by Japanese soldiers who not only checked identification papers but made it clear that no one was to leave until the ceremony was over. As if this were not contrast enough with the annual meetings held by the Dutch, the gathering had little to do with administrative subjects and simply made the heavy-handed point that the Japanese Army was now firmly in power. It may well be that, as one non-pangreh praja in attendance noted, the regents appeared frightened and preoccupied with the prospects of saving their own skins,[104] but it is also probably true that most were not especially impressed with the Japanese as serious rulers.

At the second conference, held on 16 June, only 10 regents appeared compared with 39 at the earlier event.[105] This time the program followed Dutch lines more closely, each regent presenting a short report on political activities in his region. The group then lunched with the military commander in Surabaya's best hotel. The afternoon was devoted to a motion picture showing Japanese victories at Pearl Harbor and Hong Kong. A concluding speech by the commander emphasized that with rust en orde now restored, it was time to get down to the business of supporting the war effort. He complained frankly about the lack of cooperation from the regents, and reminded them that they were now considered employees of Japan. They were expected to behave accordingly. The impression on the pangreh praja was even more negative than before. The Japanese called for information which every Dutch official had known by heart, and failed to discuss pressing local problems and solutions. Pangreh praja also had no trouble observing that the Japanese gave them greater responsibilities but, at the same time, less respect than had the Dutch. It was not difficult to conclude that the pangreh praja were in danger and their privileged position in Indonesian society likely to erode rapidly.

In Surabaya's kampung at this time, inhabitants felt both a sense of relief and a vague uneasiness. Many had fled the city with the onset of the bombing, and several months passed before they returned to their homes. The majority were able to return to their old jobs or similar work, and this reestablishment of old patterns was an important factor in the initially neutral kampung attitude toward the Japanese order. Fears of destruction were put to rest, but other concerns remained. It had been commonly believed in the kampung that the Japanese would bring with them improved economic conditions, especially in the form of inexpensive consumer goods. Their experience during the first few months of occupation indicated that this might not turn out to be the case. There was apprehension also about the implications of actions such as the setting up of loudspeakers at various points in or near kampung throughout Surabaya.[106] For the most part, however, kampung life gave no signs of having suffered appreciable damage, and the arek Surabaya wanted to see if the future might hold anything different for them than the past.

■ Administrative and economic changes

Seldom new in appearance and often disappointing to those who had awaited it, Japan's order nevertheless bore within it the unmistakable germ of change. In addition to the practical impetus to win the war, the Japanese were driven by the hope of sparking in Java the same kind of development process they themselves had experienced since the Meiji Restoration of 1868. Even during the early months of the occupation, when little consideration was being given to implementing substantive changes, public opinion in Java was deliberately turned toward the Meiji dream and the Japanese model of modernization.[107] Intellectuals, who were often sufficiently familiar with the general story of Japan's economic growth to be excited by it, were encouraged. For a brief time a few writers were even moved to discuss expansively in print the promise of changing times and revolutionary improvement inherent in the New Order.[108]

As yet poorly understood, however, was the distinguishing characteristic of the "revolution" the Japanese had in mind: a subtle blending of the themes of continuity and change. When Japanese leaders in Surabaya spoke publicly of the Meiji transformation, they did so in terms of strong, sustained change that brought with it no serious dislocations and a spirit of revitalization both highly charged and carefully measured.[109] In an exhibition propagandizing Japan's intentions, other aspects of the message came through. Under a photograph of a Japanese woman in modern dress standing beside a traditional doll figurine was printed the legend, "People must be modern so as not to be left behind by the times, but their traditional culture should not be discarded in the process." Beneath a picture of a Japanese eating rice appeared the words, "They eat rice just as we [Indonesians] do, so why are they stronger?"[110]

The principles of change and continuity so successfully wed under the aegis of Meiji modernization were fully complementary in Japanese eyes, but in the context of occupied Java they seemed difficult bedfellows at best. The fundamental source of conflict lay in Japan's contradictory roles of liberator and ruler, but there were others of less encompassing nature. The military leadership was sensitive to conflicts inherent in the occupation and its policies, but realized that little could be done about most of them until the war's end. In some respects the fact that Japanese goals often ran counter to each other prevented the majority of occupation policies from reaching extremes. The government's need for order and discipline, for example, certainly limited efforts to awaken and mobilize the population in support of the Greater East Asian War, as enthusiasms stirred up in such a campaign might prove difficult to control. At least in part on this account, Surabaya's occupation years were quiet ones, both for the Indonesians and for the Japanese themselves, who tended to view the city, far from the front, as a kind of paradise in which one could drink real coffee with sugar, and not worry a great deal about the "lovely, impotent" indigenous population.[111]. Yet, beneath the surface of city life, inconsistency and discord began to take their toll and eventually to produce an uneven ferment of enormous potential force.

Some of the dilemmas the New Order posed for both Japanse and Indonesians in Surabaya began to reveal themselves after six months of military rule. In August 1942 the official return to civilian government was announced, and along with it the formation of Surabaya *shu*, a division equivalent to the earlier Residency.[112] Although regulations issued at the start of the occupation had called for no changes in colonial administration, in fact a number of important alterations were made. These followed two general principles. First, dualistic features of Dutch rule—by which, for example, the Dutch assistant Resident's powers overlapped with those of the indigenous regent—were abolished. Direct chains of command with no duplication of responsibilities were established. Second, the confused tradition that had allowed urban areas, such as Surabaya, to be governed partly by regents and partly by a mayor was no longer condoned. What lay inside the city limits was the responsibility of city officials, who thereby gained authority but also were tied more directly to the shu, as opposed to the central, administration. The purpose in all this was to give clearer lines to the bureaucratic system and to reverse the development of the city as an independent colonial unit.[113]

Under the new scheme, the officer of chief importance to Surabaya was no longer one in the municipal structure, but the *shuchokan*, or Resident. The position of mayor became more technical or managerial, and after September 1942 was entrusted only to Japanese.[114] Surabaya's Resident was Yasuoka Masaomi, a forceful but unpretentious retired army officer who had served in China.[115] He established a reputation for being reasonable and patient, and has been credited by Indonesians acquainted with his office with preventing in Surabaya the kinds of excesses said to have occurred in other cities. Yasuoka also was considered to be, despite his aloofness, sympathetic to Indonesians. He was one of very few upper level Japanese administrators in Java to make a serious attempt at speaking the Indonesian language in public, and he became fond of paying visits to nongovernmental offices and kampung schools throughout the city.[116]

When Yasuoka arrived in Surabaya on 31 August 1942, the Residency office over which he was to preside had already been moved from temporary military headquarters to the old governor's office, where it had begun to function as a regular, largely civilian, administrative center. The municipal building nearby had operated in the usual fashion for some time. At that moment and for the next few years there were surprisingly few outward signs of change. The city (with the exception of military installations) was little damaged, and even tram schedules remained relatively undisturbed. Most municipal services continued uninterrupted, and despite a reduced budget efforts continued to expand the city's transportation network and to improve its supply of water and electricity.[117] The precinct system inherited from the Dutch was modified slightly by reducing the number of divisions to ten; kampung boundaries remained as before; a new census of the city was completed; and to no one's apparent dismay the municipal council was not revived.[118] Otherwise municipal structures and services continued much as before. One Dutch official's impression that after six months of Japanese rule "the kampung had spread everywhere" reflected a superficial problem with rubbish collection rather than a deeper transformation of Surabaya under Japanese auspices.[119]

More subtle modifications proved to be of greater importance in the long run, however, especially in the ways they affected Indonesians. Japanese administrators, for example, clearly hoped to employ as many Indonesians as possible, both because this was often practical and because there was a genuine feeling behind "Asia for the Asians" ideals. Considerable effort went into attracting former personnel back to work and having them begin courses in elementary Japanese. At the same time, those responsible for hiring were conscious of the problem they faced in trying to run the city properly without adequate technical and managerial aid, and this practical consideration also was compelling. In several instances the Japanese temporarily released Dutch officials from internment to train Indonesians to take their places in the administration.[120] For the most part, however, Indonesians did not fall heir to Dutch supervisors' jobs, as the Japanese did not hesitate to burden experienced individuals with two or more jobs, call experienced persons out of retirement, or hire Chinese and Eurasians before Indonesians to fill especially important positions.[121]

Indonesians were therefore not unduly impressed with the new opportunities the occupation presented. It was commonly believed that the Japanese were more interested in training individuals already on the payroll than in hiring new people, and that advancement under the Japanese was more difficult than it had been under the Dutch.[122] While it is likely that the municipal workforce did increase during the occupation, and that the majority of new places were filled by Indonesians,[123] the negative perception of what was occurring was more significant than the reality, as it failed to inspire loyalty and led to disillusionment.

A similar situation developed with respect to the maintenance of law and order in Surabaya. The city's great importance to the Japanese—as a military and economic center, as a possible focus of unrest, and as the residence of the majority of civilian and military Japanese in East Java—was reflected in the special attention given to law enforcement. The sheer number of police in Surabaya shu was impressive, accounting for approximately one-tenth of the total civil police force on Java.[124] By the end of the occupation the municipality employed approximately 1,500 regular police (in addition to army and navy military police), a force more than 60 percent larger than in prewar days.[125] Although several organizational changes were made in Java's police structure, including the clear separation of pangreh praja and police ranks, these had little effect on circumstances in the city, where the functioning of the municipal police and other branches continued much as before.

The PID, now known formally as the *tokoka*, or special service police, was reconstituted early in the occupation under military supervision, but later operated as it had earier.[126] Its highest ranking Indonesian officer from the Dutch period was placed in charge, and principal agents assumed broader powers of arrest. Police operations of all kinds made it possible, as the Japanese fully intended, for the city to remain peaceful during the occupation. But as had been the case under the Dutch, dependence on police power had the drawback of frequently producing the very restlessness it sought to forestall. Under the Japanese this tendency was heightened by the sharpened suspicions and tensions of wartime, and the greater role that force and cruelty came to play in police work. In short order the prewar concern over an omniscient PID was replaced by a deep-seated fear of a highly generalized and certainly overwhelming *kempeitai*. The word meant "military police," was commonly was used by Indonesians during the occupation to indicate police in general.[127]

That this should happen in Surabaya was particularly ironic. Among police officials who had some basis for comparison, Surabaya's PID and other police were considered to have been more closely controlled than similar groups elsewhere during the occupation period.[128] To the arek Surabaya and many of the new priyayi, however, kempeitai headquarters, located directly across from the former governor's office in what had been the Dutch Court of Justice, became the occupation's most fearful symbol. Kampung residents believed the Japanese to be cruelly arbitrary in contrast to the Dutch, and their distrust and fear of the "kempeitai" outstripped by far their ill will for the municipal government. Indeed, it inspired a host of savage rumors, many of them unfounded, about the horrors of the Japanese police.[129]

In economic matters the government's policies for the period following the early occupation were focused on rural Java, but cities were neither ignored nor unaffected. In general, Japanese thinking about Java's economy was based on the long-standing image of the island as a source, given the proper treatment, of enormous productive strength, and on the belief that the Japanese were intuitively capable of improving on the already creditable performance of the Dutch in this regard.[130] The bulk of occupation propaganda aimed at increasing saving, hard work, and productivity. Especially after late 1943, official determination to raise production became intense everywhere, even in urban areas. In Surabaya, Dutch and Eurasian youngsters who managed to remain outside internment camps recognized the employment theme as the most innovative and insistent of the occupation; city dwellers read in their air raid practice instruction booklets that factory and shop workers should ignore sirens and other danger signals lest industrial production drop.[131]

Three aspects of the Japanese drive for greater productivity were of special significance to Surabayans. The first concerned the collection and distribution of the annual rice crop. Here the Japanese faced severe problems. The new government had to replace an intricate Dutch-built system that was already in a state of collapse and that, in any case, Japanese agricultural experts considered scandalously inefficient.[132] There was also the complication that the Japanese replaced a potato- and wheat-eating ruling group with a rice-consuming one, thereby straining an already burdened agricultural sector.[133] Although there is reason to suspect that the occupation was much less disastrous for rice production than the Dutch later believed,[134] urban residents certainly did not see their situations improved in comparison to prewar days.

Yet the arek Surabaya appear to have enjoyed greater security with regard to their rice supply than most of their rural neighbors. Japanese planners were thoroughly aware of the city's vulnerability where footstuffs were concerned, and out of self interest as well as a determination to see the municipal administration work smoothly they took steps to counteract it. Surabaya, like several other major cities, became a center for rice storage, the Japanese holding large reserves there for themselves and for the use of the local population.[135] Government workers down to the level of the lowest office clerk received rice and other basic food rations regularly throughout the occupation period.[136] Surabaya's kampung folk, except for the lowest-paid coolie laborers and recent immigrants from the countryside, were far from going hungry. Rice and, especially, meat and produce, frequently were limited in quantity, but the city population in general cannot accurately be depicted as going through the occupation in a seriously deprived state.[137]

Surabaya's people were unhappy with their lot, however. They resented the rationing system instituted by the Japanese because it strictly limited the rice purchases of all residents, regardless of what they were able to afford. The feeling of being uncomfortably restricted in this way was common among the arek Surabaya,[138] and it was a sensation to which they traditionally reacted strongly. It is also likely that the unfamiliar situation of having money but not being able to spend it freely was more difficult to accept for the arek Surabaya, particularly the kampung middle class, than the reverse.[139] Rice processors and retailers, more of whom were Indonesian in the New Order than under Dutch rule, were especially concerned because Japanese regulations often made it impossible to realize a profit or even to avoid operating at a loss.[140] Continual tampering with a deteriorating distribution network earned the occupation authorities no friends in Surabaya, where by late 1943 people had begun to eat maize and cassava on a regular basis, more because rice was strictly rationed than because it was unaffordable.[141] The arek Surabaya drew the simple conclusion that the New Order, at least in this particular and basic respect, was inferior to the old.

Occupation authorities were also keenly aware of the degree to which Java under the Dutch had depended on imported manufactured goods, and of the reality that such items would be scarce during the war. No attempt was made to mask this circumstance, which often figured in speeches as the fault of Western domination and a burden all must learn to bear for the duration of the war. Serious efforts were made, however, to promote local inventiveness and industry. Indigenous business life was encouraged to adjust to the new conditions and to expand without dependence on outside forces or goods. Surabayans quickly made use of the disappearance of Western competition by manufacturing from local ingredients or materials, and selling, for example, tooth powder to replace the popular imported toothpastes, and bicycle lamps for the market formerly reserved for European models.[142] Other business-minded individuals saw money-making opportunities in such items as soda pop, *kecap* (a Javanese sweet soy sauce), and cooking utensils, large quantities of which had previously been made in other areas of Java but were not difficult to obtain.[143] Finally, existing industries only partly in Indonesian hands before the war generally improved financially as they fell more completely under Indonesian control. Among these were textiles, paper (usually *merang*, a type made of rice-straw), leather, soap, brick, lumber, and ceramics.[144]

Many Surabayans, especially those from the kampung middle class, were able to take advantage of the favorable business conditions, and most realized that their economic situation was far healthier than that of the rural population,[145] yet there was considerable discontent. Although indigenous businesses were often stimulated by the conditions of the occupation, they also were hindered by Japanese restrictions on the movement of raw materials and by the government practice of purchasing many products at artificially low prices. Government interference occasionally went so far, indeed, that even privately owned Japanese firms were forced out of business.[146] The arek Surabaya were especially irritated at the close watch the authorities kept on small enterprises, and at the increased regulations and paperwork imposed on them. Resentment over the unavailability of consumer goods also ran deep, particularly since it was widely and with some justice believed that the Japanese themselves had access to warehouses filled with all manner of commodities.[147] One obvious conclusion arek Surabaya drew was that whatever benefits the occupation had initially or potentially brought Indonesian businesses, these might be further enhanced by the removal of Japanese rule.

A final characteristic of the wartime struggle for production was the great attention paid by government officials to labor mobilization. Emphasis on hard work in field and factory was, after early 1944, placed in an even more urgent context than previously. Not only had the war crisis become acute, but the government had become frustrated with the tepid response to its calls for dedication from the masses. The arek Surabaya were chided in print for being "fooled by the tranquility they felt around them" and for having no understanding of the critical stage the Pacific conflict had now reached.[148] Propaganda to stimulate production reached a shrill pitch, now under the banner of a new labor association established by the Residency government.[149] Also during 1944, the work week for most urban employees was officially extended from 6 to 6½ days, and taking time off from work during the Moslem fasting month was prohibited. These changes were so thoroughly unpopular that even officials directly under Japanese supervision were brave enough to complain aloud.[150]

The most widely known and notorious innovation of the labor campaign, however, was undoubtedly the *romusha*, literally "volunteer worker" but by connotation (and often in fact) a forced laborer.[151] In common usage, "romusha" referred to anyone pressed or enticed into working for the Japanese or on Japanese projects, generally in some sort of manual labor. More precisely, these people ought to be divided into several distinct groups. Most prominent was the comparatively large number of skilled and semiskilled workers transported from Java to other parts of the archipelago and Southeast

Asia.[152] The majority in this category were attracted to recruitment programs by the pay offered and by the prospect of steady work; conscription was in fact rare.[153] Other varieties of romusha were assembled for projects on Java. Many of these, who were far more numerous all told than the laborers shipped overseas, were drawn by force and at random from poor areas where food production was low and the jobless rate high.[154] Still other romusha were part of a host of part-time, short-term workers on local sites, most of them cajoled or pressured in petty ways into participating.[155] A final category of workers, frequently referred to as romusha by Indonesians but never by Japanese, were school children and members of mass organizations who were mobilized to take part in local projects.

On the whole the labor recruitment effort was a disappointment to the Japanese, whose requirements never seemed to be met and who complained continually about Indonesians being a fainthearted people "lacking in the will to struggle."[156] To the people of Surabaya, however, Japanese labor recruitment appeared both successful and pervasive, and it became the most feared aspect of the New Order. Comparisons with the despised corvée of Dutch colonial rule were commonplace, and it was believed that rural society was torn apart by the brutal shanghai methods of the Japanese. Such notions certainly exaggerated the truth and were in any case not based upon the experiences of the arek Surabaya themselves, who were sheltered from the most abusive types of labor mobilization. Indeed, one of the most important attractions the city offered migrants during the occupation was an environment of relative anonymity and freedom from harassment by local officials. That a source of income might also be found in the city was often secondary to the goal of escaping what many rural poor saw as the likelihood of being pressed into service. In the city, kampung leaders were regularly asked to send given numbers of volunteers to clean streets or to do other chores for which they received no remuneration—labor which arek Surabaya lumped generally under romusha activities—but few additional demands were made.[157] Most kampung passed through the occupation undisturbed by Japan's search for manpower, except insofar as residents signed up voluntarily for jobs outside Java or joined a group involved in "volunteer" work within city limits.

Yet discontent generated by the romusha issue was serious among the arek Surabaya. They resented government intrusion into kampung life, and found required participation in public (and extra-kampung) cleanup or repair projects degrading and oppressive to a degree they had not known under Dutch rule. This restiveness was heightened by the tales of refugees from rural East Java, which filled kampung residents with dread and convinced them that their own safety was threatened. Many arek Surabaya came to view the urban atmosphere as increasingly unstable. In some areas of the city it became an article of faith that the only anchor in this gathering storm, the only protection against intrusion on kampung society, was to have one or more native sons—usually middle-class young men risen to new priyayi-type jobs—placed in government offices where they could make special appeals to the Japanese.[158] The more propaganda kampung residents heard about kampung recruitment or the necessity of increasing production, the more they tended to feel threatened. In this way, despite the New Order goal of keeping urban society as untroubled as possible, specific aspects of Japanese governance frequently worked against this general design.

■ Urban society and the growth of discontent

The uncertain and sometimes internally contradictory pattern of Japanese influences in Surabaya was reflected also in aspects of social and cultural life. The New Order, for example, appeared at first to promote a society shaped quite differently from the one preceding it in at least one respect, that of racial discrimination. Not long after the Dutch surrender, the majority of the city's movie theaters and hotels, customarily subject to restrictions against Indonesians, were opened to the public. Despite a few exceptions—a notable one being the Simpang Club, which became an exclusive Japanese officers' club—the change was widespread and its symbolic importance received immediate recognition.[159] Similarly, the gesture of sweeping away the colonial dual-track educational system, streamlining and Indonesianizing what remained, bore an obvious significance to all who had aspired to an education under Dutch rule. Finally, many Surabayans quickly grasped that the circumstances of the occupation sometimes offered remarkable social opportunities which might be taken advantage of by a clever individual with backbone, perserverance, and a certain amount of flexibility.[160] Yet the promise and hopefulness went largely unfulfilled, and results turned out rather differently from what either Japanese or Indonesians expected. Although the Japanese removed some of the barriers separating the Dutch from the indigenous population, for example, they did not prevent altogether the appearance of such problems in the New Order. Language difficulties and a certain naiveté about the Indonesian world prevented most Japanese from interacting meaningfully with their new "younger brothers," and where these were not serious factors a well-developed Japanese sense of superiority made its distinct impression. From the Indonesian point of view, relations with the Japanese were at best businesslike and frequently were touched with an unkind humor of which most Japanese were unaware.[161] The prospects for achieving social or financial mobility under the changed conditions also were subject to limitations. The Surabayan who, in the first weeks of the occupation, advertised his willingness to teach the Indonesian language to Japanese at the royal fee of f. 60 a month clearly was making the most of circumstances, as were individuals who discovered that they could learn elementary Japanese relatively easily to talk their way glibly into a job about which they knew little but the Japanese knew even less.[162] Opportunities of this sort, however, were more the exception than the rule, and comparatively few Indonesians were able to seize them successfully. Furthermore, positions gained in this manner were closely tied to the fortunes of the Japanese; as a result, those who held them seldom felt secure. Experience also showed that while the Japanese spoke a great deal about the significance of self-confidence and "modern" thinking, they were annoyed by Indonesians who did not appear to know their "proper place" in the New Order, or who seemed insolent in the way they spoke and wrote.[163]

In education, too, popular disaffection gradually resulted from the application of Japanese policies. From the beginning, occupation authorities favored Indonesians who had good basic educations, and there can be little doubt that they were serious about creating a school system offering a high-quality, Indonesian-run program. The respected language teacher Sutan Mohammed Zain, for example, was appointed director of Surabaya's single government high school and given considerable freedom to create a curriculum for it. At the same time, however, the vision of the New Order did not include using education to enlarge substantially the indigenous intellectual class. The Japanese were hesitant to open up government-sponsored (or, even less, privately run) schools to a broader clientele than had the Dutch; emphasis was placed instead on agricultural and vocational institutes, which found a certain receptiveness among some arek Surabaya but did not answer the persistent demand for "regular" schooling.[164] Both government and private schools in Surabaya underwent careful scrutinization by the Japanese, who kept them closed between March and August 1942. When the reopening finally was announced, it appeared that the number of government schools had been reduced, and entrance to them was restricted to those students who could prove previous attendance.[165] Private Indonesian-run schools of the type so popular before the war were treated even more cautiously. Their academic offerings were examined very closely and judged against strict government standards.[166] Most such institutions did not survive, and the reins of education were kept taut in Japanese hands.

Disappointing as it was, this situation was further complicated in a number of specific ways. The changes made by the Japanese in the administration of education, for example, caused much confusion. Teachers' expressions of discontent, which came early and vigorously, caught authorities by surprise.[167] In addition, the curriculum quickly fell victim to language problems, among them the compulsory use of the Indonesian language, in which many teachers exhibited little real facility where complex vocabulary and grammar were concerned, and the teaching of Japanese, for which teachers were poorly prepared, and for which native Japanese instructors rarely were available.[168] The daily school schedule became impossibly crowded with early morning calisthenics in the Japanese manner, military-style drilling, and a surfeit of "voluntary" work projects. Before long it commonly was judged that Surabaya's schools had turned disorderly and academically weak. On this account, and because government jobs seemed to follow government schooling less regularly than before, the appeal of the schools faded. Parents often wished to avoid school because it seemed to tie their children to a regimented program which had few rewards and was difficult to comprehend. The new priyayi, who realized fully how much their involvement in education was weakened by the new arrangement, found it easy to permit their interest in it to subside temporarily. Such repercussions were unsettling to urban society in ways and to a degree that the Japanese had not expected.

Finally, in cultural affairs a similar pattern gradually emerged. Here it is necessary to point out initially that, despite the contrary opinions often expressed later by Europeans,[169] there is little reason to think that the Japanese believed it possible or even especially desirable to Nipponize Indonesians. Efforts to teach Indonesians elementary Japanese language skills were motivated chiefly by the necessity of assuring that some communication occurred in that tongue. Language workshops and crash courses were, in Surabaya at least, limited for the most part to Indonesians who already possessed considerable education and a position in municipal or other government offices. Perhaps the real intent of the Japanese cultural policy was made clearest in newspapers and periodicals, which—aside from understandable attempts to introduce Indonesians superficially to Japanese ways of thinking and doing things—devoted their attention predominantly to Indonesian matters, signaling that the New Order was in fact far more Indonesian than the old. This is not to say that the Japanese perceived Indonesian cultural development as taking place entirely independently of Japanese guidance, but to emphasize that there were limits, and relatively narrow ones at that, to the occupation government's desire to impose Japanese culture on Indonesians.

A second point worth making is that there were limitations, as well, on the effectiveness with which the Japanese monitored and attempted to channel Indonesian culture. Their principal tool in this regard was the *sendenbu*, literally the Department of Information, under which both censorship and propaganda activities were gathered. Though it had arrived in Java with an embarrassment of propaganda riches, the sendenbu was throughout the occupation both understaffed and underfunded for the job expected of it.[170] The Surabaya branch employed about five Japanese and ten Indonesians, including one or two staff members connected with the subsidiary bureau for mail censorship.[171] The office as a whole had the responsibility of checking newspaper texts and overseeing the preparation of materials used in the Indonesian press. Even this task was somewhat circumscribed, however, because the Surabaya office was one of three similarly sized sendenbu centers on Java, and because their Japanese staffs lacked a sensitivity to nuance in the Indonesian language.

All newspaper copy was required to pass through sendenbu hands before publication, but little actual censorship occurred. Indonesian journalists and editors operated under the basic assumption that nothing overtly anti-Japanese could be printed, and that no war news except that taken from Japanese wire services could appear. Experienced at working under the Dutch system, most writers had little trouble adjusting to the more stringent but not otherwise very different one of the New Order; truly sensitive materials almost never reached sendenbu readers, who in practice accepted a wide variety of other materials with no objection.[172] In theory texts used in the performing arts and public performances of all kinds also required checking, but through Jakarta headquarters rather than the Surabaya sendenbu staff. This time-consuming process was insisted upon only for major events and performers, smaller local groups either consciously practicing self-censorship or acting cautiously out of a generalized fear. Such fear was in fact widespread in Surabaya, to the chagrin of the authorities. Printers of all kinds in the city seem to have believed, for example, that sendenbu or some other Japanese officials had to approve calling cards, stationery, business forms, and all manner of other everyday printing jobs, and continued to do so despite repeated officials denials and published requests that printers stop submitting proofs of these items.[173]

So it was in less direct and obvious ways that occupation policies affected Indonesian culture, usually by stimulating forces already at work. The best example probably is the expansion of the Indonesian language, which the Japanese consciously and unconsciously promoted as both an official language and a language suited to modern intellectual life. This phenomenon became as important to kampung dwellers as to intellectuals. In newspaper publishing, for example, *Soeara Asia,* the direct successor of *Soeara Oemoem,* and the only replacement for several large Dutch dailies and a host of smaller Indonesian papers, saw its daily press run quadruple to 40,000. Much of the increase was due to a new kampung audience that now found the paper both more affordable than before, and of more compelling interest.[174] In the less obvious area of the popular arts, changes also took place, some deliberately encouraged by the Japanese and others appearing unsummoned by occupation policy. In wayang and ketoprak a range of stories rarely played in Dutch times because of their anti-Dutch connotations—"Sawunggaling," "Untung Suropati," "Diponegoro," and others of that sort—came to the fore, and a new genre of historical drama grew rapidly. Likewise, a fledgling modern stage drama received encouragement in its treatment of social themes, particularly the value of labor and elite devotion to the masses, while ludruk was further enlivened with new subject matter and stage techniques.[175] The occupation is also often considered to have given birth to the Indonesian cinema, and although this view is strictly speaking inaccurate, it does reflect the popular perception of an increased number of truly Indonesian (language, story, setting) films and heightened public interest in seeing these productions.[176]

The new and distinctly Indonesian aspects of these cultural developments were not lost on the people of Surabaya, who were sensitive to the advances they represented, but neither were the limitations that Japanese rule imposed upon them. The arek Surabaya appear to have recognized, before the occupation was far advanced, that the Japanese, unlike the Dutch, often attempted to change Indonesians' ideas (rather than merely prohibiting the exchange of certain kinds of information or ideas). Skeptical and independent-minded to begin with, Surabayans were not inclined to take anything but a highly cautious attitude toward such efforts, especially in printed form. Though interest in reading increased, much written material was evidently mentally discarded. Messages in dramatic performances came to be considered predictable, especially when the performing troupe was known to have close government connections; urban audiences could not help but notice, furthermore, when plots took unfamiliar, Japanese-inspired turns or when propaganda speeches turned up in the midst of well-known dramas.[177] And, if these indications of Japanese interference were not obvious enough, it also became painfuly clear that police surveillance of public performances of all kinds was substantially increased.[178]

Beyond this sort of niggling interference, however, Surabayans had a special reason to be aware and deeply resentful of the Japanese where cultural matters were concerned. Sometime in the last half of 1943, Cak Gondo Durasim's ludruk troupe, one of the few in the city which declined to place itself under Japanese patronage, and which continued to present tangy social commentary in its performances, began to reflect Surabayan discontent with the conditions of wartime occupation. Performances included barbs aimed directly at the Japanese, and despite a number of police warnings Durasim persisted. At this time a number of pithy Surabaya couplets circulated in the city's kampung areas, and many were attributed to Durasim. Translated freely, the best known of these—still well-remembered in the 1970s—said, "If you thought things were bad before [under the Dutch], look how much worse they are now under the Japanese."[179] This line and the ditty in which it was set became so popular that it could not be passed over by the authorities. One evening after a show in the town of Jombang, Durasim was forced off stage by police and asked to report the next day to headquarters in Surabaya. There he was detained and apparently tortured. Durasim died not long after returning to his home in Kampung Genteng Sidomukti. Nearly all arek Surabaya heard about this incident at the time, and the sense of outrage seems to have grown at each repetition.

The seeds of urban discontent germinated rapidly; that they might become strongly and deeply rooted is plainly indicated in the institutional history of two particular programs the Japanese attempted to apply to the arek Surabaya, with results they could not foresee. The first involved the owners and drivers of the city's *dokar*, or horse-drawn taxis, and *becak*, or pedicabs. Seemingly an unlikely group to be affected in any significant way by administrative changes under the occupation government, these people nevertheless became the focus of much official attention and, subsequently, of serious unrest in Surabayan society.

Even before the Japanese entered Surabaya, most cars and trucks had been requisitioned by the colonial government or retired from use because of the prohibitive cost of gasoline. The once-popular dokar enjoyed a revival, and in 1941 was joined by a new competitor, the becak. The origin of this vehicle, handcrafted of steel piping and three bicycle wheels, is obscure. Some say it first appeared in Singapore, others that it was essentially an Indies invention, coming to light first in Medan, Ujung Pandang, or Jakarta.[180] Whatever the case, becak certainly were suited to survive in financially difficult times. In the course of less than five years they all but replaced the dokar. A becak cost about f. 50 in 1942 or 1943, while a dokar and a proper horse to pull it were worth four times as much and the animal required care and feeding in addition. In Surabaya, where the becak was first seen in late 1941, the number of these new man-powered cabs rose to 100 in less than a year, to 2,000 in eighteen months, and to 2,400 by mid-1943.[182].

The operation of vehicles for hire was an occupation that embodied most of the economic and social values dear to the arek Surabaya. Owning dokar and driving them were honorable livelihoods, calling for entrepreneurial skill and hard labor while assuring good pay and a certain individual freedom. Though owners never drove their own vehicles, preferring to lease them on a daily basis to those who could pay the price plus a deposit, ownership did not confer a director's or boss's rights. Eager and resourceful drivers could make their own schedules and use their own techniques to drum up business. Handsome profits were the reward for business acumen of this kind.

Except for paying a vehicle tax to the municipal administration, the dokar enterprise was free of government control in Dutch times, and drivers, who were nearly all Indonesians,[183] had few responsibilities to anyone other than themselves. The same was true with the becak business when it began. Many of these vehicles were built in Chinese garages and owned by Chinese small-scale investors, but drivers were always local Indonesians, who retained a keen sensitivity to their autonomy. The low capital requirements for becak drivers, the heady urban transportation market in the early 1940s, and the instability of the times made becak operation a popular and rewarding, if often excruciatingly difficult, occupation.[184] It soon acquired a distinctive élan closely wedded to the traditional spirit of the arek Surabaya. The independent, free-wheeling character of becak drivers became stereotypical. The dokar driver, usually identified by the Dutch-derived term *sopir*, was distinguished from his new colleague the becak driver, who was styled *tukang*. The word means, roughly, a specialist or expert in a craft, and it acknowledged in a thoroughly

Indonesian way the skill, determination, and rough individualism that becak drivers were reputed to possess. "Tukang," furthermore, contrasted sharply with the foreign sound of "sopir" (from "chauffeur") and another Dutch-derived word used for dokar drivers, *kutsir*. Perhaps for this reason, becak drivers came to be popularly addressed as *cak*, which carried with it that sense of populist honorific the arek Surabaya reserved for each other. Dokar drivers were rarely if ever so designated.

What disturbed the Japanese about dokar and, in particular, becak drivers was their unaccountability and apparent lack of organization. The Japanese were accustomed to a highly ordered public transportation system and tended to judge other peoples by their own standard. Apart from this general consideration, Japanese military and civilian customers in Surabaya were indignant to find themselves at a disadvantage in dealings with brazen pedicab drivers, who set no firm rates and were quick to take financial advantage whenever possible. There was also concern over incidents in which enlisted men ran off without paying for their becak rides, incurring drivers' fury and resulting in feuds between the city's drivers (among whom word spread fast) and the Japanese military authorities.

The Japanese planned to solve these difficulties by bringing all transportation enterprises, owners as well as drivers, under the wing of the municipal government. They dealt first with the becak situation, which was regarded as the most disorderly. Existing traffic laws were changed to include becak specifically, provision even being made for a dress code for drivers.[185] A second step was to set fares and require all becak to have licenses and to display identifying numbers.[186] When these measures appeared to be less than satisfactorily complied with by drivers and owners, city authorities drew up more. In early 1943 the word was spread that at some point in the near future all of Surabaya's becak concerns would be centralized and placed under the control of a government-run cooperative. Preparation for this major change was begun by holding a gala becak parade, complete with prizes for the best-decorated vehicles, presumably designed to coax unregistered becak out into the open. Officials also announced that a school for teaching becak drivers elementary Japanese and basic traffic etiquette would soon be established.[187]

On 1 May 1943 the becak cooperative officially opened under the sponsorship of the police and the city administration.[188] From the beginning, however, the effort was visibly controversial and incomplete. Though the pressure to conform must have been great, the owners of nearly half the becak in Surabaya refused to join, at least initially. Lengthy newspaper accounts made clear that there was serious opposition to the cooperative plan, and left the impression that no matter how much Japanese officials threatened there would be no general agreement to the new regulations.[189] The Japanese appear eventually to have succeeded in convincing a majority of owners and drivers to give in, but their acceptance was a grudging response to considerable official pressure.

Why the resistance? The question seems to have genuinely puzzled Japanese municipal officials, who devised the system not to make money,[190] and certainly not to ease their administrative burdens, but to benefit the public and bring public transportation in the city into line with modern standards as the Japanese saw them. The problem was not in the financial provisions of the system, which gave owners a regular income based on the number of vehicles they turned over to cooperative control, and provided compensation for any becak damaged while under cooperative supervision. Drivers dealt with the cooperative on an equal basis. Although the rates (both rental and fares) were set at the lower end of the range earlier observed, the ill effects of bargaining and highly competitive pricing were eliminated. Drivers received additional benefits in the form of free medical check-ups and vaccinations. Owners and drivers both received special food and clothing distribution privileges through the cooperative.

The chief difficulty lay in the manner in which these regulations transformed, or sought to transform, the men who accepted them. Owners, for example, became office personnel rather than entrepreneurs or investors. They were given no opportunity to make real decisions as to how their business was run; some worked at salaried desk jobs for the cooperative. Drivers' roles also were altered. They were no longer independent businessmen, masters of their own schemes to earn a living. They particularly resented being forced to wear numbered armbands and have their working hours set, to say nothing of being prohibited from bargaining with prospective passengers. In short, Japanese methods of controlling the becak trade unwittingly challenged fundamental Surabayan values and caused difficulties more serious than officials imagined. Nor was dissatisfaction limited to a relatively small occupational group, for owners and drivers communicated their views to the rest of kampung society, finding them echoed and reinforced by similar opinions already prevalent there.

A second Japanese program in Surabaya drove more directly and even more disturbingly to the heart of kampung society. This was an effort to influence the bulk of the city's population by methods which stood in sharp contrast to those used in the Dutch period. Though the wartime approach to altering the relationship between kampung and the municipal government was, in comparison with the becak experiment, more carefully founded on existing institutions, it nevertheless proved problematic. This Japanese endeavor, furthermore, ended on a distinctly ironic note. At the same time as it promoted a long overdue transition integrating kampung society more completely into an increasingly Indonesian urban world, it struck a note of profound unease and even rebelliousness in the face of change.

Occupation authorities showed from an early date a strong interest in establishing better communications with kampung residents, almost certainly because, as numerous newspaper items straightforwardly complained, official regulations and announcements seemed to go unheeded among them. Conditions in this colonial city were different from those in Japan, where the media and other communication tools were developed more fully. The comparison can only have frustrated Japanese administrators, most of whom had little or no colonial experience. Initial attempts to improve the situation did not succeed. The celebrated "singing towers" erected throughout the city in 1942, for example, never had the desired effect of reaching arek Surabaya with information.[191] Most of these radios-on-poles were set up on main streets rather than in kampung alleys, and the sound of their broadcasts did not penetrate the majority of city neighborhoods. Even where it managed to do so, many instruments soon broke down and were not repaired. After the first comprehensive air raid practices of the occupation proved to be poorly attended and executed by kampung dwellers, the need for a more effective method reaching the neighborhoods rose even higher on the Japanese priority list.[192].

The principal innovations the occupation brought to urban social organization were the *tonarigumi*, a neighborhood association with a basis in traditional Japanese concepts, and the *keibodan*, a voluntary civilian guard or "vigilance corps" of a type common in Japan since the mid-1930s. Both terms were generic, and although theory provided for single, over-arching organizations, reality was much closer to self-contained, local organizations bearing the same names and operating in similar fashion throughout Java. Much about the functioning of the tonarigumi and the keibodan in Surabaya remains unclear. The dates of founding, for example, are uncertain and so variously recorded even in official sources that it seems best simply to note that both groups rose to importance after mid-1943, occupied much of the administration's time for approximately eighteen months, and then began to fade in significance.[193] The two organizations were not spread uniformly throughout the city, contrary to what official data and accounts suggest.[194] Some kampung appear to have had no keibodan at all, while others were bound up in their activities; some kampung residents paid close attention to the installation and growth of the tonarigumi, but others saw too little change even to mention. Finally, both organizations as a rule had only the haziest images in popular thinking. They often were confused by the arek Surabaya with any number of other groups: the *bokagun*, or fire-fighting corps, for instance, or each other.[195]

Yet the effects of these two occupation institutions upon kampung life are clearly discernible. The tonarigumi, though it seemed to be nothing much different in broad outline from the familiar sinoman, implied alterations that kampung residents could not ignore. Institutionally the tonarigumi did not echo the unique circumstances of each kampung in which it became established, but the needs of the government to which it owed its existence. The tonarigumi, unlike the sinoman, was part of a centralized system, and its existence precluded the displacement of the "unorganized and traditional" arrangements the Japanese professed to see in Surabayan society.[196] Thus the tonarigumi was in reality the ground level of a pyramidal structure designed to bring municipal government directly into the kampung. At the top stood the *lurah*, the lowest ranking individual in the pangreh praja hierarchy on whom the Japanese now depended to appoint trustworthy section heads (*azacho*) in the city. These individuals, who were expected to make monthly reports to the lurah, were required in turn to search discretely for heads of neighbrohoods (*tonarigumicho*) in their own areas and to arrange what might loosely be called an elective process by which these persons could be recognized as kampung leaders. Each tonarigumi was to hold a regular series of meetings for the purpose of furthering community solidarity, distributing government rations, and passing on news of governmental regulations.[197]

In application, all of this fell somewhere between Dr. Soetomo's earlier efforts with the Sinoman Council and Dutch attempts to exercise control over the kampung by establishing a precinct system. On the one hand, the Japanese set the sinoman notion on its head, with the municipal government bringing kampung within its reach rather than being challenged by kampung interests. On the other hand, however, the tonarigumi scheme avoided some of the more serious difficulties inherent in the Dutch administration, with its dual lines of responsibility, and tapped with some success the resources of kampung society. Pangreh praja generally approved of the new system, which appeared to them mercifully uncomplicated by questions of who had jurisdiction over what. Kampung residents seem to have appreciated the scheme's orderliness and its useful role in the distribution of foodstuffs. As a rule kampung people also exhibited considerable tolerance for the individuals who found themselves, often quite unexpectedly, in the difficult positions of section chief or neighborhood leader in the new system. Petty abuses of power generally were ignored, and it was noted then and later that the persons involved had been forced to take their positions.

On the whole, however, the arek Surabaya found it hard to accept the pyramidal system of which the tonarigumi was a part, especially because they considered it to be applied from above. There were few overt expressions of discontent, as it was feared that the Japanese would deal harshly with open refusal to cooperate. But uneasiness about the tonarigumi was in fact widespread. The Japanese had great difficulty promoting the system in Surabaya throughout 1943 and 1944, and they do not appear to have been satisfied at any time with the way it functioned.[198] Many kampung merely arranged to accommodate their existing sinoman with the general framework of the new system, and then refused to accept any further changes. Other kampung altered their ways more completely, but without any genuine commitment from residents.[199] For the bulk of the urban populace the tonarigumi seemed more an irritation than a sign of progress, and it did not narrow appreciably the gap between kampung and the city government.

The keibodan, the second Japanese innovation, was a vaguely defined institution that operated in a variety of ways depending upon circumstance. Essentially an auxiliary group promoting civilian preparedness in the areas of first aid, fire-fighting, and keeping the peace during an emergency, the keibodan was conceived of as operating through the combined efforts of pangreh praja and the police.[200] In Surabaya's kampung, organizational responsibilities fell most often to section heads, neighborhood heads, and a number of individuals with experience in the Dutch LBD. Training was the task of the police and, occasionally, members of the military.[201] Devised primarily to engender the spirit and organizational habits which the Japanese believed necessary for self-defense, and to encourage cooperation with municipal officials, the keibodan was unarmed and, except at the highest level, entirely in Indonesian hands.

In some respects the keibodan appears to be a good example of a successful Japanese exercise in mass mobilization in Surabaya, but in practice it never performed as its designers expected. It also failed to earn the loyalty of the kampung folk who were to have been its back-bone. There were many reasons for the keibodan's unpopularity with the arek Surabaya, among them the customary sensitivity to imposi-tions from the municipal government, and a relatively poor under-standing of the organization's purposes. There also were problems resulting from the keen competition for manpower among a host of occupation organizations in the city: workers who belonged to de-fense groups at their factory or workplace (also called keibodan) nor-mally refused to take part in the neighborhood versions. In some areas section heads contented themselves with simply pulling together a few individuals to act in case of fire or air raids.[202] Loud objections arose also over the keibodan training sessions, both the type involv-ing large numbers of people and mass exercises, and ones held for smaller groups in special dormitory quarters over a period of three or four days. In the first type, practices were sometimes so realistic that kampung residents panicked and abandoned their duties, intent upon saving themselves and their families from certain destruction; in the second, arrangements usually included a rigorous program of calisthenics or marching, tedious bucket brigade practice, and dietary changes.[203] Few kampung residents thought well of these activities, which they considered humiliating and unnecessary besides. Not long after the establishment of the keibodan, kampung residents learned to make themselves scarce when the practice sirens sounded, and to avoid in any way possible being asked to attend one of the training sessions held in dormitories.

Despite considerable Japanese effort, the tonarigumi and keibodan in Surabaya could not be made to perform satisfactorily. Initial evi-dence that the organizations were getting off to a slow start prompted special training sessions for Japanese and Indonesian leaders, public admonitions that persons in important kampung positions should "show good character and be friendly," and attempts to dismiss un-cooperative kampung leaders; participants were even to be identified with special insignia so they might "avoid difficulties in carrying out their responsibilities.[204] The changes did not have the desired effect. A city-wide alert and training day that was observed by visiting Japa-nese military dignitaries from Jakarta proved an embarrassing fiasco. On 29 July 1944 much-rehearsed drills in fire-fighting, neighborhood evacuation, and first aid application broke down completely. Water supplies failed, kampung residents did not cooperate, and even spe-cially trained squads were not able to carry out their tasks: the major-ity of arek Surabaya in the practice area were frightened and ran to their homes during the air raid simulation, leaving empty lots where shelters were to have been erected. Two days later it was announced with obvious chagrin that "the training . . . was no better [than earlier sessions] and in some places was even worse.[205] Intensified drilling followed, along with a greatly increased number of meetings designed to perfect the tonarigumi system. As late as April 1945, however, after nearly two years of operation, the keibodan still was considered by Japanese officials in Surabaya to lack the proper drive. Its performance was poor and the authorities did not disguise their continuing disappointment.

Thus discouraged with the results of their kampung activities, the Japanese concluded that for the most part urban Indonesians were backward and incapable of functioning in a modern, integrated society.[206] The arek Surabaya, however, looked at things in quite a different light. To kampung residents the occupation appeared as an extended and often threatening period of confusion, in which the keibodan and tonarigumi came to represent the forces of disorder and intrusion rather than, as the Japanese intended, the opposite. The arek Surabaya's response was avoidance and irritation, which together became the basis for a rapidly multiplying hatred of the New Order version of colonial rule. In addition, neighborhood stress enhanced local cooperation and feelings of unity, while intensifying rather than beginning to heal kampung hostility toward the municipal government.[207] Indeed, Japanese attempts to involve kampung directly in municipal life and break down kampung isolation seem to have provoked Indonesians far more seriously than Dutch efforts in nearly the opposite direction. At the highest level of generalization it seems fair to say that for the majority of Surabayans the occupation years brought not so much transition as intensification of established patterns and attitudes.

■ Notes

1. SO 10-28-37; SP October 1940:127.
2. SP March 1940:37 and 84.
3. SO 8-24-41; IPO 1940 No. 48 (Nov. 30): 114. The latter suggestion

never got past the discussion stage, but it is interesting to note that the Dutch at least considered doing what they later complained bitterly about the Japanese accomplishing.

4. Dutch accused Indonesians of defiling pictures of the Dutch queen and of plotting secretly against them. Much of the difficulty and fear was generated, however, from within the Dutch community itself, where debates raged over how to treat the natives during the crisis, whether the army and navy could be relied upon, whether the colonial government was effectual, and whether fascist sympathizers ought to be jailed. For some examples, see ARA MvK Mr 1108secret/1940; SH 11-25-40; SP May 1940:151-52; SO 1-14-41; and IPO 1941 No. 42 (May 22):805-06; RvOIC 000387-32:1-4. That all of this made a deep impression on Indonesians who followed events is clear from both printed accounts (for example SP March 1940:86) and from interviews, for example with police officers who watched Dutchman arrest Dutchman for the first time during their service.

5. SO 1-21-41.

6. SP October 1940:120; IPO 1940 No. 40 (Oct. 4):899-901.

7. SH 10-31-40 and 12-18-40; RvOIC 000387-68; RvOIC 028977:7-8.

8. RvOIC 015406-7; SH 11-26/27-1940.

9. SO 3-4-41; SH 11-5/12-40; RvOIC 034101; RvOIC 062945:15.

10. This account is based on reports in SO 1-22-41 and 2-6-41.

11. Information in the remainder of this paragraph, except where cited otherwise, is drawn from SO 3-11-41, 4-18/19-41, and 5-29-41.

12. IPO 1940 No. 19 (May 19):330.

13. For example, SO 3-27-41; based also on kampung interviews, 1971.

14. Interviews in 1971 with employees at municipal and PID offices.

15. Predictions of conflict between the Japanese and Europeans abound in the writings of nearly all pergeraken figures. One of the earliest was Tan Malaka (see McVey:317), but see also Mohammad Hatta (1952):65 and (1953) I:27 and 78; Sukarno:116-25; and Mangkupradja:105-34. Dr. Soetomo was so certain in 1937 that war would break out and alter Indonesian's situation that he bid his followers to relax and allow events to take their course. ARA MvK Mr 230secret/1938:12.

16. SO 5-10-41; see, for example, the use and explanation of the phrase in SSW December 1941/January 1942:1-2.

17. SP May 1940:143-44, and June 1940:159-60; SO 4-5-1941 and 7-1-1941.

18. *Abdulgani MS*; interviews with several individuals who left the city to await developments, and knew many others who did the same.

19. SO 2-25-41.

20. ARA AAS 97b/XXII/45d, *passim*.

21. MBZ IA XV/9/Mr 699/APO secret:4; interview with the Dutch mayor of Surabaya at the time, 1970.

22. ARA MvK Mr 199secret/1940:9.

23. Interviews in 1971 with both former PID officers and a Japanese par-

ticipant in these meetings in Surabaya. It is unclear whether there were Japanese in the employ of the PID as spies, but former Surabaya PID officers noted in the same interview that they believed this would have been impossible, at least in East Java.

24. Interview with former PID officer, 1971; ARA MvK Mr 199secret/1940:21.

25. Takeda:250–51.

26. ARA MvK Mr 559secret/1940, Bijlage 3:2; and Mr 893secret/1937:1; interviews with a Japanese resident of Surabaya in those days, 1971.

27. A general reflection of Japanese ideas can be seen in the many items listed in the Irikura bibliography. More specific information is contained in ARA MvK Mr 70secret/1939; Takeda: 249 and *passim*; and in Okano's autobiographical work. I have drawn also on 1971 interviews with Okano Shigezo and several other Japanese who had economic interests in Java at the time.

28. Interviews in 1971 with two Indonesians who gave such lessons in Surabaya. Japanese were well aware of Dutch sensitivities in these matters, and deliberately shied away from any behavior which might arouse the suspicions of the colonial government.

29. Interviews in 1971 with a number of Japanese having experience with Indonesians in the 1930s, two of them experienced businessmen in Surabaya and East Java; and with a group of "Indonesia hands," mostly journalists for various Japanese news services. Though the Japanese approved of nationalism in the abstract, there was comparatively little real sympathy for Indonesian nationalist feelings, even during the occupation. There were exceptions, however. Thus the unusual career of Ichiko Tatsuo, who teetered on the thin divide between being a Japanese expansionist patriot and "going native" in Indonesia, and who died fighting the Dutch during the revolution. See Goto (1976) and (1977).

30. The only serious instance of Japanese-Indonesian collusion uncovered by the Surabaya PID was a suspected effort of Japanese newspapermen to buy or heavily influence the Parindra-associated paper *Soeara Oemoem*. Little came of this except a tentative agreement that the Indonesians would use some Japanese dispatches in future issues. Nevertheless, four *Soeara Oemoem* directors were interviewed by the PID, to whom they related every detail, and the Parindra executive committee engaged in a furious argument with the newspaper directors on the issue of the paper's freedom to act as it wished. ARA MvK Mr 230secret/1938, Mr 4secret/1939, Mr 317secret/1939, and Mr 1114secret/1939.

31. Slogans of this sort were posted, for example, on the walls of the Surabaya Japanese youth organization. ARA MvK Mr 70secret/1939.

32. Interviews in 1971 with a Japanese who was there, and with the former Japanese consul in Surabaya.

33. An account from the Japanese perspective is given in SH 4-24-42. See also Takeda:249. I have been unable to locate a published Dutch or Indonesian account, but have been aided by a former Dutch resident in 1970.

120

34. RvOIC 000387-53:5.

35. Eyewitness accounts of the bombings are found in RvOIC 072775, 000387-68, and 000387-53.

36. ARA AAS 97b/XXII/45i:2; RvOIC 015183.

37. NICJ Vol. 7:15.

38. RvOIC 015183.

39. RvOIC 005309.

40. RvOIC 000387-32:6.

41. RvOIC 000387-53:32; and 028254, No. 20.

42. Interview in 1971 with a former PID officer; also ARA AAS 97b/XXII.45e:3.

43. ARA AAS 97b/XXII/45g:1.

44. The best account is in NICJ Vol. 7:134ff.

45. MBZ IA/XV/9 Mr 699/APO secret:6; RvOIC 012920:2 and 0003309:4.

46. Interview in 1971 with former pangreh praja serving in the Mojo-kerto region at the time.

47. ARA AAS 97b/XIV/5b:85.

48. *Abdulgani MS* and Ruslan Abdulgani (1972a):15. Ruslan Abdulgani evacuated his family from Surabaya to Kediri at the end of February 1942, and from that vantage point saw the effects of rampok in areas outside the city. He was deeply impressed by the unleashing of destruction, concluding that it was an expression of "economic nationalism" on the part of the masses.

49. RvOIC 028254, Nos. 28, 64, and 68; 064547:2-3; 028977:7.

50. Drawn from ARA AAS 97b/XXII/45h, *passim.*

51. RvOIC 004685; 004684;00387-53:12.

52. NICJ Vol. 7:136.

53. RvOIC 000387-31:12-19, 050577:1-3; and 000387-31:1-6.

54. RvOIC 000387-53:15.

55. NICJ Vol.7:148; RvOIC 002436:1-2.

56. RvOIC 047309:27-30 and 83.

57. RvOIC 000387-68.

58. SP February 1940:61-62; September 1940:241.

59. MBZ IA/XV/9 Mr 699/APO secret:5-8.

60. For a contemporary report see SH 3-25-42; a later judgment (dated 3 August 1946) by an eyewitness is RvOIC 047309:46.

61. RvOIC 000387-53:20.

62. Virtually all Dutch officials in East Java cooperated with the Japanese until being interned on 22 April 1942. Two individuals attempted to flee their positions, but were dismissed by the then powerless Dutch provincial governor for doing so. Only in Bojonegoro Residency were there large-scale refusals to continue in office, and the majority of ranking Dutch officials there were executed by the occupying forces. ARA AAS 97b/XXII/45i:5.

63. One such view is expressed in RvOIC 047309; another is contained in RvOIC 071420, which reveals the admiration a Dutch judge had for Japanese harshness in administering justice to petty law-breakers.

64. The account here is drawn from RvOIC 047309, apparently the only extant eyewitness record.

65. RvOIC 062994:3.

66. The majority of Dutch inhabitants remained indoors and did not watch these events. Many have continued to deny that Indonesians cheered the Japanese troops, but eyewitness reports and photographs make clear that a moderately large crowd of Indonesians was on hand. RvOIC 028254, No. 50; and 000387-53:17–18; ARA AAS 97b/XXII/45f:1 and 45i:3.

67. ARA AAS 97b/XXII/45g:1.

68. RvOIC 047309:34ff; 015474:1; and 028254 No. 123. The fate of this particular kampung was to be severely damaged by a roving Japanese patrol called to the scene by Dutch police.

69. Interview in 1970 with a former Dutch official who accompanied the Japanese. The occupation authorities were well aware what alarm the news of Radjamin's appointment would create among the Dutch, whom they wished to keep as quiet as possible, and of its symbolic worth among Indonesians. One can hardly help feeling, however, that Radjamin was merely to fill space until civilian Japanese arrived. Interview with the former Dutch mayor in 1970; RvOIC 029292:10; 000387-53:33; PP 9-11-42.

70. ARA AAS 97b/XXII/45h:1–2; 45i:3–4.

71. For the text of the regulations see SH 3-28/29-42, and Gunseikanbu (1944a):5ff.

72. SH 3-25/28-42 and 5-5-42.

73. In East Java 21 bridges were damaged or destroyed by Dutch demolition teams, 7 in Surabaya Residency. PP 9-18-42.

74. Shocked that complete railroad inventories had apparently never been drawn up by the Dutch, for example, the Japanese promptly set about this task. The data was quickly put to good use in restoring and even improving train service in many areas, as chagrined Dutch had an opportunity to note. RvOIC 000387-42:10.

75. SH 3-23/25-42. It was unclear to the new rulers why so many city residents seemed to ignore the newspapers and the regulations printed in them. SH 4-10-42.

76. SH 5-4-42.

77. The prices of January 1942 officially were announced as the new ceilings on most goods, and additional limits were placed on such items as taxi rides and servants' wages. The levels were not necessarily adhered to, and soon after the original announcement appeared, permission was given to raise prices on many items. SH 3-13/14/18/19-42 and 5-2-42.

78. ARA AAS 97b/XXII/45e:3; RvOIC 029292:6; SH 5-11-42 and 12-23-42.

79. SH 4-11/15-42.

80. See, for example, SH 3-27-42, 4-4-42, and 6-9-42. Rural rampok continued into May in some areas. SH 5-16-42. On both Madura and Java, religious conflict in villages was sparked by the rampok phenomenon, resulting

in hundreds of deaths and the stripping clean of Dutch plantations and sugar mills in a fury of anticolonial feeling mixed with village conflict. SH 4-10/15/16-42; RvOIC 000387-68.

81. By 8 April 1942, 500 cases of rampok had been handled by Surabaya's lower courts. Police investigation and arrests continued as late as July. SH 4-9-42 and 7-9-42.

82. Interviews with both the Dutch mayor at the time and a Japanese reporter who was close to the military, 1970–71.

83. RvOIC 032780:4; Vermeer-Van Berkum:9ff.

84. Interview with former mayor Fuchter, 1970.

85. RvOIC 050577:7; 000387-32:8; 028254 No 66; 060750.

86. *Enquêtecommissie*:1062.

87. RvOIC 029292:9.

88. RvOIC 062511:17.

89. The chief administrative official with the Japanese forces had been known in Surabaya in prewar days, when he worked at the Japanese Consulate. He was widely thought to dislike Indonesians and to prefer hiring Eurasian servants in his home. During the early occupation he entertained Europeans on a regular basis, especially the wives of high-ranking government officials who had been interned. Interview in 1970 with the former Dutch mayor. On his first meeting with Parindra leaders, this same Japanese official said frankly that he did not feel Indonesians were good for much else besides looting and being put to work. MBZ IA/XV/9 Mr 699/APO secret:9.

90. *Abdulgani MS*; kampung interview, 1971.

91. Interview with Roeslan Wongsokusumo in 1971. It was widely thought that Dr. Soegiri, a prominent Parindrist, stepped forward to offer assistance as the Japanese entered Surabaya, thus giving his party a special advantage. There is no evidence that this actually occurred, however, and no Indonesians seem to have met with the Japanese until at least a day after the city fell under their control. These initial contacts seem to have been persons responsible for publishing newspapers, but in the case of *Soeara Oemoem*, at least, the Japanese approached the wrong individual. Interview in 1971 with Moh. Ali, who was on the *Soeara Oemoem* staff at the time. MBZ IA/XV/9 Mr 699/APO secret:6.

92. Interview in 1970 with former mayor Fuchter.

93. Interviews in Surabaya, 1971–72.

94. Doel Arnowo, for example, was made the chief Indonesian employee at the Japanese propaganda service in Surabaya because of his journalist background and his ability to speak some English. Ali Sastroamidjojo became not only an employee in an economic affairs office but a principal translator for the local Japanese command in Surabaya, not because he knew any Japanese but because he spoke English comparatively well. Interviews with these two men in 1971 and 1972.

95. Interview with an individual who was obliged to register, 1971.

96. See *Osamu Seirei* Nos. 3 and 4 (20 March 1942).

97. MBZ IA/XV/9 Mr 699/APO secret:14. The Malang affair, in which about seventy Parindrists were involved, was apparently the result of the Japanese commander and the Dutch mayor feeling pressured by political groups and considering them responsible for rampok in the area. Most of the Indonesians who were detained stayed in jail until August 1942. In April 1942, in the wake of these events, the entire leadership of the party in Surabaya narrowly escaped being jailed on the charge of spreading communist, anti-Japanese propaganda. ARA AAS 97b/XIV/5b:85; RvOIC 032868:5; MBZ IA/XV/9 Mr 699/APO secret:10; and a 1971 interview with an Indonesian arrested in the affair.

98. MBZ IA/XV/9 Mr 699/APO secret:13; SA 7-2-42; *Abdulgani MS.*

99. SA 7-27-42.

100. On the warning, see PP 8-?-42. (The date is clipped from the original, but internal evidence indicates either 9 or 10 August.) The best account of the drive is in ARA AAS 97b/XIV/5b:47. For a sense of the atmosphere from the perspective of worried new priyayi, see Ali Sastroamidjojo:129–33.

101. There were two series of arrests. One occurred in September 1942, the other in January of the following year. The well-known arrest of Amir Sjarifuddin took place on the later date according to his own account, which says that 54 persons, all members of the PNI, PKI, and Parindra, were detained. It is possible that this account is in error and confuses parts of the two events. In the PKI, for example, Sukajat, Abdul Aziz, and Abdulrachim were detained in Semptember, Pamoedji and others in January. Sidik Kertapati:28; Leclerc:26.

102. Based on interviews during 1971–72 with three former pangreh praja serving in the Surabaya region at the time the Japanese entered.

103. The account given here is drawn principally from SH 4-24-42 and SA 4-23-42. RvOIC 000387-53:44–45 gives another perspective, showing that the Japanese appear to have used trumped-up accusation of anti-Japanese activities in order to make the interning seem justifiable.

104. Interview in 1972 with Doel Arnowo, who attended.

105. This account is taken from SH 6-16-42 and SA 6-17-42, and interviews in 1971 and 1972 with former pangreh praja.

106. SH 5-12-42.

107. For example, AR 4-30-42.

108. See, for example, the famous article by R. Samsoeddin in AR 4-29-42.

109. PP 11-4-42.

110. Examples are taken from the account of the exhibit in PP 10-22-42.

111. Interviews in 1971 with two former military officers posted in Surabaya.

112. The former provinces were abolished, but the remainder of the Dutch administrative divisions were retained under a new terminology. The regency (*regentschap* or *kabupaten*) became the *ken*; the district (*kewedanaan*) became the *gun*; and the subdistrict (*kecamatan*) became the (*son*). Villages or *desa* were known as *ku*, while city precincts (*wijken*) were called *shiku.*

113. See *Osamu Seirei* No. 12 (29 April 1943); PP 11-2-42 and Benda, et. al.:87.

114. Radjamin was relegated to the position of vice-mayor (*fukushucho-kan*) and Surabaya became one of the three cities on Java—Jakarta and Semarang being the others—not to go through the occupation with an Indonesian mayor. PP 9-11-42.

115. Information on Yasuoka is taken from the biographical coverage in AR 12-24/29-42, and personal interviews in 1971 and 1972 with Indonesians who worked close to him.

116. His effort in a speech to a gathering of municipal employees in mid-1943 was said to be one of the first times a ranking Japanese official did not use Indonesian translators in public in Surabaya. PP 8-12-43. For other activities, see PP 9-23-42 and 1-23-43.

117. Duparc:71-72.

118. PP 6-15/19-43, 7-7-43; SA 9-23-43; interviews with former municipal employees, 1971. The pangreh praja and city employees were in favor of the majority of the Japanese changes.

119. Interview in 1970 with a former Dutch municipal official. The military government, indeed, complained in late 1944 that cities in general were continuing to act too much like autonomous administrations and to behave too closely to the pattern established in Dutch times. Gunseikan, Naiseibu:5–6.

120. Interview in 1970 with a former government employee who was released for this purpose, and knew others who were.

121. Interviews in 1971 with former city employees; RvOIC 028254, No. 54.

122. Kampung interview in 1971.

123. In 1932 the Netherlands East Indies government counted 186,891 Indonesians among its 209,696 employees (*Statistische zakbeokje*:59). In August 1945 Japanese reports to Allied forces listed 220,726 Indonesians in the Civil Administration of Java and Madura alone (RvOIC 012614:6). If the two sets of figures are based on the same definitions of "government employee," an increase of considerable magnitude is indicated. Information on Surabaya seems to point to a more modest but still significant expansion. The same Japanese source cited above mentions 4,026 Indonesian workers in Surabaya Residency. It is fair to assume that at least one-fifth of these, or about 800, were employed in the city. If the number of Indonesian municipal workers in Dutch times was about 660 (a total of 749 less approximately 25 percent Europeans), the increase in question is a shade less than 20 percent, providing again that Dutch and Japanese figures count the same categories of employee. It is quite possible that, especially in municipal government hiring patterns, movement to upper ranks was sufficiently limited by strict requirements to give the impression that advancement was difficult. The bulk of new employees would have been hired at middle and lower levels.

124. RvOIC 005197 lists a civil police force as of September 1945 numbering 26,998 on Java and 2,639 for Surabaya Residency.

125. The percentage of Indonesians employed in the city police force almost certainly increased greatly. Even within the category of military police,

150 out of 204 were Indonesian auxiliaries. RvOIC 005197. Though actual figures were not given, the Japanese drew attention to the increase of the number of Indonesians in upper police ranks. PP 6-2-43.

126. Information on the PID at this time is drawn from interviews in 1971 and 1972 with two former officers.

127. The enormous fear that a mythologized kempeitai awakened among Indonesians deserves study in its own right. There were in fact only 697 Japanese kempeitai and 958 Indonesian *kempeiho*, or auxiliaries, for all of Java's 55,000,000 people. RvOIC 005197.

128. Interviews with former PID officers, 1971.

129. This is not to say that the cruelties later reported by so many persons were nonexistent, or that torture, for example, was not practiced by the police forces of the occupation. Clearly these things existed and the Japanese period was in this regard both quantitatively and qualitatively different from the period before it. The incidence and nature of police cruelty under the Japanese have been vastly exaggerated, however, in a manner not unlike that by which the fear of being taken away as a romusha mushroomed beyond reasonable bounds. It is also almost certainly true, though peripheral to this particular issue, that a significant portion of what torture and other acts did take place were committed by Indonesians acting to one degree or another independently.

130. PP 12-7-42 and 3-8-43.

131. As one Eurasian schoolboy wrote in 1946, "The Japanese had something new, namely [the idea that] everyone had to work." RvOIC 028254, No. 106. Also Gunseikanbu (1943a):38.

132. One Japanese wrote that methods of rice culture used in Java were so inefficient that 3,400,000 hectares of land were required to produce a crop that should by Japanese standards need no more than 1,400,000. He recommended that rice lands be diminished and the areas left over turned to cash crop production. Hamaguchi:310. The Japanese also tended to feel that Europeans did not take rice agriculture seriously enough to make the investments necessary to its success. At a cost of f. 750,000 and using a reported 2,000,000 laborers, occupation authorities completed the enormous irrigation project in the Popok area of Kediri, East Java, which the Dutch originally had planned but abandoned in the 1930s because of the projected cost. RvOIC 051163:28.

133. There were about 65,000 Japanese on Java at the end of the war, far fewer than in 1943–44. RvOIC 000664 and materials in Kanahele (1967):59 and 65. This number is considerably less than the previous total European population, even counting only those interned and remaining on Java throughout the occupation. But the drain on rice supplies was significant, particularly since the Japanese stockpiled enormous supplies for their own emergency use, and because all European internees had now to be fed from the same rice harvest as well.

134. Rice harvest figures for the war years are extremely unreliable and difficult to interpret. But what the Dutch in 1945—not without a touch of conceit—saw as sheer disaster caused by Japanese ineptitude or malice, and

by the abandonment of Western expertise, may have been the result of bad weather, widespread hoarding, and deliberately inaccurate reporting. While it is true that the Japanese began importing rice to Jakarta from occupied Malaya toward the end of 1942 (Nakamura:25 citing Kuroda:82–83), this probably reflected uncertainties about collection during the first harvest of the New Order rather than actual production levels. Contrary to popular belief, no rice left Java for Japan during the war, though some quantities went to Navy territories in the Outer Islands. According to some accounts, production remained relatively steady until the poor harvest (due principally to drought) of 1944, when it dropped about 20 percent for Java as a whole. At the end of the occupation, the Japanese command figured that 60 percent of the rice harvest would be hoarded or sold on the black market, well beyond government control. RvOIC 005374. This was probably a conservative guess. As far as Surabaya is concerned, East Java's *recorded* rice production was steadier than that of Central and West Java, dropping only 9 percent between 1943 and 1945, as opposed to 56 percent and 13 percent, respectively. RvOIC 051163:26. Especially in East Java's case, therefore, it is not difficult to imagine that *actual* production was higher at the end of the occupation than before it, contrary to Dutch estimates.

135. In 1945, government plans called for collecting 700,000 tons of milled rice for local civilian rationing and 200,000 tons for Japanese use. RvOIC 005374. Huge stores already had been put by for emergency use. Most of these appear to have been in Surabaya and in several strongholds built in the hills of East Java after mid-1944.

136. Interviews in 1971 with several former municipal employees.

137. Kampung interviews in 1971 and 1972; RvOIC 051163:29 gives the usual view. The matter needs more intensive study. A great many figures are available on price index, livestock slaughter count, and the like, but interpreting them—even supposing they are accurate—is difficult at best. One may easily see, for example, a decline in slaughtering; but how much was the drop due to withdrawal of the European population from the urban meat market, and how much slaughtering was done illegally?

138. Kampung interviews, 1971.

139. Kampung interviews, 1971. Exactly for this reason, though without much success, the Japanese tried to encourage saving among both rural and urban Indonesians.

140. RvOIC 020118:4–5.

141. RvOIC 020118:1.

142. PP 10-12-42 and 2-20-43. The latter "invention" won first prize for a Surabayan entrepreneur in a government-sponsored "Made in Java" contest.

143. Interview in 1971 with two intellectuals who themselves went into business, and knew others who did the same at this time.

144. RIPDT:235-238.

145. Kampung interviews, 1972.

146. RIPDT:236 and 346-48.

147. Thus at a time when even middle-class kampung residents were in

rags because of the scarcity of textiles, the Japanese received five meters of locally made cloth every three months, and had stockpiles for several years at this rate of distribution. Interview in 1971 with an Indonesian employed at Japanese warehouses in Surabaya, and responsible for much administration in the city's distribution system. One measure of the stores originally built up by the Dutch and held by the Japanese is the fact that, though liberally drawn on by the Japanese in early 1945 and pillaged by Indonesians in September and October, Surabaya warehouse supplies were ample to feed and clothe thousands of returning Dutch internees in November and December of the same year.

148. SA 1-26-44.

149. SA 1-30-44.

150. For examples see SA 4-14-44, 8-14/17-44.

151. See especially RvOIC 039357, which also appears in Brugmans, et. al.:501-02.

152. Wertheim (1956):228 gives a figure of 300,000 romusha sent overseas, but this is almost certainly too large. The recruitment of such laborers began rather early in the occupation, but success in finding persons to fill the jobs, most of which had specific requirements (carpentry and tinsmithing skills, for example), was fairly limited. Furthermore, interisland and long distance sea travel became risky after mid-1943. The search for this type of skilled labor, to which the label "romusha" does not appear to have been applied at first, should not be confused with the drive for workers to complete projects on Java, which intensified in late 1943 and reached a peak when Sukarno took a cameo role in the recruitment program in August 1944. SA 8-18-44, The word "romusha" seems not to appear in newspapers until about March 1944.

153. Unskilled villagers were not at all desirable, and most recruits were probably urban residents with building or mechanical skills of some kind. Newspapers were used heavily for recruitment in the city, listing explicitly what sort of people were required. Kampung interviews in 1971–72, and discussions in the same years with two doctors who were required to examine recruits from Surabaya, were helpful in assembling this view.

154. In East Java the chief sources seem to have been Blitar, Tulungagung, and Bojonegoro. These laborers were picked up by the truckload under false pretenses and often by force. Interview in 1972 with a former government official.

155. There was also considerable corruption in the program. Romusha sent to work on locations in Java frequently ran off, but their disappearance customarily went unreported by Indonesian supervisors, who then pocketed the surplus wages and food allotments. Interview in 1972 with a former official close to government offices responsible for such programs.

156. SA 6-24/28-44.

157. Kampung interviews, 1971.

158. Kampung interviews, 1971.

159. Interviews in 1971–72 with both kampung residents and intellectuals in Surabaya at the time.

160. See, for example, the article "Menginsafkan diri," SA 5-11-44.

161. Interview in 1971 with an Indonesian who worked closely with Japanese officials in Surabaya. Indonesians of this sort frequently found Japanese rather comical, and they privately ridiculed Japanese accents, physical features, and airs. See Ajip Rosidi, passim.

162. SH 4-2-42; interviews in 1971 with former city workers who had precisely these experiences.

163. Thus, for example, although Ajat Djojoningrat's *Tekad* contained ideas very much in line with many of those espoused by the Japanese, who were conscious of promoting "modern" thinking and who went out of their way to combat "antiquated" behavior, it also was considered to encourage Indonesians to be insolent and offensive. For the latter reason *Tekad* was banned. Interview in 1971 with Ajat.

164. No figures are available on the actual number of students in Surabaya during the occupation. Though many schools were closed, European students, of course, did not attend, and at higher levels this meant a substantial number of additional places for Indonesians. On the other hand, these were probably taken largely by students coming to Surabaya from localities in which such schools were no longer continued. It seems likely that the number of Indonesians (though not necessarily Surabayans) in government schools remained roughly the same as before 1942, while numbers in private schools declined sharply. Interviews in 1971 and 1972 with former teachers support this impression.

165. PP 8-15-42.

166. PP 9-12/15-42.

167. For example, PP 5-7/14-43.

168. Students accustomed to learning largely or entirely in Dutch, as many were, naturally had great difficulty with the change to Indonesian, as did teachers. Textbooks were an additional serious problem. To make things worse, Japanese was a required second language, but teachers were at best inadequately trained to pass on even basic knowledge of that complex language. Interview in 1971 with a former school inspector; RvOIC 028254, No. 128.

169. A strong example of this view is RvOIC 059679. Despite gestures such as setting Java's clocks to agree with Tokyo's and replacing Dutch holidays with Japanese, occupation authorities do not seem to have believed it possible or even especially desirable to "Nipponize" Indonesians. When they wrote or spoke of making Indonesians into a "second Japanese people," they invariably did so from the point of view of improving spirit and strength, but not out of a desire to teach all Indonesians Japanese or force them to borrow the material trappings of Japanese culture. A strong thread running through occupation policy, indeed, was that of recognizing and, for the most part respecting, religious and cultural differences. See Benda, et. al.:26 and 73–74.

170. ARA AAS 97b/XIX/27b. The budget for the entire sendenbu on Java was only f. 250,000 in 1943, and only half that sum was to be spent on materials.

171. Except where cited otherwise, information in this and the following paragraph is taken from a 1971 interview with a former sendenbu official.

172. Interviews in 1971 with two former *Soeara Asia* editors. It was also understood that prepared Japanese releases could not be refused or altered appreciably without bringing down a more exacting sendenbu evaluation of the paper as a whole.

173. SH 3-25-42; interview in 1972 with the Indonesian owner of a kampung bookstore and small printing business.

174. *Soeara Asia*, successor to *Soeara Oemoem*, began publishing on 1 June 1942 and increased its subscriptions from about 10,000 to 40,000 by 1943. Interview in 1971 with Mohammed Ali, long-time editor of the paper. Even considering that by this time Dutch-language newspapers had disappeared and other Indonesian papers fallen by the wayside, the increase is remarkable. One reason for it may be that the Japanese, in an effort to build up the press as a tool of communication to the public, dropped the price of newspapers to less than half the prewar level. SH 6-15-42; PP 8-22-42. From the kampung point of view, the lower cost was not the only factor. People were anxious to see if they could determine the course and outcome of the war, and showed a greater interest in learning to read Indonesian than before. One kampung resident, in a 1971 interview, reported that in a neighborhood of about 200 families, where previously only a handful took newspapers, during the occupation nearly 50 did so.

175. Interviews in 1971–72 with ludruk players and a dalang active in this period.

176. After the first months of occupation, foreign films ceased to be shown. In addition to the many Japanese films, most of which were dubbed or subtitled in Indonesian and concerned with virtues as such as bravery, national pride, and discipline, Indonesian-made films began to appear after 1943. These apparently were funded from Japanese sources, private or government. They used entirely Indonesian casts as well as production staffs and subject matter. Themes were usually very much the same, however, with bravery and discipline in the face of grave crisis heading the list. See, for example, the film "Berdjoeang" [Struggle] as reviewed in SA 2-29-44 and 3-2-44; and the account in Salim Said:31–36.

177. Kampung interviews, 1971–72. As, for example, in the drama "Kali Seraya," in which a traditional Indonesian plot suddenly ends with the recognizably Japanese—and thoroughly un-Indonesian—resolution of the lovers jumping together to their deaths in a river. PP 4-2-43. Sendenbu writers found traditional Indonesian stories difficult to tamper with, and sometimes attempted only the crudest grafting of Indonesian and Japanese story lines. Frequently they merely injected a propaganda pitch at a convenient interval. Interview with a former sendenbu bureau chief, 1971.

178. One obvious indication was that PID agents' seats remained empty until the last moment. Interviews in 1972 with ludruk players active at the time.

179. The line goes, in Javanese, *bekupon omohe doro, melu Nippon tambah soro.*

180. Everyone has his own theory, but interviews with Indonesians and Japanese resident in Indonesia during the late 1930s and the occupation seem to pinpoint the immediate prewar period.

181. Here and below, except where cited otherwise, information on dokar and becak is based on interviews in 1971 with two arek Surabaya, one a former dokar owner and the other a long-time owner of a becak business.

182. PP 10-9-1943; 11-27-43; and 5-3-43. It is fairly clear that the increase was at least to some degree connected with the wave of bicycle thefts (which supplied wheels for the new vehicles) that accompanied the general rampok phenomenon of the early occupation. See, for example, SH 4-7-42 and 5-12/18-42.

183. In 1943, ownership of Surabaya's 72 dokar stables was divided more or less equally among Armenian, Arab, and Indonesian families. PP 7-3-43. Drivers, however, were virtually all arek Surabaya.

184. Many people who lost their jobs due to the war switched to becak driving because it was an expanding business and often the only job available. Some individuals feared being taken off as romusha. When proper air-filled bicycle tires became unavailable, the job became physically extremely demanding.

185. PP 7-9/17-42.

186. PP 10-5-42.

187. PP 3-11/18-43 and 4-15/20-43.

188. PP 5-3-44.

189. For example, see PP 4-21-43 and 5-10/13/14-43. It is difficult to determine where Indonesian intellectuals stood on this issue, but the tone of articles in the press, and the very fact that the problem attracted so much attention, suggests that writers saw in it an admirable example of bravery in the face of Japanese pressure.

190. The city did collect taxes on individual becak, to be paid annually by the owners, and there was some financial benefit for the municipal government in having all vehicles registered. But the program that officials devised must have eaten into the amount collected, and it seems likely that the total effort cost more than it brought in. Owners of becak never once complained that the Japanese were making money, unfairly or otherwise, from the cooperative, so that does not seem to have been considered an issue by anyone.

191. Kampung interviews in 1971.

192. PP 8-20-42.

193. The keibodan was founded officially on 20 March 1943, though an organization with the same function and name was announced in Surabaya in March 1942, and was said to have played a role in air raid practices held shortly thereafter. The tonarigumi is given in one source as being officially established in Surabaya on 25 September 1943, but in another on 17 January 1944. RvOIC 004980; SA 1-17-45.

194. In theory there was to be one tonarigumi for each twenty families in the city, a ratio that would have yielded, according to Japanese estimates, 30,000 neighborhood associations. No actual count seems to have been made, but there is no indication that Surabaya's tonarigumi reached anything like the estimated number.

195. This is certainly the impression gained from numerous kampung interviews in 1971 and 1972, which virtually all indicate that confusion was common at the time and not merely the product of hazy memories.

196. Gunseikanbu (1943b):1-2.

197. This and the next paragraph are based upon kampung interviews in 1971-72 with persons formerly associated with the tonarigumi in several neighborhoods.

198. Periodic complaints appeared in the press that the tonarigumi system was still not functioning properly. For example, SA 12-21-43. An official pamphlet was written to remedy the situation. Gunseikanbu (1943b).

199. It is probably on this account that kampung residents frequently considered sinoman to have "continued under a different name," or failed altogether to notice any change at all. Kampung interview in 1971.

200. On keibodan regulations, see *Kan Po* 5-10-43:17-23.

201. Interviews in 1971 with pangreh praja close to these activities; see also *Sedjarah singkat:*33.

202. In one Kampung Plampitan keibodan group, for example, only two persons took an active part. Interviews with residents, 1971.

203. Interviews in 1971 with kampung residents and several intellectuals who observed the programs at work.

204. SA 9-21/25-43, 12-21-43, 2-23/28-44, and 3-17-44.

205. This account taken from SA 7-31-44, 8-3-44, 9-30-44, 10-30-44, and 11-1-44; also from a 1971 interview with an eyewitness.

206. See, for example, SA 8-28-44, in which an editorial echoed this concern by noting that "to exist in a living, moving society and be thoroughly involved in it . . . that is what it means to live in a country that is awakening and worthy of respect."

207. Kampung interviews in 1971-72. Thus, for example, the Japanese were in 1944 faced with a group of tonarigumi leaders bold enough to demand progress toward Indonesian independence, for which they said they would trade their cooperation. The reply was that if Japan did not get cooperation now, there would be no consideration of independence in the future. SA 10-5-44.

■ Chapter Four

New Priyayi and Youth in the Japanese Order

■ The new priyayi and the New Order

The unfolding of the new Japanese order in Surabaya did not affect the city's new priyayi uniformly. They reacted in a variety of ways that depended as much on personality as ideological or other differences. Most intellectuals spent the occupation discovering, through trial and error, the limitations as well as the opportunities inherent in the new conditions. For the most part they charted a cautious course. Despite the largely peaceful nature of the occupation period, for the new priyayi it was tinged with an uneasiness that occasionally bordered on silent terror. This fear can be traced to the threat of internal upheavals that had accompanied the change of government, as well as to popular tales of the kempeitai and romusha, but a more powerful factor was an awareness that Japanese seldom treated Indonesian intellectuals as even approximate equals, or bothered to mask their contempt for what the Japanese viewed as the Indonesians' lack of stamina and mental toughness. Educated Surabayans appear to have subscribed rather widely to the belief that the Japanese planned eventually to annihilate most of them,[1] though in retrospect hard evidence for this notion is lacking. These and related anxieties troubled intellectuals profoundly; few were able to escape being touched emotionally by the dangerous environment they perceived around them.

Occasionally the combination of the threat of violence and the abrupt challenge to the old and largely Western order had an electric effect on individuals. An extreme example is Dr. Moestopo, whose life appears to have been fundamentally altered by the advent of Japanese rule.[2] Moestopo, born in 1913, was the son of a minor aristocrat and a graduate of Surabaya's school of dentistry. Evacuating to the interior of East Java in March 1942, he was stopped by troops from the occupying army, who mistook him for a European because of his light skin and sharp features, and because he was wearing an LBD helmet at the time. Only with difficulty was Moestopo able to convince his captors of his true identity and obtain permission to continue his journey. The episode was apparently traumatic. Moestopo, reputed even in his student days to be a nervous, emotional person with no interest in pergerakan affairs, brooded on it for several days in solitude. He emerged an apparently changed individual, dressing in traditional Javanese style rather than in his usual European clothing, using only the Indonesian language rather than speaking in his customary Dutch, and so on. He was observed to both fear and admire the Japanese greatly, responding with apparent enthusiasm, for example, to the opportunity to train (however briefly) in the Japanese-initiated Indonesian defense force, or Peta, in which he received the semihonorific appointment of battalion commander. Friends concluded that Moestopo had fallen victim to acute emotional stress. They were able to recognize the symptoms because these were shared, though in far less severe form, by a number of fellow new priyayi; for them the occupation soon came to resemble *jaman edan,* the time out of joint mentioned in classical Javanese literature and prophecy.[3]

Other intellectuals, uneasy yet somehow less dramatically affected by the arrival of the Japanese, merely nurtured the skepticism about colonial rule that they had developed under the Dutch. This attitude was seen clearly first in connection with the Three A Movement, a hastily devised propaganda effort aimed at the general populace and planned around the slogan, "Japan the Light of Asia, Protector of Asia, and Leader of Asia."[4] Although it was prominent for a time in the capital and in areas of West Java, the Three A Movement does not appear to have been strong in East Java generally, or in Surabaya in particular. One explanation for this may be that local military and police officers were still nervous, between April and August 1942, about the political situation and therefore reluctant to allow in their area an activity approved elsewhere. But it is also true that Surabaya's intellectuals themselves failed to view the new organization with much enthusiasm. They studied the Three A Movement carefully because it had attracted attention from pergerakan colleagues in Jakarta and elsewhere, and because it was at the time the only remotely political activity sanctioned by the Japanese authorities. On the whole, however, they were unimpressed. Unike many former Parindra figures elsewhere, those in Surabaya hesitated to become involved; PNI and other leaders from the prewar era were equally cautious and refused to make themselves available to the Three A Movement. It was, they seem to have agreed, a transparent attempt to propagandize the Indonesian public, and one which exhibited vividly Japanese clumsiness and ignorance of Indonesian nationalist sensibilities. Could the Japanese really be as competent as their military victory had first suggested? In some ways they seemed more naive, and far less predictable, than the Dutch. Here lay the foundation of a gradually building cynicism about the New Order and its chances for survival.

For all the fear and uncertainty represented in these responses, the Japanese were not viewed entirely negatively by Surabaya's intellectuals, many of whom perceived from an early date that the occupation, whatever its dangers, held certain opportunities for Indonesians. The humiliation of the Dutch naturally and immediately encouraged the idea that change along lines established under the pergerakan might now, despite other dangers, take place. Japanese efforts to curb Chinese economic activity, streamline the educational system, encourage indigenous manufacturing, disseminate new rice-growing methods in the countryside, rationalize administrative structures, curb pangreh praja privilege, and mobilize mass opinion represented New Order policies which intellectuals could both approve of and work for; most of these policies, indeed, echoed closely those endorsed by the pergerakan before the war. Few were naive enough not to see that Japanese policy and practice were often far apart, but equally few felt compelled to take an either/or approach to Japanese rule. For the majority of new piryayi, the occupation was a clichéd best and worst of times, in which difficult, severely pragmatic decisions guided day-to-day activities and the future appeared alternately bright and grim. Although some were deeply shaken by the sight of migrants begging and even dying in the streets of Surabaya,[5] and others were highly invigorated—in administrative positions in the New Order—by the exercise of real (if still restricted) authority, new priyayi on the whole approached the occupation with uneasy restraint and viewed it in tones of gray. Whatever elements of a "kabuki style" there might have been in the Japanese occupation, these were limited in fact as well as in the perception of intellectuals, who did not see the period in quite the dramatic terms scholars sometimes have assigned to it retrospectively.[7]

Much about the role and attitudes of Surabaya's new priyayi in the Japanese period is revealed in an examination of Putera, occupied

Java's first major government-sponsored mass organization.[7] Putera's full name (in Japanese, Jawa Minshu Soryoku Kisshu Undo, or Movement for the Total Mobilization of the People of Java; in Indonesian, Pusat Tenaga Rakyat, or Concentration of the People's Power) indicates its general purpose. The effort to elicit broad support from the Indonesian population, however, was expressed more frequently than not in terms of specific functions rather than goals in the wider sense, and it is fair to say that the precise aims of Putera were unclear from the beginning. The organization was designed for Indonesian intellectuals, especially those with pergeraken experience. There was no membership in the usual sense, only directors and a limited number of staff members working under them. The primary leaders chosen by the Japanese were Sukarno, Mohammad Hatta, K. H. Mas Mansur, and Ki Hadjar Dewantara; virtually all leadership positions at the local level were filled by individuals of a similar type and regional stature. Apparently the Japanese had decided that the risks involved in dealing with new priyayi were outweighed by the potential benefits, especially in the area of mobilizing the populace through the use of nationalist appeals. When Putera was inaugurated officially in early March 1943,[8] it attracted a gratifyingly enthusiastic response, particularly in areas where popular pergerakan leaders were given ample opportunity to make public appearances and speeches. Some intellectuals even remarked that Putera seemed to revive in a government-approved form the essence of the pergerakan, and to represent the first step toward a truly Indonesian government.[9]

Surabaya's branch of Putera was not established until July 1943, four months after the ceremony at the capital.[10] This delay was caused in part by local police and military tendency, as in the case of the Three A Movement, to see the new organization as a threat to law and order. But another important factor was an unpublicized struggle among several of the city's pergerakan groups to have specific individuals named to directors' posts.[11] The organization that eventually took shape possessed a membership adroitly balanced in age, experience, and political background. Of the individuals on whom information is available, the average age was 36 years, and all but one person had been involved in prewar pergerakan organizations.[12] A wide selection of interests and backgrounds was represented. Although Sudirman was appointed Putera chairman in Surabaya, and a number of other staffers had been affiliated (not necessarily exclusively) with the Parindra, that party did not enjoy a particularly powerful role, considering its prominence in the city and region before the war. All Putera directors serving under Sudirman, regardless of their political leanings, had held some form of public or government-associated position under the Dutch; only one had been arrested for political activities, and he had returned quickly to Batavia's good graces. The Japanese authorities clearly attempted to find moderate new priyayi for Putera, and to arrange them in a symmetrical, cooperative configuration. Before long some Putera officers became dominant in the organization while others provided mostly a symbolic representation, but the original appearance of the group was one of careful equilibrium.

Appointees had their own reasons for accepting roles in Putera, one of which was the suspicion that to do otherwise might be dangerous.[13] Some held notions that Putera would serve the drive for Indonesianization of government and, ultimately, independence. There was also a modest salary attached to Putera jobs, and few intellectuals could afford to pass up this additional income without strong reasons. Many agreed from the start that Putera was a compromise, a risk worth taking. Sukarno's leadership held some promise, after all, and it was perhaps preferable to become involved in such an organization than to stand entirely idle. Despite these notions, and a surprising show of interest in Putera from Surabayans,[14] intellectuals continued to be cautious about the organization. Few were certain why they had been appointed or by whom, and most had trouble comprehending what they were expected to accomplish. Lacking other specifics, new staff members viewed their assignments chiefly as they recalled prewar interests, such as aiding the unemployed, combating illiteracy, and encouraging thrift and cleanliness. Familiar and difficult to fault, these activities nevertheless seemed insufficient to account for the government emphasis on Putera, and this circumstance worried new priyayi.

One aspect of Putera, however, did attract intellectuals' attention, as it offered them an entirely new opportunity to address, in person as well as through the press, large audiences and nationalist themes. Crowds had of course gathered in the Dutch period, but they had done so relatively infrequently, and only rarely for events other than athletic contests, holidays, or special religious ceremonies. In the 1930s, pergeraken-associated meetings were circumscribed and hampered by colonial authorities. Sudden access to large audiences and relative freedom to discuss before them previously forbidden themes—anticolonialism being the most obvious—represented significant changes from the past, of which new priyayi might make good use.

The full extent of this opportunity was not recognized immediately in Surabaya, partly because intellectuals there adopted a wait-and-see attitude to Putera and partly because a personal visit by Sukarno to the city on Putera's behalf was delayed.[15] When Sukarno finally reached Surabaya in August 1943, however, the effect was spectacular. The key event was a giant rally held in the open air.[16] Mass gatherings were still a great novelty after eighteen months of Japanese rule, and they captured the imaginations of many intellectuals. Sukarno's performance was especially encouraging because the tone remained strong despite the obvious presence of two Japanese military companions. "The fate of our people is in our own hands," he said, "and not in those of others." Was this not proof that, whatever compromises had to be made, the heart of the pergerakan survived and beat in Putera?

In Surabaya Putera spent much of its energy on committee work and small projects, but there also was propagandizing to be done. Most of the subjects were familiar to new priyayi: the value of discipline, the evils of capitalist colonialism, the importance of hard work, the need for national pride and sacrifice. While the sendenbu sketched out the themes and format of propaganda campaigns, Putera employees enjoyed considerable freedom to fill in with what essentially were pergeraken vocabulary and imagery. Great emphasis was placed on words like "perjuangan" (struggle) and "semangat" (will, spirit), and on the prospect of a bright future. While it is true that many key phrases acquired from the occupation atmosphere a harsh urgency they had not possessed earlier—"perjuangan," for example, began to suggest actual combat rather than a more internalized struggle—this change was gradual and by no means imposed by the Japanese.[17] Journalistic techniques developed by intellectuals in the 1930s for use under Dutch censorship required only minor adjustments and polish to serve admirably in the New Order. The classic example of the effective use of double entendre during the occupation was the continued use of the phrase "kemenangan akhir," or final victory. This expression had always implied in the pergerakan context an Indonesian victory in the search for independence, but after about 1939 it had been applied also as a translation of the "final victory" of the Allies during the war. Under Japanese rule the words became the stock rendering of a projected Japanese triumph in the Pacific, all the while continuing to remind those familiar with earlier conventions of the drive toward an independent Indonesia.[18]

Whatever its possibilities, Putera disappointed both Indonesians and Japanese before long. Intellectuals working for the organization realized that the effect of rallies and propaganda on the kampung population wore off quickly. The arek Surabaya reacted positively to government policies early in the occupation, but quickly lost interest as they saw the city's economic situation worsen, and as fears about labor conscription rose. Kampung residents tended to dismiss what they heard or read about Putera and Putera-sponsored activities, and eventually new priyayi themselves grew skeptical of the utility of their efforts. By November 1943 even the routinely overstated promotional articles in the daily press were forced to describe public enthusiasm for Putera as moderate at best.[19] Surrounded by rumors that Putera was after all nothing but an arm of the sendenbu, and by complaints that its leaders were saving their own skins while everyone else suffered, intellectuals were made aware of the liabilities in their endeavor.[20] Quietly, whenever and wherever possible, they withdrew their support or channelled their energies in different directions.

The Japanese grew concerned when they saw Putera staff members turn their interests toward projects such as charity fund raising, establishing an all-Java soccer league, and running an employment service, rather than propagandizing in the way originally intended. Some military officers questioned whether or not Putera was serving the nationalist interests of Indonesians more than the war effort, and suggested greater emphasis on propagandizing of all kinds. But it was only when intellectuals complained aloud about too much propaganda work, and even distanced themselves from Putera activities, that consideration was given to ending the organization altogether.[21] For the Japanese there was more than a touch of chagrin in the abandonment of Putera; they seem not to have understood why or how Indonesian intellectuals could have allowed it to fail.

Barely six months after its inauguration in Surabaya, Putera's official life was ended by occupation authorities. Scholars have tended to view the event as marking either a great defeat for the new priyayi or the completion of an important step toward independence.[22] Surabayans directly involved in Putera's activities, however, have not seen matters quite so clearly, recording more than anything else their puzzlement over the sudden cancellation of the organization and, ultimately, their lack of real interest in its fate.[23] This vagueness may be due in part to the fact that Putera in Surabaya was never clearly disbanded. Official announcements of the disbanding of that organization and the founding of the People's Service Association (Jawa Hokokai, Perhimpunanan Kebaktian Rakyat) noted the change, but without fanfare.[24] Following this announcement, Putera's offices were moved rather than closed down altogether. Their new location was in the old Governor's Office building, where they shared space with Residency administrative offices and where they appeared to become part of rather than to be replaced by the Hokokai.[25] Though not recognized generally as official staff members of the Hokokai, which was placed entirely in the hands of Japanese officials and the pangreh praja,[26] pergerakan intellectuals continued to play a notable role in the city's public events, especially where speech-making was involved, and to be seen by Surabayans as prominent and even powerful figures.[27] This suggests that, with Putera, the new priyayi had embarked on an important transitional experience, moving from a restless, oppositional colonial elite to something closer to a class of leaders ascending over their own society. Although this change was made possible in the most immediate sense by the circumstances of the occupation, the speed with which it occurred and the shape it assumed were influenced heavily by continuities from the pergerakan past.

■ The solidification of new priyayi leadership

Though intellectuals often supposed the contrary, their role in government and public life was more secure after Putera than before. Even as Putera in Surabaya embarked on its first tasks, the occupation authorities announced the beginnings of what Japanese Premier Tojo had termed "political participation" or *seiji sanyo,* which also might be styled "administrative advising."[28] An initial step was the formation in September and October 1943 of advisory councils at the central and Residency levels. These devices were not designed to wield real power, and in this respect compared unfavorably even with the councils of the Dutch period. Indonesian participants hardly can have missed the limitations of the councils, but as in the case with Putera most individuals, when asked, felt they could not refuse to serve. It could also be argued that the councils represented a more acceptable prelude to independence than Putera, a view the Japanese implicitly encouraged.[29] Whatever the case, the councils were dominated by the new priyayi rather than, as had so often been the case in the prewar era, the pangreh praja.[30] The central body, called the *chuo sangi-in,* gathered a startling array of figures, a great many of whom had pergerakan backgrounds. From Surabaya, Roeslan Wongsokusumo (next to Sudirman, who was otherwise engaged, the ranking Parindrist) and Iskaq Tjokrohadisurjo (at the end of the Dutch period a Parindra member, but also Surabaya's ranking PNI figure) joined the group, which met periodically in Jakarta. The Surabaya Residency council or *sangi-kai,* was limited to six persons, three of whom were intellectuals with strong pergerakan experience: Sudirman, Iskaq Tjokrohadisurjo (who thus held dual council membership) and Doel Arnowo.[31]

Few if any of these pergerakan-seasoned individuals were naive enough to take the work of the councils very seriously, as it consisted largely of responding to questions the Japanese posed about how Java might be governed more successfully. Some were forthright with their criticism of occupation policies, though it was believed generally that such commentary fell on deaf ears. Experience and a pragmatic outlook, however, led intellectuals to see other advantages in participating. Though the councils met infrequently, members were not only paid salaries and accorded special attention in the press, but they were given a large measure of legitimacy within the political structure of the occupation. New priyayi who had remained outside the Dutch colonial structure can only have seen this change as an improvement, whatever its limitations. And whether the Japanese intended so or not, new priyayi who took council seats frequently became pivotal in an informal way to the making of official appointments of Indonesians elsewhere in the government, both in the capital and in the regions. Council members were, after all, well-positioned to know about openings in the administration and to place colleagues and followers. Such powers may have been ill-defined, but they were real and, for the most part, they were exercised with remarkable evenness across prewar party lines. Here was another step in the building of new priyayi as participants in the governmental order.

The security of intellectuals in the Japanese period was further enhanced by the difficulties experienced by the Hokokai. Although some Putera members and other intellectuals were either included in or associated wtih the Hokokai in Surabaya, and accepted seats on its board of directors,[32] in general the organization did not receive the support of new priyayi because it sought to emphasize the leadership role of the pangreh praja. Intellectuals' reception of Surabaya's Hokokai was cool from the start. Sudirman was the first to indicate his disillusionment when he gave his inaugural speech as vice-chairman of the Hokokai and mentioned neither that organization nor Japan even once.[33] Thereafter Sudirman did less public speaking, and at the first meeting of the Hokokai directorship the vice-chairmanship was split between him and another individual, probably a Japanese. In the following months other intellectuals only grudgingly aided the Hokokai, and this lack of support may have been crucial to the organization's eventual poor performance.

The failure of the Hokokai in Surabaya's urban setting is indicated

141

not only in critiques that appeared in the press, but in statistics. Unlike Putera, the Hokokai was established as an organization with a dues-paying membership, and its progress is therefore more easily charted. An initial drive for enrollment resulted in a total of 3,239 members, 600 of them Japanese, by the end of March 1944.[34] The great majority of the Indonesian members seem to have been municipal and other government employees, who were subject to considerable pressure to join. A full four months later the membership figure had increased only slightly to 3,481, which Japanese authorities considered much too low. It was noted, for example, that there were 3,900 heads of tonarigumi in the city, but few had stepped forward to join the very organization which had been designed with them in mind. No membership figures were published after mid-1944, but it seems unlikely that they rose significantly. In August 1944 the Hokokai entered a propaganda campaign in support of "volunteer" labor and the policy of working during fasting month,[35] programs toward which the arek Surabaya were already antagonistic. Thereafter the organization seems to have been involved in a dwindling number of activities, with far fewer references in the press.

The Hokokai was never disbanded officially, but by the end of the first year it could claim to be little more than an empty shell. One of its chief goals had been to unite all of the various mobilization efforts in a single structure, but in Surabaya this did not occur. Groups and sub-groups tended instead to resist functioning as part of a well-oiled operational whole.[36] Intellectuals often fitted themselves into sections of the Japanese-planned framework, but used their positions to maintain contact with colleagues or to build personalized local followings, activities that naturally ran counter to Japanese expectations. The failure of the Hokokai also made it possible for the new priyayi to repeat a suggestion they had made to the Japanese long before: that the mass of Indonesians could not be reached effectively without the help of pergerakan forces and people. This was a notion the occupation government appears finally to have taken to heart, perhaps especially in Surabaya. The successor organization to the Hokokai, known as the Gerakan Rakyat Baru or New People's Movement, clearly returned to the principle of new priyayi leadership, a shift that might have been more significant had it not been initiated so close to the end of the war.[37]

Intellectuals found secure footing during the occupation in not only competing with the pangreh praja for influence, but actually beginning to displace them. This eventuality, which in the prewar period had been feared by the colonial government and implied in many pergerakan attitudes, was made possible largely by a convergence of new priyayi and Japanese opinions of the pangreh praja. Both felt the tradition of a priyayi-aristocratic administration to be "feudal" and in need of reform. They considered the pangreh praja to be wedded to Dutch power, morally as well as fiscally corrupt, and inefficient. As might be expected, the Japanese and the new priyayi drew their conclusions from somewhat different perspectives, but the differences were considerably less important than the substantial areas of agreement.

While it has been suggested frequently that the Japanese and the pangreh praja worked out an alliance on which the occupation government was based and a fundamentally similar colonial rule continued,[38] the argument both overstates and oversimplifies the case. Though the Japanese knew they could not govern without the cooperation of the pangreh praja, they never were entirely happy with this inheritance from Dutch rule. Their attitude was mirrored in the way they treated the pangreh praja, which was not only less preferential than the Dutch method, but was in some respects downright humiliating from the pangreh praja point of view.[39] Thus, pangreh praja were summoned to periodic training sessions during which incomprehensible lectures in Japanese and hard physical exercise in public were required; pangreh praja wives were forced to propagandize new rice-planting techniques by wading in paddies, an unforgivable assault on status; and pangreh praja in general were criticized in the press and, when found guilty of misconduct, severely punished in the public eye. Though it is not possible to get a sharp statistical picture, relatively large numbers of low and middle level pangreh praja in East and Central Java lost their positions during the occupation, often because they were considered incompetent. And in the first twenty months of Japanese rule, the regents of Pamekasan, Probolinggo, Bojonegoro, and Purwakarta were removed from their positions for refusing to carry out Japanese orders.[40] Beginning in early 1944, pangreh praja in Panarukan and Bondowoso were executed, and those in four nearby regencies jailed, for suspected pro-Dutch activities.[41] Surabaya pangreh praja do not seem to have suffered any such attacks, but the fear that these events spread throughout pangreh praja ranks in the Residency was considerable.

The Japanese cannot have been eager to worsen the already sharp rivalry between intellectuals and the pangreh praja, but frustration over the cleavages in Indonesian society and a desire to reach the masses effectively led the occupation authorities to enlist intellectuals' aid in pressuring the pangreh praja for reforms.[42] Despite the original prohibition against Putera involvement in pangreh praja matters, for example, Putera staff in Surabaya were soon attending pangreh praja gatherings called by the Japanese Resident and, presumably with official encouragement or at least permission, making suggestions as to "how things might be improved."[43] In November 1943 the higher ranks of Surabaya Residency pangreh praja were several times lectured to by Japanese and Putera spokesmen, all stressing the same message: civil servants should accept the challenges and responsibilities of the New Java, and should strive to become true "fathers to the masses."[44] This phrase and much of the scaffolding of ideas around it, which were in fact lifted straight out of the pergeraken, had been borrowed by the Japanese Resident himself soon after his arrival in Surabaya,[45] and it later became convenient for Japanese and Indonesians to note that devotion to the masses was extremely important under the circumstances of wartime. It was against this standard, government announcements made clear, that pangreh praja would now be judged.

A model pangreh praja in Japanese as well as in many new priyayi eyes was R. M. T. A. Soerjo, who in the Dutch period had served as the district head of Magetan, East Java, and who had enjoyed a reputation as a progressive, bold individual.[46] During the occupation he attracted attention at least in part because he did not hesitate to stand up to forceful Japanese officials, yet managed to gain the respect of Japanese rather than stir their suspicions. In November 1943 he was appointed Resident to Bojonegoro and lionized in the press as the ideal pangreh praja. Dressed in a trim but plain military-style uniform rather than the traditional clothing usually worn, Soerjo was said to spend much of his time talking to the masses, personally investigating village affairs, and even walking in rice fields to emphasize his determination to break away from the aloof and overbearing attitude he felt pangreh praja had exhibited in the past.[47] He received the praise of both intellectuals and Japanese authorities for embodying the spirit of the New Order, though perhaps from different perspectives. Soerjo was quoted as saying, for example, that "in addition to working hard and sacrificing dearly to reach the final victory ["kemenangan akhir"], we need to understand also the fundamentals of our traditional philosophy in order to build the inner strength necessary to overcome all obstacles."[48] In many ways Soerjo seemed to characterize perfectly the kind of change in pangreh praja thinking that new priyayi had suggested for a long time; perhaps he was even the kind of pangreh praja they themselves might be, were they given the opportunity.

Many new priyayi had opposed the traditional civil service system more as a matter of rote than on the basis of personal knowledge. By bringing the pangreh praja and the new priyayi face to face, however, the occupation tended to deepen the commitments of the latter rather than shake their determination to compete.[49] As intellectuals were quick to see, administrative and other changes made by the Japanese encouraged competition by offering opportunities to change the pangreh praja system by becoming part of it. In particular, New Order efforts to bring pangreh praja into the framework devised for other government employees, and to ensure that pangreh praja advanced on a merit system based on open examinations, seemed attractive to new priyayi of many types. They saw the possibility of gaining positions of prestige and security, as well as a chance to practice what they had, or had heard, preached so vigorously under pergerakan auspices.

In Surabaya Residency and East Java generally, the majority of higher pangreh praja positions continued to be filled from traditional ranks during the occupation; toward the final year of the war, however, these offices seem frequently to have been filled with "unorthodox" figures, not all of them even new priyayi. In Kediri, for example, a local Moslem leader became regent for a time, and new priyayi were placed as regents' immediate assistants in Bondowoso and several other areas.[50] The best example of this sort of individual is Ismoetiar, who was in the 1930s, a prime Parindra mover and organizer of Rukun Tani in East Java. Though of small town origin, modest social background, and vernacular school education, he rose to new priyayi status through his ability to organize middle class farmers, and was chosen by the Japanese to become the *patih*, a sort of vice-regent, in Pasuruan.[51] In addition, at least two new priyayi figures in Surabaya took posts as regents outside East Java: Iskaq Tjokrohadisurjo in Banyumas and Dr. Murdjani in Indramayu.[52] For the most part, however, it was the lower and middle levels of the pangreh praja hierarchy to which intellectuals had access most frequently. Pergerakan followers who could claim no particular leadership or administrative experience before the war took the necessary examinations and frequently received appointments. Teachers from both government and private Indonesian prewar schools, many of whom lost their original jobs, seem to have been especially suited for this type of change, filling positions of district or sub-district head in many areas around Surabaya.[53]

Alterations of this type did not take place without some difficulty, however. There was, on the one hand, a stiff resistance from the pangreh praja themselves, who not only saw their social standing and sphere of responsibility encroached upon as a result of intellectuals' calculated planning,[54] but had little that was positive to say about intellectuals' capabilities as civil servants. While this hostility generally was controlled, it can only have made the rural administrative system more difficult. In the wake of the Indramayu Revolt of 1944, which purportedly was the result of Japanese mismanagement, continued tension and decay in the rural administration of Indramayu were alleged by pangreh praja to have been caused largely by the appointment as regent of the Surabayan Dr. Murdjani, who was said to behave in too egalitarian a manner and to encourage the people not to pay taxes.[55] On the other hand, it is probably fair to say that most of the intellectuals who took pangreh praja positions during the occupation were not only bothered by the cold reception they received, but were taken aback by the enormous responsibilities they had to bear. Even those who had sought pangreh praja jobs with more than simply a notion of safeguarding themselves and their families were dismayed by the tasks and the compromised positions in which they were left. The primary school teacher who, after he had succeeded in getting an appointment as a subdistrict head, returned to teaching in Surabaya as soon as he was able, is probably not unique.[56]

Other individuals, however, whether because of greater pergerakan experience in administration, the nature of the authority of their positions, or personal factors, were better able to take their new positions in stride. They often filled pangreh praja duties with distinction. Among Surabaya's intellectuals the best example is the durable Sudirman, who ended his series of wartime appointments by being selected in March 1945 as assistant Resident.[57] The promotion made Sudirman the highest-ranking Indonesian in local government service, and although the post he held was not strictly speaking a traditional pangreh praja stronghold (in prewar days it was always filled by a Dutch official), it did offer a vantage point from which authority over the civil service could be exercised.

Sudirman's rise in the New Order was based largely on his reputation as a pergerakan leader and then on his past experience as a customs official or on his quiet, thoughtful demeanor. The pangreh praja in Surabaya interpreted his appointment as yet another example of Japanese disregard for the time-honored civil service and the bloodlines, training, and experience on which it was built. Particularly because of Sudirman's well-known background in the Parindra, the pangreh praja reacted defensively to the notion of his wielding power over them and, at least in the beginning, withheld their cooperation. As it happened, however Sudirman approached his task with far greater responsibility and acumen than the most optimistic pangreh praja expected. Wise enough to appreciate his own weaknesses, he attempted to hire an aide from among a number of younger, relatively progressive pangreh praja officials in the Residency. When his effort foundered on their hard feelings, Sudirman sought a person with pergerakan leanings but expertise of the type necessary in establishing strong administrative office. The choice fell to Sutadji,[58] who was employed at that time in the Residency financial office, and the two made a team appropriate to the time and circumstances. Together they possessed the skills, the refinement of character, and the confidence to gain the trust of the pangreh praja, for whom they soon began to act as welcome intermediaries with the Japanese authorities. At the same time, Sudirman and Sutadji both were determined to change administrative practices wherever necessary and possible, and to reduce what they believed were the exclusivist, arbitrary aspects of traditional pangreh praja rule.

At least in part because the Japanese had begun to lose much of their interest in doing more than hold the status quo, Sudirman and Sutadji discovered that they possessed great freedom in their new positions. Sudirman insisted on making tours of the entire Residency to see conditions for himself, and he did not hesitate to exercise his authority when he felt it necessary. Nor did he balk at attempting to convince pangreh praja that changing times required cooperation rather than hesitancy. Sudirman also took care that the general population became aware that he, rather than a Dutch or Japanese official, sat in a position of leadership. He encouraged those with complaints to bring them to his desk, and he personally took a hand in investigating even the anonymous accusations that had been so frequently ignored in the past. In this fashion Sudirman acquired a renown and respect that few others in Surabaya could equal.

Sudirman's experience was exceptional, but other new priyayi made passages that were essentially similar though less dramatic. While this was not the case with all new priyayi, a substantial portion did undergo the transformation from pergerakan adherents to participants in government. Even Parindra followers, who perhaps had been best prepared for this change, seem to have felt uneasy at the shift in perspective. It was no simple matter to recall Dr. Soetomo's advice of a decade earlier, much less to carry it out. Age and growing independence, he had said, would alter the kinds of responsibility his generation would be forced to bear; it was natural for the coming generation to take up the burden of outward, visible, and even physical activism, and for authority and activity to be balanced off between younger and older members of the movement.[59].

In the context of the occupation, the change that Dr. Soetomo and others viewed as inevitable could not occur without certain complications. One of the most serious was that intellectuals remained separated from the kampung population, unable to move beyond the uncertain relationship developed under Dutch rule. Very occasionally the kampung provided a place of refuge or a barometer for the new priyayi in the Japanese period, but far more frequently the demands of the day led intellectuals further from the arek Surabaya than ever. Relatively few kampung residents recognized the names of Putera and the Hokokai, for example, and those who did tended to visualize those organizations as belonging entirely to the sphere of the elite.[60] Propaganda events, while they put intellectuals on display and were for a time interesting to the urban public, soon lost their attractiveness to the kampung population. The most common attitude toward mobilization efforts seems, after the first months of occupation, to have been one of indifference, and whatever initial enthusiasm there had been was soon replaced by a linking of antipriyayi and anti-Japanese feelings.[61] The few intellectuals who, with Japanese encouragement, reached out to kampung residents became increasingly uncertain of how they were being received by the arek Surabaya. When one Putera worker with much prewar experience in charity programs finally succeeded in bringing an adult literacy course to several Surabaya factories, she was disturbed to find workers' reactions lukewarm at best. "We never knew," she recounted many years later, "whether the people understood [what we were trying to accomplish] or not."[62]

Such a response suggests that the new priyayi's relationship with the existing order was fundamentally changed, and that the pergerakan was tamed to a considerable degree. As critics then and later pointed out, new priyayi frequently seemed to have sacrificed the understanding of not only much of the general population but also of their own younger intellectuals in order to grasp a place at the helm of Indonesian society. The central pergerakan goal of independence was not lost nor the anticolonial determination shaken; indeed, perhaps these dreams were strengthened by the atmosphere of the occupation and by intellectuals' courage in stirring others' hopes with nationalistic speeches and the like. But in truth there had been a price to pay. Intellectuals now saw the future differently than before, and new concerns crowded their thoughts. With a stake in and a grip on the immediate future of the state, the outstanding question was not so much what could be done to hasten independence as what preparations needed to be made for its arrival. Pergerakan instinct told them to trust in themselves and their ability to stand on their own feet; it also reminded them of the important role youth might play.

■ The Japanese and Surabaya's youth

During the earliest months of the occupation the Japanese did not single out youth for special attention. It may be that there were no clear plans to do so, and in any case authorities seem to have been absorbed in restoring order to Surabaya. Nearly all of the city's many youth groups bowed to the same pressures that ended the pergerakan political parties and other organizations. Only the KBI was permitted to continue. Scouts from this group had been encouraged by the dawning of the New Order and had occasionally taken advantage of the initial disarray by confiscating equipment from Chinese scouting groups, admonishing them that now Indonesians had greater rights in their own country than foreigners.[63] In June 1942, KBI leaders announced that a Japanese police officer had offered to train scouts according to police methods, a suggestion that was accepted eagerly.[64] Perhaps on this account, the KBI in Surabaya was permitted to continue its activities and, in September 1942, to celebrate its twelfth anniversary.[65]

The occupation government's first cautious approach to Indonesian youth began when Jakarta announced the formation of the Barisan Pemuda Asia Raya (Greater East Asia Youth Corps, BPAR) in June 1942.[66] The Japanese elaborated on their own prudent view of the course youth might follow in the New Order, noting that while it was desirable for the younger generation to possess the spirit of sacrifice and a sense of courage, they also must be aware of their responsibilities and should act with "quiet strength" and the approval of their elders.[67] These notions, and the prospect of continuing with scouting groups, convinced some intellectuals, particularly in Jakarta and Semarang, that the BPAR was worthy of support and that the Parindra's Surya Wirawan might become its nucleus. In Surabaya, however, the BPAR did not gain acceptance. No BPAR branch was established, and no Youth Day, such as that celebrated in some towns of West Java, took place.[68] Surabayans from the Parindra as well as from the PNI studied the BPAR plan carefully, but concluded that it lacked substance.[69] At least in part because much of the pergerakan concern about the younger generation was still fresh, new priyayi were content to limit their involvement to forming sports leagues and stressing the need for moral guidance in education.[70] This was a stance the Japanese found at least temporarily acceptable, and there the matter rested.

The first clear indication in Surabaya that the occupation government might seek a closer relationship with Indonesian youth more vigorously came in March 1943 with the formation of the Surabaya Youth Committee under the sponsorship of the propaganda corps.[71] The immediate goal of this new group was to unite the pemuda in the city to erect a monument dedicated to the sacrifices made by the Japanese in conquering Java. Money for the project was to be raised by selling soccer match tickets and postcards. The efforts culminated a month later in an impressive ceremony attended by 4,000 young Surabayans, most of whom had signed their names in a book honoring those who worked for coprosperity under Japanese leadership. Though it had been staged carefully by the Japanese, the gathering did not fail to impress new priyayi onlookers, and to worry them as well. The Japanese, it was now obvious, had taken an interest in cultivating the younger generation. What is more, the success they had in gathering what was probably the largest number of young Indonesians ever brought together in the city was not simply dramatic but rich in ominous overtones. Speeches made by youths during the ceremony, however, implied strongly that the pemuda themselves resented the Japanese efforts.

The formation of the Surabaya Youth Committee precipitated the city's intellectuals into belated action. On the day following the monument dedication, the Parindra leader Dr. Soegiri, who had a long-standing interest in athletics and youth training, was announced to be in charge of a planning group to form a BPAR unit, described as a continuation of the Surya Wirawan.[72] This news item is more than a little curious, since by the date on which it appeared the BPAR had vanished from the rest of Java, and its parent organization, the Three A Movement, had been replaced by Putera. Dr. Soegiri's efforts received mention several weeks later, but this time in the context of a powerful new youth organization of Japanese design, within which he was listed not as a director but as a member of the administrative committee.[73] Thereafter he disappeared from view where youth activities were concerned, and new priyayi in Surabaya lost whatever initiative they might have retained in pemuda affairs.

Japanese attempts to establish deeper ties with youth became more evident with the founding of the Youth Corps or *seinendan* at the end of April 1943. Although some important spadework may have been done by a few pergerakan figures, including Dr. Soegiri, to produce a membership of 280 the day after the organization was inaugurated in Surabaya,[74] it was apparent that a major government objective was to keep the city's pemuda at a convenient distance from the intellectual leaders. This policy originally had been emphasized when Putera by design had excluded youth, and when the Japanese actively discouraged even sports association relationships between Putera leaders and pemuda.[75] In Surabaya's seinendan as it originally was formulated, no Putera leaders were among the directors and advisors. To futher underscore the aim of separating new priyayi and youth, the Surabaya KBI was, shortly after the launching of the seinendan, required to disband. The May 2 ceremony held for this purpose was small and inconspicuous.[76]

By the time of the inauguration of the seinendan, a number of developments affecting the role of the younger generation in society could be observed, none of which was more important than the changed implications of the term "pemuda." In the context of the prewar pergerakan, this designation had acquired a fixed and narrow meaning: it was applied to young intellectuals or those headed in that direction, for the most part students at Western-style schools and invariably participants in pergerakan-associated youth organizations. Additionally, these pemuda were well defined in age (in most groups 21 or 22 was considered the limit for membership) and social background (new priyayi and the upper level of kampung middle class). The New Order changed this in several ways. Earlier confines of social class, for example, were loosened during the war, partly because the Japanese, who disapproved of what they saw as elitist social divisions, tended to address a broader younger generation than had come under the pemuda umbrella earlier. Youth groups of the occupation still emphasized educated youth, but a greater variety of levels and types of education came to be represented. Occasionally, deliberately and otherwise, the Japanese also threw rural youths together with the schooled children of urban intellectuals and pangreh praja. For Indonesians of pergerakan experience these changes were acceptable, fitting with the prewar activities of groups such as Indonesia Muda which had sought to abolish social distinctions among its members.

The age brackets implicit in the term "pemuda" also underwent some alteration. In addition to students in regular schools, agricultural institutes, and vocational programs, the Japanese took an interest in many others. Perhaps most important was the apparently large number of older individuals who either graduated from school after about 1937 and remained unemployed or in low-ranking jobs, or who were unable to remain in school and turned to employment in a variety of industrial and governmental offices. These people were frequently well over 21 years of age—in some cases they had reached 29 or 30—yet in 1943 they continued to be catalogued as pemuda and, despite experience as youth leaders, they did not accede to positions of adult responsibility. They were a source of special concern to the Japanese because they did not fit neatly into the ranks of the seinendan and yet had to be accommodated in some way. Also, a substantial number of these older pemuda avoided both school and employment as long as possible during the occupation, and shied away from government-sponsored activities. They also were known as pemuda, but in their case the word took on a strong pejorative sense.

But if pemuda-dom had become both larger and considerably less easy to delineate than before, it also showed signs of coalescing and gaining focus. The disbanding of prewar political groupings and the youth organizations that accompanied them removed some important barriers to further unification of youth activism. The war and occupation came as rude shocks to many urban youths and drew them together with new urgency. The added sensation of being separated increasingly from pergerakan intellectuals, many of whom then were tied to positions in the New Order, gradually convinced pemuda leaders that youth would have to rely largely on their own past experiences and present energies in meeting the future. Under these conditions and at roughly the same moment, pemuda rediscovered the power of ideas originally introduced under the pergerakan, and they were moved by the vivid realities of the New Order. Far from conflicting, these stimuli moved in the same powerful line, forming a current in which the drifting youth of earlier years were slowly caught up and moved along.

The exact purpose and nature of the newly established seinendan were unclear to intellectuals in Surabaya, who could surmise only that the organization was another reflection of the occupation government's desire to mobilize all sectors of Indonesian society. Opinions on the desirability of bringing the younger generation under such a scheme were mixed, some being cautious and distrustful, others more attracted to the concept. One early assumption on the part of several Surabaya leaders was that the seinendan was intended to have a military-like function. In a brief announcement of the organization's forthcoming inauguration ceremony in the city, one writer declared his understanding that the seinendan's goal was "to teach youth how to bear arms and defend the nation."[77] As intriguing as such a notion may have been to many new priyayi, and despite assertions made later by some Japanese and Western scholars of the occupation,[78] the premises on which the seinendan was founded had, in fact, little to do with training a fighting force.

The Japanese authorities had no intention, understandably enough, of taking steps likely to radicalize youth in any way. If they sought to energize young people in the same general fashion in which they sought to energize Indonesian society as a whole, they were also obviously determined to discipline that energy and put it quite literally and unglamorously to work. From this perspective, the seinendan appears as a mechanism designed to deal effectively with a younger generation that was potentially both troublesome and useful. Thus the organization's full regulations indicate that it fell under the control of Japanese or Indonesian civil servants in conjunction with police officers; intellectuals were not included.[79] The seinendan goal was to "build sound minds and bodies for young people in a truly organized fashion, encouraging the desire for self-development and the will to work cooperatively and be united in every way." Far from taking part in military activities, seinendan branches were to engage in such exercises as providing volunteer labor for public work projects, developing pemuda desire to work hard and strengthen production, training for air raids and earthquakes, and holding drills. Even the oath that all seinendan members were asked to repeat placed overwhelming emphasis on discipline, physical and mental fitness, and devotion to hard work, making only one fleeting reference to "honoring the homeland."[80] When photographs of Java's first functioning seinendan group appeared in print, they showed pemuda marching through Jakarta's streets with refurbished Surya Wirawan caps on their heads . . . . and hoes on their shoulders.[81]

During the seinendan's early days, any connection the organization had with the development of patriotism was left implicit. The conclusion that joining the seinendan represented a service to the nation was not discouraged,[82] but the absence of an effort to attract a membership by appealing to nationalist sentiments is noteworthy. This may be the principal reason behind what the Japanese considered Surabaya's poor response to the seinendan during its first three months. Largely by pressuring former scout leaders and recruiting in government offices, authorities managed to collect nearly 500 members by the time of the first oath-taking ceremony in May 1943.[83] Similar methods, with an emphasis on younger employees in the government and in the private sector, and on school youth, probably accounted for the rise to 1,200 members reported at the end of the month. But there was no progress after that time, and with considerable chagrin a total membership of only 1,130 was announced the following August. Japanese authorities in Surabaya made no secret of their dissatisfaction, nor of their determination to turn the disappointing situation around.

In pursuit of a more effective recruiting program, and under the influence of the excitement created by Tojo's speech and visit, the Japanese first made deliberate appeals to youth in the name of patriotism, and then added the attraction of possible paramilitary training. In Surabaya, municipal officials made several unsuccessful attempts to interest youths in activities such as registering radios and acting in propaganda skits, but attention soon turned toward building the confidence of pemuda as the hope of the nation and as a key element in the New Order.[84] The slogans and approaches were very much in the pergerakan style, for intellectuals were permitted to play a modest role in delivering the message to youth. References to the special strengths of youth frequently were combined with those of defense of the homeland. The boldest step taken at the time was the order that, beginning in mid-August 1943, seinendan members would be given paramilitary exercises as part of their regular activities.[85] This opportunity, and the prospects offered by the formation of Peta several months later, became the basis of a new brand of occupation propaganda designed especially for a body of largely unattached, uncommitted, and often unemployed pemuda. It was also effective, of course, with many of those youths who had followed the pergerakan path.[86]

The new approach, however, neither secured a greatly enlarged seinendan membership in Surabaya nor eased growing Japanese frustrations with the city's youth. By the end of December 1943, the total number of seinendan youth was much the same as it had been four months earlier. Despite the establishment of several asrama, or training centers, only 400 seinendan members had gone through the short training course provided.[87] Warnings went out that pemuda ought to stop wasting their time and behaving aimlessly, and allusions to "snails" and "leeches" loitering about the city made it evident that youths were reluctant to add their names to seinendan rolls.[89] After several months of complaining, municipal officials launched a campaign to search all kampung in Surabaya for pemuda who were neither enrolled in school nor registered in one or another government sponsored organization, primarily the seinendan; youths who had been trained in seinendan asrama earlier apparently had drifted away from government control also, and efforts were made to locate them.[89] Using data gathered in this fashion, a seinendan membership drive was started with the goal of establishing branches of the organization in every ward of the city and in every subdistrict of the Residency.[90] Greatly increased expenditures were devoted to the seinendan, most of which supported new asrama and refresher courses covering what pemuda had been taught at the first sessions.[91] By April 1945 the Surabaya seinendan counted 4,100 members, but that figure was not particularly large compared to the prewar scouting membership in the city, or even to the number of youth the Japanese had gathered together for one occasion prior to the founding of the seinendan.[92] Clearly the expectations of the Japanese—which seem to have been that anywhere from 200,000 to 1,000,000 Indonesian youths might be mobilized on Java alone—were far from being reached in Surabaya, and any hope of deeply stirring the younger generation either to support the war effort or to behave more as the Japanese thought appropriate went largely unrealized.[93]

One reason for this state of affairs was that the linking of patriotic themes and ideals to the seinendan did not change appreciably the day-to-day nature of the seinendan. The organization remained a combination of work troop and scouting association, in which discipline and control were cultivated above all else.[94] Seinendan activities were far from glamorous, though marches in uniform, which some found stirring, were organized occasionally.[95] Both asrama training sessions and regular practices included calisthenics and jogging, along with a certain amount of philosophizing about the importance of building strong bodies. Afterwards, there was labor of some sort, generally a menial task such as road repair, street sweeping, castor bean planting, or wood cutting in a location outside the city. Kampung youth also were assigned guard duty on a regular basis and asked to take part in projects to help the needy; lectures and discussion on "character building" filled spare hours. All of this aimed to encourage self-reliance, boldness, and pride as well as loyalty to principle and the Japanese.[96] The goal was to impress the younger generation with the need to balance action and will power on the one hand with control and obedience on the other. As was explained at the time, "steel must be tempered while it is red-hot; youth must be trained while still impressionable."[97]

Sometimes described as a military organization, the seinendan was in reality something less than that term implies. No modern weapons were issued to seinendan units, even for training or parade purposes. At best it can be said that the defensive use of the bamboo spear was taught after mid-1944, and that in Surabaya seinendan youths carried spears and, occasionally, dummy wooden rifles in infrequent marching exhibitions. Physical exercises were often reminiscent of training in a vaguely military style, as were the manner and tone of leadership, whether in Japanese or Indonesian hands. But in general the seinendan resembled closely the scout groups of the 1930s and did not alter those patterns sufficiently to warrant the military label. Kampung residents looked on the seinendan as a scouting group, and although it clearly was recognized as being different from the prewar sort in that it was controlled by the occupation government, the seinendan seemed to them a natural successor to organizations such as Surya Wirawan.[98] Those groups also had possessed a military flavor, and it was common for kampung folk to equate scouting activities with military training even before the occupation, perhaps because any program that built the physical and psychological strength of Indonesians was seen as arming them.[99] But there were no illusions about the mundane nature of what seinendan members actually were called upon to do, which was guard kampung and some municipal facilities, and clean or repair Surabaya's streets. The latter tasks in particular were invariably done under the supervision of Japanese guards. Western and other writers on the Japanese period in Indonesia frequently have pointed to Japanese inculcation in youth of the notion that willpower or semangat was the key to everything; quite to the contrary, pemuda in Surabaya's seinendan groups found it difficult to ignore the message that semangat, however strong, could never entirely replace hard work, training, and cooperation.[100]

The seinendan did not enjoy the enthusiastic support of Surabaya's kampung youth. A small number of individuals found the organization attractive either because of its toughening, challenging style or because of the opportunity it offered for small pay and fringe benefits such as cigarettes, extra rice, and even the possibility of finding a government job.[101] The majority, however, did not consider these appeals compelling, and they resisted becoming members for as long as they were able. Unemployed pemuda hid or pretended to be occupied with petty trading ventures in order to escape serving in the seinendan, particularly since rumor held that joining was much the same as becoming a romusha.[102] Youths who worked in factories and offices generally preferred to follow the less rigorous and high-handed training offered by seinendan branches at their places of employment, avoiding the kampung seinendan altogether. Those unable to escape in this way—often youth with some education who were neither employed nor attending school—tended to resent seinendan activities deeply. It was said that the attraction of seinendan uniforms and activity was greater for newcomers from rural East Java than for the arek Surabaya, and that perhaps the majority of those who participated in the marching and calisthenics were country youths newly come to the city.[103] The disquiet of the kampung public over the seinendan was such that in many Surabaya neighborhoods branches of the organization were never established. For while residents approved of youth guards, parents were uncomfortable with the idea of kampung sons being forced to labor under the pretense of training; they could not commit their children to the seinendan because they did not feel its purpose was sufficiently clear.[104]

■ The new priyayi and the younger generation

The new priyayi remained largely separated from the younger generation for much of the occupation, though they did make use of the opportunity provided by the Japanese turn to patriotic propaganda. The Japanese acquiesced and permitted a nationalist, pergerakan-style appeal to youth only when it appeared necessary. Even then, contact between new priyayi and youth was monitored carefully until early 1945. On this account, and because their own roles were undergoing change, intellectuals continued to have an ambivalent approach to the younger generation. Until late in the occupation much journalistic commentary on the position of youth in the New Order sounded as if it had been written years earlier, when pergerakan leaders freely expressed their distress over a straying younger generation. One writer poked fun at the difference between the youthful (sexual) urge (*semangat muda*) and the "true spirit of youth" (*semangat pemuda*), while another noted that the role of youth in the New Order was not to sit back but to be tempered and trained to take creative, productive action."[105] Others suggested that pemuda who simply loafed about the city "dressing up in fancy clothes and making passes [at girls] . . . [had] no semangat at all [and did] not want to join in the struggle; [perhaps they were] better off dead."[106] There is no indication that these were Japanese views foisted on intellectuals to appear under their names in newspaper columns. Intellectuals had always believed discipline and organization necessary to a younger generation preparing to enter new priyayi ranks, and they maintained this view during the occupation. They neither understood nor approved of youth who did not wish to follow more or less in their footsteps, and they did not hesitate to say so.

New priyayi did not choose the methods the Japanese used to attract and train Indonesian youth, but they did observe them carefully and, especially because they feared too heavy a Japanese influence, interjected themselves whenever possible. There was much about the seinendan that intellectuals could applaud; the emphasis on hard work, the insistence on physical exercise, and the balanced treatment of semangat, to take only the most obvious examples, were familiar elements that had been developed amply in prewar thinking. Additionally, the seinendan sometimes provided defensive skills for youth, skills not easily come by otherwise. On these accounts, intellectuals in Surabaya discovered that they were able to encourage the seinendan in good conscience. When Japanese requested that intellectual leaders give talks to seinendan groups in city asrama, they began to do so with less reluctance than when, for example, they were asked to take part in propaganda rallies.[107] Their message to pemuda was that however demanding the seinendan program might be, and however much the youths might dislike having their home life or jobs disrupted by special sessions, the experience was certain to prove worthwhile. Youths were urged to put themselves to the test of tough physical standards, though some intellectuals worried privately whether these might be too exacting. Pemuda complained bitterly about the sessions, but their elders advised them to continue, harden themselves, and learn the lessons carefully in order to meet what were euphemistically called "personal goals" or vaguely referred to as "the needs of the homeland."[108]

The majority of youths whom intellectuals met in their visits to seinendan asrama in Surabaya had filled scouting ranks in the Dutch period. They were the educated sons of new priyayi and kampung middle class families, and they either attended school (which was generally considered a prerequisite for seinendan membership) or held regular office jobs. While many prewar pemuda leaders appear to have been able to avoid these training sessions, those who did attend were familiar with pergerakan scouting and its principles. The Japanese do not appear to have attracted a new clientele in the urban seinendan; for the most part they continued with a group already reached by intellectuals earlier.

During the occupation some of these youths maintained contact with pergerakan scouting leaders or intellectual figures in informal ways, for example when the elder individual was employed in an office or with an organization to which younger persons could become attached. More frequently, however, informal social networks bound youth to new priyayi mentors. The most common of these took the form of circles comprising an older intellectual surrounded by several extended family members of varying ages, as well as young friends and political kin. Variations included groups of loyal ex-students around popular teachers or scout leaders. Thus Ir. Darmawan Mangunkusumo and Dr. Samsi Satrowidagdo, both of whom remained in the background of pergerakan politics, continued their "advisor" roles during the occupation; R. Widjajadi, who as Pak Doho was a well-known scouting leader, enjoyed a loyal following in the Japanese period and at one time was saved from financial ruin by the young people around him.[109] Bonds of this sort were strong, and while it is difficult to reconstruct the precise intellectual content of these relationships, they seem to have consisted largely of reviewing pergerakan lessons and applying them to the realities of the occupation, and to an imagined future. In most instances it was a joint enterprise, with the elder figures supplying the framework for thought and as much information as they could gather. Young members contributed different sorts of information gleaned from their places of work and on their wanderings about the city; occasionally, as well, they were able to make visits to small towns and even villages in East and Central Java, bringing back impressions from those areas. In this fashion new priyayi and pemuda together assembled a more complete and thoughtful view of their surroundings than either could have done alone.

Yet at the same time as they sat with their elders (or, in a few cases, more experienced colleagues) in a roughly "father-son" or *bapak-anak buah* relationship, these pemuda began to strike out on their own and to rely less completely than before on the guidance of their pergerakan teachers. The most important reason for this was the altered position of intellectuals, both within the structure of occupation affairs generally and with regard to youth. A second reason was the galvanizing effect certain aspects of Japanese rule had on educated youth. The occupation represented a far more palpable crisis than they had been able to imagine in the late 1930s, creating fear and resentment. Fueled with renewed pergerakan ideals and stimulated by much New Order propaganda, they soon acquired a direction and energy distinctly their own. Third, the occupation often provided new environments and broader horizons to educated urban youth. Both because of and despite school closings and Japanese mobilization efforts, youth from markedly different backgrounds were thrown together, and pemuda with pergerakan experience had more chances than before to proselytize and develop their ideas.

In late 1943, after much initial confusion related to the founding of the seinendan and the Peta, Surabaya's educated youth began very tentatively to form small, local groups with shared interests. This activity was largely unplanned, taking place along social and political lines already well established and having purposes that were at best only dimly perceived. For these reasons, and because recollections have tended to fade in the light of the more spectacular events which followed, a precise account is impossible. But a few examples convey a reasonably accurate notion of the sort of development that was underway among many pemuda in the city.

At the former Batavia Petroleum Company and several other oil concerns in Surabaya, the established pergerakan figure Djohan Sjahroezah began to circulate quietly, discussing the political aims of prewar activists and very carefully sharing a sense of discontent over Japanese rule.[110] Sjahroezah, closely linked to Sutan Sjahrir—a founding member of the so-called "new PNI" in 1931—and in the early occupation Mohammad Hatta's secretary, sought out individuals in their mid-twenties or older (he was 31 at the time), educated to roughly the MULO level or better, and acquainted with political activity of some kind. No formal organization was proposed, largely because this was thought likely to attract unwanted Japanese attention, and the group survived on what might be described as a loose emotional and intellectual camaraderie. This seems to have extended gradually to younger employees in a number of other private and government offices.

A different but not entirely dissimilar group centered on Ruslan Abdulgani, who was then 29 years old.[111] Firmly anchored in the New Order both as a government office worker of better than middle rank and as a widely recognized political figure, Abdulgani was cautious but restless under the Japanese. As the dust of the first year of occupation began to settle, he became the nucleus of a loosely constituted study group very much like those he had instigated several years earlier. Participants were young men in their mid-twenties or older who were family relations, personal friends, or colleagues from Indonesia Muda days. One or two were actually a year or two older than Abdulgani himself, but all customarily called him "Captain" out of respect for his education and wide reading. Books, indeed, were an important part of the shared experience of this small group, and Abdulgani abstracted for the others a variety of works in Western languages. One example was W. Hendrick van Loon's *The Liberation of Mankind*, which provided inspirational and intellectual guidance. But there were other important aspects to "meetings," which were irregular and often held in unlikely places such as roadside food stalls. Here a generalized discontent was shared, as well as a range of ideas about the effects and long-term meaning of the occupation. Special attention was paid to the question of how prewar yearnings for independence and involvement with the masses might fit into the framework of the Japanese order.

A third cluster of young men formed in the Surabaya branch of the government's Bureau of Cultural Affairs.[112] Several older pergerakan figures including Ali Sastroamidjojo and Dr. Soegiri were appointed by the Japanese to oversee this office, but for practical purposes its daily administration fell to others with fewer demands on their time. Among these were several young artists such as Karjono, then about 25 years old, and a group of journalists which included Abdul Aziz and Bagus Sulaimanhadi, who were about the same age. These men had shallow roots in the pergerakan and their understanding of events was only lightly shaded in political hues. They were, and consciously styled themselves as, "free spirits" whose discussions revolved around cultural matters, philosophical gleanings from Western-language works, and thoughts about the Indonesian state and society which were likely to emerge from Japanese rule. Considering themselves progressive thinkers, Karjono and his colleagues shared a dislike of what they saw as Japanese-imposed limits on their freedom, and it was largely on this basis that they condemned the New Order.

These and other similarly small and tentative groups did not represent the beginnings of an underground movement against the Japanese, much less a revolution. Membership was neither large enough nor sufficiently widespread throughout the city to draw together a critical mass of educated youth to begin such an undertaking. Furthermore, the subject of mounting an effort to oppose the Japanese seldom came up for discussion, and when it did it was soon set aside out of fear or a sense of helplessness. Yet, at the same time, many of these pemuda circles harbored the potential for more independent and volatile activity. They were, however indebted to new priyayi mentors, largely unrestrained by them; the intensity of anti-Japanese and pro-independence feelings grew steadily and began to acquire a distinct pemuda stamp. After early 1944, when Putera was replaced by the Hokokai and mobilization efforts intensified, pemuda appear to have become more difficult for the government to control, as even seinendan leaders evaded their responsibilities and parents resisted further recruiting efforts.[113] What is more, the new Japanese policy of cultivating the younger generation with patriotic sentiments and new priyayi nationalism seems not only to have built pemuda confidence, but to have convinced many that independence was a real possibility in the near future and that youth was to be an important part of the movement toward it. Changes of this sort were important in quickening the currents carrying pemuda. The Japanese did not miss them, and sensed a growing restlessness and resistance among the youth they wished most to utilize. The new priyayi, who also saw the changes and encouraged them in subtle ways, believed they might spell the emergence of a generation of pemuda willing and able to answer the cries of a "sick Motherland," a nation in need of sacrifice.[114] By mid-1944 pemuda sentiments were rising and, though they had little real power to act, small groups among educated pemuda had begun to multiply.

■ Pemuda and the waning of Japanese rule

Japanese authorities were not slow in attempting to contain pemuda activities and to reassert direction of them. On 4 October 1944 a Surabaya Residency Youth Committee was established with the help of the sendenbu.[115] Leadership of this new enterprise was to be exercised by Malikin, a 25-year-old arek Surabaya whose Dutch technical education had helped him to secure a position as foreman at a supply yard run by the Japanese Naval Air Corps.[116] Malikin's family was entrenched firmly in the kampung upper middle class, and he reportedly was a nephew of the Surabaya-born Moslem pergerakan figure, K. H. Mas Mansur. Other individuals named as officers in this group were probably from similar economic and social backgrounds.[117] In addition to bringing younger government office workers together in a single organization fostering the ideals of the New Order, the Youth Committee apparently had intentions of making a public announcement—as an example to all youth—of its members' devotion to duty, the Greater East Asia War, and eventual Indonesian independence.

Less than two weeks later, the Japanese sponsors of the Youth Committee found themselves struggling to control it. The precise course of events cannot be traced because of insufficient information, but two general developments seem clear enough. The first was an escalation of patriotic rhetoric among pemuda, made possible by increased Japanese willingness to permit pro-independence expressions, and stimulated by Sukarno's lively performance before a Surabaya audience, including many pemuda, on 6 October 1944. His rousing speech centered on the theme "Indonesia is ours, we must be free" and, without so much as mentioning the Japanese, emphasized that Indonesians had to "find the door to independence" by themselves.[118] For the first time since the earliest days of the occupation,

Surabayans sang the anthem "Indonesia Raya" in public, and ended the mass meeting with the old pergerakan cry of "Hidup!" A second concurrent development was that of a critical, competitive spirit among pemuda, singly or in groups, who feared that the Japanese guided Youth Committee might lead in the wrong direction or overshadow the efforts of others. The founding of the committee was interpreted as a challenge rather than, as the Japanese had hoped, being accepted as a channel into which pemuda energies might flow without eroding the surrounding landscape.

Much affected by these circumstances, the Youth Committee soon showed more independence than its initiators had counted on, and its first efforts to arrange a city-wide youth rally were cancelled by nervous officials.[119] In the midst of pressure to reschedule the event, the Japanese apparently were convinced to allow a public observation of the 16th anniversary of the Youth Oath.[120] The ceremony was modest, but it marked the first commemoration of a key pergerakan event during the occupation, and therefore attracted considerable attention. One youth used the opportunity to deliver a lively speech explicitly linking the ideals of the 1928 oath with the activities of the younger generation in the 1940s, after which his audience was asked to swear allegiance to a free and united Indonesia.[121] Two mass gatherings of pemuda followed in rapid succession. During the final moments of one, led by the Youth Committee, Malikin announced his desire to send a pemuda delegation to visit Sukarno in Jakarta. At first refused by the Japanese, this request was later granted and the group soon met with pemuda leaders in the capital, where they pledged their loyalty to Sukarno. Surabayans were ready, one speaker noted, "to face any eventuality whatsoever in order to achieve Indonesia Merdeka, a free Indonesia."[122]

The new priyayi took careful note of the surging pemuda interest in the prospects for independence, not least because circumstances had given them an opportunity to foster it. The new enthusiasm seemed to confirm activist pemuda as the legitimate offspring of the pergerakan, and to provide evidence that the younger generation was at last finding its direction. Particularly for intellectuals who had been critical of pemuda aimlessness before the war, the change was welcome. Mohammad Hatta's satisfaction that youth had developed a new, stronger attitude and now "felt responsible toward the nation and its people" was probably widely shared.[123] In Surabaya, intellectuals' commentary on pemuda activity became almost uniformly positive. Sudirman suggested his new confidence in pemuda when he spoke to young office workers about their taking advantage of favorable "present opportunities . . . to eliminate all obstacles to the realization of Indonesian independence."[124] New priyayi assumed greater roles in certain aspects of the seinendan and its extension, the Barisan Pelopor or Pioneer Corps, and it became commonplace for new priyayi leaders to point out proudly that recent pemuda actions in Surabaya set an admirable example of courage for the rest of Java and were not fully backed by the confidence of their elders.[125] Thus there were ample signs that the younger generation might assume a position of importance in the changing New Order, moving in the same direction as the new priyayi and with their blessing.

By the end of 1944, however, much about this new pemuda role remained obscure, in part because pemuda leaders themselves continued to behave cautiously, and in part because, even at this late date, Japanese and pemuda interests were often difficult to distinguish. It is unclear, for example, whether the primary organization of this period, the Angkatan Muda (Younger Generation), sprang first from pemuda energies in the West Java city of Bandung, or whether it formed mainly at the behest of Japanese officers, among them the curious figure of Shimizu Hitoshi.[126] What may have seemed obvious to those close to the scene in Bandung and Jakarta was fuzzy at best to pemuda leaders in Surabaya, who had never heard of the Angkatan Muda when Jamal Ali and Sam Kawenke visited East Java in December 1944 to locate potential supporters there.[127] Ali, a journalist in his late twenties with an activist background in Indonesia Muda, sought out several of Surabaya's former IM leaders, among them Ruslan Abdulgani.[128] The contact, however, was cursory; Abdulgani and several close associates were suspicious, and refused to commit themselves. The uncertainty did not disappear after Abdulgani returned in January 1945 from a fact-finding trip to Jakarta, made at the invitation of Hokokai leaders. There he perceived a struggle for a foothold in pemuda circles between Hokokai leaders on the one hand and sendenbu officials, Japanese as well as Indonesians, on the other. No guidance was forthcoming from the established new priyayi. Mohammad Hatta reportedly told Abdulgani, when asked what stance Surabaya's pemuda ought to take, that it was "up to them," they would have to figure things out for themselves. Abdulgani's report to his circle of associates precipitated heated debate but no firm plans for action.

Then, in March 1945, Chaerul Saleh and Sukarni, both 28 years old and experienced political youth leaders who had managed to find a niche during the occupation in the offices of the sendenbu, visited Surabaya. Their purpose was to establish a branch of the Angkatan

Muda and to invite delegates to an all-Java youth conference planned for several months hence. At a meeting of barely a dozen young men, the two leaders explained their outlook in some detail.[129] Japan was weakening, they pointed out, and the Indonesian people were in a desperate situation. It was up to youth to do whatever it could to hasten the arrival of independence and devote effort to the betterment of the masses, especially in rural areas. The relationship to Indonesia Muda was plainly visible, as expressed in slogans such as "we must give to the masses rather than take from them."[130] As in prewar thinking, the "rakyatism is radicalism" formula was played upon with effect.[131] The group listened attentively, but agreed to appoint a leader before taking any steps. The choice of those present, including members from each of the three small pemuda circles which had formed earlier in Surabaya,[132] was Ruslan Abdulgani, who had declined to attend the meeting altogether.[139] His prestige was great enough, however, that Sukarni and several others went to his home, urged him to reconsider, and met again the next day to make matters official.[134]

Under these circumstances, Abdulgani could hardly refuse the appointment, but his acceptance was hedged with doubts.[135] He agreed that the group would engage in illegal activities, primarily carrying propaganda to kampung and, when possible, rural villages, behind a more open type of organizational effort aimed at pulling together like-minded youths.[136] To safeguard the group, Abdulgani distinguished it from the Jakarta-Bandung organization by using the name Angkatan Muda Committee, and chose as working partners only individuals he knew well from prewar days.[137] The new committee kept its distance from the Chaerul Saleh-Sukarni organization, and no official delegation was sent to the May 1945 pemuda meeting at Villa Isola, outside of Bandung.[138] Wary of becoming too deeply involved in a group manipulated by the Japanese, and haunted by Allied radio broadcasts describing the Dutch vow that Indonesian collaborators would be punished as traitors after the war, Abdulgani and most of his colleagues considered their options carefully before acting.

Hesitant though they were, Abdulgani's committee did bring together representatives from the three major pemuda circles in the city, and they were much affected by the tension building at the time. The changed atmosphere had gripped the new priyayi, and one Jakarta leader even went so far as to announce, in March 1945, that the Indonesian people "now lived in a time of revolution."[139] Alert pemuda were influenced deeply by such opinions, and they gradually came to the realization that events were reaching a critical stage. The conviction spread that the need for pemuda activism was growing. For the majority of those who took a vigorous role in pemuda gatherings at this time, such notions appear to have been more intuitive than based on a knowledge of actual conditions, but they were nevertheless genuine and intense. Most important, the impulse to action took hold with special force because it was rooted securely in the ethos of the pergerakan. Japanese rule had not replaced old concepts but it had brought about a pemuda revisualization of those stressed, though perhaps not as completely embraced, under the very different conditions of Dutch rule. The intellectual and social debt was acknowledged by Abdulgani and many others, who dedicated themselves anew to principles of long standing.

In mid 1945, with Japanese power on the wane and an increasingly favorable environment for pemuda outspokenness, the time for action had arrived. The steps eventually taken by the Surabaya Angkatan Muda Committee constituted the only significant nongovernment youth effort in the city until after the Japanese surrender. The nature of this action was influenced heavily by the social and intellectual perspective of the committee's leaders, which was essentially that of younger new priyayi.[140] Ruslan Abdulgani's background is already familiar. His kampung origins merely enhanced his reputation as an intellectual, and as a government employee of some importance he was tied reasonably securely to the New Order. Abdulgani's closest colleague in the new group, both personally and socially, was Bambang Kaslan, a friend from Indonesia Muda days.[141] Kaslan, who was 32 years of age in 1945, was a true arek Surabaya. His father—who was related to Abdulgani's father and like him had been involved in Sarekat Islam activities several decades earlier—had been a draftsman for the colonial navy and had urged his sons through HIS, MULO, and several Indonesian-run vocational schools in Surabaya. Kaslan did not command the overwhelming respect that Abdulgani enjoyed, but he acquired similar status through pergerakan friendships and activities. While maintaining more kampung contacts, especially among business families, Kaslan, like Abdulgani, had made the transition out of the kampung world.

Other committee officers could lay claim to far less humble roots, and represented even more clearly a kind of next half-generation of new priyayi. Krissubanu, who was about the same age as Kaslan, was educated to the MULO level or higher and came from a family of high social standing in Surabaya.[142] He was the younger brother of Bambang Suparto, who carried the title Kiyai Ngabei and bridged aristocratic and new priyayi groups. Krissubanu was involved throughout the 1930s in pergerakan youth groups, and he knew a number of Jakarta counterparts. Kusnadi, who was nearly 30 years old in 1945, had a Dutch middle-school education.[143] He worked throughout the occupation as a customs official, and like his associates he spoke the Dutch language well. Kustur was a nephew of the high-ranking pangreh praja Suprobo Reksodiprojo, one of whose daughters was married to Ruslan Abdulgani.[144] About 28 years old in 1945, Kustur had come to Surabaya after finishing HIS in outlying Krian and discovered that he fit in rather well during the mid-1930s with the educated youth then clustered around Abdulgani. Murdianto was a son of the prominent Dr. Sumadijono, who was a passive pergerakan sympathizer and a close friend of Ir. Darmawan Mangunkusumo, Abdulgani's chief mentor.[145] He was about the same age as Abdulgani and, like Kustur, spent most of the occupation employed as a physical education instructor at the Surabaya high school; a brother, Murdiono, worked under Abdulgani and Darmawan at the Office of Economic Affairs. Finally, Gatot Gunawan, by far the youngest of the group, was the 18-year-old brother of Abdulgani's wife, and thus related to both Abdulgani and Kustur.[146]

Sometime in May 1945, Abdulgani, at the urging of Kustur and Murdianto, began meeting with groups of high school students.[147] Most were the children of government workers, pangreh praja, and new priyayi, but a number came from kampung middle class families. Many were hopeful doctors and lawyers for whom no specialized schooling was available at the time. The Angkatan Muda Committee became convinced that these students, all in their late teens to mid-twenties, were ripe for the same kind of tutoring in pergerakan ideas that had been carried on under Indonesia Muda auspices in earlier years. News of a revolt in a Peta barracks in Blitar on 15 February 1945 had filtered down to these students, who were then undergoing self-defense training with bamboo spears under the newly formed student defense corps (*gakutotai*), a kind of Peta-seinendan designed especially for students. A significant portion of their time in this organization was spent collecting scrap metal in Surabaya's kampung and sweeping streets, activities which were not at all popular. Sometimes openly in Japanese-sponsored question-and-answer sessions, and sometimes in private with small groups of friends, committee leaders focused attention on two interrelated themes: the critical situation of the masses, and the necessity of achieving independence before anything else. The ideas and accompanying rhetoric were well-worn, but suitable for the time and place. The hostility to the Japanese which underlay this talk was obvious, if expressed in less than obvious ways.

Students were asked to spread the word throughout Surabaya's kampung among less-educated youth.

As all this was proceeding, the foundation was being laid for a more spectacular project, a public meeting for educated urban youth at which some of the new spirit could be brought out into the open. It is difficult to say who arranged the event. Ruslan Abdulgani, even by his own account, seems not to have taken a major role in the planning. Kustur and Murdianto were perhaps most directly involved, but they leaned on the assistance of several contemporaries such as the journalist Bagus Sulaimanhadi, and Bambang Suparto, who maneuvered behind the scenes.[148] Judging from the results, there also may have been some Japanese contribution to the decision-making. Whatever the case, the 1 July 1945 gathering was advertised as a meeting of the student defense corps, but it attracted attention from many other organizations in which younger Indonesians were members.[149] Those in attendance probably made up a roughly representative body of the city's educated youth; included in the bargain were numbers of middle class pemuda who had participated in the seinendan and other groups.

Speakers at the meeting were predominantly new priyayi leaders. Doel Arnowo, Roeslan Wongsokusumo, and Sudirman gave presentations, along with several other individuals acting as honorary leaders of groups such as the special police corps. All stressed the role of activist pemuda in the future and in determining the fate of the independence movement. A handful of students, most of them drawn not from the high school but from Japanese language schools and the like, also made speeches on the same theme. Japanese officials in attendance seem to have realized toward the end of the planned program exactly what was afoot; the Angkatan Muda Committee in Surabaya was growing in size and moving beyond the point at which it could be controlled. Just before Ruslan Abdulgani was scheduled to deliver the closing message, the authorities ordered a halt to the meeting, and turned on air raid sirens to disperse the crowd.[150]

The Angkatan Muda Committee took credit for the 1 July assembly and the expression of pemuda semangat which issued from it. To many who were unacquainted with the group, it must have seemed a great deal more effectively directed than was actually the case. Some members became overenthused at the newspaper treatment of the event, probably written by Bagus Sulaimanhadi, but as Abdulgani reflected much later, while the meeting showed that Surabaya's pemuda were capable of an impressive show of spirit on behalf of independence, it also indicated that the Japanese were still on top of events. A few days later Abdulgani was called before the Japanese chief of the municipal police and questioned intently. He came away more certain than before that the war's end was not far away, but he was equally certain that further public activities by youth would be dangerous and for all practical purposes impossible.[151] Abdulgani was content to mull over the long-term significance of the reaction elicited from urban pemuda, which had taken him by surprise in much the same way as, ten years earlier, he had been astonished by the "radicalism" of kampung youth. His attention also was diverted from these matters by an offer from Dr. Samsi to teach a few mini-courses in economics at a Japanese-sponsored institute to be held at the old Dutch resort town of Nongkojajar.[152] The Angkatan Muda Committee in Surabaya quickly lost coherence, and toward the end of July Krissubanu, Kusnadi, Kaslan, and Sumarsono went to Jakarta at Chaerul Saleh's request to discuss what to do about it.[153]

The Angkatan Muda Committee was the principal concentration of young activists in Surabaya, but there were lesser centers of energy whose importance did not emerge until later. One such group was focused loosely on Sutomo, the 25-year-old son of a middle class kampung family who unwittingly stood on the threshold of fame greater still than that of the doctor whose name he shared.[154] Sutomo was one of those individuals who had improved his position during the occupation, rising in the field of journalism to become second in charge of the Indonesian desk at the Domei news agency in Surabaya. Like many of the Angkatan Muda Committee followers, however, he was uneasy about some aspects of Japanese rule, and by early 1945 he could not help puzzling over the future. The prospects for independence, whether under Japanese or Dutch sponsorship, were discussed earnestly by Sutomo and a handful of acquaintances from prewar days, among them Malikin, Asmanu, Amiadji, and Sumarno. They were all roughly the same age, all from new priyayi or upper kampung middle class backgrounds, and all experienced in prewar scouting groups or pergerakan associations. The latter attribute was considered essential by the members of this circle, a proof of loyalty or sign of trust.

Sutomo was hardly unknown among Surabaya's educated young men, and when in June he received word that he had been chosen for membership in the New People's Movement that was to replace the Hokokai, no one seems to have been surprised.[155] In July 1945, at the same time as the Abdulgani group was considering the outcome of their meeting, Sutomo was in Jakarta taking part in discussions on the new organization. By nature strong-headed and by circumstance

rather sheltered from a view of how the new priyayi leadership functioned during the occupation, the young Surabayan reacted sharply
to what he saw as the plush, too-cautious life of new priyayi in the
capital city. Sutomo played the cocky arek Surabaya to perfection,
and in a matter of days made a name for himself as a vividly outspoken personality. By his own account, he was congratulated by several prominent leaders for daring to quarrel with no less a figure than
Sukarno himself. Though the New People's Movement was scuttled
by pemuda in Jakarta, Sutomo returned home with a greater reputation than when he had left.

There is no indication that Sutomo was spurred by this experience
to plan a course of action. The most that can be said is that his Jakarta
encounters brought him to reconsider the implications of an Allied
victory and the subsequent return of the Dutch. The crisis he now
began to visualize more clearly seems to have occasioned his rededica-
tion to the rakyatist principles he had inherited from his pergerakan
involvement.[156] The deteriorating condition of the masses, impatience with the Japanese, and a sense of expectation about independence broke together over Sutomo as a single wave. On the one hand,
the experience was a lively awakening, and on the other a stunning
blow from which he did not immediately recover.

In addition to Sutomo and the Angkatan Muda Committee,
there were in some Surabaya kampung clusters of young men who
met periodically but informally for drills and who, in the early
months of 1945, seem to have thought increasingly of a time in the
near future when the occupation would draw to a close.[157] It is impossible to pinpoint satisfactorily the number and nature of these
groups. Some participants look back on them as having commonly
acknowledged leaders, training programs, and goals, while others do
not. In careful retrospect, the likelihood that such order existed is
small. A more reasonable picture may be one of vague coteries, some
large and some limited, of young men and boys from the age of about
25 down to 15 or so. Most groups formed in central city kampung
with strong middle class populations. A common and believable pattern was of some kampung youth sharing with others their seinendan
or similar experiences at school or work, but informally and with
their own purposes in mind, and often with the help of an older man.
The Japanese, if they were aware of these groups at all, may have been
inclined to treat them as extensions of the self-defense groups they
had spent much of the war trying to promote throughout the city.

It was natural enough, considering the environment in which they
appeared, for these groups to begin to consider themselves protectors

of their kampung, and to take this role seriously. The leaders were men with some education and, often, scouting experience. A few individuals had personal links to circles of better-educated pemuda outside the kampung. Perhaps in a few minds there existed a rough sense that all this might be one day useful in a struggle for independence, but this almost certainly was not a widespread notion until the last few months of the occupation. The main ingredients of the crisis to which kampung pemuda began to react were the uncertainty of their future and the tension caused by kampung restlessness under Japanese rule. Direction and action were still absent.

The fading light of the New Order revealed in Surabaya a complex and in many ways tenuous set of circumstances involving the younger generation. Pemuda had become discernibly energized during the occupation years, and pemuda attitudes gradually had begun to acquire a focus and grit that were previously lacking. It also might be argued that from early 1945 an emerging group of young leaders gathered a momentum of their own in urban life. Yet a universally and dramatically transformed generation of youths, stirred by a traditional sense of imbalance as well as the effects of Japanese tutelage, such as that visualized in many Western studies of the period,[158] did not exist in Surabaya. Nor is it possible to speak of a younger generation alienated or cut adrift from older mentors. The realities were both more uneven and more intricate than such generalizations allow.

Whatever may be said about Surabaya's pemuda and their outlook at the end of forty months of Japanese rule, it seems wisest to incorporate in them an understanding that the social and intellectual development of the pemuda was indissolubly linked to the pergerakan and the processes it originally called to life. At the same time it is clear that the occupation represented rather different phases of growth for new priyayi and pemuda. For the former, the Japanese offered opportunities for consolidation and security on the way to fulfilling long-held goals. For the latter, however, the effect was less definitive. Youth leadership, with neither an anchor in the passing order nor a sharply drawn role in whatever might emerge from it, still searched for a vantage point in the rapidly flowing stream of events. Instinctively moved by the excitement of approaching independence, youth nevertheless faced the prospect of Indonesia Merdeka with great uncertainty. As word of the 17 August 1945 proclamation of independence spread throughout Java, it remained to be seen what part Surbaya's pemuda might seize or be given in the new age that at last was dawning.

■ Notes

1. Abu Hanifah:124; "Riwayat Moerdjani"; interviews with Surabayan intellectuals, 1971-72.

2. This account is drawn principally from ARA AAS 101b/210, a military intelligence report clearly written with the help of a close personal friend of Moestopo's. The essence of the story is repeated in B. Anderson (1972):429, using information from Indonesian Department of Education biographical files.

3. On this subject see Kamadjaja; Day; and Quinn:21ff.

4. The most comprehensive account of the Three A Movement is contained in Kanahele (1967):45-52. The account given below is based upon 1971 interviews with Surabayans acquainted with the movement; the *Abdulgani MS*; MBZ IA/XV/9:11; and de Bruin (1967).

5. *Abdulgani MS*. Many interviews confirm that the specter of a ravaged rural population and countryside both touched and frightened intellectuals profoundly during the occupation, particularly as it was seen from the relative comfort of upper class urban life.

6. Depictions of the Japanese occupation as exciting, dramatic, and soaked in vivid color surely overstate the case. This is particularly so where intellectuals and the first three years of occupation are concerned. The best example of this romanticized view is B. Anderson (1966).

7. The most complete treatment of Putera is contained in Kanahele (1967):72-77, which notes that the organization was first discussed in November 1942. The most detailed eye-witness account is Mohammad Hatta (1971). For statements of purpose and functions, see Benda (1965):136-39; for a Japanese point of view, see Kishi:352-55.

8. The official date of founding is usually given as 9 March 1943, but announcements were made the previous day, which was the anniversary of the establishment of Japanese rule on Java. AR 3-8-43 and 3-9-43.

9. See especially RvOIC 005798; G. Pakpahan:27; and the *Abdulgani MS*. Sukarno's well-known inaugural speech, in which he said he himself was "a *putera*, a native son" helped convey this impression strongly. The text was carried in SA 3-13-43.

10. Mohammad Hatta (1971):72 indicates that Putera's branch chairmen were installed in Jakarta on 25 May 1943, but that the Surabaya branch did not hold a local ceremony until 20 July. Surabaya newspaper accounts show that activities took place before the local inauguration, as early as 1 July 1943. PP 7-2-43; SA 7-2-43, 7-16-43, and numbers in the following week.

11. *Abdulgani MS*.

12. The two most complete listings of Surabaya's Putera staff, one noted in Mohammad Hatta (1971):10, and the other in SA 7-5-43, overlap. Included in both lists are: Sudirman (Chairman), Mr. Ali Sastroamidjojo, Dr. Moh. Suwandhi, Mr. Iskaq Tjokrohadisurjo, K. Ng. Bambang Suparto, Nj. Sribudiutami Sumantri, Sjamsu Harya Udaya, Ruslan Abdulgani, and Dr. Moes-

topo. Those given only in the latter source are: H. Moh. Tahir Bakri, R. Tjokrohandoko, R. Widjajadi (Pak Doho), Munadi, Ismoetiar, R. Roeslan Wongsokusumo, and Kusno. The first group consists of uniformly powerful new priyayi pergerakan leaders, while the second is more mixed. The total of sixteen individuals still does not fill the staff complement mentioned by Mohammad Hatta, which came to about thirty persons. Except where noted otherwise, information on appointees is taken from listings in *Orang Indonesia*; SA 7-24-43, 7-27-43, and 7-28-43; and interviews in 1971-72 with several of the original members of Putera in Surabaya, and close acquaintances. The pergerakan affiliations of the members (for those known) were: no affiliation, 1; Parindra, 3; PNI, 2; PNI-Parindra, 2; Taman Siswa, 1; PNI-Taman Siswa, 1; Taman Siswa-PNI-Parindra, 1; Muhammadiyah, 1; Nahdlatul Ulama, 1; kepanduan (mostly KBI), 1. While it has been suggested frequently by Dutch and other writers that the Japanese heavily favored Parindrists, implying that this was further proof of the party's connivance with Japan in prewar days (see especially Sluimers [1968]:348ff.), in Surabaya such a view is not justified. Mohammad Hatta (1971):37-39 notes that the aim was a balance of parties and groups, and looking at the original nine Putera members in Surabaya the impression is of almost perfect balance, with Sudirman being the only thorough-going Parindra leader.

13. Information here and below on the Putera staff reactions is taken from interviews in 1971-72 with three former members of the staff, and several of their close acquaintances. Noehadi:17 also contains pertinent information.

14. For example, a flurry of local organizations, among them old and new business associations, began to "surrender themselves" to Putera even before that group was formally established in Surabaya. Perhaps the hope was that they would be protected in some way or reap some measure of benefit by doing so. SA 3-21/26/29/31-43, 4-1/13/15/17-43, 5-25-43, and 6-18-43. Perhaps on this account too, and because it was officially defunct anyway, the Parindra donated its office furniture and supplies to Putera, SA 7-10-43, 9-1-43, and 11-4-43.

15. SA 7-16/17/21/22/23/-43. Sukarno had to be in Jakarta in July to greet the Japanese premier, Tojo Hideki.

16. This account is taken from the *Abdulgani MS* and SA 8-17/19-43.

17. Significantly enough, aside from a spate of administrative terms, few Japanese or Japanified words entered into the language of propaganda or, for that matter, everyday conversation. What proved to be the most widely used of the Japanese coinages—*berjibaku*, from the Japanese *jibaku*, "suicide explosion," and meaning to sacrifice oneself—did not enter general use until the early revolution. The coinages *rapat raksasa* and *rapat samudera*, indicating giant public rallies, were not based on Japanese terms. With the exception of these and a handful of less important terms, the vocabulary of the occupation was to a striking degree that of the pergerakan.

18. Mohammad Hatta (1971):5.

19. SA 11-18-43.

20. Mohammad Hatta (1971):60–61.

21. See the argument in Mohammad Hatta (1971):13–20.

22. On the basis of nearly identical sets of materials, these opposing views have been advanced, respectively by Dahm:246–47 and Kanahele (1967):80 and 241–42.

23. On this Mohammad Hatta (1971):114 and the *Abdulgani MS* agree very closely.

24. SA 3-1-44.

25. Interview in 1972 with a former Surabaya Putera member.

26. For contemporary announcements see SA 1-28-44 and 2-8/9-44. Kishi:397-99 discusses the details of structure, while Benda (1965):145-63 gives a complete account of regulations and purposes.

27. As a rule intellectuals continued to be used as public speakers in urban areas, while rural propagandizing was turned over (much against their will) to pangreh praja. The Japanese feared, in the same way as the Dutch before them, an urban-rural link forged by pergerakan activists.

28. Tojo's speech was made in the Japanese Diet on 16 June 1943, shortly before his departure for Java. A translation of the portions of the address concerning the future of Java—"Indonesia" was never mentioned—can be found in Benda (1965):49–52.

29. AR 8-2-43; SA 10-18-43; *Osamu Seirei* Nos. 36 and 37; *Osamu Keirei* Nos. 5–8; *Kan Po* No. 26, 1943. Persons holding government jobs were specifically prohibited from holding office and taking part in the appointive process.

30. Information on the councils used here is taken from SA 9-18/20/21/22/23/24/27-43.

31. Doel Arnowo replaced H. Abdulwahab Kasbullah, a principal Nahdlatul Ulama leader. Other members were Dr. Moh. Saleh (a nonactivist pergerakan sympathizer in the Dutch period), H. Fakih Usman (a youth group leader), and Lim Sik Tjo (a Chinese).

32. The Surabaya Hokokai was constituted as follows: Chairman, Yasuoka Masaomi; Vice-Chairman, Sudirman (later shared, almost certainly, with a Japanese who was not named); Directors: Dr. Samsi Sastrowidagdo, H. Abdulwahab Kasbullah, Tukul Surohadinoto, a Japanese, and a local Chinese; Advisors: seven Japanese from various government offices, Iskaq Tjokrohadisurjo, Dr. Moh. Salih, Mr. Soewardi, Dr. Soegiri, Nj. Moesono, Ch. F. Hakkers, and Liem Thwan Tik; Others: two Japanese officials and Bambang Suparto. SA 3-4-44.

33. SA 3-11-44.

34. SA 7-22-44.

35. SA 8-14/17-44.

36. Interviews in 1971-1972 with former Putera members.

37. The New People's Movement, announced in early July 1945, generally has been discussed in the context of the growing importance of youth groups and leaders in occupation activism. B. Anderson (1961):39–41 and 53

is a good example of this line of thinking. But the movement also serves as a reminder, if one is needed, that the Japanese experiment of relying heavily on the pangreh praja for leadership did not work out to the government's satisfaction, and that intellectuals and a few educated youth were being looked at again in terms of their usefulness to the Japanese.

38. See especially Sluimers (1965):350 and B. Anderson (1966):18. Mohammad Hatta (1971) indicates that he too felt such an understanding and working arrangement had been arrived at.

39. Information in the remainder of this paragraph is taken from RvOIC 032508; *Peraturan dasar*:5–7; and interviews in 1971–72 with former pangreh praja serving in the Surabaya areas, as well as with two employees in their offices.

40. RvOIC 032508.

41. *De Vrije Pers* 9-1-49; interviews in 1971–72 with former pangreh praja.

42. SA 8-30-43.

43. *Kan Po* No. 17, 1943; SA 10-19-43.

44. SA 11-16/21/27-43.

45. PP 10-6-42 and the strong editorial in SA 7-11-43.

46. Information on Soerjo in this and the following paragraph, except where cited otherwise, is based on interviews in 1971–72 and 1978 with Sutomo and Ruslan Abdulgani, who were in close contact with Soerjo in 1945–46; with several pangreh praja who worked under him at various times; and on Sutjiantiningsih's biography.

47. SA 11-24-43.

48. SA 2-22-43.

49. Interview in 1971 with Sutadji, who was Sudirman's closest colleague at the time; the same view is implicit throughout Mohammad Hatta (1971).

50. Interview in 1971 with pangreh praja who served in or near these areas. Unfortunately, it does not appear possible to compile from available records a completely accurate list of occupation period changes in the pangreh praja, and what is more sufficient social information on new appointees is lacking in records which do exist. Benda (1958):270–71 argues, with only slight hesitation, that the pangreh praja was little changed during the occupation. While the kind of data that might clinch the point seems lacking, my impression, and the conclusion of Kurasawa Aiko (1986), is that in most areas of Java considerable change did in fact take place.

51. Interview in 1971 with Roeslan Wongsokusumo.

52. "Riwayat Moerdjani," see note 54 below.

53. Interviews in 1971 with pangreh praja who knew colleagues of this sort, and one who had the type of experience described.

54. There was some justification for this, beyond prewar experience. "Riwayat Moerdjani" notes that his appointment as regent was the result of Sukarno's personal intervention, and that Mohammad Hatta himself had urged intellectuals to take pangreh praja positions lest the Japanese think

that Indonesians possessed no talent for leadership of that sort. The latter point is born out in Mohammad Hatta (1971.)

55. ARA AAS 97b/II/17:16-20.

56. Interview in 1971 with a middle-ranked pangreh praja who had this experience.

57. Information in this and the following pararaph is based largely on interviews with Sutadji in 1971 and 1972.

58. On his background, see above, pages 48–49.

59. Soetomo (1959):125–27.

60. Kampung interviews, 1971–72.

61. For example, the word *fujinkai,* which actually referred to the Japanese-sponsored women's auxiliary later connected to the Hokokai, was used derisively and with mistaken syntax as voguish slang for a high-class prostitute. Imbedded in this was a round hatred of the Japanese, as well as a dislike of the priyayi elite, since only upper-class women were thought to belong to the organization. Kampung interviews in 1971.

62. Interview in 1972 with Sribudiutami.

63. RvOIC 000387-68.

64. Sa 6-2-42.

65. SA 9-14-42.

66. The founding of the BPAR is given detailed treatment in de Bruin (1968):11–19. Information here is drawn from this source, except where cited otherwise.

67. SA 7-11-42.

68. At least I can find no record of such events in local newspaper accounts or private diaries. Copies of SA 7-7/8-42 are missing from all available collections, however, and there is some possibility they might contain references to youth activities.

69. MBZ IA/XV/9:12; *Abdulgani MS.*

70. Associations such as the Indonesian Sports League (Ikatan Sport Indonesia, ISI) had attempted with some success in the late 1930s to unify the major Indonesian soccer clubs of Java. Led for the most part by doctors in their early thirties, the ISI stressed many pergerakan values in a nonpolitical setting. It survived the early occupation, and associations like it continued in one form or another throughout the war years. PP 7-6/19-42, 9-9/18-42. Intellectuals were somewhat less familiar with moral guidance in the curriculum, but their interest in guiding the younger generation along proper lines led them to think that some effort of this type was necessary in the schools.

71. The account here is taken from PP 3-1-43 and 4-11-43.

72. PP 4-10-43.

73. PP 5-1/3-43.

74. PP 5-3-43.

75. Mohammad Hatta (1971):52–54.

76. PP 5-4-43.

77. PP 4-27-43.

78. For example, Kishi:191.

79. This and the following material on goals and structures is taken from PP 5-4-43.

80. The youth corps oath is found in SA 9-3-43 and, in a slightly revised version, in SA 5-16-44.

81. PP 5-1-43.

82. For examples see SA 7-20-43.

83. PP 5-3/27/28-43 and 8-21-43.

84. SA 8-6/11/14-43 and 9-6-43.

85. There were two orders, one given on 18 August 1943 and the other on 6 September 1943. Both mention various types of defensive military-style training. The second of the orders appears to have been intended as a reinforcement of the first. O. D. P. Sihombing:122-23. Full implementation of the policy was not scheduled, however, until March 1944. De Bruin (1968):37-39.

86. Shortly after the announcement that seinendan members would be defense-trained, a *Soeara Asia* editorial noted with special enthusiasm that the original tasks of the seinendan had been set in times of peace, but now that a period of danger and national threat had begun, youth would be in the forefront of the defense effort. SA 8-24-43.

87. SA 12-28-43. This source makes it apparent, too, that a number of those engaged in this asrama training were much older than seinendan regulations set down as age limits for members.

88. SA 12-8-43, 1-4-44, and 3-6-44.

89. SA 5-10-44 and 6-13-44.

90. SA 5-22-43 and 6-3-43.

91. SA 6-26-44 and 8-18-44. Funds for the seinendan were more than doubled from f. 19,000 to f. 40,000 between 1944 and 1945. SA 4-11-45. If comparable figures for Surabaya regency are any guide, the city seinendan also nearly doubled between 1943 and 1944.

92. SA 4-11-45.

93. In early 1945, Jakarta announced that it hoped for 190,000 seinendan members as an absolute minimum, but there is no indication that even this level was reached on Java. On the numbers issue generally see de Bruin (1968):25-40.

94. The seinendan was in practice divided into a number of separate groups centered on factory employees, government and other office workers, kampung residents, and the like. Each tended to have a different character and program of activities, though generally they had much in common. Members tended to limit their involvement to one seinendan group, for example the one established at the place of work, which often was less demanding, and to ignore others, such as that at the kampung level. In any case, not all workplaces or kampung had seinendan branches, and probably relatively few had branches that functioned regularly or at full strength.

95. Except where cited otherwise, the description of the seinendan given here and below is based upon interviews in 1971-72 with seven individuals who saw the Surabaya seinendan at close range, either as lecturers or participants.

96. SA 7-17-44 and 9-4-44.

97. SA 9-4-44.

98. Kampung interviews, and interviews with former Surabaya seinendan members, 1971–1972.

99. Based on a 1971 interview with Dr. Angka Nitisastro, who followed seinendan affairs closely and frequently was asked to speak to seinendan groups in asrama.

100. SA 11-13-43, 12-3/23-43.

101. O. D. P. Sihombing:127; kampung interview. 1971.

102. Interview in 1971 with Sifun, whose own experience this was and who knew others who did the same thing.

103. De Bruin (1968):88; kampung interviews, 1971.

104. Based on interviews in 1971–72 with kampung dwellers.

105. SA 8-27-42; PP 4-2-43.

106. SA 2-12-44.

107. Information and opinions in this and the following paragraph are drawn, except where cited otherwise, from an interview in 1971 with Dr. Angka Nitisastro, who gave such talks and had friends who did also.

108. In the same vein, see the remarks of Sukarno and an unidentified Indonesian journalist after watching seinendan training. SA 7-20-43 and 5-20-44.

109. *Abdulgani MS*; Ali Sastroamidjojo:73ff.; 1972 interview with Widjajadi.

110. On Djohan Sjahroezah's activities see B. Anderson (1972):126 and 417–18 and the sources cited there. An interview in 1978 with Sumarsono (who was of course close to Sjahroezah) has been helpful as well.

111. This account of Ruslan Abdulgani's activities is taken from the *Abdulgani MS*; Bambang Kaslan, "Kisah sedjarah":4; and interviews with Abdulgani and Kaslan in 1972, and in 1973 with Kustur, their close associate at the time.

112. The account given here depends on information given in a 1971 interview with Karjono and a 1972 interview with Ali Sastroamidjojo.

113. SA 6-13-44 and 8-28-44; kampung interviews, 1971.

114. SA 8-15-44.

115. SA 10-6-44.

116. Biographical information is taken from a 1972 interview with Sutomo.

117. No detailed biographical information is available on the remaining leaders mentioned in newspaper accounts, who were Usman Burhan, Slamet Sarwo, Saleh Said, and Luktaningsih.

118. SA 10-7-44.

119. SA 10-19/20-44.

120. SA 10-31-44.

121. SA 10-28-44.

122. SA 11-7/14-44.

123. SA 10-3-44.

124. SA 11-2-44.

125. The Barisan Pelopor was founded almost immediately after the Koiso resolution in early September 1944. It apparently was conceived of as a paramilitary arm of the Hokokai and was placed largely in Indonesian hands, though Japanese controlled the parameters of activity and the highest decision-making. Kanahele (1967):166–67. In Surabaya the Barisan Pelopor stirred little more interest than the seinendan, except in that it brought a small number of youths closer to a few new priyayi figures, such as Doel Arnowo, who were given responsibility for the group. The activities the Japanese had in mind for the Barisan Pelopor were identical to those of the seinendan. Interviews in 1971 and 1972 with two persons who joined the group.

126. The origins and nature of the Angkatan Muda are obscure, and there is no entirely satisfactory account of this organization. Part of the problem may be that the name was borrowed by a number of different pemuda circles for their own purposes, with or without contacts in the group which originally used the name. Also, the name lent itself to generic use; it was easily repeated orally and in the press without necessarily indicating an organization. To say one belonged to the Angkatan Muda seems to have been another way of saying that one shared a certain vaguely defined state of mind. This pattern by which ad hoc groups spread or appeared to spread was common in the 1930s, and became prevalent in the early revolution as well.

127. Djen Amar:33ff.

128. The information in the remainder of this paragraph is taken from the *Abdulgani MS*. Many figures, young and old, in Surabayan political circles seem to have been increasingly uneasy about initiatives coming from Jakarta as the war continued. A major contributing factor was disapproval among new priyayi leaders of several of Sukarno's actions, especially his apparent support of the romusha program.

129. Unless cited otherwise, this account is taken from Bambang Kaslan "Kisah sedjarah":5–6.

130. Djen Amar:32.

131. Interview in 1973 with Ruslan Abdulgani.

132. Those present were: Chaerul Saleh, Djohan Sjahroezah, Sumarsono, Ruslan Widjajasastra, Kusnadi, Margono, Susiswo, Bambang Kaslan, Asmanu, and Krissubanu, at whose home the meeting was held.

133. Interview in 1973 with Kustur.

134. Present at this second meeting were: Sukarni, Krissubanu, Murdianto, Kustur, Abdul Aziz, Sumarsono, Dimyati, Ruslan Widjajasastra, Kusnadi, Margono, and Bambang Kaslan.

135. *Abdulgani MS*.

136. Bambang Kaslan "Kisah sedjarah":5.

137. The name probably was intended to cause some confusion over the exact state of the group as far as the government was concerned, and also made the group easy to mistake for the Surabaya Shu Youth Committee, circumstances that were thought to protect Abdulgani and his efforts.

138. *Abdulgani MS*. There are claims that a delegate from Surabaya did in

179

fact attend. (B. Anderson [1972]:51 and sources cited there.) Abdulgani says these are in error. In a 1971 interview, Karjono claimed that he, Sumadji, and another youth, the son of the editor of *Soeara Asia*, went to Villa Isola. That is not verified in any published material.

139. SA 4-8-45.

140. There appears to have been no clear delineation of Angkatan Muda Committee leadership, and different written and oral accounts list different individuals in a variety of orders of importance. It seems safe to conclude, however, that the five or six people at the core of the group were Abdulgani, Bambang Kaslan, Krissubanu, Kustur, Kusnadi, and Murdianto. Others mentioned are Gatot Gunawan and, more marginally, Abdul Aziz and Sumarsono. This list has been drawn up on the basis of statements in the *Abdulgani MS*; Bambang Kaslan "Kisah sedjareh":5; and interviews in 1972 and 1973 with Bambang Kaslan and Kustur.

141. Information on Bambang Kaslan is taken from the *Abdulgani MS*; and from interviews in 1972 and 1973 with Bambang Kaslan and Kustur.

142. Information on Krissubanu is taken from the material cited in the previous note and from materials cited in B. Anderson (1972):425.

143. Information on Kusnadi is taken from a 1972 interview with Bambang Kaslan.

144. Information on Kustur is drawn from a 1973 interview with him, and from the *Abdulgani MS*.

145. Information on Murdianto is taken from the *Abdulgani MS*. Darmawan was the younger brother of the well-known pergerakan figure Dr. Tjipto Mangunkusumo. Active in political affairs during the late 1920s, Darmawan preferred to take a mentor's role behind the scenes in later years. He chose as proteges Abdulgani and a few others, who referred to him as "Oom D" or "Uncle D."

146. Information on Gatot Gunawan is taken from the *Abdulgani MS*.

147 The account in this and the following paragraph is based, except where cited otherwise, on material in the *Abdulgani MS*, a 1970 interview with Abdulgani, and a 1973 interview with Kustur.

148. Interview in 1973 with Kustur.

149. SA 7-2-45, which provides the basis for the following paragraph.

150. A short account of this event is given in Kahin:122, which notes inaccurately that the meeting took place in June. Kahin says that 4,000 persons were in the audience, but there are no published or other verifications of that number, which in any case seems far too large for the building used.

151. Interview in 1972 with Abdulgani.

152. This activity apparently was suggested by Rear Admiral Maeda Tadashi, whose motives have been the subject of much speculation, for example in Kahin:115–19, and B. Anderson (1972):44–46.

153. Bambang Kaslan "Kisah sedjarah":7.

154. Material in this and the following two paragraphs is taken from 1972 and 1973 interviews with Sutomo. A more detailed biographical treatment of Sutomo and his close associates is found in Chapter Five.

155. Sutomo had no idea who appointed him to this position. He later recalled that he was told on one occasion that Sukarno was responsible, and on another that Mohammad Hatta and the Muslim leader Wachid Hasjim had singled him out.

156. Sutomo was vague when tracing his thought during the Japanese period, but the rendition here is based on interviews with him in 1972 and 1973 and on Sutomo (1946):8-11 and the *Sutomo MS*:4-5.

157. Material in this and the following paragraph is based on a 1971 interview with Sifun, who was involved in such a group, and on kampung interview in 1971-72.

158. The most complete expression of such a view is B. Anderson (1972):1-34.

■ Chapter Five

Independence and Changing Leadership

■ First reactions to independence

News of the proclamation of Indonesian independence was not long in reaching Surabaya. The famous noon broadcast did not reach many people, but by the following evening the majority of the city's new priyayi intellectuals knew of the August 17th ceremony in Jakarta and many others had heard rumors of such an event.[1] The immediate response, even among the best-informed, was one degree or another of doubt. Not only was the truth of the news frequently uncertain, but the questions of who had sponsored this independence and what it really meant were difficult to answer.[2] As the message spread from the city to the countryside, it was greeted with hesitancy as well as a certain warmth.[3]

Leading new priyayi figures appear to have dispelled many of their original doubts after a day or two of efforts to confirm the proclamation story, but they remained cautious in their views of the immediate future. Sudirman, for example, expressed his pleasure over the announcement when it appeared in the Surabaya press on 20 August, but he pointed out that the difficult course ahead would require discipline and sacrifice from all.[4] Other leaders had messages of similar content, stressing the necessity of taking responsibilities seriously and of remaining calm. Intellectuals also implied that they viewed themselves as heirs to positions of authority, and in that capacity hoped for a smooth transition to a fully Indonesian state, one without colonial rule. Less obvious were the reactions of Surabaya's chief

182

pemuda figures, who remained tied to the opinions of the established new priyayi. When pemuda did express views, they were both less certain and less comprehensive than the ones on which they were clearly modeled. Even Ruslan Abdulgani, of all the pemuda leaders perhaps the most likely to have worked out beforehand his own opinions on the matter, merely echoed in print the thoughts of Ir. Darmawan Mangunkusumo, from whom he had sought counsel.[5] Other younger leaders looked to friends in Jakarta or questioned prominent Surabaya acquaintances before hazarding a judgment on the state of affairs.[6] At this stage no pemuda group in Surabaya appears to have devised contingency plans or burst into activity.

Part of the reason for intellectuals' self-possessed response to the proclamation was that they had planned, however vaguely, for such a moment over the years of pergerakan involvement. Intellectuals' faith that independence would indeed come, the habits of restraint and pragmatic calculation that they acquired during the prewar period, and the more secure position they gained during the occupation, produced in them a balanced concern, rather than any thoroughgoing confusion, over what lay ahead. Pemuda leaders, often less directed by prewar experience and less certain of themselves at the end of the occupation, found it more difficult to assemble a coherent view. They were, perhaps, more concerned than others that the announcement of independence stood for a time by itself, unaccompanied by any notion as to the fate of the Japanese and the New Order. *Soeara Asia* did not print information on Japan's surrender until 22 August, and then the news was more surprising and difficult to believe than that of the earlier proclamation.[7] Under these circumstances Surabaya's pemuda, like much of the general populace, simply suspended their credulity and awaited events to reveal the true state of affairs.

For city residents in general, neither the proclamation nor the surrender seemed genuine until the wartime curfew and blackout regulations were lifted on 23 August; some time passed before Surabayans reaccustomed themselves to the night markets and the other evening activities which had been so much a part of prewar city life.[8] The city lights seemed to burn especially brightly, symbolizing a new era, but the common reflex was still hesitation. This caution was mirrored particularly well in the use of the already circulating term *bersiap* or *siap* (be prepared be at the ready). Although occupation rhetoric lent this word a challenging ring, in late August 1945 to be siap was to be defensively alert but calm.[9] When Sukarno appealed, in his first major post-proclamation speech, for all Indonesians to be "ready and willing to struggle for a free Indonesia," he explicitly stated that this meant remaining quiet and cool-headed, exercising all possible self-control and discipline.[10] For intellectuals this reading was familiar with pergerakan days; for the general urban population it merely seemed to fit the broad and common desire to await clarification of the course of events. Thus it was that the so-called *bersiap-tijd* or bersiap period, a designation frequently given in Dutch works to the chaotic and violent days of the early revolution, had at first a rather different character.

Surabaya remained peaceful well beyond the first week of proclaimed independence. Accounts from a variety of different points of view agree that the city was quiet for an extended period, functioning at least outwardly in a normal fashion and lacking any signs of acute tension or sharp breaks with prevailing conditions.[11] One reason for this state of affairs was that the proclamation and surrender occurred during the first part of the Moslem fasting month (*puasa*), a religious occasion Surabayans took seriously. During puasa the city acquired a subdued tone as people gave precedence in their lives to religious concerns. As the month proceeded, the air filled with subtle expectation—in 1945 highly compatible with growing public anticipation over the prospects of independence—but puasa's dominant characteristics of reflective sobriety and a general slowing down of life cannot help but have affected the events of August and early September. Fasting was scheduled to end on 7 September.[12]

A second powerful factor accounting for the maintenance of a certain equilibrium was the continuing authority of the Japanese. The surrender agreement determined that Japan's forces on Java should be responsible for keeping the peace until Allied forces landed.[13] In Surabaya this task was taken seriously. Even before the surrender announcement, notices appeared saying that although the war was over, the Japanese continued to be in charge and would deal strictly with those who disturbed the peace.[14] Japanese commanders followed other Allied orders by preparing to send the majority of their troops to selected repatriation centers in inland East Java, but they also strengthened the military guard at key installations and in areas of the city likely to be of special interest to Allied troops when they landed. While this show of force was not dramatized, it did indicate a firm intention to hold the status quo. This was effective in keeping administration moving forward as if the New Order were still in place, and is likely to have discouraged both political activities and ordinary lawlessness.[15]

Urban life during these initial weeks gained cohesion in a more positive way from the popular focus on symbols of merdeka, above all the red-and-white flag. The exact timing is difficult to establish, but well before the end of August 1945 red-and-white stickers and small flags had appeared in the city and soon flooded it.[16] Households every-where sewed their own patches in red and white, ordered out to local tailors, or purchased small sample flags from a host of entrepreneurs who already had spotted a strong market for these new goods.[17] Becak drivers were among the first in Surabaya to give wide exposure to the national emblem, displaying thousands of small red-and-white stickers pasted on their vehicles.[18] The appearance of the flag in this way confirmed visually a popular mood and a link with the not-so-distant past.[19] Under the circumstances, the symbol was powerful enough to bring city residents together and create something like a common interest, despite the uncertainty over the future. On this ac-count above all, the interregnum of August and September 1945 was markedly different from that of February and March 1942.

Intellectuals and kampung dwellers alike observed the unfolding realities of the new situation with restraint. By the middle of Sep-tember parts of the city had experienced trouble with petty thievery and the like, but such incidents were limited by vigorous police activ-ity and by kampung guardedness. Urban Indonesians of many types feared disorder; deliberately and intuitively they took whatever steps seemed appropriate to prevent it. After the surrender announcement, many Surabaya kampung held ceremonial meals (selamatan) at which independence was praised, order and solidarity pledged and every word of the proclamation read aloud and reviewed for what it might reveal of the future.[20] Teachers in kampung schools required their pupils to discuss the meaning of independence and to pledge allegiance to Indonesia Merdeka, being especially careful to distin-guish between these exercises and the ones sponsored earlier by the Japanese.[21] In many neighborhoods by popular consent the precinct head no longer was recognized, and the prewar sinoman head was reinstated in a position of leadership.[22] Kampung residents also sought general guidance from better-educated, middle class neigh-bors as to the implications of merdeka, took votes in sinoman fashion as to whether or not independence should be recognized, and ap-peared ready to organize their own affairs. Excitement was unques-tionably in the air, but so also was a keen sense that order was likely to be in everyone's best interests.

The majority of new priyayi did not share kampung dwellers' sense of wonderment about independence, and they worried considerably about the lack of sophistication which they believed this wonderment revealed. The kampung conversation that defined merdeka as "a time when taxes did not have to be paid,"[23] must have provoked concern, and the issue of keeping the public peace in confusing times is likely to have seemed urgent, especially with the 1942 rampok phenomenon still fresh in memory. Holding onto independence rather than simply declaring it was now the goal. *Soeara Asia,* operating with only intermittent and much less insistent Japanese supervision, editorialized nervously against what it saw as a tendency for urban residents to spread rumors and "act as they wished."[24] While in many other respects intellectuals wanted to wait and see how conditions developed, nearly all expressed themselves freely on the issue of public peace. They believed that in it lay the key to remaining free of colonial rule. The notion that roughly parallel (if not especially sophisticated) sentiments might have existed among kampung folk seems not to have occurred to intellectuals, and in view of their separation from kampung life since the mid-1930s the omission is hardly surprising.

New priyayi also were concerned that efforts at establishing a new government be unified. Intellectuals in Surabaya struggled to keep abreast of rapidly moving events, both by listening to radio news broadcasts and by keeping in close contact, often by telephone and telegraph, with friends positioned to know the latest developments in Jakarta and in other centers.[25] It was hoped that local actions could, as a result, reflect those initiated elsewhere. This approach was aided by the continued functioning of residency and municipal governments, and by the tendency of most of the other segments of urban society to look to Jakarta for signals. The capital was so broadly recognized during this early period as the energized core of independent Indonesia that a surprising number of Surbaya's leaders felt compelled to visit Jakarta as quickly as possible and to speak directly with authorities there. Some individuals were soon as well informed about what was taking place in the capital as in their own city and environs, and perhaps for this reason they echoed Jakarta's calls for calm and restraint.[26]

■ The emerging structure of new priyayi authority

For some time the bureaucratic and other government functions in Surabaya remained little changed. The problem facing intellectuals, particularly those with pergerakan backgrounds and positions with or related to the occupation government, was how to drain authority from the Japanese regime without appearing to do so and without creating or permitting disorder in the process. Efforts toward this end proceeded on the basis of trial and error, but long before Jakarta announced on 25 September that civil servants could accept orders only from it,[25] the groundwork had been laid in Surabaya for building a new and thoroughly Indonesian structure of authority.

The principal vehicle through which power was to be consolidated in new priyayi hands was the National Committee (*Komite Nasional Indonesia*, KNI). Since no comprehensive or detailed study of the KNI exists, it is difficult to say how or whether the KNI in Surabaya fit into a broader pattern.[28] What is clear, however, is the short-term significance of this body and its intimate involvement in setting the stage for the early struggle for independence. The KNI reflected, in more concrete ways than had yet been possible, pergerakan instincts to build a state within a state. While the KNI represented neither political nor bureaucratic authority in any strict sense, the intention was that the body would link both the political and the administrative currents of urban Indonesian leadership, and attract increasing power and political support.[29] The KNI, therefore, was not only an emergency arrangement, but one designed to effect as smooth a transition as possible from colonial to indigenous rule. The purpose and form were understood widely among the new priyayi, and owed at least as much to their thinking before the occupation as to their activities during it. Indeed, there is some evidence that prototypical bodies, often using the identical name of Komite Nasional, had been drawn together in a number of Java's towns during February and March 1942 to deal with the crisis brought on by the lifting of Dutch rule.[30]

As in other urban centers, a Surabaya KNI was formed in response to the 23 August 1945 announcement that a Central KNI (*KNI Pusat*, KNIP) had met in Jakarta and that similar groups should be established at the regional and local levels.[31] There were, however, no instructions as to how these local KNIs were to be pulled together, and the process was improvised within the framework of an unspoken understanding of goals.[32] On 23 or 24 August, a telegram was received from the KNIP, addressed to the "regional government" in Surabaya and requesting it to oversee the creation of a KNI for that area. At the time the regional government, exclusive of Japanese personnel, consisted largely of a bureaucracy and Sudirman, who as the assistant Resident was the logical individual to receive the official message. There are sharply conflicting views as to Sudirman's reaction to the responsibility thrust upon him,[33] but in any case a series of meetings attended by leading new priyayi from 25 to 27 August 1945 grappled

187

with the questions of who should become a member of the KNI and what that institution's sphere of activity might be. Early in these sessions Doel Arnowo came to play a leading role, more likely than not because he was mentioned by Sukarno (who knew Arnowo as a prewar PNI loyalist) and because he was quite acceptable to Sudirman,[34] who apparently saw his own role as being "above politics." Satisfied that Jakarta's request was being carried out, Sudirman left Surabaya for the capital on 26 August in order to acquire a better understanding of the direction in which events were moving.[35] Arnowo presided over long and arduous debates held in an atmosphere of increasing concern that the Allies would land in a week or two.[36]

Doel Arnowo's priority was quite simply to create a mechanism of government capable of reflecting accurately decisions made in the capital, and at the same time capable of commanding popular respect. He began by gathering acquaintances from a variety of prewar pergerakan groups,[37] and discussing with them the goal of the KNI and the composition of its eventual membership. At each session attendance increased, until 60 or 70 persons were involved. To accommodate them, meetings were moved from the governor's office— where they must have had at least the tacit approval of the Japanese, who did not realize their significance—to a more spacious building with the added advantage of being further removed from kempeitai headquarters. No clear record survives of how nominations were made or decisions taken during these gatherings. Later comments of some individuals who were present indicate strongly that the procedure combined election with appointment by acclamation. The idea was accepted generally that the KNI, as it was then being constituted, was of a temporary and emergency character. Few if any serious quarrels arose over appointments, and conflict over issues such as political ideology or collaboration with the Japanese was put aside in favor of a unified effort to safeguard independence.[38]

The official founding of the Surabaya Regional KNI (*KNI Daerah*, KNID) took place on 28 August 1945; a slate of 32 members had been announced the evening before.[39] This list adroitly brought together diverse elements of the city's new priyayi leadership, and graphically showed that the chief concern in the KNI planning sessions had been to collect as many strands of authority as possible into the hands of intellectuals, weaving from them the essential fabric of local government. Little thought was given to the political positions members might espouse under the new circumstances, perhaps in part because intellectuals of all stripes tended to feel ideologically uncertain at this time. Planners devoted their attention to satisfying a need for a well-rounded council of advisors capable of providing informed and practical opinions on every aspect of urban life. For this reason, care was taken not only to represent the obvious groups, such as municipal employees, former pergerakan leaders, and Moslem figures, but to insure that medical and legal expertise, for example, were close at hand.[40].

The KNID membership did not constitute a roll of Surabaya's most prominent or powerful new priyayi figures. There are several explanations for this, first among them being that some noted individuals had already accepted positions elsewhere. A number of persons also may have wished to avoid the burden and limelight of membership, particularly since the future seemed so very uncertain. But the most pressing factor was probably the determination of leaders like Doel Arnowo to fit together a council that was both practical and broadly representative. If reaching this goal required leaving out well-known intellectuals, so be it; the public peace and solid establishment of government were at stake.

Still, there was no mistaking the KNID for anything but the product of new priyayi thinking and planning. No persons with pangreh praja functions were included, and all of the Moslem figures concerned fit easily within the bounds of pergerakan-associated intellectual groups.[41] Pemuda were not neglected, and two members of the Angkatan Muda Committee were on the KNID list. While it is true that the average age of KNID members was between 40 and 45 years, with the majority of individuals having been active in the pergerakan during the 1930s, there was no particular hostility to younger and less experienced individuals. Many appointees shared the opinion that pemuda generally lacked a sufficiently balanced, pragmatic view of the world to calculate the benefits and risks involved in the difficult circumstances of the day, but few identified themselves as part of an "older generation" or some other group sharply delineated from pemuda. Many, indeed, were moved deeply by the proclamation and propelled by a sense of now being involved in "radical" events. The buoyant spirit that filled such people had little to do with physical age, and more often than not it made generational boundaries less important than they frequently had been during the prewar pergerakan.

The new priyayi obviously were feeling their way and operating on the basis of pragmatism and a vague like-mindednesss in forming the KNID in Surabaya,[42] but the new body gave every sign of being adequate to the job at hand. During the KNID's first days, steps were taken to support the flying of the Indonesian national flag and to further regularize government. It also was proposed at an early date that Sudirman be named the chief government official for the Surabaya region. As there was no serious opposition to this arrangement,[43] Jakarta was informed of the local preference. On 3 September, before confirmation could be received from the capital, Sudirman became the principal authority of the "Residency of Surabaya, part of the territory of the Republic of Indonesia."[44] While he was still in Jakarta, Sudirman's name appeared under a crisply worded *Soeara Asia* announcement clarifying the changed state of affairs and laying down seven basic requirements of the public, most of which emphasized the need for calm and observance of the law.[45] When Jakarta confirmed Sudirman's appointment several days later, the KNID moved back to the governor's office, which now flew the red-and-white flag from its highest tower.[46] Doel Arnowo, presiding over meetings that heard reports of conditions elsewhere on Java and announced plans for public rallies as well as administrative conferences,[47] was led to wire Sukarno early in September that since all was peaceful in Surabaya there was no need for the Allies to land there.

The establishment of the KNID evoked a strong positive response from ordinary Surabayans, and within days miniature KNIs were being founded at the kampung level throughout the city.[48] After a week or so KNIs bloomed everywhere, even in the becak cooperative, which claimed to represent over 5,000 people. While no doubt aided by the media and, to a lesser extent, new priyayi and pemuda proselytizers, the phenomenon was for the most part spontaneous. Many kampung rapidly produced their own version of the republican government by appointing KNI heads and committees at their level to handle activities such as information dissemination and defense. In a few exceptional cases, elaborate ceremonies honored these changes and special gatherings of kampung residents considered the appropriate attitudes and actions for sinoman members.[49].

All available accounts of the spread of KNIs in Surabaya's kampung indicate that the movement possessed two quite different but complementary characteristics. One was a strong and unabashed anticolonialism. The arek Surabaya saw the installation of KNIs as a concrete expression of their desire to resist interference from outsiders. The notion that part of KNI activities included a struggle against Dutch and Japanese authority seems never to have been far from their minds.[50] In the eyes of some kampung residents the KNIs so clearly expressed this aspect of independence that they came to underlie a sudden psychology of expectation and courage. The other characteristic, however, was an inclination to partake of the unfolding new order and to recreate elements of it at the kampung level. Thus neighborhood KNIs spent time regularizing kampung guards and improving food distribution systems, arranging these and other tasks along lines suggested by what was known about the KNID and the various branches of government.[51] On the whole these activities, coupled with a new sense of confidence in the kampung, kept life in the city's neighborhoods on an even keel.

Not long after the appearance of the kampung KNIs, an intermediate-level organization known as the Municipal KNI (*KNI Kota,* KNIK) was formed in Surabaya. The central government originally had encouraged KNIs at all administrative levels, but in several respects this municipal group was unusual. At its initital meeting on 11 September 1945, the KNIK announced its chief interest as promoting the establishment of KNIs everywhere in the city,[52] an activity already well under way. No other goals were mentioned, and if additional topics were addressed, nothing was said about them publicly. The group also apparently had no involvement with coordinating or taking over administrative functions in the city. The KNIK seems instead to have owed its existence to what some intellectuals perceived as a neglect of specifically municipal affairs, and to competitive feelings regarding the KNID. The self-appointed leader of the KNIK, Roeslan Wongsokusumo, has recollected a sense of being separate from and beyond the authority of Doel Arnowo and the KNID.[53] At the time he thought this a desirable state of affairs since "[we] had our own ideas [of how to do things]" and since the new formation seemed to open up the possibility of political action at the municipal level. The KNIK, however, captured few imaginations and never emerged as an important force in the city. Working from the beginning in the shadow of the KNID, it eventually faded from view altogther.

Although their hold on events and personalities was often tenuous, the new priyayi persisted in their movement toward coordinated, comprehensive action. Their efforts included encouraging the growth of a unified Indonesian military body in the Surabaya region. The Peta had been disarmed and disbanded by the Japanese as late as 20 August and was not easily resurrected. In a process fostered by Sudirman, the KNID, and a number of pemuda leaders, a People's Security Organization (*Badan Keamanan Rakyat,* BKR) began to take shape out of remnants of the Peta, seinendan, and Barisan Pelopor.[54] Debate and compromise in which Sudirman and the KNID were deeply involved, brought Moestopo, Sungkono, and Jonosewojo recognition as Surabaya's principal military figures.[55] There were personal and organizational rivalries among these three, and a fully uni-

191

fied military apparatus into which they might fit was still lacking. But it can be said the BKR and civilian leaders in Surabaya were closely acquainted and in some ways linked at this stage, and their shared new priyayi background seems to have provided the basis for a considerable degree of cooperation in governmental matters.[56]

Sudirman and his colleagues concentrated much effort on wooing municipal employees and, with more difficulty, the pangreh praja. Municipal office staff heard Sudirman emphasize in early September that although they were still technically working for the Japanese and obliged to show this outwardly, in their hearts they should realize that they were working for the Indonesian Republic, which soon would inherit full authority.[57] During the following week Radjamin Nasution, acting as mayor of the city, held ceremonies and made official announcements affirming the loyalty of his employees to the Republic.[58] As for the pangreh praja of the Residency, they were visited from 6 to 12 September by Sudirman, who made the unusual gesture of traveling to their offices and asking for their support. At the end of this trip Sudirman wired Sukarno that the pangreh praja in the Surabaya region had all agreed to back an independent Indonesia. *Soeara Asia* editorials already had begun to prepare the public for this rather new, because implicitly anticolonial, view of the pangreh praja.[59]

The deliberate reach of Sudirman and other new priyayi leaders also extended to existing pemuda organizations, which still hesitated to announce any actions of their own and remained dependent for the most part on the advice of more experienced intellectuals. In an effort to sort out the confusion brought on by the proclamation of independence, informal but frequent meetings were called in pemuda circles after 20 August 1945.[60] Most accounts of pemuda involvement in the activities of this period—in Surabaya as well as the rest of Java— supply few details and are content to portray a blur of activity and to imply that much of this was directed against, or at least differently from, the efforts of the more established leadership. In Surabaya, however, a handful of detailed sources indicate that intellectual figures and the more prominent pemuda were in constant communication, working together in various ways. Thus Ruslan Abdulgani came to be valued not only as an intellectual force but as a point of contact with new priyayi authorities such as Sudirman and those in his circle, who controlled public facilities like meeting-halls and playing fields, and who could provide varied kinds of support for pemuda efforts to build public enthusiasm for independence.[61] When the Djohan Sjahroezah group held its first meeting on 21 August, its leaders first made a point of securing both the blessing of and aid from Sudirman, Bambang Suparto, and Doel Arnowo.[62]

These and other established new priyayi put a hand in pemuda affairs for a variety of reasons. Not least among them was a concern over youth and those who, while not particularly young, occupied a status close to that of the new priyayi. Intellectuals also probably hoped to encourage the potentially valuable activism that seemed likely to emerge from pemuda groups. Whatever the case, Surabaya's first large-scale pemuda convocation after the proclamation of independence took place on 26 August 1945 as the result of hurried behind-the-scenes work by Bambang Suparto, Doel Arnowo, and Bambang Kaslan. Invited guests were mostly persons associated with the old Putera and Hokokai, members of the Barisan Pelopor, as many former enlistees in the Japanese army and Peta as could be called together, and an assortment of delegates from government offices and private firms. By no means could all be classified, either by age or by pergerakan experience, as pemuda. Personal relationships may have been the single most important determinant in deciding who attended.[63] This meeting was orderly, but undeniably different from the assembly held concurrently not far away to discuss the founding of the KNID. Talk ran to serious and detailed considerations of how power might be seized from the Japanese. Physical attacks on military headquarters in the city were at least mentioned as a possibility. New priyayi leaders apparently did not find these suggestions unthinkable, for they did not react negatively and discussion proceeded at great length. Toward the end, however, Bambang Suparto noted that no firm decisions could be taken without Sudirman. Doel Arnowo, who arrived late because of his duties at the KNID meeting, spoke briefly and agreed with Suparto's conclusion. There being no objections, the conference drew to a close. Despite their differing focus, therefore, the two gatherings appeared to move together toward a new order of independence.

■ The reemergence of Europeans

By early September the essentially quiet atmosphere in Surabaya was disturbed by the return of Dutch and Eurasians to the city from internment camps elsewhere on Java. Although a small portion of the city's European population had managed to remain free throughout the occupation, the majority had been imprisoned and relocated.

When they began to return to Surabaya during the last week of August 1945, the ex-internees' rapidly growing numbers and plainly difficult adjustment to a changed urban environment brought on a mood of, at best, strained accommodation.

As one former colonial official put it, the Dutch in 1945 were "looking into a completely dark room."[64] Those returning to Surabaya had a limited notion of what had occurred during their absence, and their first impressions were linked intuitively to the past. Some found the city "very much Easternized,"[65] while others were reminded distinctly of the calm but unstable situation they had known in the year before the Japanese attacked.[66] Most Dutch who stepped off the train in Surabaya after 26 August discovered that the Indonesians they encountered were much less cordial than expectd, or than had been the case in the countryside and the small towns where internment camps had been located.[67] Few Europeans went as far as one woman, who saw the new Indonesian state as a "Parindra-created Javanese republic with a lot to answer for,"[68] but there was a widespread tendency to dismiss merdeka and all that went with it as theatrics no more worthy of being taken seriously than the prewar pergerakan.[69] Dutch diaries and government intelligence reports compiled during this period suggest a close relationship between these attitudes and the tendency for returnees to have nothing to do with Indonesian leaders or municipal authorities, and to ignore or defy their regulations and announcements altogether.[70] Their oversimplified and generally hostile attitude proved to be the foundation of increasing frustration and, eventually, conflict.

The principal instinct among returning Dutch, the earliest of whom were mostly women and children, was not merely survival but the reestablishment of the life and community they had known previously. They mobilized people and resources in a fashion highly reminiscent of that used during the early occupation. Although the first arrivals found no one to greet them, for example, within a few days a Red Cross loosely organized under the Swiss counsel was providing all ex-internees with food, shelter, and a variety of basic services.[71] All of this was accomplished without reference to Indonesians. Even the most prominent leaders in institutions such as the KNID were ignored. Returning Dutch also paid scant attention to municipal regulations, even when these were known. Where face-to-face meetings with Indonesians in authority—police, railroad personnel, hospital staff, housing officials—could not be avoided, disagreement and tension were the result.[72]

The first signs of serious trouble were not long in coming. The birthday of the Dutch Queen Wilhelmina fell on 31 August, one of the days Surabayan authorities had designated, in response to the example of Jakarta, as "Indonesia Days" on which the Indonesian flag was to be flown everywhere.[73] Perhaps as early as 25 August, a small group of Eurasians and Dutch is said to have announced at the office of the municipal police its intention of recognizing the royal birthday by flying Dutch colors. When they were told several days later that this could not be permitted because of directives from Jakarta and the KNID, the Dutch became very angry.[74] At least partly as a result of the furor raised by this issue, incidents began to crop up in which young Eurasians ridiculed the Indonesian flag in public. They also tore down pro-independence posters, wrote anti-Indonesian slogans on walls, attempted to set up military-style guards outside public and private buildings, and displayed a bitter militancy in many other ways.[75] For most Indonesians who had even passing contact with these Eurasian youths, the immediate impression was of arrogance and racial hatred, a dismissal of Indonesians as people. Clashes were for some time prevented from developing into larger disputes, but increasing numbers of Dutch returning to the city made it less likely that tensions could be kept under control.

At the end of August, Dutch and Eurasians formed their own self-support group. This step, predictable and not particularly noteworthy in its own right, soon added a new and dangerous dimension to the already tense situation. The Social Contact Committee (*Komite Kontak Sosial*, KKS) was established by several early arrivals in Surabaya, among them the lawyer and prewar Eurasian political figure, V. W. Ch. Ploegman.[76] The KKS quickly exhibited a strident, competitive approach to helping former internees, so much so that it came into conflict even with the Red Cross.[77] The "contact" of the organization's name, furthermore, referred to relations between the Dutch community and the Japanese, not Indonesians. The clear intent of KKS leaders was to encourage Japanese protection and support, in which they were successful. Only a few days after its founding, the KKS received a small cash donation from kempeitai headquarters in Surabaya, and in the next two weeks contributions from Japanese military units and business firms poured in, culminating in a gift from the Japanese Resident amounting to f. 50,000.[78] Indonesians had little trouble perceiving the ominous nature of the Dutch-Japanese link thus being forged. It was a blatant reminder of the often surprisingly cordial dealings between Dutch and Japanese at the beginning of the occupation. It also suggested that the two forces might together threaten Indonesian independence and its gradually assembling order.

The specter of a Dutch colonial world revitalized through Dutch-Japanese collusion alarmed widening circles of Indonesians in Surabaya, and it was enhanced by the fear that Dutch government might be restored under Allied auspices. Indonesians close to sources of short-wave radio news were aware at a relatively early date of the existence of the Netherlands East Indies Civil Administration (NICA), established in Australia in late 1944 by the colonial government in exile.[79] By mid-September the same people were also probably informed of Australian landings on Timor and Kalimantan, with NICA detachments.[80] An obvious conclusion to be drawn was that a reoccupation pattern was being established and that Surabaya could expect similar treatment under the British in the near future.

Those who interpreted the NICA as a vehicle by which the Dutch colonial regime intended to regain its former position were not mistaken, and a brief characterization of the organization is helpful in understanding attitudes and events in the early days of independence in Surabaya.[81] The purpose of the NICA was to do as much as possible to replant colonial structure at a time when the Netherlands was weak militarily. The relationship between NICA units and the Allied command was at best difficult to understand, therefore, and at worst deliberately obscure. British commanders soon learned that efforts to land NICA personnel with Allied troops and advance Recovery of Allied Prisoners of War and Internees (RAPWI) teams left them open to accusations of providing cover for Dutch colonialism. This produced Allied discord as well as confusion. But it was also true that the precise nature of the NICA was unclear even in Dutch circles. The question of whether the organization was military or not confounded the highest leadership as well as ordinary staff. In this respect the NICA recalled some of the more serious difficulties of prewar Dutch defense groups, carrying with it not so much the seed of colonial rule as that of confusion and instability. Finally, and perhaps of greatest immediate importance, the NICA depended heavily on former internees, most of them returning to their prewar homes and nearly all of them selected on the basis of their prewar functions as civil servants, especially police.[82]

None of this escaped the notice of watching Indonesians. Surabaya's intellectuals and pemuda leaders grasped the threat early, and the arek Surabaya were by no means left in the dark. What their understanding lacked in sophistication was made up in intensity. Europeans had never disappeared entirely from city life, but from the kampung perspective they were long absent. A common belief was that Dutch people had been taken to some unknown location far beyond Java, and when ex-internees began to arrive back in the city kampung dwellers often assumed they had arrived by ship, making the sensation of watching a recolonization process especially strong.[83] Not did arek Surabaya fail to notice that, although returning Dutch and Eurasians were worse off than before the war, they still possessed trunks and suitcases filled with goods—particularly clothing—which was in short supply locally.[84] Some arek Surabaya sought out Europeans they had formerly served,[85] but more commonly Dutch returnees were greeted with astonishment and fear. Even at the kampung level, the impression had begun to spread that the colonial urban society of the 1930s might somehow be reimposed.

■ Urban tensions and the flag incident

The city as a whole was not shaken outwardly during the first half of September, but the impact of tensions created by returning Dutch residents was felt everywhere. New priyayi leaders were aware of this undertow, but for a variety of reasons did not react quickly to it. They were deeply involved in establishing a government, in which they already had large personal stakes and for which they were rapidly assembling the necessary institutional authority. They were also confident of their ability to deal with a Dutch presence, both because they were accustomed to the ways of a Western-oriented urban world and because they found it extremely difficult to believe that, after the Japanese occupation, Dutch supremacy could ever be reinstated. To many it seemed that the time at last had come for the "inevitable" passing of colonial rule.[86]

Pemuda leaders watched developments from a somewhat different vantage point. They were less comfortable with the Dutch presence, as they had less experience with it. They also possessed a far smaller stake in the new republic as a governmental or administrative order. In addition, pemuda were sometimes better acquainted with kampung opinion than were the majority of new priyayi leaders, and they often had first-hand knowledge of the effects Dutch and Eurasian returnees were having in many areas of the city. Those who were informed through radio and the wire services about the movements of

Allied forces, therefore, tended to be especially sensitive to this news and to feel that the intellectuals now in responsible positions were blind or indifferent to the danger.

On the strength of such attitudes, pemuda restlessness began to emerge out of hesitancy and indecision. On 3 September, the same day on which Surabaya was declared a part of the republic, the city's better-educated youth gathered once more at the high school building.[87] This meeting had been called by Ruslan Abdulgani upon his return from several days in Jakarta, largely because he was shocked to discover that many Surabaya youth were still uncertain about the proclamation and its meaning. Abdulgani began by giving a long and, to some, condescending address outlining the course of events since 17 August and describing the formation of the independent Indonesian government. He announced that his Angkatan Muda Committee had been making organizational plans and had begun to lead the rakyat by talking to kampung leaders. Before he was finished, however, Abdulgani was interrupted by several members of the Sjahroezah group, who jumped on tables and chairs and shouted that being called together for such a purpose was insulting. What the pemuda of Surabaya really needed to do, they said, was to prepare to oppose the Japanese and the Dutch, who were threats to independence; to that end pemuda ought to unite and mobilize as much assistance as possible. This outburst received an excited response from older and generally well-schooled pemuda employed in government and private offices. It was precisely this group that had been cultivated by Sjahroezah and his colleagues, and what they saw as the growing interest of other youth made the time ripe for more organized activity.

Three days later an Action Committee (Komite van Actie) was formed under the leadership of two members of the Sjahroezah circle, Sumarsono and Kusnadi. The Dutchified name of this committee, which clearly reflects the educational status of its founders, is curious in light of its goal; it was probably meant to imitate the name given to a similar group established on 1 September in Jakarta by Angkatan Muda leaders.[88] Meeting in a Kampung Plampitan home, the Komite laid plans for a massive rally to be held on 11 September, after the end of puasa, on Tambaksari athletic field.[89] The purpose of this assembly was to bring together as many potentially influential groups in the city as possible, and to foster among them not only a sense of unity but a desire to oppose both Dutch and Japanese forces. The effort was not limited to pemuda, as Komite members appear to have seen their role predominantly in terms of providing liaison and initiative. They deliberately included new priyayi leaders of many types in their plans, and leaned heavily on key figures such as Sudirman and Doel Arnowo in carrying them out. Both the KNID and the fledgling Residency government were carefully informed of the group's activities. The new priyayi responded guardedly, agreeing to take part in the rally and quietly giving other types of support.

Despite Japanese efforts to prevent it,[90] the Tambaksari rally was held and sparked a number of smaller gatherings throughout the city during the following week. There is no indication that these public occasions radically changed the prevailing urban calm, but they did test the Japanese (who finally declined to oppose the rallies with force) and accomplished much that new priyayi could not in the way of tapping public support for independence and the republic. Individuals like Sudirman, who had feared that mass displays of activity might provoke the Japanese into precipitous action and thereby jeopardize progress toward real independence, were pleased on the whole with the effort, which had been aided by one of Sudirman's children.[91] The exercise did not bring appreciably greater unity to the pemuda however. The initial inclination of Komite leaders to collect a number of separately identified groups of young office workers under the rubric of the Angkatan Muda Committee was unsuccessful. Shortly before the 11 September meeting it was decided further that attendance at Tambaksari would be in a private capacity only, rather than representative. Surabaya's pemuda still were tied to small, personal circles, intellectual mentors, or shared places of work. The struggle for a larger structure or pattern of leadership would not be easy and had only just begun.

By mid-September pressure in Surabaya had been building for several weeks against the popular Indonesian desire to avoid confusion and violence. The resulting tension was undeniable, but it had neither the weight nor edge to break the new priyayi-controlled flow toward a fully ordered Indonesian state. On 16 September, however, a handful of parachutists landed on the outskirts of the city and in a stroke seemed to confirm the worst fears voiced in previous weeks.[92] These first Allied representatives were apparently British officers, part of the RAPWI effort. They established themselves quickly in the centrally located Oranje Hotel, still styled the Yamato, where they received the protection of a Japanese military guard and urgent visits by anxious Dutch and Eurasians. Although members of the Allied team wisely attempted to keep a low profile, their presence could not be missed by either the Dutch or Indonesians.[93] The results were dramatic indeed.

On the morning of 19 September 1945, several small groups of former internees clustered near the Oranje Hotel and the Red Cross headquarters across the street.[94] Many of them appear to have been young Dutch and Eurasians spoiling for a fight. They were armed crudely with tire irons, bicycle pumps, and similar weapons.[95] There is no clear explanation for their presence, but in general they seem to have been encouraged by circumstances to strike a blow for Holland. They knew that Indonesian youngsters returning home from school at mid-day could easily be goaded into combat on what then appeared to be favorable ground.[96] School-boy rivalries had been intensive in the prewar period, and now they were exacerbated because there were no longer schools for Dutch children; the atmosphere also bristled with frustrated Dutch nationalism, the darker side of which found expression in the rumored formation of "Kill All Natives" groups that were to roam Surabaya's streets.[97]

The following events transpired rapidly in a setting so confused at the time and so heavily mythologized afterwards that a thoroughly trustworthy reconstruction is probably impossible. A band of Dutch youth, urged on by the appearance of a Dutch flag outside the Red Cross office,[98] entered the hotel and raised a small red-white-and-blue banner on the building's flagstaff. This gesture called forth a burst of activity on the part of Ploegman and other KKS members, who gathered in front of the hotel, and was followed by a hastily contrived parade of Dutch children carrying little Dutch flags.[99] At the same time, one of the British RAPWI personnel was persuaded by Eurasian leaders to raise a large Dutch flag,[100] and from that moment control was lost. A crowd of Indonesians, most of them students and young teachers, gathered before the hotel. They soon faced a line of Japanese soldiers with unsheathed bayonets, who had been summoned to protect what was then designated as Allied headquarters.[100] This was too much for the crowd, and stones began to fly. Shots were heard from behind the hotel. Suddenly several Indonesian youths, seeing the Dutch and Eurasians retreat inside the hotel, rushed the building to scuffle with them and attempt to reach the Dutch flag. During the fracas Ploegman was clubbed with a pipe; he died several days later at the municipal hospital.[102] A number of youths succeeded in scaling the outside of the hotel, reaching the flagpole, and ripping the horizontal blue stripe from the Dutch flag to create an improvised Indonesian one of red and white.[103] The republic's national banner then waved proudly over the Oranje Hotel and its European guests with a symbolic force that was lost on few Surabayans.

The flag incident of 19 September holds an honored place in Surabaya's revolutionary lore, and indeed that of the nation. Although later retelling of the story has led to considerable embellishment,[104] the core importance of the event is genuine. A few interpretive comments are warranted, however. Most students of the affair, including Surabayans with an opportunity to reminisce in print or over a cup of coffee, treat 19 September as the landmark date on which independence, with all of its energies and hazards, became a reality in the city; it was a time when "the people began to catch the scent of blood"[105] and, by implication, the moment at which the turmoil of the revolution commenced. Yet the bulk of first-hand evidence suggests strongly that this is not the case, and that while the incident astonished Dutch, Indonesian, and Japanese alike, it did not in fact signal the immediate outbreak of general violence. Surabaya continued to be described, even by persons not inclined to look benignly on the situation, as calm and peaceful.[106] Tensions were increased, and the legal order was strained, but continued conflict was avoided. Rather than initiating disintegration, the shock of the flag incident initially served to harden existing patterns of organization and test them to the limit.

The Japanese observed the events of 19 September with grave concern. Previously more melancholy than genuinely anxious, they then were gripped with the realization that their position between the Allies and Indonesians was dangerous and could worsen quickly. Neither side was likely to be satisfied with compromise positions, and adopting a neutral position between them was already impossible, leaving Japanese throughout the city vulnerable to attack.[107] The flag incident also brought many Japanese, perhaps especially those in the military, to question for the first time whether they had ever really understood Indonesians. They began to look upon local inhabitants with, rather than the usual condescension, distrust and fear.[108] In this frame of mind the Japanese took the final steps in preparation for the Allied landings, evacuating more than 10,000 troops and administrative personnel to locations in the interior of East Java, assigning 500 extra military police guards to the Oranje Hotel, and posting small contingents of soldiers in areas of the city frequented by Europeans and near the entrances of centrally located kampung.[109] Posters were hung everywhere proclaiming that the kempeitai would not tolerate disturbances of the peace in any form.[110] There was no Japanese effort to contact Indonesian leaders and solicit their aid in maintaining public order.

With these activities still under way, several new groups of Allied representatives arrived in Surabaya.[111] On 21 September a RAPWI team headed by the Dutch officer P. G. de Back appeared and established headquarters in the Oranje Hotel, where they began to hold interviews with a stream of Dutch and Eurasians. They ordered the Japanese command to devise a comprehensive scheme for the protection and support of ex-internees, who were still arriving in large numbers, and were impressed when this was done effectively within a day's time. On 23 September another team arrived under D. L. Asjes, the head of the Dutch Office of Displaced Persons, and entered the city with the protection of a Japanese honor guard. Asjes soon was satisfied that conditions were, from his point of view at least, better than anywhere else on Java. Later the same day a third team arrived under P. J. G. Huijer, another Dutch officer, who believed he was acting as the personal representative of both the Dutch and British high commands. He spoke directly to the Japanese Army and Navy commanders and left three days later for Jakarta.

These visits contributed heavily to a ballooning sense of crisis in the city. They did not soothe the European community, but they did intensify the poster and slogan competition raging between Dutch and Indonesian youths, and prompt some former internees to reestablish a barricaded women's area in Darmo as a protection against Indonesian violence.[112] The visits also attracted hostile reactions from Indonesians. The Allied groups were not large, amounting to some 36 persons in all, but the identity of their members became an immediate cause for concern. The groups contained largely Dutch nationals, most with experience in Surabaya before the war. De Back, for example, brought with him a former teacher at the medical school, then a captain in the military, and Huijer's staff included several career military men as well as C. C. J. Maassen, who had been Resident of Surabaya in the 1930s and was designated a political adviser to Huijer and "Governor of East Java." Huijer's interpreter was the same individual who had acted as translator at the Dutch-Japanese meeting in Sidoarjo in March 1942. A crowd of hangers-on from among the ex-internees, including former Resident Pastoors and former assistant Resident Samkalden, quickly attached themselves to the RAPWI teams.[113] The popular image of RAPWI as the NICA in disguise was sharpened by the widespread, and probably accurate, notion that written plans for the reoccupation of Surabaya by military force were being reviewed by the Europeans gathered at the Oranje Hotel.[114]

■ Creating a pemuda order

New priyayi leaders were surprised by the flag incident. Journalists on the scene ran to the KNID headquarters asking for information or opinions, only to find that no one there had an inkling of what was happening.[115] Sudirman, who later showed up to try to calm the crowd which had gathered,[116] knew nothing of the incident until it was nearly over. But these can be little doubt that the implications of 19 September were recognized quickly, well before the additional Allied teams landed. The question of what to do about the Allies and returning Dutch, previously considered of secondary importance, now leaped to the foreground of the KNID's attention. On 21 September Doel Arnowo conducted a meeting in the open hall of the GNI to examine the alternatives.[117] KNID members actively debated the risks of attempting to attack the Oranje Hotel and listened to Moestopo, who already had begun to call ex-Peta recruits to Surabaya from East and Central Java,[118] deliver an angry promise that he and his BKR troops would take the Dutch-Allied headquarters in the morning whether the KNID chose to agree or not. No decision on the matter was taken. Moestopo is said to have overslept and missed his chance for action the next day. Be that as it may, intellectuals appear seriously to have considered military action of the sort advocated by Moestopo, and to have vowed to support any moves eventually made by the BKR.

On the same day in another part of the same building a second meeting took place, this one of pemuda leaders and representatives. The main issue before their assembly was identical to that facing the more established leaders, and it proved equally controversial. As Bambang Kaslan later recalled, youth from government and private offices were jolted out of a "standby mentality" by the flag incident. Ruslan Abdulgani advocated preparation for hostilities and possible disarming of the Japanese, while others talked more heatedly about opposing the Allies and gathering up firearms for that purpose. There was no unity of opinion, however, and this pemuda gathering differed from the one going on nearby in that there was stormy disagreement over questions of organization and leadership. Some in attendance preferred to support Abdulgani and his Angkatan Muda Committee, which after all had been in existence for some time and carried with it a measure of intellectual respectability. Most of the Djohan Sjahroezah circle considered themselves at least loosely associated with that group, and since virtually all pemuda present on this occasion were educated, politically aware individuals, Abdulgani's appeal was strong. At the same time, there were others who were genuinely appalled at the committee's hesitancy, and some who instinctively realized that the situation offered remarkable opportunities to improve their own standing in pemuda ranks. There was much posturing as individuals vied for influence in the meeting. At one point, for example, Krissubanu rose and shouted that his word ought to be heeded because he reflected the views of the masses; he represented, he said, the vegetable sellers and marketplace vendors all over the city. This was so patently ridiculous a claim that the whole assembly burst out laughing and hooted Krissubanu down.

The outcome of this crucial meeting mixed compromise with a certain decisiveness. The issue of what to do about the looming threat posed by the Dutch (along with the Japanese and the Allies) was resolved by rejecting the preparatory approach and encouraging active opposition to the Japanese. It is unclear whether this decision was made on strategic or other grounds, but the obvious point that the Japanese were the only source of large numbers of weapons in the city must have been examined. The issue of leadership and pemuda organization was treated more cautiously and in a manner that reflected the position these youth occupied with respect to new priyayi leaders. Despite the more militant position favored by the gathering, Abdulgani remained the majority choice as leader. But for reasons that are still unclear—some have spoken vaguely of a failure of nerve— Abdulgani and the committee officers decided to step down in favor of others. The assembly heard Abdulgani suggest Sumarsono as a likely successor, as he was a member of the Sjahroezah group acceptable to everyone. This individual was a moderate and, except for his advocacy of immediate action where the Japanese and Dutch were concerned, not very different from Abdulgani in his estimation of the circumstances. Though not as well educated as Abdulgani, Sumarsono's background and wartime experience (see below) placed him squarely within the community of intellectual and politically aware youth. He accepted the draft to leadership. Considering his mandate to be essentially to continue the Angkatan Muda Committee under a more up-to-date name, he chose Krissubanu and Kusnadi as his chief officers in what became known officially as the Youth of the Indonesian Republic (*Pemuda Republik Indonesia*, PRI).[119] With the advent of this group, events seemed to push forward with a new impetus.

The PRI was not established for the purpose of opposing the KNID or competing in any direct fashion for the position of leadership held by the new priyayi in Surabaya. There was in some quarters at this time an unmistakable impatience with KNID cautiousness, but this impatience was not universal and was not limited to pemuda. Many KNID members, after all, had gone home on the evening of 21 September fully expecting to be wakened in the morning and handed a pistol with which to join in the storming of the Oranje Hotel.[120] A statement of PRI goals and philosophy was not published when the group was founded, but later accounts leave the impression that two objectives were especially clear in the minds of its leaders. First, there was a strong desire to organize pemuda energies, particularly since conflicts with Dutch and Eurasians were intensifying and seemed to call for a more coordinated response. The flag incident, moreover, had suggested to experienced youth leaders that there was greater potential for large-scale pemuda activity in the city than they originally had guessed. Organization was all that was required. Second, pemuda leaders desired more strongly than ever to contact the masses. They were influenced in this regard by prewar populism as well as a sense that older intellectuals were preoccupied with the business of government. Their notion lacked a methodology, to say nothing of a definition of the "masses" they wished to target, but it nevertheless possessed a real moral voltage.

These goals were rooted in pergerakan experience, and the PRI neither denied this nor attempted to cut itself free from prewar intellectual and social ties. Once the organization had been formed, special efforts were made to firm up contacts with established figures in the KNID and elsewhere, who now more than ever were considered to be advisors. Perhaps the most influential of these at this stage was Sudirman, but Doel Arnowo and Moestopo carried considerable weight, and many others had important parts to play.[121] Formally, the KNID and the Resident's office appeared neutral and unwilling to become involved, but informally many new priyayi leaders seem to have known about and supported PRI activities. More likely than not they saw the organization as offering young and less established Indonesians the complementary, activist role that the pergerakan had considered natural, and as performing the important task of mobilizing support from the urban populace, for which established new priyayi had little time or enthusiasm to spare.

At the very least it can be said that the PRI did not strike the new priyayi as a threat. The group rapidly worked out an organizational scheme based on existing municipal administrative divisions, and arranged itself into departments in much the same fashion as prewar political parties and the KNID. A PRI headquarters was installed in a former Dutch home a few blocks from the Oranje Hotel, on a street renamed Jalan Merdeka, or Independence Street, for the occasion. Not all KNID members were aware of developments concerning the PRI, but no move was made to assert the KNID's authority, limited though it may have been, over the new organization. Constant communication between PRI leaders and the executive committee of the KNID encouraged new priyayi confidence that they might exercise whatever influence seemed necessary through indirect, informal means.[122] Besides, KNID members cannot have missed the interest the PRI evoked from kampung residents of all types, who treated PRI headquarters as if it were another center of pro-Indonesian authority in the city, looked upon the group as a source of help and protection, and even began forming PRI "branches" in the kampung.[123] If there was no precise coordination between the PRI and KNID, there was adequate communication and no serious friction; the two bodies moved in often intuitively complementary ways toward an assumed common goal.

Additional insight into the PRI and its relationship with the new priyayi can be obtained from a closer look at the backgrounds of the group's leaders.[124] The chairman, Sumarsono, appeared to some activists in 1945 to leap to prominence from nowhere. Doel Arnowo, however, knew his name prior to the founding of the PRI, and people informed about the activities of youth working in government offices recognized him as one of the more thoughtful individuals in Djohan Sjahroezah's circle. Sumarsono was born in about 1921 (no precise record exists, and it seems likely that the actual date could be several years earlier) in Kutarjo, near Magelang, Central Java. His father was a health official (a vaccinator) for the colonial government; his mother was of "ordinary" social background and illiterate. Young Sumarsono received primary schooling that gave him access to the Dutch-language system, and then received a scholarship to attend a missionary secondary school, where he converted to Christianity. At this institution he ran afoul of the principal, whom he happened to see molesting a female student, and was forced to move to Jakarta, where he attended a privately run Dutch-language trade school. After his father's death at about this time, Sumarsono supported himself by working and with some help from an older brother and an Englishman. Aiming for a position in government or business, he found temporary work in the colonial Department of Finance. Then, still in his teens, he worked for Borsumij, one of the best-known firms in the Netherlands East Indies.

As a boy Sumarsono had gone to listen to Sukarno speak in Kutarjo, an adventure for which he was punished by his father, and realized that he possessed a strong anticolonial urge. But he received no introduction to political thought until 1938, when he was invited by an artist neighbor in Jakarta to attend a meeting. The well-known Amir Sjarifuddin was present, and there was much talk of working for the Allies for the cause of democracy, fighting fascism, and the like. Sumarsono became interested and soon took an active role in the Gerindo. Then in 1942 he happened to meet Sukarni, whom he knew to be an Indonesia Muda leader, on the train from Solo to Jakarta. They became friends, and Sumarsono subsequently was introduced to Chaerul Saleh, Djohan Sjahroezah, and many others. They did a lot of reading under Sjahroezah's direction, mostly the works of Mohammad Hatta and Sukarno. Then in 1943 a group of 80 young men including Sumarsono followed a course given, under Japanese tutelage, by Sukarno and other Putera leaders. For six months they listened to what they perceived as Greater East Asia propaganda mixed with nationalist messages, and argued among themselves about the distinctions between the two. In early 1944 Sumarsono married the daughter of a Christian preacher from Kudus, Central Java, and then received orders to move to Surabaya, where he was given a job at the Batavia Petroleum Company offices and where he soon was accorded a position of leadership in Djohan Sjahroezah's group.

Sumarsono's recollection many years later was that he and his colleagues were asked to organize a "popular movement" (*gerakan rakyat*) in Surabaya, but that in fact this meant a movement of educated youth in the city and, in the areas beyond, school teachers, police, and even pangreh praja. The general notion was that the rakyat eventually might be contacted through these leaders, but no one could be certain whether or how soon such efforts might be successful. In Surabaya's kampung Sumarsono's group attempted to approach youth through the government-approved tonarigumi heads, and received the distinct impression that kampung residents did not need to be coached to oppose the Japanese; they were, if anything, more deeply resentful of Japanese rule than the pemuda themselves. Long after 17 August, however, the chief effort continued to be to bring together young office workers of the Batavia Petroleum Company and a number of similar companies and government offices. The focus remained on the Japanese, little or no attention being paid to the Dutch until more than a month after the proclamation of independence.

In this context Sumarsono built a modest following. He was trusted by Sjahroezah and known among his peers as a rather shy, cerebral person who was not at all given to emotional speech-making or overstatement. By his own assessment, he was politically naive and unaware of some of the fine distinctions in political philosophy among various pemuda figures. In addition he was, partly out of necessity, rather isolated from youth from other circles in Surabaya. For example, he was not well informed about the ideas and activities of Ruslan Abdulgani's organization, despite feeling in some vague manner that he was "part of" it.

In addition to what has already been said about Krissubanu, Kusnadi, and Bambang Kaslan, it should be noted that these three older, better-educated individuals had in common experience with the pergerakan and a degree of political sophistication formed over a decade or more. In this respect they too were part of the small pemuda elite developing on the fringe of new priyayi-dom. A similar profile, though including less activist experience, was shared by several other PRI leaders. Supardi, who was about 35 years old when he became the group's assistant secretary, came from a teacher's family and was educated in Western-style schools to the junior high level. His Dutch, like that of the others, was excellent, and partly because of it he was able to work before the war at the Van Ingen publishing company in a low managerial position. Supardi's pergerakan activities, however, had been limited to a light involvement with scouting, and he only came to the PRI because of his wartime friendship with Kusnadi. Less is known about Kusnandar, a relative of Doel Arnowo's who grew up in Kampung Peneleh in a well-off, aspiring family that owned a large brass works. About 25 years old in 1945, Kusnandar was a graduate of Taman Siswa schools, and in the late 1930s he worked in the offices of the municipal electric company. A member of Pusura and, just before the occupation, of Gerindo, he was arrrested by the Japanese in 1942 but later released to resume his job.

Hasjim Amin, who shared with the little-known Wahab the position of PRI treasurer, appears to have differed from his companions in a number of ways. At 21 he was by far the youngest of the PRI officers; with a mixed education in government and private schools, including three years in a madrasah, he was also the least well educated, although he had passed his preliminary examinations for government service. Hasjim Amin also was unusual in that he had arrived in Surabaya only in 1943, from his home town of Samarinda, Kalimantan, where his father was a moderately well-to-do interisland trader. Adjusting quickly to big-city life, the young man found a job in the offices of a trading company with branches in Kalimantan, and joined a seinendan group consisting of pemuda working in his and a few neighboring firms. Though his contacts with trading families throughout the city were of great value, Hasjim Amin first came to Kusnadi's attention through his enterprising manufacture of small red-and-white flags for kampung dwellers immediately after the proclamation of independence. When he collected funds for and manufactured the huge flag used during the 11 September rally, his reputation spread as an energetic and financially resourceful individual.

Other leaders of PRI sections (Defense, Information, and so on) or branches in different parts of the city generally fell within the same social boundaries as the persons already described. European observers later tended to speak of the PRI as an assemblage of ignorant youths or "non-thinking former Japanese soldiers,"[125] but these assessments were mistaken. The majority of PRI officers had at best only cursory training under the Japanese, and only a few had seinendan or Peta experience. Since the PRI had no formal membership,[126] fine distinctions cannot be made, but on the whole individuals who considered themselves part of the organization and took an active role in it were educated, pergerakan-influenced children of new priyayi and, in a few cases, kampung middle class backgrounds.[127] The daughter and three sons of Sutan Mohammad Zain, for example, were not alone among fellow PRI activists in possessing superior schooling and polished, though not artistocratic, social credentials. On the whole, youth with less education and political understanding followed the lead of others.[128] Values commonly discussed were self-reliance, personal courage, and dedication to the masses, all derived more or less directly from pergerakan sources. Foremost in PRI minds, however, was a vision of independence and the threat which outside forces posed to it.

If the PRI fed in large measure on ideals cultivated during the pergerakan and ripened in the summer of the occupation, the group was also very much influenced by the mood and activities of the urban population after the flag incident. Pemuda leaders did not represent a common social denominator for the city, but they often were both more interested in and better positioned to know about what was taking place in Surabaya's kampung than most new priyayi figures. During the last week of September, even KNID members recall sensing the welling up of what they loosely identified, in Dutch, as *massa geest*, a "spirit of the masses,"[129] and pemuda often saw with their own eyes the building hostilities and fears that entered kampung life at the time. These must have been particularly apparent in the dozens of small spontaneous demonstrations in centrally located kampung after 19 September, and in the even more numerous kampung meetings called to discuss tensions in the city and rumors of an impending Dutch attack.[130]

The PRI leadership devoted its energies largely to organizing office youth, including youth from other walks of life as and if the opportunity presented itself. Kampung connections were not vigorously pursued, and when they were sought the goals often were vaguely perceived. Nevertheless, pemuda soon saw that Surabaya's kampung responded sensitively to even the informal and indirect attentions paid them by the PRI. Many central kampung set up local PRI "offices" and boasted "representatives," most of whom were self-appointed.[131] The BKR also rather suddenly sparked kampung imaginations in a similar way, and a number of neighborhood leaders announced that they represented that group locally. In a few cases, kampung residents with the nerve to put themselves forward in this fashion actually were recognized by the PRI or, less frequently, the BKR, and given encouragement and the elements of a uniform.[132] But a far more common pattern was for kampung groups to be quite independent of their namesakes and to function according to the rhythm and needs of the neighborhood.

Kampung interest in the PRI and BKR appears to have been due primarily to a belief that these organizations were powerful and both willing and able to provide protection in the face of attacks from Japanese or Dutch. "Joining" the PRI or announcing that one lived in "a BKR neighborhood" were ways of building a defense and of saying that kampung interests now had support from sources outside kampung walls. Before long kampung became the scenes of reprisals against former colonial police officers, often perceived as being pro-Dutch and therefore a threat to the neighborhood, and of frequently violent quarrels between arek Surabaya and Eurasians or Christian Indonesians (mainly Ambonese youths—over republican flags and graffiti that then festooned the city, including kampung walls.[133] On these occasions kampung leaders called for aid from neighboring kampung as well as from PRI and BKR headquarters.[134].

The pattern of organization and leadership emerging at the upper levels of Indonesian society in Surabaya not only touched kampung people but attracted them toward its orbit. In these circumstances the PRI functioned as an intermediary. It did not represent a departure from new priyayi leadership, but intentionally supplemented the capabilities of the KNID and developed popular enthusiasm for the republic and the maintenance of independence. Undeniably the PRI—leaders as well as followers—came to exhibit a vibrant energy and willingness to act that made them a unique and moving force. At the same time, however, this force arose out of tendencies already abroad in an urban society under stress, and could not have been effective without reflecting them.

■ Linking new priyayi and pemuda leadership

After 21 September word spread rapidly through Surabaya that the groundwork was being laid for an uprising against the Japanese. The message was passed by PRI followers, but was also carried on its own momentum along new priyayi and kampung networks. The preparation further darkened the mood that gripped Indonesians throughout the city, and over the period of a week tension was brought to a high pitch.

While it attempted to maintain a dignified bearing, the KNID found itself caught up in the new atmosphere. When Moestopo returned to the group's executive meeting vowing that the BKR was ready to help lead an attack on Japanese forces, Sudirman replied that he would have the full support of the KNID for any action he had the courage to launch.[135] To several individuals who requested recognition as leaders of new groups, the KNID not only provided services such as printing and other publicity, but did much to bring the new arrivals into the informal cooperative power arrangement between the PRI, BKR, and KNID. In this way, for example, M. Sapiya's self-styled "Ambonese branch" of the Angkatan Pemuda Indonesia sought and got recognition from Sungkono (BKR) and Sudirman (KNID). Bambang Suparto, acting for the KNID, arranged to have 5,000 flyers printed announcing Sapiya's group and its support for the republic, and a special session of the KNID brought Sapiya together with PRI leaders. The two groups soon merged.[136]

The kampung population was even more deeply stirred by the changing climate, and reacted with special excitement when BKR and PRI members pulled down Japanese posters and announcements beginning on 27 September. Confrontations between kampung folk and Japanese proliferated. These scuffles, which seem to have occurred most frequently near kampung gates, resulted in the Japanese soldiers fleeing or being killed, and their weapons falling into the hands of the attackers.[137] All of these early incidents appear to have been initiated by kampung residents, and not necessarily youths; the PRI found out about most of them, but on the whole observed rather than participated, and apparently did not acquire control over the weapons wrested from the Japanese. Only later did PRI adherents actively become involved in such events.

Two incidents, similar in nature to those just mentioned but far more serious in outcome, illustrate vividly the importance of the actions of the arek Surabaya, and of the manner in which pemuda and new priyayi authority worked together. The first took place on 29 September 1945, near Pasar Blauran, a crowded commercial area.[138] A Japanese military vehicle carrying an officer and his chauffeur collided with a dokar, seriously wounding the Indonesian driver and his family. In an instant the automobile was surrounded; an angry mob pulled the occupants out and beat them nearly to death. PRI representatives from a nearby branch were called to the scene, arriving quickly enough to prevent the murder and taking the victims to their headquarters for medical aid. But the rakyat in this central city area could not be pacified. That night Japanese patrolling the streets in trucks near where the incident occurred were attacked by mobs; the Japanese panicked and abandoned their vehicle and firearms. PRI youth, who were not the instigators of this violence, joined in only toward the end, perhaps primarily to gain control of the weapons involved.

Beginning on the same day but drawing to a climax on 30 September, a second example of mob action drew the attention of not only the PRI but the KNID, BKR, and police.[139] When a large crowd of residents from surrounding kampung began to surround the Don Bosco barracks, used by the Japanese as a warehouse for weapons and other supplies, several PRI representatives rushed to the spot from a nearby post. Among them was Sutomo, then active in the PRI Information Section. His forceful, persuasive character, in addition to his ability to speak some English, led to his being able to take the role of chief negotiator between the tense Japanese and the excited mob shouting for weapons and revenge. Attempting to arrive at a peaceful solution, Sutomo discovered that the crowd was adamant and would settle for nothing less than all Japanese arms. Toward nightfall a compromise was achieved, the rakyat promising to return in the morning if Sutomo would bring authorities of the republican government with him. The next day a larger crowd of arek Surabaya gathered, along with Sutomo, Moh. Jasin from the Special Police, and representatives of the KNID and the BKR. After four hours of threats and debate the Japanese, whose taut psychology Sutomo and Jasin played on effectively, caved in. A substantial cache of firearms, food, cloth, and other materials was turned over to Jasin in the name of the republic. Most of the items were then distributed to the BKR, PRI headquarters, and kampung guards.

The Don Bosco "formula" was applied to a number of key locations throughout Surabaya. The motor pool of the Japanese Army, the city's main broadcasting facility, the military hospital, and other facilities were turned over to representatives of the regional government in rapid succession.[140] On most of these occasions the role taken by the urban rakyat was crucial, though it is clear that PRI and BKR soon got the idea that what had begun as spontaneous involvement of the rakyat could in fact be encouraged and channelled. And it seems worth remembering that the takeover phenomenon went far beyond a few dozen brazen and potentially explosive confrontations: a typical if unsung experience was that of a young kampung individual who, after witnessing the Don Bosco drama, returned to the Japanese-run bean curd factory at which he worked, demanded in the name of the republic that the boss hand over his ceremonial sword, and then dispensed to coworkers and friends what goods and few small firearms were found in the building.[141]

The popular role in these events surprised both new priyayi and pemuda leaders alike, for whom outbursts were more widespread and more heated than they could manage easily. The Japanese viewed these circumstances as proof that conditions had degenerated into chaos, and Europeans, though aware that the hostility was directed against the Japanese rather than themselves, were too frightened by what they saw going on around them to believe that the situation had not veered entirely out of control.[142] Yet a rough pattern of leadership connecting new priyayi government, PRI and other auxiliary forces, and kampung actions had emerged. The regularity with which crowds called for and in general obeyed new priyayi and pemuda authorities during the takeover incidents shows how widely the new roles of these authorities were recognized and how, in many important respects, urban society had acted together in this crisis rather than been torn apart. The order thus achieved may have been turbulent and tentative in nature, but it was an order of a certain kind, with a certain social logic.

The power of this enfolded and largely intuitive unity was fully revealed only after the scattered takeover actions had proved effective. Late in September posters had begun to appear in various city locations declaring that 1 October would be "butchering day for the Japanese dogs," and kampung rumor had generated widespread public anticipation of this event.[143] The precise origin of the idea behind this day of reckoning is uncertain, but in all likelihood PRI leaders were largely responsible for it; certainly the PRI was involved in distributing posters throughout the city, and PRI members did a great deal to assure that the news spread by word of mouth as well. These efforts also may have been responsible for the sudden and ominous silence that fell over Surabaya on the evening of 30 September. But the preparations were by no means exclusively in PRI hands. The BKR, by all indications, was well informed about the event and almost certainly took a major role in organizing assaults on specific targets and in supervising arms use and distribution.[144] The KNID and the leading new priyayi in general also appear to have been aware of the plans being laid, and Sudirman apparently not only approved the movement but synchronized his own activities closely with it. At 1:30 a.m. on 1 October he is said to have given his final blessing to the PRI and BKR leaders who were directing the assault,[145] and shortly after daybreak he had a succint note delivered to the office of the Japanese Resident. It read:

1) The time has arrived for us to run every aspect of the government ourselves. Effective immediately, all administrative functions in this region are under our control. We will respond only to the commands of the Government of the Republic of Indonesia.

2) Henceforth all matters of concern to the Allies, whether regarding the state, the populace, or private and public property, must be negotiated with us.[146]

By 8:30 a.m. whole sections of central Surabaya were flooded with posters, flags, and screaming Indonesians brandishing bamboo spears, swords, and firearms.[147] Despite the wild and largely undirected appearance of these demonstrations, their deliberate nature came through to thoughtful Japanese officers. They called what was taking place a coup d'état and had few illusions about the seriousness of its intent or likely effectiveness.[148]

In two days of negotiations, mob action, and often bitter fighting, the entire Japanese civilian and military authority in Surabaya was brought to its knees by Indonesians. Japanese accounts record the horror with which their authors viewed the violence that swirled about them, and discuss the painful and frequently dangerous decisions that had to be made.[149] In large and small actions several dozen Japanese were killed and wounded, and thousands were placed in jails or detention camps.[150] The greatest of the Indonesian victories took place on the afternoon of 2 October. At that time the infamous kempeitai headquarters, located near the governor's office, finally surrendered after 36 hours of siege and ferocious fighting. The attack was led by the BKR and Special Police, supported by armed PRI members, and joined by large mobs of excited arek Surabaya; the Japanese surrendered to Sudirman and a few others representing the republican government.[151] One of Surabaya's most powerful symbols of colonial rule, Dutch as well as Japanese, was then held firmly in Indonesian hands.[152]

The events of the first days of October 1945 shattered dramatically the coherence of the tense order which had reigned in Surabaya since the proclamation of independence, and replaced it with something at once more powerful and more brittle. The struggles with the Japanese gave new substance to the transition from colonial rule, and from kampung to KNID residents of the city sensed both the raw excitement and the changed structure of unity that prevailed. A newspaper editorial noted with obvious satisfaction that "the history of the new Indonesia had begun brilliantly," while on the opposite page a boxed slogan cried, "Blood . . . Blood . . . the blood of Indonesians has been spilled in Surabaya for Indonesian freedom, for a republic of the people."[153] The battles indeed produced the first fallen heroes of the revolution in East Java. Sudirman and his closest colleagues acted quickly to establish a special burial ground in the center of Surabaya for those who had died in the fighting, and the afternoon of 3 October at the former Cannalaan field, now renamed Taman Bahagia, 24 heroes were laid to rest with full ceremony.[154] Huge crowds looked on, waving innumerable red-and-white flags as the Special Police fired an honor salute. Sudirman, Radjamin Nasution, and Doel Arnowo made speeches. Local religious figures read prayers for the fallen, and the observance was closed with the phrase, reminiscent of pergerakan days. "Hiduplah Indonesia Merdeka!"

Although some KNID members later claimed not have have attended the ceremony or known about plans for it,[155] there is little doubt that the martyrdom celebrated in this fashion became an important ingredient in Surabayan thought and emotion during the following month.[156] Special rites were held for individual victims by family, coworkers, neighbors, and friends; flowers and other offerings were brought daily to the gravesites by the general population; the Taman Bahagia became a prime sight for visitors from outside the city; and on 17 October, the anniverary of two months of independence, a highly emotional ceremony was held for thousands of people at the burial grounds. The sacrifice represented by the deaths required little deliberate promotion to attract and hold the attention of the public.

In addition to the nationalist message they conveyed, the burial ceremonies carried a social one of considerable force. The times were recognized broadly as bringing forth the actions and interest of the masses—it was no accident, for example, that on 1 October the former *Soeara Asia* appeared under the title *Soeara Rakjat*, or Voice of the People—and Taman Bahagia became a powerful symbol of popular involvement in the struggle for freedom. At the same time, the pemuda component also was emphasized heavily in the speech-making and discussion surrounding the burials. Most of the victims appear to have been identified as pemuda of the type that joined the PRI, belonged to the BKR or the Special Police, or worked in one or another city office. Most were described carefully as having had good educations, and several were the sons of prominent Surabayans. Yet there was no conflict between the two sides of the symbolism. Although the truth of the matter may be that the Taman Bahagia memorialized heroes who were sons of the new priyayi and, to a much lesser extent, the kampung middle class,[157] the remembrance seems to have focussed on the egalitarian aspects of the battles and the heroic deaths in them. The theme of popular unity under the banner of pemuda energies and courage captured the imagination of urban society and, in one manifestation or another, came to characterize not only the early October struggles but, as it turned out, the intense period which followed.

The principal goal of Sudirman and KNID leaders was to take the opportunity offered by the new solidarity, however vague and emotionally based it may have been, and extend the framework of leadership already established. Shortly after the kempeitai building fell into Indonesian hands, the Resident's office issued a decree in the name of the republican government. Its six points read:

1) As of today we promote the BKR to the status of an agency of the Government of the Republic of Indonesia, under the leadership of the Resident of Surabaya. The PRI will assist in carrying out the work of the BKR.

2) Official guards bearing the insignia of Military Police areas of today abolished.

3) The emblem of the "Rising Sun" on police caps will be replaced with red-and-white badges.

4) The BKR headquarters will be relocated in the former kempeitai building.

5) Japanese will be interned in the former Marine headquarters and on the grounds of the Jaarmarkt.

6) Arms and ammunition acquired thus far are requested to be turned over to the Government of the Republic of Indonesia, Surabaya Region, at the office of the BKR in the former kempeitai building, or at the headquarters of the Special Police, on Coenboulevard.[158]

The intent behind these points is clear, and they are to be interpreted as details in the broader new priyayi effort to gather authority further under their auspices. The KNID joined in publishing a notice asking people to obey the BKR, and together with the Resident's office began connecting pangreh praja to the growing Indonesian government apparatus.[159] *Soeara Rakjat* editors, though unabashed in their enthusiasm for the recent turn of events, also showed their concern for the established order by printing in semiofficial format three rather surprising reminders:

1) The police of the Republic of Indonesia are official[ly approved] and respected; they have the full respect of society.

2) The pangreh praja of the Republic of Indonesia are the true fathers of the People.

3) The administrators [*pegawai*] of the Republic of Indonesia are truly leaders of the People.[160]

The position of the PRI leadership with regard to the framework of government is of particular interest. This new force in Surabayan affairs moved its headquarters on 4 October to the spacious and richly symbolic Simpang Club in the heart of the city.[161] Almost certainly this change took place with the blessing and perhaps even active help of Sudirman, who shortly afterward announced that the executive committee appointed to help with the everyday governing of the Residency comprised, in addition to the KNID members Doel Arnowo, Dwidjosewojo, Angka Nitisastro, and Bambang Suparto, the young labor leader Sjamsu Harya Udaya, and the chairman of the PRI, Sumarsono.[162] A statement appearing in *Soeara Rakjat* over the PRI endorsement indicate that the moment of self-determination had arrived, the public order should be guarded, and all religions, races, nationalities, and customs should be protected by law.[163] Concurrently, the PRI established its own training program for pemuda, complete with asrama, and began perfecting its internal organization as well as giving official recognition to branches in Surabaya and elsewhere in East Java.[164] In these and other ways the PRI was fitted, and began to fit itself, into the new priyayi establishment.

The anatomy of an important working relationship between PRI leaders and government bodies in Surabaya was apparent in the handling of Japanese and Dutch in the city during early October. The relationship was based at least in part on the inability of the KNID to act on its own, and the inadequacy of the BKR to undertake all of the activities that Sudirman and KNID members believed were necessary. The PRI, organized and led by young men who, for all their insistence upon direct and strong measures, were nevertheless part of the same pergerakan stock as the new priyayi figures, naturally filled a role that was activist yet complementary to the new priyayi leadership.[165] In part, too, the status of the PRI and the relationships stemming from it were founded on the hard rock of physical strength. An enormous arsenal had fallen to Indonesians between 2 September and 2 October in Surabaya, by some estimates a full fifty percent of all the weapons controlled by the republic on Java.[166] Of this amount even the commander of the BKR in retrospect estimated that half or more was held by the PRI, making it equivalent to the government's principal armed body in applicable force.[167]

In some areas it was the impression of close observers among the Dutch that the PRI actually controlled the BKR,[168] and while this is probably an overstatement, the two groups did operate, after 2 October, on something approaching an equal footing. In the task of interning military and civilian Japanese still remaining in Surabaya, for example, the PRI took major responsibility.[169] Much of this operation occurred on the afternoon of 2 October, at the same time as the BKR-led battle against the kempeitai was brought to a climax, and it required much planning as well as a large, reliable body of armed men. Only the PRI was able to supply the necessary numbers, and new priyayi leaders relied on these pemuda with little hesitation. Likewise, when the majority of Japanese civilians were released from custody the next day, and attacked by mobs and kampung gangs, it was the PRI that located survivors, protected them against further assault, and brought them back to prison areas.[170] These were not the acts of pemuda on the rampage, or even at fundamental odds with the republican government coalescing under new priyayi watchfulness; they are best interpreted, instead, as links between two related and complementary sources of leadership, working within a common framework.

■ Notes

1. There is some question as to exactly when individual figures in Surabaya received the news. Ruslan Abdulgani, for example, has written variously that word of the proclamation reached the city on August 17 and on the following evening. Ruslan Abdulgani (1963):32; *Abdulgani MS.* It seems clear from 1971 interviews with a number of prominent Surabayan intellectuals, however, that some persons either heard the original broadcast or were told about it in their office. Soebagiyo I. N.:61 notes that the Antara news agency office received the original broadcast and spread the news.

2. Interviews in 1971 with intellectuals active in Surabaya at the time.

3. Apparently middle-ranking pangreh praja, most of whom tended to disbelieve the proclamation story and to assume it was a Japanese fiction, nevertheless sent the news out to village administrations via a courier system that had been developed during the occupation. Interview in 1972 with a former pangreh praja who not only did this himself but knew colleagues who did so as well.

4. Except where stated otherwise, information in this paragraph is taken from interviews with prominent Surabayans as they appeared in SA 8-20-45 and 8-21-45.

5. *Abdulgani MS.*

6. Interview in 1972 with an individual who was at that time a leading member of a youth group.

7. *Abdulgani MS*; SA 8-22-45.

8. *Abdulgani MS*; Ruslan Abdulgani (1974c):13; SA 8-29-45.

9. See, for example, SA 9-25-43 and 8-9-45.

10. The full text is given in SA 8-24-45.

11. Dutch, Indonesian, and Japanese first-hand views all give largely the same impression. See *Bakti* 8-19-45 and 8-20-45; RvOIC 005140; van Sprang:7; and Nishimura (1962):3.

12. Puasa was scheduled to last from the evening of 8 August until the evening of 7 September 1945. SA 9-6-45.

13. B. Anderson (1961) cites the original instruction, dated 18 August 1945. Reiteration of the principles, dated 5 September 1945, is treated in OBNIB I:88-89.

14. SA 8-21-45.

15. Interviews in 1972 with several pangreh praja posted in rural and urban areas at the time.

16. SA 8-27-45, 8-28-45, and 8-29-45; RvOIC 062073.

17. Interview in 1972 with an individual who aided such activities; RvOIC 00387-32:41; Thomson:65.

18. Kampung interviews, 1971.

19. Some idea of the continued strength of pergerakan symbolism at this time can be gathered from an announcement by Sukarno in late August that as of 1 September 1945 the prewar nationalist greeting of "Hidup!" should be

replaced with that of "Merdeka!" Apparently many city residents were not yet accustomed to changing times. SA 8-31-45.

20. *Sutomo MS*:6; Sutomo (1951):3-4.

21. M. Sapiya (1946) *Bakti* 17:17.

22. Kampung interviews, 1971. Some neighborhoods in which the kampung head had never really relinquished authority during the occupation experienced little or no change in leadership at this time.

23. Interview in 1970 with a Eurasian who lived in Surabaya for many years before 1945.

24. SA 9-12-45.

25. Interviews with several Indonesian doctors and journalists present at the time, 1971.

26. Interview with Sutadji, 1971.

27. Smail:53 and the sources cited there.

28. B. Anderson (1972):85ff examines the KNIP (the highest, national level), and Smail:39-41 looks at the situation in Bandung, but not in great detail. To my knowledge there are no other published studies in any language of the KNI as an institution.

29. Reid (1974):34.

30. Kanahele (1967):29-30.

31. The announcement, though fairly widely known because it was mentioned in Sukarno's 23 August broadcast, was not published in Surabaya until two days later. SA 8-25-45.

32. There is insufficient printed information on the founding of the Surabaya KNID to produce an entirely satisfactory picture, and memories of participants has weakened over the years. The account given here amounts to an educated guess based on several conflicting reports. With only a few exceptions, points of controversy have not been emphasized for the reader. Except where cited differently, information on the KNID in the next three paragraphs is based on the *Abdulgani MS*, the *Kaslan MS*:13-15; and interviews with three surviving members of the KNID, 1971-72.

33. Ruslan Abdulgani claims that Sudirman had to be goaded by the Angkatan Muda Committee, and assigns a prime role in events to that group. No other source mentions this relationship, however, and it is difficult to see why Sudirman would have wished to ignore Jakarta's request, or how he could have delayed very long, since the first meeting was held on 25 August 1945.

34. Interview in 1971 with Dr. Suwandhi, who was close to the individuals and the situation.

35. Interview in 1971 with Sutadji, who was close to Sudirman and soon after became his private secretary.

36. Interview with Ruslan Abdulgani, 1970.

37. One member recalled much later that the number was 17, as a symbolic remembrance of 17 August, but Doel Arnowo only recollected that "about 20" persons were present at the first meeting. Interviews, 1971-72.

38. Ruslan Abdulgani has pictured the collaboration issue as being ex-

tremely important to his group. There is no other evidence, however, that the subject was brought out sharply at any of the meetings, which, it should be noted, only one or two persons from the Abdulgani group attended.

39. Actually only 31 persons were named, one slot being reserved for an as yet undecided individual. The list ran: Chairman: Doel Arnowo; first vice-chairman, Bambang Suparto; second vice-chairman, Mr. Dwidjosewojo; secretary, Ruslan Abdulgani; members (in the order originally published), R. A. A. Soejadi; Soebakti Poespanoto; Setiono; M. Masmoein; Radjamin Nasution; Goesti Majoer; J. H. W. Tampi; Dr. Siwabessy; Liem Thwan Tik; Alaydroes; Ir. Darmawan Mangunkusumo; Ir. Soemono; Ir. Salijo; Dr. Moh. Suwandhi; Soebakto; Kustur; Anwar Zen; Dr. Angka Nitisastro; H. Moh. Tahir Bakri; another person from the Masyumi (the Moslem council formed in late 1943); H. Abdoelkarim; H. Zarkasi; Soedomo; Notohamiprodjo; Abdul Wahab; Nj. Soemantri; Soepeno; and Soedji. SA 8-28-45.

40. Thus Dwidjosewojo is said to have been chosen solely because he was thought to be the best legal talent available, and advice on the law was assumed to be necessary in any confrontation with the Dutch.

41. Interview in 1971 with a Moslem intellectual figure who watched these events closely.

42. This point was made especially clear in a 1971 interview with Dr. Angka Nitisastro.

43. Even among those responsible for this decision—Dr. Angka Nitisastro, Dwidjosewojo, Doel Arnowo, and several others—there was some concern that Sudirman might not be sufficiently tough-minded. It was also acknowledged, however, that no one else possessed the experience and skills necessary for the job.

44. The public announcement did not actually attach the title of Resident to Sudirman's name, as that might appear to be usurping Jakarta's prerogative. *Abdulgani MS.* Confirmation of the post came several days later. RIPDT:909–10 gives the most complete report.

45. SA 9-4-45. The seven points, which reveal much about the thinking of Sudirman and his colleagues at the time, were: 1) strong measures will be taken against any act contrary to the Government of the Republic of Indonesia; 2) only the national flag of Indonesia may be flown throughout the Surabaya region; 3) public peace and order will be strictly observed, according to the laws that remain in effect at the present time; 4) those who break the laws just mentioned will be held strictly accountable by the authorities; 5) all government offices, departments, and works will continue as before; 6) the entire populace is ordered to go about its daily business calmly and properly, observing full discipline; 7) all labor groups and other organizations are ordered to continue working in an atmosphere of togetherness, thereby supporting the public peace and well-being.

46. The *Sutomo MS*:7 reports that younger employees in the governor's office had earlier attempted to raise the red-and-white there and lower the Japanese flag. When told to stop by Japanese guards, a compromise was arranged whereby the Rising Sun continued to fly in the usual place, but the

Indonesian flag also hung in a more or less improvised fashion from another tower of the same building.

47. SA 9-6-45.

48. Accounts of kampung and other KNIs can be found in SA 9-1-45, 9-2-45, 9-10-45, 9-13-45, and 9-14-45. Unless cited differently, material in the following two paragraphs is taken from these sources.

49. One kampung in the Peneleh area put on a selamatan for 1,000 people and announced the four duties of every kampung resident; fly the national flag, know the words to the national anthem, wear a small red-and-white emblem on the lapel, and use the "Merdeka!" greeting. In addition, the head of the kampung KNI telegraphed congratulations to the Jakarta government. SA 9-3-45.

50. Kampung interviews, 1971–72, RvOIC 071224.

51. Kampung interview, 1971.

52. SA 9-12-45.

53. This section is based on interviews held in 1971 and 1972 with Ruslan Wongsokusumo, who was central to these events. It is unclear exactly how many members originally sat on the KNI Kota, though Wongsokusumo mentioned "about 10." SA 9-12-45 records the executive committee of the KNIK as consisting of Ruslan Wongsokusumo, Soetijono, Dr. Soegiri, Djokosangkolo, and H. Goefran Fakih.

54. The BKR was officially inaugurated on 6 October 1945, utilizing most of the same officers and men trained in the former Peta. There is disagreement over whether the Peta may properly be called the basis of the eventual Indonesian Army, via the BKR, although that is the generally accepted view. The most detailed work of this subject is Larson; studies emphasizing the discontinuities are Nugroho Notosusanto (1979a) and (1979b).

55. *Sam Karya*:48–50.

56. Interview with a career military officer based in East Java at the time, 1972.

57. SA 9-5-45.

58. RvOIC 005148.

59. SA 9-5-45 and 9-12-45.

60. The first such gathering on record was Abdulgani's of 20 August 1945, as noted in the *Abdulgani MS*.

61. Interview in 1971 with a former pemuda group leader.

62. *Kaslan MS*:13–14. The account in the following paragraphs is based on this source.

63. Thus Kaslan notes that the pemuda types present were mostly those who, like himself, had been associated loosely with the Barisan Pelopor, which in turn had been rather vaguely under the guidance of Doel Arnowo during the last year or so of the war. The pemuda attending were: Krissubanu, Soedjani, Kustur, Abas, Bambang Kaslan, and Moh. Bakri.

64. *Enquêtecommissie* C II:1515.

65. RvOIC 062073:7.

66. RvOIC 000387-32:45.

67. RvOIC 068665:1 and 030905:1.

68. RvOIC 062945:48.

69. K'tut Tantri:165.

70. Scarcely one of the dozen or more Dutch and Eurasian diaries available in archives mentions the name of a single Indonesian city leader at this time, and few Dutch seem to have bothered to obtain and read *Soeara Asia*, which continued to appear until mid-September. Netherlands Forces Intelligence Service (NEFIS) reports compiled as late as December 1945 could not identify Bambang Suparto and had precious little information on Sudirman, who was characterized briefly as a "Japanese-colored extremist." RvOIC 070851 and 070882.

71. RvOIC 032780:11; ARA AAS 97b/XXII/45:5; Schouten:118.

72. Yoga:11; RvOIC 032780 described, for example, the housing situation to which Dutch returned in August 1945. The office set up in 1942 to handle the occupation of European homes by Japanese had been turned over to an Indonesian, and most of the homes had by that time been taken over on a temporary basis by Indonesians and a few Chinese. One can imagine how returning Dutch felt when confronted with this situation.

73. "Indonesia Days" were proclaimed on 28 August in Surabaya, after announcements had been made several days earlier in Jakarta that from 29 August to 1 September only the Indonesian flag was to be flown.

74. *Sutomo MS*:11; Yoga:12, 18, and 23.

75. RIPDT:910; interviews with eye-witnesses, 1971.

76. "Soerabaya mempertahankan"; Yoga:12; RIPDT:910.

77. Schouten:118. This source gives the impression that the KKS actually was founded by the Japanese to encourage Eurasian-Dutch action against Indonesians and to oppose the neutral Red Cross.

78. SA 9-1-45, 9-6-45, 9-11-45, 9-14-45.

79. Van der Wal (1979) I:3 and the sources cited there. Ruslan Abdulgani, for example, recalls that knowledge of the NICA was already a prime cause for worry in early 1945 and became even more so after mid-July. *Abdulgani MS*.

80. Long:553–55.

81. There is no satisfactory study of the NICA, though as an institution it illustrates very neatly the variety of ways in which prewar colonial administration and outlooks tended to live on after the occupation. The core of information on the NICA is contained in ARA APG 180; there is also material on the British-NICA relationship in *Enquêtecommissie* 8 A:650ff. Further sources on the British-Dutch quarrels over the NICA and RAPWI are Schouten, *passim*; Kirby V:243ff.; OBNIB I and II; and PRO WO203/4366.

82. See the list of individuals, mostly from prewar West Java government offices but including high police authorities from Surabaya, in RvOIC 005369. There was a widespread understanding among returning Europeans that a NICA "Army" was avidly recruiting (ARA AAA 97b/XXII/45c:1), and indeed the official NICA handbook prescribed that as near as possible to half of the staff of each local unit be police personnel.

83. Kampung interview, 1971.

84. Clothing and cloth had become increasingly scarce for Surabayans during the war, and the appearance of Dutch people returning from imprisonment with trunks still filled with clothes, which were valuable items of barter, caused many Indonesians to rankle at the inequities and the reminder of the colonial relationship.

85. RvOIC 030905:2, and 062945:49–50.

86. Interview with Dr. Angka Nitisastro in 1971.

87. The account given here and in the next paragraph is drawn from the *Kaslan MS*:15–18; and interviews with Bambang Kaslan in 1972 and Sumarsono in 1978.

88. B. Anderson (1972):118–19.

89. Present at this meeting were Sumarsono, Kusnandar, Ruslan Widjajasastrà, Djohan Sjahroezah, Nurullah, Bedjo, Hasjim Amin, Krissubanu, Bambang Kaslan, Saleh Said, Abdul Wahab, Mansur Burhan, and several others. These individuals were all employed in offices in the city, predominantly government-affiliated but in some cases private.

90. Japanese authorities went so far as to have it announced in *Soeara Asia* that the rally planned for September 11 was postponed, with no reason given. SA 9-10/11-45.

91. Interview in 1972 with Sutadji.

92. I have been unable to locate an adequate account of this event. It is mentioned briefly in RvOIC 071004:1–2; *Enquêtecommissie* 8A:603; and ARA AAS 97b/I/23a:1–2, which is also excerpted in OBNIK I:486–87.

93. The parachutists were unaware that less than 24 hours before their arrival a Dutch-language pamphlet heralding the return of Dutch armed forces had been dropped on Surabaya. *Abdulgani MS*; Kinoshita:82.

94. Interviews with two eyewitnesses, 1971.

95. ARA AAS 97b/XXII/45b:5–6.

96. Schools in Surabaya had been given extended puasa holidays and did not open until 17 September. SA 9-6-45.

97. *Sutomo MS*:16; that the Dutch and Eurasian returnees were primarily responsible for creating the precariously tense situation is confirmed on the Dutch side in RvOIC 005144, and is implied in many other Dutch and Japanese sources, which certainly would have no good reason to blame Dutch rather than Indonesians.

98. RvOIC 005140:1.

99. *Enquêtecommissie* C II:1183.

100. The junior officer was sent back to Jakarta and demoted two ranks. Kinoshita:83; *Enquêtecommissie* C II:1183.

101. *Sutomo MS*:12.

102. RvOIC 005140:1.

103. The identity of the person who actually lowered and tore the Dutch flag was not recorded at the time and is not likely to be known with any certainty. It is common in Surabaya to claim that the youth "came from this

very kampung," or "was my close friend," and every arek Surabaya seems to have his own idea of what sort of person this hero was. For some recent journalistic efforts to make an identification, see Suhadi; "Siapa sebenarnya"; and "Ketika warna biru." Among the personal accounts is Barlan Setiadijaya. Nugroho Notosusanto (1985):25 cites work done by a team of historians to identify the individual or individuals responsible. These sources do not discuss the same individual, but they do seem to agree on a general description of a well-educated young man from a lower new priyayi or upper middle class background, with, in the case of the last work mentioned, a job as a city employee.

104. For example, the frequently depicted scene of a large crowd, armed with a variety of weapons and whipped into a frenzy, is overdrawn. Contemporary photographs and written sources close to the event indicate relatively small numbers of people and very few real weapons, even bamboo spears. Participants were very largely schoolboys, dressed in the familiar white cotton outfits. RvOIC reports only about 30 Dutch and several hundred Indonesians involved at most, with no spears, guns, or knives in the crowd.

105. Ruslan Abdulgani (1974c):16.

106. *Enquêtecommissie* 8A:596; Schouten:119.

107. This difficulty is brought out particularly well in the memoirs of Admiral Shibata Yaichiro, especially chapter 7, some of which is translated in Reid and Oki: 277–88 and 341–74.

108. Nishimura (1962):308 contains a vivid, personal view of the dawning of this realization. He notes that Japanese often were influenced heavily by young Eurasians coming to their offices with warnings that Indonesians in the city were becoming extremely dangerous.

109. RvOIC 006951; *Sutomo MS*:15.

110. Sutomo (1951):18–20; RIPDT:911; Ruslan Abdulgani (1963):20.

111. For all the reports and commentary that events in Surabaya eventually spawned on the European side, there is remarkably little certainty in such matters as dates of arrival of personnel, or the precise sequence of activities. Except where cited otherwise, the abbreviated account in this and the following paragraph is compiled from de Back's testimony and report (*Enquêtecommissie* C II:1183ff and 1407–14, and from various reports and recollections by Huijer (*Enquêtecommissie* 8A:595ff and ARA AAS 97b/I/23c).

112. RvOIC 030905:2–3.

113. Interview in 1971 with Dr. Suwandhi, who was one of the first to realize the identity of these individuals; ARA AAS 97b/I/23c:9. The last Dutch Governor of East Java, W. Hartevelt, had died in 1944 while interned, however. The last Dutch Mayor of Surabaya, W. H. Fuchter, was imprisoned in West Java and left Indonesia permanently to settle in the Netherlands in 1946.

114. K'tut Tantri (1969):179–80 mentions having seen such plans during a visit to the hotel, but it is difficult to tell from her text exactly when this might have been. RIPDT:10 also indicates a belief that such plans existed. A

document that may possibly have played the role is RvOIC 069253, which 'lists strategic targets in the city and contains maps clearly designated for use by Allied troops.

115. Sutomo (1960):12.

116. *Sutomo MS*:13; interview with a kampung resident who was there, 1971.

117. There are no published accounts, contemporary or otherwise, of either this meeting or the one held concurrently with it, as described in the paragraphs below. *Soeara Asia*, which might have carried some of the news, stopped publishing on 14 September, and its successor paper did not appear until 1 October. Memories with respect to dates and personalities, to say nothing of the subject matter of debates, have proved shaky. The picture sketched here, therefore, is of necessity grounded on a good deal of extrapolating from recollections of several participants, long after the events. Except where cited otherwise, material in this and the following paragraph is drawn from the *Kaslan MS*:18, and interview with Ruslan Abdulgani, Dr. Suwandhi, Dr. Angka Nitisastro, and Bambang Kaslan in 1971–72, and Sumarsono in 1978.

118. Several contemporary Dutch reports mention numbers of Indonesians dressed in military-type uniforms, heading by train toward Surabaya during the last ten days of September. RvOIC 032385:1 and 032388:1.

119. The PRI is generally believed to have been founded on 23 September 1945, as mentioned in B. Anderson (1972):6 and the sources cited there. Here Bambang Kaslan's unpublished account, which uses 21 September and the occasion of the GNI meeting as the occasion of the PRI's birth, is followed since the author was involved personally and has proven reliable on similar matters. Sumarsono, in a 1978 interview, also noted that the official announcement of PRI's founding followed by a few days the actual day, though he hesitated to fix a date.

120. Interview in 1971 with Dr. Angka Nitisastro.

121. Interviews in 1971 with a former PRI officer and a doctor who was asked by the PRI to act as an advisor. The PRI not only depended on new priyayi figures for material aid, such as cloth for flags (obtainable only through those with access to Japanese warehouses), but for expertise in, for example, medical aid and social services. The *Kaslan MS*:18 gives brief attention to how this was thought out.

122. Interview in 1971 with Dr. Angka Nitisastro.

123. *Kaslan MS*:19.

124. Biographical data is difficult to come by for many PRI figures. Information in this and the next five paragraphs is drawn, except where noted otherwise, from inteviews in 1971–72 with Bambang Kaslan, Abdulrazak, Welisudjono, Sifun, Hasjim Amin, Hardjadinata, Doel Arnowo, and Ruslan Abdulgani; and in 1978 with Sumarsono.

125. RvOIC 032385:1.

126. Somewhat later PRI identification cards were used, especially by local branches, but no membership lists appear to have been kept, and cards were readily forged. There is no indication that anyone at this stage conceived

of the PRI as an embryonic political party with a clearly delineated membership.

127. Interview with two former PRI members well-informed about the backgrounds of their colleagues. 1971.

128. Interview in 1971 with a doctor who served the PRI.

129. Yoga:16.

130. RvOIC 005140:3.

131. This account is based on a number of kampung interviews, 1971.

132. ARA APG 803.

133. ARA AAS 97b/XXII/45a:3, and 97b/XXII/45b:8; RvOIC 005192; Sutomo (1951):26.

134. Some kampung appointed special "scouts" and couriers to inform residents whenever a fight or some other threatening action erupted nearby. All who were able then rushed to the spot. Kampung interview, 1971; Yoga:28-29.

135. Interview in 1971 with Sutadji, who was very close to Sudirman.

136. M. Sapiya (1946) *Bakti* 18:12-14.

137. Sutomo (1951):26.

138. This account taken from the *Kaslan MS*:19.

139. This account taken from the *Kaslan MS*:20; the *Sutomo MS*:21-23; and Sutomo (1951):26-28. Kaslan gives the date of events as 30 September, while Sutomo, without mentioning a date, says that things happened over a two-day period. The affair certainly was over by 1 October, so the dates given here are probably accurate.

140. RIPDT:911-12.

141. Interview in 1971 with the individual who did this; a similar experience is mentioned in the *Sutomo MS*:17-18.

142. Interview in 1971 with a Japanese who was there; ARA AAS 97b/I/23c:2; RvOIC 030905:3; Stevens and Grevedamme:10-12.

143. Kampung interviews, 1971-72; interview with an eyewitness and participant, 1969; *Kaslan MS*:10.

144. Virtually all sources, including Dutch, agree on, without especially emphasizing, the dominant role played by the BKR. This is given special emphasis in Nugroho Notosusanto (1985):27-28.

145. ARA AAS 97b/I/23c:2 notes that Sudirman "gave the orders" for an uprising, and van Sprang:10 uses a similar phrase. Wehl:51 agrees, saying that the orders were broadcast by Sudirman. Sudirman was not responsible for all the planning involved, but he does seem to have been both informed and in agreement with it, taking a clear leadership role.

146. SR 10-3-45.

147. *Kaslan MS*:20; van Sprang:12-13.

148. Kinoshita:99ff.

149. In addition to the personal, diary-like renditions of Nishimura, Kinoshita, and Shibata already cited, see also RvOIC 006870 and 059381.

150. Figures published in SR 10-3-45, and accepted as official in Japanese reports of the period, were 22 known dead, 25 wounded, 6 captured, and many

missing. RvOIC 058803:16. The actual death toll was probably considerably higher. A. H. Nasution (1979) I:372 says 18,000 Japanese were imprisoned at this time, and van Sprang:13 uses a figure of 10,000. RvOIC 006958:7 guesses that only about 4,000 Japanese remained in the city, however, and on the whole this figure seems more likely, though it may underestimate by 1,000 or so.

151. *Kaslan MS*:20. The 23 September date assigned to this event by some Indonesian sources and repeated, for example, in Parrott (1970):89 is erroneous.

152. This stunning achievement was never forgotten by Surabayans. It was originally suggested—by the PRI, Sudirman, and the KNID—to dismantle the building as a way of underscoring the victory and its symbolism. *Kaslan MS*:21. This was not done, however, and the BKR used the structure as its headquarters starting the day after the battle. The building was largely destroyed in the fighting of November 1945, and the ruins pulled down in the late 1950s, when the present Heroes' Monument was erected on the site.

153. SR 10-4-45.

154. SR 10-4-45. The spot was later renamed Taman Kusuma Bangsa, which became a common name for cemeteries of this type.

155. For example, Dr. Angka Nitisastro in a 1971 interview.

156. The account in this and the following paragraph is based on information in SR 10-8-45 to 10-18-45. It is both ironic and curious that the ceremonies are mentioned in no published treatment of the early revolution in Surabaya. Presumably they were forgotten in the blinding light of subsequent clashes and losses. But the initial impact of the 3 October rites is clear from contemporary accounts.

157. A few of the 24 heroes were unidentified, which may indicate more modest social origins. Several more dead were later buried at Taman Bahagia and were identified by level of education, while others were interred in different graveyards, such as those reserved for Christians or particularly devout Moslems. As it turned out, Taman Bahagia was a modernist, at least partly secular and distinctly kaum terpelajar rendition of a memorial to the dead. It seems likely that the official death count of 25–30 (and 60 wounded) reflected only new piryayi and middle-class victims. More ordinary kampung folk killed in the fighting may well have remained unsung, and buried without city-wide fanfare in kampung graveyards; kampung interviews, however, never mentioned this.

158. SR 10-3-45.

159. SR 10-3-45, 10-4-45, and 10-12-45. Pangreh praja of the Residency were asked not only to confirm their loyalty to the republican government, but to form an executive committee in order to facilitate closer communications with the KNID and Sudirman. The great influence Sudirman had on events is evident not only in the manner in which his decrees and regulations overshadowed both in number and comprehensiveness the relatively few coming out of the KNID, but in the 4 October announcement that a Central KNI for East Java had been established a week earlier. The chairman was

Sudirman, and the vice-chairmanship was shared by Doel Arnowo and Mr. Surjadi, a well-known lawyer and KBI leader living at the time in Bondowoso.

160. SR 10-4-45.

161. *Kaslan MS*:21. In a curious bit of continuity, the old steward of the society, and most of his staff, were kept on in their jobs by PRI leaders.

162. SR 10-6-45.

163. SR 10-5-45.

164. SR 10-6-45; *Kaslan MS*:22.

165. This is not to say that the PRI always was viewed with equanimity. Ruslan Abdulgani has noted in interviews (1971–72) that the PRI after 2 October seemed too extreme and violent to most members of his Panitia Angkatan Muda. At a final meeting held sometime between 2 and 9 October, that group decided formally to part ways with the PRI. Bambang Kaslan was the only individual close to Abdulgani who shifted allegiance, but several other lesser figures took more than a passing interest in PRI activities. Surely new priyayi figures, especially members of the KNID, also entertained doubts about the PRI. In fact, however, the PRI was much closer to these people and their ideas, to say nothing of the republic's organizational framework, than was often apparent at the time.

166. PRO W0203/2289; A. H. Nasution (1956):78 estimates that 10,000 weapons fell into Indonesian hands in Surabaya before the Allies' arrival. Kirby:331 gives a more detailed listing of about 31,000 weapons, including 25,000 rifles.

167. Interview in 1971 with the commander, Jonosewojo.

168. ARA AAS 97b/XXII/45b:12.

169. *Kaslan MS*:22.

170. ARA AAS 97b/XXII/45b:4.

■ Chapter Six

Youth and the Urban Masses in Revolt

■ The pemuda and new priyayi authority

Although the widespread Japanese (and European) view was that Surabaya had fallen into disorder, a perspective that made no distinctions between BKR and PRI forces on the one hand and mobs of arek Surabaya on the other, the cooperative relationship—leaning heavily on PRI strength—remained workable for some time. PRI leaders did not contribute visibly to the complicated negotiations in which Admiral Shibata effectively surrendered the few remaining uncaptured Japanese weapons and military staff to the Allies via the BKR and the KNID.[1] At the time they were engaged in posting armed checkpoints throughout the central city that even the Dutch agreed with run in an orderly, proper manner.[2]

On October 6, PRI leaders encountered a severe test of their determination to hold order.[3] An enormous crowd of kampung dwellers gathered outside the Simpang Club headquarters of the PRI, angry that PRI men were involved in the reimprisonment of the Japanese, and demanding a chance to seek revenge. A handful of PRI leaders rushed to the nearby Bubutan (Koblen) jail and saw another enraged crowd facing a small group of government personnel, most of them KNID members. Sudirman was present, as were Bambang Suparto, Doel Arnowo, Angka Nitisastro, Bambang Kaslan, Dr. Suwandhi, Sumarsono, Hardjadinata, and others. While the PRI and KNID representatives discussed possible courses of action, a small part of the gathered mob broke past the PRI guards who were in charge of the prison. Several Japanese were grabbed and, forced at swordpoint to a position in front of the crowd, executed on the spot. The frenzied crowd watched as the killers proceeded to confront the new priyayi leaders with the bloody sword, ordering them to lick it. Terrified, some pretended to do so while others edged away. Talks continued briefly, but at a crucial moment when the prison seemed about to be stormed, a heavily armed unit of PRI men frightened the crowd into dispersing and refused—at considerable risk to themselves—to let any more Japanese prisoners fall into the hands of the rakyat, the urban masses.

This incident has acquired a certain amount of notoriety, especially since it has been used to dramatize the nature of a generalized pemuda phenomenon, pitting pemuda against leaders of the older generation.[4] Later recollections of three important pemuda figures, however suggest that some finer distinctions need to be made. Bambang Kaslan, for example, has said that the PRI leaders were utterly taken aback at the proceedings and felt themselves pitched against a rising tide of mob action which they did not understand and in which they could not join.[5] A very similar picture emerges from the recollections of Sumarsono and Ruslan Abdulgani.[6] It is, of course, possible that perspectives have altered over time, but Ruslan Abdulgani in particular would have no reason to be retrospectively gentle on the PRI leadership, and the accounts of all three individuals seem to ring with authentic horror. There may have been youths among the killers, but they were not leaders of the reigning pemuda groups and their actions or state of mind cannot accurately be used to characterize those of the pemuda leadership, whatever they may reveal about kampung youth at large.

If this is not clear from interviews or other autobiographical material, it is confirmed by the actions taken subsequently by pemuda leaders, who appear to have been determined to prevent anything of the sort from happening again. The PRI information section was mobilized immediately to spread the word to the city's kampung that physical attacks on Japanese and other foreigners were to cease, and PRI guard units made particular efforts to protect Chinese and Eurasians.[7] In addition, Sumarsono and his closest associates, who seem to have realized suddenly that the majority of persons their organization had attracted in recent days had only the haziest notion of its nature and function, set about trying to define the PRI and its goals more closely. On 9 October 1945 they drew up for the first time a constitution, spelling out organizational structure, intentions, membership, and regulations.[8] The document revealed a PRI with a disciplined

231

attitude and political goals, and the hope of speaking for the rakyat in the manner of a political party. Eleven statutes maintained a balance between supporting the republic and the forces of order on the one hand, and bearing the standard for the less predictable "revolutionary spirit" and "will of the masses" on the other. While emphasis fell on the dynamism and revolutionary character of PRI pemuda, the group's posture was to "protect and aid official organizations to defend the rights of the Republic of Indonesia." A special goal was the nurturing of a united people, "a rakyat [molded by] iron discipline and socialist ideology."

On the following day, PRI leaders also officially inaugurated their new Simpang Club headquarters in a remarkable ceremony designed to make the point that they viewed themselves as defending both an independent Indonesia and an orderly transition to peacetime.[9] Acting on an idea that Bambang Kaslan has recollected as being first voiced by two Eurasians and Kundan, a prominent member of the city's Indian community, PRI youth invited representatives of all foreign groups in Surabaya to meet at the Simpang Club with pemuda and new priyayi leaders. The theme of the gathering was mutual understanding, and Sumarsono emphasized the message that the PRI intended to defend Indonesian independence without bloodshed or disorder. Sudirman gave a keynote speech reiterating Sumarsono's points, aiming his remarks especially at Europeans and Chinese. Despite a few strident calls for total war against the Dutch, one Indonesian reporter wrote, the PRI was not going to let a few "barking dogs" get in the way.

The PRI's firm opposition to the return of Dutch colonial rule was not altered, however. On this there could be no compromise, and at several points the spirit of cooperation was punctuated with allusions to NICA and the hostile attitudes of Europeans. If anyone were found aiding the restoration of prewar conditions, several speakers warned, PRI protection would cease and appropriate action be taken. Thus the October 10 gathering politely served notice on Surabaya's non-Indonesian communities that times and the balance of power had changed.

The approach was acceptable to most new priyayi figures. On the same day, Radjamin Nasution used his new authority as mayor to call for the registration of all Dutch residents, as provided by law; Sudirman supported this announcement.[10] Implicit government approval was given to PRI-initiated searches of selected Dutch and Eurasian homes, and to a PRI-popularized boycott against European customers in the city's markets.[11] It would be easy to conclude that rising pemuda power, in addition to the recent spectacle of mobism, as the primary cause of new priyayi willingness to support or at least acquiesce in PRI's actions. However, neither new priyayi nor, more importantly, pemuda sources encourage such a belief. The evidence of cooperation between PRI leaders and Surabaya's new priyayi leadership suggests strongly that the latter group hardened its own attitudes independently. Or, to put it more precisely, PRI members repeatedly brought new information to government figures, who gradually formulated harsher views than they had held earlier of the threats posed by NICA and the Dutch. Such an evolution of opinion was made even more likely as new priyayi came to see the restoration of Dutch rule as a direct threat to their own ascendancy.

Sudirman, for example, appears to have been convinced even before October 10 that the Allied representatives in the city, who were overwhelmingly Dutch, could not be trusted, and he took a firm stand on the issue. Earlier in the month PRI leaders had discovered that Pastoors, a member of the RAPWI committee, had been a Resident in the colonial system before the war, and they successfully pressured de Back to take him off the committee.[12] A few days later Sudirman dropped his earlier conciliatory approach and directed a polite but unflinching communication to P. J. G. Huijer, who seemed to carry the status of chief Allied officer in the region, accusing the RAPWI of being the forerunner of NICA and denying all further Indonesian assistance until detailed instructions were received from Sukarno in Jakarta.[13] This letter marked the final step in Suriman's effort to seize authority in urban affairs. The BKR, known since October 5 as the TKR (People's Security Force, Tentara Keamanan Rakyat), and the PRI were given duties to carry out on behalf of the government. TKR personnel became responsible for controlling and searching Red Cross offices and staff; PRI units were to be responsible for controlling former internees. Both organizations were involved in the planned arrest of all RAPWI representatives on October 10 and 11.[14]

■ The rakyat phenomenon

As their role in the battles with the Japanese, the burial ceremonies at Taman Bahagia, and the Bubutan prison incident indicated, an aggressive, violent atmosphere was building among the arek Surabaya, who became an increasingly decisive force in the changing urban scene. In the absence of firsthand, contemporary accounts by ordinary kampung dwellers, and of anything but rather impressionistic subsequent reminiscences by those close to kampung realities, it is difficult to know why, how, and at what speed the urban populace came alive in the way it did. A general picture, however, shows a potent response coming from the city's kampung after the fighting of 1–2 October 1945. Much of this response has been characterized, especially in Japanese eyewitness accounts, as wild, unleashed fury or untargeted and exceptionally violent rioting. The looting of warehouses and unoccupied Dutch home by bands of Indonesians was common at the time, as was the phenomenon of whole kampung erupting when Japanese or Europeans passed by.[15].

In some respects the situation might be compared with that prevailing during the rampok-filled days of March 1942, but in other ways the rakyat phenomenon of October 1945 was distinctive. It was unmistakably urban in character and did not spill into the countryside until much later. Additionally, the surge of mass sentiment was far more intense and dangerous than anything that had appeared earlier. During the first week of October centrally located kampung rang with the sounds of "training sessions" and the clang of hand weapons.[16] At night, neighborhood guards with simple but threatening weapons stood at the alert, and kampung residents threw stones and homemade bombs at Dutch and Eurasian homes when these happened to be nearby.[17]

The most significant feature of the October kampung risings, however, was their position in the context of new priyayi and, especially, pemuda affairs. In 1942 rampok had appeared in isolation from the typical responses of urban Indonesian leaders to the crisis of that time. Now, however, actions of the arek Surabaya seemed to flow in the same rough current as leaders' thoughts, lending them teeth and perhaps even a inspirational force. While in truth both KNID and PRI figures were quick to realize and worry about the uncontrollable aspects of mass involvement—even to abhor what they discovered of its murderousness—few such persons could truthfully say that they did not possess a measure of respect for this outburst of popular spirit. Doel Arnowo, for example, complained that the public had gotten out of hand, and warned all Surabayans that they should trust the government to do what was right.[18] Yet at the same time *Soeara Rakjat*, which tended to reflect the views of Doel and his colleagues with great consistency, editorialized approvingly that the rakyat were the motor of the independence movement and noted sympathetically that the urban masses justly were enraged at the prospect of a revived colonial rule.[19].

Whereas the new priyayi viewed the kampung world from a customarily detached position, pemuda leaders watched the winds of change blow over the urban masses with a deeper and more complex sense of involvement. Interest in the rakyat was already developed, and it sharpened with the advice older pergerakan figures frequently dispensed on the subject. Even schoolgirls who intended to become activists by joining the PRI were told by women with pergerakan experience to stop worrying about high ideals and simply get closer to the common people, to do whatever possible to unify the upper classes with the lower.[20] Educated pemuda who worked in factories and offices were reminded to serve the masses,[21] and everywhere young people seemed to pursue an outwardly egalitarian style, calling each other "saudara" and applying the same term to workers, kampung folk, and all but the most prominent of new priyayi figures.[22] The whole exuberant value system of scouting also came into play here: self-reliance, courage, forthrightness, and confidence were part of pemuda proselytizing in kampung and workplace alike.[23] Educated pemuda were involved also with the broad changes affecting kampung society in other, perhaps more substantial ways. The most important of these was the widespread and varied process best, though somewhat awkwardly, termed *golongan*-ization, the formation of smaller common-interest groups in or under the name of larger, society-wide bodies. This phenomenon shares some of the characteristics of the formation of *aliran*,[24] but is distinct. The word "golongan" as used here, and as it seems to have been used in late 1945, refers to a group that is limited in numbers and founded upon narrow, concrete commonalities such as neighborhood, occupation, or acknowledged leadership. Educational background was also sometimes a factor binding a golongan, but political party or ideology seems to have been of little or no consequence. Golongan encompassed individual kampung and factories, municipal workers in general, employees of particular types of industries, and a range of other classifications large and small. Underlying their formation were the different but complementary motives of adjusting to the new national order on the one hand, and providing for local order and defense on the other.

In its early stages, golonganization in Surabaya occurred at least partly spontaneously, in response perhaps to the activities at what came to be dimly perceived as a national or local-national level. The tendency of kampung, printing plant workers, and all manner of other groups to jell around the idea and name of the KNI is a good example, and the early spread of PRI membership into kampung areas had many of the same characteristics. Measuring the exact pemuda role in bringing about these responses is difficult, but it seems virtually certain that as carriers of information and opinions, PRI leaders had considerable effect in central city neighborhoods. The arek Surabaya appear to have felt the need to form groups of a size and type that offered both safety and familiarity, and yet reflected higher national or local orders.

Yet there was another side of the golonganization coin which, especially after the early October conflicts with the Japanese, glinted with the realization that the power of the KNID and the new priyayi was in practical terms still rather limited. Fearing disorder and aware that no single authority reached into kampung life, daring kampung personalities and, increasingly, small committees took on an unaccustomed importance. They seemed to see themselves in a scaled-down world in which their own priorities and defense were of paramount interest. These bodies were neither founded upon opposition to the new priyayi order nor intent upon promoting any ideological point. Vigorous self-defense was the primary goal. For better or worse, past a certain point golongan and their leaders tended to become mini-organizations in their own right rather than, as might be imagined from the names they chose for themselves, integral parts of a larger arrangement.

Broadly speaking, the formation of golongan was a phenomenon of the kampung middle class, and one in which youth were as much acted upon as actors. The most prevalent example of the spread of golongan outside of the kampung was the manner in which offices, businesses, and factories were taken over by employees, declared *milik Republik Indonesia* (property of the republic) and run independently. This so-called "milik movement" occurred first in government offices, probably under the influence of educated pemuda working there, but it spread rapidly elsewhere. Sometimes single places of employment formed golongan, but more often such groups jelled further into larger entities, such as the Young Surabayan Teachers' Group or Chauffeurs of the Republic of Indonesia.[25] In such cases the pattern was not one of ordinary laborers rising to take control, despite the common use of the term *buruh* to describe participants, but of white collar workers taking the lead, agreeing on a leader, and striving to close all ranks around him.[26] The circumstances called forth many of the qualities admired most by the arek Surabaya's kampung middle class, and for plucky individuals surely seemed rich with opportunity.

Within kampung walls a roughly similar course seems to have been followed. In September, individual residents identified themselves with the PRI, the BKR, and other organizations, and whole neighborhoods announced their founding of KNI branches. By the first week of October, however, kampung residents began to think more narrowly of their own safety and leaders made comprehensive changes. For example, kampung leaders called formal meetings to decide which residents would act as directors of the TKR in the neighborhood and which would send sons to join the PRI.[27] Kampung guards were armed and set on rigorous schedules. Some of these alterations were undoubtedly the result of outside contacts, especially the receipt of arms and instructions from PRI members, but for the most part they seem to have been brought about by kampung concerns and kampung methods of dealing with them. While kampung dwellers' thoughts occasionally still touched on the KNID and even Sukarno in Jakarta,[29] they were devoted for the most part to immediate realities.

The meaning of golongan formation of this type was simply that the authority of the KNID, as well as that of bodies such as the TKR and the PRI, weakened rapidly at the kampung and factory level. Golonganization consolidated small- and medium-sized groups, and it also gave them the energy and encourgement to act independently, even threateningly. Rakyat energy, increased and atomized in this way, soon became unharnessable. Even *Soeara Rakjat* complained that the general order was unraveling.[29] Kampung forced all who wished to enter to wear red-and-white lapel buttons, chauffeurs' groups established their own armed units, barricades appeared randomly in the city, and rampok was on the rise.

■ Mass Violence and the pemuda response

That golongan formation had begun to alter the pattern of Surabayan affairs was clear by the second week in October. The KNID, whose members were sensitive to the fragmentation of authority around them, went about its duties with a growing sense of helplessness.[30] Sudirman made perfunctory efforts to tie golongan in factories and offices to the regional government by requesting that they file financial reports,[31] but nothing was done about the kampung or the majority of ordinary Surabayans. The executive committee was expanded and readjusted to appear to represent more large golongan, at least in part because Sudirman and others feared what the Allies might do if they received an impression of divided authority when they landed in Surabaya, but in fact the committee revolved around the same individuals as before and was effective only in bringing the TKR and police further within the government fold.[32] No special attention was paid to the kampung population, which new priyayi leaders seem to have believed was reachable only through a slightly revised tonarigumi system[33] and a small number of pemuda. Weakened and confused, the new priyayi government came quickly to rely on the leadership of the pangreh praja figure R. M. T. A. Soerjo, who was appointed governor of East Java by Sukarno and arrived in Surabaya on 12 October 1945.[34] Initially frightened and uncertain, Soerjo was received by Sudirman and Doel Arnowo, who offered personal assurances of safety.[35] Soerjo's stern character and anticolonial stance eventually won him support among the new priyayi and from many PRI leaders as well.

The PRI leadership was less alarmed than the new priyayi by the rise of kampung activism, and less concerned about the disintegrative effects of the formation of golongan at the kampung level. Perhaps in part because the PRI itself bore some of the distinguishing marks of an extended golongan, its chief officers seem to have been convinced that whatever dangers were involved in doing so, the energies of the rakyat could be turned to good advantage. Even after the shock Sumarsono and his colleagues received outside the Bubutan jail on October 6, the characteristic PRI response in the kampung during the following week was continued support for PRI branches and subbranches centered in the city's neighborhoods; continued distribution of weapons and training in their use; and continued urging of kampung heads to strengthen defenses against Europeans and other potential enemies.[36] The new priyayi tended to flinch from the willfulness and sudden heat generated by the arek Surabaya in those October days; PRI leaders, whatever other concerns they may have had, were undeniably drawn toward and inspired by rakyat activism, challenged by the manner in which its glow appeared to illuminate their populist vision.

The strength of the pemuda-rakyat alliance and the compatibility of the PRI leadership's thinking with the forces sweeping Surabaya's kampung were soon tested. The issue was the presence of Allied representatives and Dutch ex-internees in the city, and it came to a head rapidly. PRI searches of RAPWI offices and European dwellings on October 10 and 11 are said to have yielded damaging evidence: attack plans, radio instruments, maps of communications systems, instructions from the Dutch colonial government in Australia, and large amounts of Japanese currency.[37] These materials deepened existing suspicions that a Dutch attack on the regional government was in the offing. It also may have been learned that the tentative date set for an Allied landing in Surabaya was October 14, only a few days away.[38] Sudirman and the KNID, however alarmed they may have been, were restrained by instinct and out of loyalty to Jakarta, which ordered that Allied troops be permitted to disembark and that "iron discipline" be maintained by the regional government.[39] The PRI leadership, on the other hand, was unfettered by commitments to the capital and keenly sensitive to kampung sentiment against the returning Dutch. The urban populace had already shown itself to be supportive in boycotting Europeans' food supply and in standing up to Dutch and Eurasians who ridiculed the Indonesian flag or other nationalist symbols. Armed and led, pemuda leaders reasoned, the rakyat could be transformed into both a remarkably effective weapon against the Dutch and a necessary extension to pemuda forces, which were in fact limited numerically. PRI officers therefore set out on their own course, convinced that the circumstances required more drastic acts than registering all Europeans, and they counted on the support of the urban masses in all they undertook.

Several days after the house searches and the inauguration of the Simpang Club headquarters, PRI leaders decided to pressure the regional government into preventing the formation of a NICA army. Pemuda representatives appeared at the offices of the regional TKR commander, Jonosewojo, and requested that he use his men to arrest and imprison all ex-internees over the age of sixteen.[40] Jonosewojo refused, partly because the order was a tall one and partly because he, like many other TKR officers, tended to be cautious and to wait for instructions from civil authorities. Since the PRI was by this time roughly as well armed as the TKR, however, the commander did not feel he could do anything to stop the pemuda from carrying out the plan themselves. Within 48 hours, during which time a formidable organizational effort must have been made by the PRI, all was ready.

There was no advance warning of what the PRI and its followers began at midday on 15 October 1945. Dutch and Eurasians, increasingly worried about their safety and too frightened to venture beyond limited areas even in daylight, resentfully wondered whether their lot was not worse than it had been in Japanese internment camps.[41] But they gave little consideration to any danger but random mob violence, which they believed would soon be quelled by Allied troops. Therefore, when armed Indonesians, identifying themselves as PRI members, appeared before Dutch and Eurasian homes, loaded men and grown boys into waiting trucks, and headed for unannounced destinations, neither the means nor the wit for resistance came readily to hand. The operation lasted long into the night and covered the entire city. Over 3,500 Europeans were picked up and jailed in the Kalisosok (Werfstraat) prison and a number of other locations.[42]

There is a great deal more to this story than statistics, however, and the intensity of the drama as it played out stunned observers on both sides. For reasons which should be sufficiently clear, the story is also one that has been either deliberately ignored (in subsequent Indonesian accounts) or misleadingly interpreted (in Dutch renditions), but it is nevertheless of central importance to an accurate portrayal of the pemuda-rakyat relationship. In particular, the ambivalent position of the pemuda leadership, in actions as well as thoughts and emotions, comes through with unaccustomed vividness.

The sight of armed Indonesians sealing off streets in fashionable European districts and driving truckloads of frightened, helpless whites down the city's main boulevards to prison triggered a spontaneous and violent reaction from the smoldering kampung population.[43] Crowds streamed from central city kampung shouting "Kill the NICA dogs!" and "Filthy Dutch!" as they followed the vehicles to their destinations. Unhitched from a larger order and burning a highly volatile mixture of emotional fuel, the kampung, which six weeks earlier had struggled to avoid overreaction and disorder, erupted in uncontrolled fury. By the time the first group of prisoners arrived at Kalisosok, a crowd of chanting arek Surabaya already had begun to gather. They brandished bamboo spears, knives, and an occasional gun, and shouted for blood. Later in the day, when other groups of Dutch men and boys were brought to the front gate, a huge mob threatened to attack the truck if PRI guards did not release the prisoners to the crowd. Fearing for their own lives, the pemuda hesitated only momentarily before forcing their captives to run a gauntlet that opened through the crowd between the truck and the prison doors, a distance of about fifty yards. During the first of these brutal trials, until PRI officers and some TKR troops managed to bring the situation under somewhat better control, virtually all the captives were killed or wounded as they attempted to reach the now ironic safety of pemuda imprisonment.[44]

This experience with urban mobism and its unprecedented, unmanageable violence surprised and awed the PRI. To some, the prospect of an unleashed, infuriated rakyat was profoundly disturbing. Others, however—leaders as well as followers in the PRI

organization—were affected differently and found themselves susceptible to the same feverish agitation that reigned in the streets.
Drawn to and pressured by a kind of mass hysteria, PRI adherents
took actions which went far beyond the bounds of the organization's
plans. Although similar incidents occurred elsewhere in the city, the
events that took place at PRI headquarters in the Simpang Club on 15
October 1945 are the best known and of greatest consequence.[45] A
central aspect of PRI preparations to deal with the Europeans in Surabaya was an attempt to sort out the "true NICA" personnel from
ordinary people. Pemuda leaders were able to identify major figures
from the prewar government—police commissioners, administrative
heads, and the like—but there was a widespread fear that many other
individuals working for the NICA were coming in undiscovered. The
original intent seems to have been to bring suspects before an investigative tribunal, determine the extent of their NICA involvement,
and then jail them separately from other Europeans. Soon after it
began, however, this procedure slipped out of control.

The tribunal at the Simpang Club, which according to most accounts was the responsibility of the investigative section of the PRI,[46]
began its work in a strict, straightforward manner.[47] NICA suspects
were brought under armed guard into several rooms, then forced to
strip to their underwear and await questioning. The interrogation
initially was merely fumbling, prisoners being asked whether they
knew van der Plas, for example, or had been members of the Vaderlandse Club. It became both more confused and more serious when
impatient kampung pemuda guards and mobs of kampung folk gathered outside the Simpang Club grounds shouting "Merdeka!" and
"Death to the whites!" It is impossible, given the nature and paucity
of existing sources, to assign any primary responsibility for the savagery that followed, but it does seem clear enough that what began as
questioning was transformed within a few hours into vilification,
torture, and murder. Uneducated kampung youth, who had never felt
themselves subject to PRI discipline and who were far closer than PRI
leaders to the frenzy which gripped the crowds of arek Surabaya, made
a major contribution to the mayhem, but the participation of some
PRI officers with good educations and new priyayi or middle class
bakgrounds is equally certain. Between forty and fifty Dutch and
Eurasian prisoners were killed, many of them in grisly and sadistic
ways, and the PRI leadership was for a time either unable or unwilling to stop the carnage.

The slaughter of Europeans at the Simpang Club was halted eventually by discreet interference on the part of several TKR figures and Sutomo,[48] who had broken with the PRI a few days earlier to form his own organization. TKR units guarded a handful of prominent Dutch who had managed to escape the first sweeps, detaining them in scattered locations near TKR posts. But the NICA hysteria did not subside, and in some areas of the city the rakyat turned with added rage against Ambonese and Madurese, whom kampung residents frequently suspected of being spies for the Dutch. To make matters worse, only a day or so after European males were jailed, news circulated that Japanese troops in Semarang, in Central Java, had launched a murderous offensive against Indonsians there, killing and wounding large numbers.[49] Encouraged by sensational flyers distributed by Semarang youths and by large banners screaming "Let's wipe out the Japs before they slaughter us in Surabaya too!" large crowds gathered before Bubutan prison.[50] There and at other locations where Japanese were detained, prisoners were dragged out and executed as they had been ten days earlier. For several days thereafter, wherever bands of Surabayans could do so they took bloody revenge on the Japanese.

Although many new priyayi and former followers of Ruslan Abdulgani's now defunct Angkatan Muda Committee believed—and continued to believe, long after the revolution—that PRI leaders encouraged the deadly events, or at least condoned and planned to do nothing about them,[51] this does not seem to have been the case. During the following ten days, amid growing anxiety over the Allied landing that was in fact scheduled for October 25,[52] the PRI made a number of moves which can only have been designed to improve control of branches and the general followership.[53] Special training sessions for individual branches and sub-branches were instituted, and clearer lines of organization arranged at these levels. As if to underscore the importance of the upper leadership, a new list of PRI officers, slightly altered from three or four weeks earlier, was printed in *Soeara Rakjat* along with addresses and telephone numbers for each. An official roster of branch headquarters locations and leaders also appeared. All branches and sub-branches were required to submit membership lists and activity reports (initially in two, later in three copies) to PRI headquarters, and strict regulations were issued governing membership cards.

That a more thorough reevaluation was going on in the minds of PRI leaders became apparent soon after these changes were made. In a message broadcast on the radio and printed in the newspaper, PRI headquarters personnel discussed the spirit of youth, or *sikap pem-uda*.[54] This was properly based, it was said, on an understanding of reality, and of the ways in which such an understanding might be used as a guide to proper action. Taking undisciplined action on the bais of rumors or hysteria was not legitimate pemuda behavior. No excuses were necessary for the desire to defend independence, but thoughtless actions stirred up the rakyat, with unpredictable consequences. Pemuda everywhere should listen carefully to their leaders before doing anything. Concurrently with this speech, orders came down from the recently formed supreme command of the PRI, saying that no PRI member was authorized to take or hold any prisoner without the command's express permission.[55]

In another announcement, PRI officers said that when they spoke of the sovereignty of the people (*kedaulatan rakyat*) they did not have in mind a rakyat unresponsive to the KNID and other government bodies, or a population broken down into self-centered and self-guided golongan.[56] Finally, at a meeting for PRI leaders at all levels, it was explained that pemuda bore within them the rakyat's hopes for a just and prosperous society, and acted as the "idea carriers" (*idee-dragers*) of the people, but the heavy implication was that interpreting or carrying out the will of the people was quite a different matter from acting on impulse, without discipline or leadership.[57] This was a far more cautious, and far more new priyayi-like, position with respect to the rakyat than had been exhibited previously. Not all agreed with Ruslan Abdulgani's notion, expressed on a radio program at the time, that the moment had come for a full synthesis of pemuda and government forces and thinking, but such an idea was obviously not entirely unwelcome to those making PRI policy.[58]

■ Sutomo and the birth of the BPRI

In mid-October 1945 the PRI gradually refined its populist position and inched away from a direct identification with the urban masses, but not all pemuda leaders agreed with these changes. There were some who saw and felt differently, and who moved, at a critical juncture, where the PRI increasingly feared to tread. One such individual, with a background and character peculiarly suited to respond to the growing tensions of the time, was Sutomo. Gathering a handful of associates, some of whom were members of a circle he had drawn together during the Japanese occupation, Sutomo resigned from his position as a minor leader in the PRI and, on October 12, founded the Forces of the Indonesian People's Rebellion (Barisan Pemberontakan Rakyat Indonesia, BPRI).[59] The name was chosen carefully to imitate that of the PRI in its spoken abbreviated form (sounded as "Bep-PRI"), but to differ markedly in content and thus reflect a changed focus. In Sutomo's scheme of things, "rebellion" replaced "pemuda" in importance, and the "rakyat" similarly replaced the "republik." This organization, stamped with Sutomo's personal style, gained instant public recognition and soon epitomized a new, fierce pemuda mentality. It projected in a uniquely potent manner a spirit of undying struggle based on a romantically ideal pemuda-rakyat union.

Sutomo was born on 3 October 1920 in Surabaya's Kampung Blauran.[60] His father, Kartawan Tjiptowidjojo, was a more or less typical kampung middle class family head, who worked first in the residency office as a clerk, then in a private Dutch firm, and finally in the municipal government as a mid-level assistant in the taxation office. Kartawan was touched by that distinctive pride of the arek Surabaya and the middle class. In family lore he counted among his ancestors Central Javanese who fled the Yogyakarta region during the Java War (1825–30) and who were close to the famed Diponegoro. In daily life a self-conscious pride was also evident. In 1940 Kartawan reported an unauthorized advertisement board put up by a Dutch business owner. Told by his Dutch supervisor at the municipal building to tear the sign down, Kartawan refused because he felt such an assignment beneath his dignity as an official. An argument ensued and Sutomo's father was cashiered without pension. He later went to work at low rank and pay for a large Dutch import-export firm.

Sutomo's father and most of his paternal relatives were aspiring office workers who seldom envinced an interest in political life or the pergerakan. His mother's side of the family, by contrast, had long been interested in such matters. His maternal grandfather, Notosudarmo, had particular influence on Sutomo. Notosudarmo came from Rembang, on the coast between Central and East Java, claimed Sundanese ancestors, and married the daughter of a Madurese religious teacher. He worked at various jobs, including that of police assistant in Pasuruan, and joined the Sarekat Islam although he was not a merchant. Sometime in 1914 he settled in Surabaya, where he sold Singer sewing machines and eventually became one of the chief distributors for that company in the Netherlands East Indies. It was Notosudarmo who exposed Sutomo to the pages of *Soeara Oemoem* and took him to pergerakan meetings to listen to Dr. Soetomo, Sukarno, and many lesser figures. It was also the grandfather who urged Sutomo at twelve years old to join the KBI, one of the most important steps in his early life. When the Depression struck, the sewing machine business plummeted and Sutomo's family, which apparently had depended heavily on the grandfather's income, found itself in reduced circumstances. Kartawan's subsequent loss of his municipal job meant that the family had to scrape to make ends meet.

Sutomo's parents insisted that he receive a good education, and instilled in him their own almost stereotypically middle class hopes for improvement and sense of individual worth. Sutomo graduated from a government primary school, then attended a secondary school but was forced to quit for financial reasons. He later took a correspondence high school course from the Netherlands, completing all but the final examinations, which had to be taken in Europe. Sutomo also had his share of practical education through a variety of small jobs that contributed to the family coffers. At one point, for example, he picked up and delivered laundry for neighbors, among them Ruslan Abdulgani's mother, and also sold newspapers to kampung customers.

Equally important was the learning experience he gained in the KBI. In retrospect, Sutomo credited scouting with not only reinforcing in him the nationalist ideas cultivated by his grandfather, but with teaching him practical skills and ideals on which to base his future life. The scouting philosophy of working hard, maintaining self-esteem, and developing leadership potential sustained Sutomo during his family's financial difficulties. The merit badge system, which rewarded a scout's efforts in assimilating a wide spectrum of practical knowledge was not an unworthy substitute for a regular education. At the age of sixteen or so, Sutomo became the KBI equivalent of an Eagle Scout, the highest honor the KBI bestowed. Only two other Indonesians had achieved this rank before the Japanese occupation.

Becoming an Eagle Scout brought Sutomo some local recognition as a young leader,[61] but scouting also made a practical difference in his life. KBI contacts introduced him to political activity, and he became the secretary of his kampung's sub-branch of the Parindra. He also took an interest in theater and eventually formed his own troupe. But in journalism Sutomo discovered an interest that suited his ability with words and served him well during the occupation years. Work for a merit badge in journalism led him to attempt to earn extra money by writing occasional articles for *Soeara Oemoem* and other papers. At age nineteen he was putting together a weekly miscellany column for Ajat's *Expres*, and he had gained local renown for writing a scrappy anti-Dutch piece on the rebel Sawunggaling, for which he was called before the PID.[62] Experience with newspaper work eventually led Sutomo, after an unsuccessful attempt at making a living acting and serving in the colonial navy, to a position with the Japanese news agency Domei in Surabaya. The work was to his liking and he rose quickly from city reporter to second on the Indonesia desk. His press card allowed him to move about freely, and he was well informed.

In the last months of 1944 Sutomo began holding informal but serious discussions with a few trusted friends about current events and the future. After the experience in Jakarta with the ill-fated New Peoples' Movement, these talks intensified, but no specific steps were taken and the small group of friends did not emerge as an influence on wider circles of opinion. Sutomo later looked back on those days immediately before the proclamation of independence and noted that the concern expressed over the future constituted the "real beginning of bersiap." Like many of Surabaya's educated youth, Sutomo and his friends were drawn to the PRI, the only organization in the city that seemed available and appropriate for them to join. Sutomo's reputation and experience, unusual for a person of his age, were recognized with a position in the PRI information section.

Sutomo's role in working out procedures by which Japanese-held buildings and weapons were transferred into Indonesia hands in late September 1945 became widely known in pemuda circles, and attracted attention to his leadership potential. Along with a few others who felt compelled to learn more about the situation, he travelled to Jakarta shortly after the fall of the kempeitai headquarters in Surabaya. In the capital he was alarmed to discover quite a different reality from the one he had left. British and British-Indian troops had landed on September 30, and by the first week in October trucks filled with Allied troops drove boldly through the streets unchallenged. The Dutch flag, long banished from Surabaya, waved above the former Japanese military headquarters in the capital.[63] Pemuda in several Jakarta groups, among whom Sutomo had made acquaintances several months earlier, seemed both pressured by Sukarno and the KNIP to contain their desires to launch armed action, and privately committed to a diplomatic strategy.

In retrospect it was probably the striking contrast between Jakarta and his native city that did most to kindle Sutomo's temper and imagination during the decisive period. By his own account, he made arrangements to meet with Sukarno and told the president about recent events in Surabaya.[64] It was possible, he emphasized, to gain control of arms by using the methods arrived at pragmatically in East Java. Sukarno was impressed sufficiently, according to Sutomo, to send out secret instructions on dealing with the Japanese to all Residents. Another idea, eventually more important, was brought by Sutomo to Amir Sjarifuddin, then the new minister of education. Suddenly acutely aware that the applied force of an entire populace, rather than merely government or pemuda organizations, distinguished Surabaya's successful struggle with the Japanese and Europeans, Sutomo conceived a plan for amplifying and channeling the power of the rakyat. Would the minister permit him to set up and operate a radio transmitter to inform and encourage the masses in Surabaya? Sjarifuddin would do no such thing, and he found unconvincing Sutomo's warning that the minister simply did not understand the rakyat. The most that could be allowed was access to broadcast facilities in government hands, and then only for programs beamed overseas.

Frustrated, Sutomo returned home on October 10 or 11 profoundly moved by a mixture of pride and disgust that "we [in Surabaya] already possessed freedom, while at the capital the Indonesian people were forced to live in fear."[65] Now on his own ground and feeling that direct action had to be taken to prevent Surabaya from sharing Jakarta's fate when the Allies finally landed, he attempted two projects. First, he announced that a mass rally would be held at Tambaksari field in order to gather the collective strength of the rakyat.[66] Second, he brashly lied to Sudirman and Doel Arnowo that Amir Sjarifuddin had given him permission to use government broadcasting facilities for the purposes he outlined. News of these proposals travelled quickly through the KNID, TKR, and PRI, where they thoroughly alarmed those in charge. Sumarsono, Bambang Kaslan, and others in the PRI were particularly afraid that Sutomo was going to try to "split the pemuda from the rakyat," since they saw his goals and methods as running counter to their own; they also reasoned that he had been in Jakarta at the time of the Bubutan prison affair, and therefore was not properly sensitive to the dangers of mobism. On several occasions Sutomo was detained or threatened with detention by the TKR and the Special Police, who believed he was a hazard to the city's precarious peace.[67] Even before the BPRI had been announced formally to the public, the new organization and its leader were the cause of great consternation among both new priyayi and pemuda leaders in Surabaya.

▪ The BPRI and the pemuda-rakyat relationship

The initial **BPRI** message which appeared in the 13 October 1945 edition of *Soeara Rakjat* was succinct and straightforward. It said that the organization was being formed because the republic's diplomatic struggle with the Allies needed the support of the rakyat, who already had shown their spirit and loyalty. The **BPRI** would work to strengthen the "extremist" nature of the masses (*semangat rakyat yang bersifat extremistis*), by which was meant their preference for direct action and a rough sort of egalitarianism. The organization already had received the blessing of leading groups among the arek Surabaya, such as becak drivers, chauffeurs, and food-sellers. "This group is extremist," Sutomo's statement proclaimed, "and together with the rakyat it will mount a rebellion, will make blood flow, if the sovereignty of the republic is threatened or the honor of our leaders is besmirched as they follow the path of negotiation." Much of the character of the **BPRI** derived from the four men who had met with Sutomo until late in the evening of October 12 at Jalan Billiton 7 to form the new group. (Two more were chosen as members in absentia, and three persons were added after the official announcement appeared.[68])

The original four were Abdullah, Sumarno, Asmanu, and Amiadji. Abdullah was between 35 and 40 years old, and had been educated at least to the secondary school level in Dutch schools. His special claim on Sutomo's attention derived from his modest kampung fame as one of the mutineers on the "Zeven Provinciën." According to several perons who knew him in the 1940s, he was full of spirit and expressed a determinedly anticolonial attitude; these attributes more than compensated for the fact that his parents were from established Central Javanese pangreh praja families. His experience in the Dutch navy made him a likely replacement in Sutomo's circle for Malikin, who reportedly had been killed while on duty. Sumarno, between 28 and 30 years old in 1945, was a native Surabayan educated in Dutch schools above the primary level. He spoke Dutch quite acceptably. The son of a Kampung Tembok resident who had managed to work himself up to the position of government school inspector, Sumarno was employed for a long time as an office worker in the Dutch sugar syndicate and, later, in the Japanese office controlling sugar and other plantations in East Java.[69] Asmanu was born in Central Java but came to Surabaya when still a child, after the death of his mid-level priyayi parents. He lived with an uncle in Kampung Kedungklinter, and he was educated in Dutch schools at least through the primary level. He belonged to the KBI, where he knew, but was not a close friend of, Sutomo. At the age of 18 Asmanu developed an interest in politics and joined the Gerindo, but he did not become involved deeply in pergerakan activities. During the occupation he avoided becoming employed or being pulled into a Japanese youth group, spending most of his time in the kampung, where he was known as an independent-minded young man and a boxing enthusiast.[70] Amiadji was a life-long resident of Kampung Tembok, who was educated in Dutch primary and vocational schools.[71] He was approximately 27 years old in 1945. The son of a Moslem leader with Nahdlatul Ulama connections, and a blue collar worker himself in Surabaya's garages and machine-shops, Amiadji had broad associations with the city's kampung middle class.[72]

The five men had concluded that "the rakyat had no understanding of politics,[73] a notion which, coupled with the fear that the PRI lacked the will to pursue an all-out struggle against the return of colonial rule, brought them to a different path of action. Aware that they would be contravening the established government and its methods,[74] the five came to depend on symbolism, rhetoric, and the spirit of golonganization to create a massive effort which, though not organizationally whole, was emotionally complete. At a time when the PRI leadership was spending much of its time contacting large and small groups, particularly those with weapons, and trying to work them into the PRI organizational scheme, Sutomo and his friends began coaxing them into existence and offering the BPRI rubric as one under which they could feel at home but not have their independence of action hindered.[75] Actual and fanciful golongan were enumerated, and an appropriate approach to each was devised. This was not precision planning, but neither was it merely a compulsive action. Largely because the original members did not believe they represented a full complement of social levels and occupations, they chose several additional BPRI leaders. The first two, Suluh Hangsono and Sudjarwo, were named in the newspaper announcement before they could be contacted, and they were not present at the initial meeting. Suluh Hangsono was the youngest and also the best-educated member of the BPRI founders. Approximately 21 years old in 1945, he was studying dentistry during the occupation. His parents were of priyayi background and his father was a well-paid office employee. This social background and rather exalted educational status set Suluh Hangsono apart from the rest, a friend of the kampung but not a kampung person. He was to be useful in contacting educated youth and their families.[76] Sudjarwo, who was about 28 years old in 1945, graduated from Taman Siswa schools and came to Surabaya from Blitar, East Java, as a boy. He seems to have been the only genuinely politically oriented individual among the BPRI leaders, but his real attraction for the founding group was his reputation as one of the first persons in Surabaya to wrest a weapon from a Japanese.

Among the three additions made a day later, Oesman (also known as Oesmanadji) was about 25 years old and had a Dutch-style primary education. His spoken Dutch, however, was comparatively poor, and Oesman was chosen primarily because he possessed a common touch and humor that was much appreciated by ordinary kampung folk. Since both he and his father were merchants, they had many acquaintances among the kampung middle class. In addition to this distinct advantage, Oesman also had a reputation for being exceptionally brave. Subedjo, whose age and education are not entirely certain, was probably in his mid 20s and a graduate of Dutch-style secondary schools. His parents were priyayi of high status, and he had worked in the municipal government for some time. Kandar, also known as Brewok, was the son of a mid-level pangreh praja. Nothing more is known about him.[77]

It is perhaps easier to say what the BPRI was not than to work out a statement of definition, a circumstance which may reflect accurately Sutomo's own thoughts when founding the organization. To begin with, the BPRI was emphatically not a pemuda group, and was certainly not built on anything like the PRI model. The differences were many, but most important were Sutomo's deliberate cultivation of persons of all ages and backgrounds, and his disregard for formal lines of organization. Although the BPRI generally has been understood—in both Indonesian historiography and in Western works on the Indonesian revolution—as the epitome of pemuda activism, and Sutomo himself as the model of a pemuda leader, this view fails to take into account Sutomo's intentions when starting the group and ignores the realities of the PRI and other pemuda organizations that preceded it. As Sutomo later made a practice of noting, the BPRI had no political sophistication or pretensions, its only goal being to prevent the reestablishment of colonial rule by means of mass action. PRI leaders, who prided themselves on at least some political understanding even if they consciously avoided making the early PRI into an obviously political association, saw such an attitude as naive and dangerous.[78] Other pemuda and new priyayi alike quickly came to consider Sutomo an agitator and something of a madman, a rallying point for the lawless, savage, and mystical elements in Javanese life.[79] This outlook was shared and embellished by the Dutch, who frequently interpreted the BPRI and Sutomo's personal magnetism in terms of a romantic unlocking of the darkest mystical and Moslem anti-Europeanism that Java had to offer, combined with the most nefarious Japanese influences.[80] The BPRI, however, was neither a Japanese product (leaders carefully chose no colleagues with either seinendan or Peta experience) nor a band of uneducated, loosely principled kampung champions (*jago*). The latter point is especially important given the emphasis in many Western studies on this "traditional," even magical, element and Sutomo's supposed familiarity with it.[81] In fact, Surabaya's central kampung, with which Sutomo and his colleagues were familiar, boasted few if any such jago figures, who frequently were considered rural or merely petty criminal lowlife. Sutomo later wrote that as far as he was aware none of his fellow leaders were anything like traditional jago types, and noted that as a group they had debated the relative merits of trying to contact such people and involve them in the struggle.[82] Considerably later in the revolution, when fighting took place far outside Surabaya, Sutomo apparently appealed for help from the *carok*—jago-like leaders—of the East and Central Javanese countryside, calling on them in some of his more imaginative speeches, but he does not seem to have attempted to address a jago audience in late 1945.

Nor was the BPRI the spontaneously authentic voice of the Surabayan people, though this was the impression its leaders wished to give. Rather, it was a calculated exercise in what might be called romantic populism, utilizing intuition on the one hand, and contemporary technology—the radio became Sutomo's main tool—on the other to create the feeling and image of a popular will united and powered from below. This did not require that Sutomo or any of his coleaders adopt a mystical or even particularly hysterical view of the world around them, but it did represent the furthest point to which pergerakan rakyatist thinking and action could be carried. In this regard it is interesting to note that Sutomo's use of the words "extreme" and "extremist" descended in nearly a direct line from pergerakan usage in the 1930s, colored by the obvious fact that in 1945 independence was at stake in a different way from 1935. The BPRI called itself extreme because, in addition to taking the position that independence for Indonesia was not negotiable, the organization wished to trust and to identify wholly with the rakyat. This was precisely what Indonesia Muda had defined as an "extreme" posture ten years earlier. In the 1930s there had been no firearms and no crisis of the type perceived at the end of the war, and the BPRI's "extremism" undeniably took on a radially different complexion, but the line of thinking was much the same.

All of this was reflected in Sutomo's unique propagandizing over the radio, which began regularly on his own Radio Rebellion (Radio Pemberontakan) on 16 October 1945.[83] In addition to news, often prsented in several foreign languages as well as Indonesian, the new renegade station carried a range of encouragements, even incitments, for groups and individuals to pull together under the BPRI banner in an unswerving struggle with the Dutch. Some of the effort was so calculated that names of individuals were mentioned on the air with the expectation that the publicity would convince them to back the BPRI effort.[84] The tactic worked more often than not. Likewise, the shouting of "Allahuakbar! Allahuakbar! Allahuakbar!" (literally, "God is great!") before and after each broadcast was a measure calculated to attract the attention of Surabaya's devout Moslems, whom Sutomo considered a potentially powerful but as yet untapped source of anticolonial resistance. Many observers have noted Sutomo's apparently special relationship with Islam, and in Surabaya it is widely believed that he enjoyed the confidence and suport of Kiyai Wachid Hasjim, leader of the famous Jombang pesantren Tebu Ireng. If Wachid Hasjim backed any special group in 1945, however, it seems to have been the TKR.[85] Sutomo, who knew Wachid Hasjim from an interview session in 1944, said many years later that he never presumed to act in the kiyai's name, and that when he did receive the religious leader's advice it was of a homespun sort such as, "Tell the [BPRI] boys not to molest Dutch women and girls, as that would be improper and immoral." Sutomo pursued popular Moslem backing and deliberately gave a moral tone to much of what he said, but he was not a religious fanatic. He took Islam seriously but did not consider himself an especially religious person.

Aware that demagoguery and propagandistic brinksmanship had its dangers, Sutomo nevertheless believed strongly that words might prove to be Indonesia's most powerful weapon, and he continued to use them to the fullest. He saw a difference between deliberate use of hyperbole and the application of what Dutch colonial laws had called *haatzaai* (literally, the sowing of hatred), but given the proper circumstance he was willing to enlist both techniques. He was prepared to urge listeners to kill all the Europeans they could lay their hands on, even when he knew this was not a very practical measure, or to announce that 10,000 Russians and Communist Japanese, or hordes of Indonesians armed with venomous snakes, were poised for attack, even when he knew this was ridiculous. Most such rhetoric was intended for Dutch ears more than Indonesian, and for effect more than sense.

To a large extent Sutomo and the BPRI founders appear to have looked at their task in psychological terms, and the general public was not the only audience on which creative staging and other techniques were lavished. Sometime in early November 1945, Sutomo arranged a conference for a large number of persons who had shown an interest in taking part in the BPRI effort.[86] Carefully planning every step for maximum effect, BPRI leaders accomplished a successful ruse to foil any spies, then had the group taken by bus to the mountain resort of Nongkojajar. There, drawing on his KBI experience with the importance of ceremony and camaraderie, Sutomo stage-managed instructional meetings in quiet, woodsy settings which, especially for city people, must have been not only cool but, after sundown, rather eerie. In the dead of night the assembly was administered an oath of loyalty to the death. At this point there was a great deal of weeping, and few participants can have gone home unimpressed.[87] There was nothing mystical about these activities, however, and Sutomo, who grew up an intensely practical person in the manner of most arek Surabaya, quite consciously looked at them as deft but not dishonest examples of manipulation, or as he called it in retrospect, *ngotakatik* or "making everything fit together" in order to get a desired result. That was his stock in trade, a technique for which he knew he possessed a natural talent.

Sutomo and the BPRI proved instantly popular in Surabaya's kampung and in outlying areas. There was much in the brash, unadorned style that appealed to the strongest of arek Surabaya instincts. The underlying principle that was perceived in the BPRI's message—standing firm against oppression, but leaving room for individual action—reflected long-held values of kampung folk. In addition, it was recognized widely that the BPRI offered a role for all people, not merely pemuda, and this answered a frustration already beginning to surface in some neighborhoods. In one kampung, for example, residents felt moved to establish a group pointedly called the Indonesian Older Generation (Angkatan Tua Indonesia). An editorial reacted to the formation of the group by saying that it underscored the obvious truth that "the struggle for independence is not at all the monopoly of pemuda . . . it is a matter of individual consciousness. No two people are the same, and each can fulfill what seem to be his own responsibilities.[88]

In kampung eyes the BPRI seemed, in contrast to the TKR and

PRI, closer to the kampung than to officialdom and less identified with the government; for the arek Surabaya this was all to the good, even with the government now in Indonesian hands.[89] In a number of Surabaya's neighborhoods, local leaders between 30 and 40 years old mobilized residents in response to the BPRI call, utilizing already existing organizational frameworks to do so. Outside the city, low and middle level pangreh praja founded or had subordinates found BPRI units in their areas.[90] What is more, kampung residents seemed to understand instinctively what Sutomo was attempting to accomplish with his rhetoric. "We had no arms," one resident of a central city kampung observed later, "so we were forced to say things calculated to build morale."[91] Thus, although it was highly unlikely that he consulted many becak drivers before announcing that they were part of the popular support behind the BPRI, Sutomo did in fact capture their imagination and rapidly became a kind of popular champion. Prefabricated or not, his efforts eventually earned him the sobriquet "Bung Tomo," or "Compatriot [Su]tomo," the romantic populist flavor of which long outlived the revolution itself.[92]

Sutomo's chief importance lay in searching for and crystallizing a singular opposition to colonial rule. Reacting to what he saw around him with as much calculation as intuition, Sutomo transformed the relatively narrow PRI approach to the problem of defending independence, which was a product of educated youth thinking in essentially new priyayi frameworks, to a mentality of a different order. In the BPRI conceptualization, pemuda leadership was clear but unspoken. No one discussed becoming "idea carriers" of the masses; emphasis was placed instead on joining the rakyat, even *becoming* the rakyat, and on expressing the popular will by acting it out. It was this distinctive attitude, and the theatrics accompanying it, which eventually came to epitomize the pemuda spirit of the Indonesian revolution, a mentality and soul which, far from being contrived, seemed to express in a single, spontaneous vision both the longings of the pergerakan and the gritty opposition of ordinary urban folk to colonial rule.

In the ten days separating the interning of Europeans and the arrival of the first Allied troops, Surabaya quietly prepared for what residents increasingly became aware must be a confrontation. The kampung and streets were not free of tension and disorder, caused particularly by the widespread fear of NICA spies and resulting sporadic violence,[93] but on the whole fighting subsided and the city returned to something like a normal state. Unaccustomed though they were to find so many Indonesians armed and confident—an attitude exemplified in the restaurant sign proclaiming boldly, "No Europeans or Eurasians allowed[94]—official government visitors from Jakarta found Surabaya

> on top of things with respect to defense and to the regulation of peace-keeping and preparative activities . . . [the population] is quiet and peaceful, but ready. Defense is truly in order . . . hopefully things will stay that way when the Allies land.[95]

Hours later on October 24, however, Sutomo's message to the arek Surabaya recommended something rather different from disciplined acceptance of Allied landings, which he said could only lead to efforts at recolonization. Reminding his audience of conditions in Jakarta, and of the experience of Diponegoro, who had been betrayed by the Dutch and taken captive while negotiating with them, Sutomo said,

> We extremists and the masses cannot now trust in sweet talk. We distrust every movement [they make] as long as the indepen- dence of the republic goes unrecognized! We will shoot to kill, we will spill the blood of all who stand in our way! If we are not given complete independence, we will destroy the imperialists' buildings and factories with the hand grenades and dynamite we have, and we will give the signal to revolt, to tear the guts out of any living creature that tries to colonize us again! It is the masses in their thousands, starved, stripped, and shamed by the colonialists, who will rise to carry out this revolt. We extremists, we who revolt with a full revolutionary spirit, together with the Indonesian masses, who have experienced the oppression of co- lonialism, would rather see Indonesia drowned in blood and sunk to the bottom of the sea than colonized once more! God will protect us! Merdeka![96]

This message suggested that in the days ahead a great deal would depend on British skill at separating their mission from that of the Dutch and their NICA.

■ The arek Surabaya and the defense of Surabaya[97]

When the 49th Indian Infantry Brigade under the command of Brigadier A. W. S. Mallaby approached Surabaya and landed there on 25 October 1945, the city was bristling in a manner that British officers had not been prepared to understand. The city lay silent, but visible on the walls and buildings just past the harbor area were painted slogans—in English—indicating a fierce desire to defend Indonesia's independence. Allied intelligence regarding Java was notoriously poor, and where Surabaya and East Java were concerned it was particularly ill-informed; the 49th brigade reached its destination still under the impression that "Surabaya would be an easier assignment than [Jakarta] because there were no Dutch to complicate matters.[98] British and British-Indian servicemen received pamphlets designed to help them understand Indonesians, warning against color prejudice, evincing some skepticism about prewar democracy, and reminding soldiers that they were "in his [the Indonesian's] country" and ought to behave accordingly.[99] But the British forces had no way of sensing beforehand the tensions that already had built up over their prospective landing in Surabaya, and knew nothing of the developments which had taken place there in government and military affairs. Additionally, there were several officers in the 49th Brigade who were not inclined to act or speak delicately with Indonesians, or to acquire an understanding of their sensitivities. This circumstance made a bad set of conditions worse, resulting almost immediately in contention. Following a strained initial exchange of signal lamp communications, Indonesians of the Naval TKR saw the British preparing to land troops. Nervously they signaled, "Before your landing wait for orders from Moestopo," but Mallaby promptly shot back, "We take orders from no one,"[100] and began debarking 3,000 to 4,000 men and their equipment.[101]

The British were faced with two very uncomfortable situations. First, every step they took on the way to performing their duties of repatriating the Japanese and aiding European RAPWI officials and former prisoners was likely to be interpreted by Indonesians as an act against them and their independence. When Mallaby sought to establish his headquarters, for example, the obvious site was the one used since September by the Naval TKR, and Indonesians were not only asked to vacate the place but to take down their flag as well. The impact of this event on Indonesian attitudes toward the Allied forces was devastating and immediately visible to all who cared to look.[102] Second, the British had no choice but to speak with Indonesian leaders, since they clearly controlled Surabaya, yet British determination to remain politically "uninvolved" dictated that they avoid appearing to recognize Indonesians as legitimate authorities. In practice British policy proved highly unsatisfactory on all sides—the Dutch were deeply disturbed that the British even spoke to Indonesian leaders—not only because it was unrealistic, but because it invited unnecessary equivocation and denied Indonesian leaders the courtesy they thought important.

In addition to the exchange already mentioned, the initial contacts of October 25 yielded other misunderstandings and one tentative agreement. Late in the morning two of Mallaby's representatives appeared at the governor's office requesting that Soerjo accompany them to their ship for talks.[103] According to Ruslan Abdulgani, who was an eyewitness, the British officers were received properly but were told by Soerjo himself that it would be impossible for him to make such an appointment, since a conference of East Java's Residents, which he had called earlier, was scheduled to begin momentarily. When the British insisted, Soerjo grew firmer in his response. Then the two visitors abruptly stood and left the room. In Soerjo's eyes this was a serious breach of etiquette, and he drew from it a Javanese conclusion. "Have no fear," he told his companions, "We have already won. It was they who first behaved badly and lost control." Despite this unhappy confrontation, Mallaby's second-in-command, Colonel L. H. O. Pugh, managed to work out a basic article of good faith with Moestopo in the early evening. This read, "For today [October] 25th, the British will stop within a line 800 meters inshore of the coastline of Tanjung Perak [harbor]."[104]

The next day a group including Soerjo met at the former British consulate and patiently hammered out the terms of what was hoped would be a more comprehensive agreement. After five or six hours of deliberation, Mallaby and Moestopo concurred on three essential points:

1) Disarmament shall be carried out only on the Japanese forces.
2) The Allied forces will assist in the maintenance of peace and order.
3) After being disarmed, the Japanese forces will be transported [from Surabaya] by sea.

Soeara Rakjat published an additional item of agreement, namely that Allied forces in Surabaya did not include any Dutch military personnel, but whether this was an official guarantee or not is unclear.[105] In retrospect these terms seem so woefully inadequate that it is a wonder either side agreed to them. For one thing, the Japanese had already been disarmed by Indonesians, and many of them jailed. For another, the second point of the agreement lacked specifics and seemed to place the Allied troops in a position of aiding rather than directing the activities of Indonesians. The welfare of former Dutch prisoners of war was not mentioned at all, perhaps because it was seen by both sides as too delicate an issue. Whatever the case, any good will existing when the agreement was signed evaporated following what Indonesians perceived as either direct violations of the document's sense or transgressions of its spirit. These were never forgiven.

Three events soon crowded upon each other and destroyed any possibility that a peaceful solution to the difficulties facing Surabaya might be reached. In the afternoon of October 26, small British and British-Indian units began to descend into the business districts of the city, occupying buildings, establishing armed command posts, and commandeering automobiles and trucks for their use. Several groups of Mahrattas[106] had even reached Wonokromo, on the southern fringes of the city, and established a formidable machine-gun nest in a kampung just before the Wonokromo Bridge.[107] It is hardly surprising that Governor Soerjo's advisors and many members of the KNID executive committee became convinced that British intentions were not simply to help keep the peace, but to occupy the city.

Later the same evening a British intelligence officer and a platoon of Mahrattas forced Moestopo to lead them to Huijer and a number of other RAPWI staff in various prisons, from which they were freed after meeting sporadic resistance from armed guards. Most of Huijer's people were reassigned to Mallaby's personal advisory group, but Huijer himself was ordered transported immediately to Jakarta, where he was held accountable for the difficult conditions the 49th Brigade encountered in Surabaya.[108] The operation did not contravene directly any of the official agreements but it had an acid effect on the fragile trust holding Indonesian and British leaders together. Moestopo, originally regarded by British officers as relatively cooperative, refused further help and, for all intents and purposes, turned over the field to Sutomo and the others who were railing for retaliation. The next day, indeed, Moestopo (who disappeared briefly at this time, probably kidnapped by BPRI followers angry at his willingness to deal with the British[109]) refused to give a planned broadcast urging calm on the populace, and in its place he offered a call to the arek Surabaya to resist.[110]

The final blow was delivered late in the morning of October 27. A military plane from Jakarta dropped thousands of pamphlets signed by Major General D. C. Hawthorn, Allied Commander for Java, Madura, Bali, and Lombok.[111] Previously dropped on Jakarta, Bandung, and Semarang, similar notices apparently had caused no great stir there, but in Surabaya their effect was disastrous. The impression conveyed by the pamphlets' eleven lengthy paragraphs was that Allied forces were proceeding with plans to completely occupy and manage major cities, and would establish themselves there by force. In particular, sections indicating curtly that "the only persons allowed to bear arms . . . [would be] members of the Allied military forces and regular uniformed police" and that "persons seen bearing arms henceforth are liable to be shot" caused alarm among Surabayans. The ultimatum that all arms be turned over to the Allied forces within 48 hours brought an angry response from PRI and BPRI leaders as well as from the TKR. Mallaby professed to have known nothing about the pamphlets before they were dropped, and some of his officers may not have learned of them until well after word of their contents had spread among Indonesians. In any case, the British felt they had no choice but to make Hawthorn's orders stick, and though Mallaby readily agreed to extend the deadline by another 24 hours, the highly unpopular provisions remained. Less than three hours after the pamphlets fell from the sky, columns of British-Indian troops moved down Surabaya's main artery, past the governor's office, posting copies of the pamphlet as they went.[112] Soerjo and those around him lost all respect for Mallaby as a commander and as a man of his word,[113] and on a broader scale the people of Surabaya joined in the conclusion that the British had broken their agreement of the day before. A sense of moral indignation seemed to grip whole segments of Surabaya's population, and this, as much as any radio broadcast, was a sign that the time for armed resistance had arrived.[114]

After a night of constant activity—rapid movement of Indonesian transport vehicles through the streets, and bold interference on the part of British troops, who confiscated weapons and trucks arbitrarily—October 28 dawned with an ominous pseudo-normality. At last, sometime between 4:00 and 4:30 in the afternoon, the tension gave way to fighting in many corners of the city. Against an opposition thought variously to number between 10,000 and 20,000 "regular" or armed Indonesians, augmented by mobs of 70,000 to 140,000, the small and scattered 49th Brigade had little chance of survival. It is enough to note here that within 24 hours many Allied soldiers had been killed and virtually every post or unit surrounded, threatened with extinction, or, in a few cases, wiped out altogether. Desperately Mallaby signaled Jakarta in hopes that the combined efforts of Su-Karno and Hawthorn could halt the battle and rescue what was left of his brigade.

The most notable feature of the bitter fighting was the role taken by crowds of ordinary kampung residents, who far outstripped in determination and savagery anything the organized groups seem to have

259

countenanced. In one opening sequence that especially horrified the British, for example, uniformed TKR men attempted to block an Allied transport caravan carrying Dutch women and children.[115] The TKR intent was to stop the traffic of Europeans, which had not yet been covered by firm agreement, and to take ex-internees into custody. Shortly after the roadblock was thrown down, however, the seventeen-truck caravan and the waiting TKR soldiers were overwhelmed by a mob streaming out of the adjacent Kampung Keputeran. This was the same kampung area which had generated such hatred of the municipal government in prewar days, and it seethed out of control and attacked the helpless whites. Early in the bloody five-hour battle TKR troops realized that, ironically, they would have to fight fellow Indonesians in order to save as many of the Dutch passengers as possible. Some were hidden in nearby houses and stores and guarded for several days from angry kampung mobs. Other passengers escaped being killed when drivers plunged through the barricades after the fighting began to subside. Between 40 and 50 women and children of the convoy's original 200 lost their lives in the incident.

Elsewhere in the city similar scenarios were acted out, involving different actors but always centering on crowds of arek Surabaya and pemuda surrounding British and Dutch.[116] Many of these isolated dramas ended in death for the Europeans, who often were butchered cruelly. The chief reason for the killings seems to have been retribution, but the level of frenzy was high and could be felt even beyond the city limits, where many Dutch and Eurasians were killed by local populations. Caught psychologically, not to say militarily, unprepared for "bestial scenes . . . [rivalling] the vilest moments of the French Revolution,"[117] the British were stunned and not inclined afterward to approach Indonesians neutrally or without bitterness. Indonesian leaders were taken aback by the storm they saw unleashed, but most could not help but see a certain justification in it. After a period of restraint in the face of provocation, they reasoned, the masses had finally lost their patience. "The rakyat has begun to move," wrote a *Soeara Rakjat* reporter, with a certain pride. "The rakyat alone, not government organizations or official groups, and the masses are now led by extremists and pemuda."[118]

The latter assertion, though generally agreed upon then by Indonesian government officials and Europeans, and subsequently by many Indonesian and foreign students of the period, calls for some qualification. It is, of couse, impossible to judge accurately the numbers of people involved or, much more important, exactly who they were. Wehl's contemporary and widely cited account, which for the events of October 28 speaks of "about 20,000 Indonesians armed and trained as regular troops by the Japanese and supported by tanks, and by an uncontrolled mob of about 120,000 men armed with rifles, swords, poisoned spears, clubs and daggers,"[119] pulls figures out of the air, and is mistaken in a number of other obvious respects. His characterization of the mobs as essentially uncontrolled, however, is more precise than he may have intended. By this time the PRI was functioning more nearly as a branch of the TKR than anything else, and does not seem to have played a role in encouraging kampung engagement in the battle, nor in leading kampung inhabitants. (Dutch accounts of this time occasionally confused TKR and PRI people, and in fact their writers frequently were protected from mob action by PRI adherents.) The BPRI and Sutomo, whose stirring radio broadcasts certainly played a major role in raising the standard of popular revolt, were not organized sufficiently, or temperamentally inclined, to take charge of the rakyat's surge in any manner that might fairly be called "leadership" on the ground.

Wehl's and others' contentions that the initial attack on British positions was anything but spontaneous is quite likely correct; it was almost certainly the product of quick planning by TKR, PRI, and police forces. But the implication that somehow the pemuda groups and others were responsible for orchestrating mass participation in the event is probably mistaken. What seems more likely is that, as had happened in early October and again in the middle of the month, the arek Surabaya were stirred to action initially by the movements of armed Indonesian groups and, energies raised to a feverish height, quickly overtook their examples in sheer fury. The ferocity of the arek Surabaya at this time was untutored, and it rapidly came to drive, rather than be driven by, pemuda forces.

Here another warning is in order. Both Europeans and Indonesian leaders in late 1945 tended, for somewhat different reasons, to lump under the rubric "pemuda" a wide variety of people. Indeed, the word swiftly was drained of what limited specificity it possessed, and was used to refer to army and youth organization leaders, members or followers of such organizations, gangs and bands of hoodlums, and more indiscriminately still to kampung mobs and crowds. In short, "pemuda" was generalized beyond any real usefulness, with the result that in some important respects the pemuda role in events came to be enlarged unrealistically. The significance of the general urban populace—the arek Surabaya—and the possibility of their acting independently and, frequently, in opposition to the established principles of pemuda organization has been seriously underestimated. Sutomo's **BPRI**, it is worth reiterating, was not strictly speaking a pemuda group, but one which extended its vision much further and sought to generate heat from an entire society. That it was successful in this task has as much to do with the state of the rakyat at the time as with the leadership of Sutomo and his group.

Sukarno arrived late in the morning of October 29 with Vice-President Hatta and Amir Sjarifuddin, "amidst a hail of bullets."[120] Long distance discussion with Mallaby produced a rough cease-fire agreement, the general sense of which began to filter down to certain groups of Allied and Indonesian soldiers in the late afternoon. The six provisions of the text were not broadcast until sometime between 6:30 and 9:00 in the evening, when Sukarno announced the truce. The key elements in this agreement, which was intended to last only until more permanent terms could be worked out with Hawthorn the next day, were that hostilities would cease and freedom of movement be guaranteed by both sides. The safety of former internees was to be guaranteed. Hatta, Sjarifuddin, and Sutomo also spoke on the radio and indicated that discipline was called for in this situation. Indonesians were not opposed to the Allies, they said, but only to those who wished to subvert the independence of the republic, and everyone knew who that was. The broadcast ended with Mallaby reading the agreement in English for the benefit of his troops.[121]

Neither side appears to have held to the cease-fire, and when Hawthorn reached Surabaya in the early morning of October 30, sporadic shooting continued. Portions of the 49th Brigade were still isolated and embattled. Indonesians were incensed because they believed they had proof that Mallaby's contingent included Dutch military men posing as British officers and even British-Indian troops.[122] At a seemingly unmanageably large meeting at the governor's office, a discussion was begun on the terms of agreement that might offer a way out of the conflict.[123] With the sounds of Indonesian-operated tanks in the street and crowds of people around the building, four main issues were gradually and tensely settled. First, the pamphlet of the 27th was disavowed and the TKR and other armed organizations allowed to keep their weapons. Second, the Allies relinquished the right to guard most areas of the city, except where their own troops were stationed in the harbor district (where guard duty was shared with Indonesians) and in the Darmo European quarter (where Allied troops held full power). Third, ex-internees in Darmo, mostly women and children, were guaranteed passage to the harbor in Allied vehicles. Last, a Contact Bureau was established, largely at the insistence of the Indonesians, who saw it as a mechanism to prevent the British from going back on their word.[124]

These terms, spelled out in some detail in eight articles, were broadcast immediately over the government radio station and Sutomo's Radio Pemberontakan. The Contact Bureau set about making plans to spread the news in other ways, among them posting hastily printed handbills. Gunfire and explosions continued throughout the day, especially where large crowds of people surrounded prominent positions taken up by Allied units, but they seemed to be decreasing. Sukarno and Hawthorn flew back to Jakarta satisfied that their journey had been successful. Hours later, however, Mallaby and several cars full of Indonesian and British members of the Contact Bureau went to Internatio Square in Surabaya's financial district. They were determined to use their presence to stop a battle that had been brewing there for some time. Under circumstances that have since caused a great deal of speculation, the car occupied by Mallaby and several others was blown up and Mallaby was killed.[125]

The British, bitter and deeply embarrassed by the loss of Mallaby and hundreds of troops,[126] took a predictably hard line in subsequent efforts to accomplish the tasks for which they had been sent. On October 31 General Phillip Christison, Commander of the Allied Forces in Southeast Asia, threatened to "bring the whole weight of [Allied] sea, land, and air forces and all the weapons of modern war" to bear on Surabaya if the perpetrators of the "foul murder" of the 49th Brigade commander were not turned over. [127] Archival material suggests strongly, however, that from that moment plans were pieced quickly together to take Surabaya by force under any circumstances. Although British officers for the most part were contemptuous of typical Dutch "die-hard imperialist" attitudes and their desire to "shoot their way back to power,"[128] they were incensed that Mallaby had been killed after the cease-fire announcement. They unrealistically treated that tragedy as a more or less planned event and blamed the Indonesian government and pemuda leaders. British tempers also were raised by the discovery that, after Mallaby's death, Indonesians everywhere seemed to have the impression that their forces had brought the British to their knees in Surabaya.[129]

On 1 November 1945 the 5th Division, with 24,000 troops and equipment that included 24 Sherman tanks and 24 armed aircraft, was ordered to head from its position off Jakarta to Surabaya and landed piecemeal between November 4 and 9. The original deadline for leveling an ultimatum at the "Indonesian rebels" in Surabaya and clearing the city had been November 5, but this was postponed in order to complete the evacuation of Dutch women and children, of whom there were far greater numbers than expected. Dutch intelligence originally had said 1,400 women and children required attention; over an eight-day period, however, more than 6,000 had been served.[130] By November 9 everything was in place[131] and the Division Commander, General E. C. Mansergh, was poised to impose an Allied peace on the city and its inhabitants. That the operation was a vengeful one is strikingly clear from the sense and general tone of reports and other communications that had followed Christison's original warning. In fairness, though, the accusation that Mansergh's purpose was blind retribution is unfounded. The most widely read Western scholarly account of the event describes as false Mansergh's contention that many European prisoners still were being held in Surabaya, and suggests that this was floated simply as an excuse for launching a full-scale attack.[132] Whatever may be said about the conclusions he drew from the information, or the way he acted upon them, Mansergh had his facts straight where even Indonesian Vice-President Hatta did not.[133] Indonesians had never relinquished control over thousands of Dutch males jailed in October, and in addition to the 6,000 or so women and children rescued in early November, Indonesians held 5,000 more in Surabaya and perhaps as many as 10,000 throughout East Java. As late as May 1946, it was estimated that 35,000 Europeans were held by Indonesians in East Java.[134] This does not take into account the thousands of Japanese held by Indonesians in Surabaya and in the interior, whose repatriation the British forces also were supposed to oversee. Almost certainly Mansergh and military personnel close to him were naive in their expectations. Reportedly, they were of the opinion that those responsible for the situation in Surabaya were "boy scouts playing with lethal weapons,"[135] but a path had been chosen and there was no going back.

On the morning following Mallaby's death, an Indonesian press photographer took a fine, evocative portrait of the commander's burned-out gray Lincoln sedan in a deserted Internatio Square. The midday scene was bright but stark, the car standing as mute testimony against a backdrop of 1920s-style Dutch colonial architecture on the left and, on the right, a large billboard that read "Once and Forever—the Indonesian Republic."[136] Similarly, the city as a whole returned to a semblance of clear-sky normality yet trembled with a sense of expectancy. Victims of the recent fighting were found and buried over a period of days, some in the Taman Bahagia used a month earlier, others in cemeteries elsewhere.[137] There were hundreds of dead, many of them unidentifiable, and kampung losses, though not immediately clear, proved to be enormous. One central city kampung, for example, took nearly a week to determine that it had suffered 193 deaths.[138] Residents of all ages and social levels were included. Municipal and government employees did what they could to encourage a return to regular city life, taking care particularly to keep businesses and markets open, and to restore municipal power and transportation,[139] but they could not dispel the atmosphere of acute tension.

Permeating the city was a new defiance, calm but firm and based upon a sensation of both unity and righteousness. Throughout the kampung of Surabaya, where residents struggled to deal with personal tragedies on a scale few had imagined possible, there reigned a certain pride and a vague perception that all classes and golongan were united. Men who had seen children trampled to death as they attempted to join in the fighting were imbued with fresh devotion to the anticolonial cause.[140] And among the new priyayi the impression grew that the events at the end of October had proved "through and through it was the rakyat who were right."[141] While there was considerable uneasiness over the application of violence, especially as it had led to the bloody extremes some had witnessed and all had heard, intellectuals gave increasing support to not only the idea of a well-trained TKR but to that of an armed rakyat as well. "In short," wrote the educator Sutan Mohammed Zain, "it is now clear that what the Dutch really want is to fight us to the death,"[142] and he encouraged all to follow the example of those who refused to compromise. In the KNID, where new priyayi leaders discussed the possibility of evacuating the entire city, hostile talk circulated about the Contact Bureau's apparent currying of favor with the British, and about Jakarta's efforts to get food supplies released to Europeans.[143] And as word raced through the city of Sukarno's remarkable October 31 address—which apologized to the British for Mallaby's death, ordered all fighting to stop, and implied that the arek Surabaya had allowed "a grain of arsenic to poison a whole glass of water"[144]—local disappointment with Sukarno and the entire national government turned to genuine anger.[145] Sutomo launched fiery, defiant speeches into the evening air, urging resistance and sarifice; the arek Surabaya not only listened but silently vowed their support.[146]

On November 7 Mansergh opened the curtain on a well-prepared skit intended to introduce the dramatic handing down of an ultimatum. He presented himself for the first time to Indonesian leaders in Surabaya, in a manner he calculated would "surprise" and cow

265

Soerjo,[147] and then issued a series of haughty, acrimonious memoranda to the governor charging him to be personally responsible for the chaos in the city and for Indonesian failure to carry out pledges made to the British.[148] Soerjo, angered at the tone and the accusations, mustered a polite but lofty reply that suggested Mansergh was himself violating the terms of the October 29 agreement, in effect ending communication between the two.[149] At 11:00 a.m. on November 9, Mansergh summoned Soerjo's aides to Allied headquarters and presented them with the text of an ultimatum that was air-dropped over the city less than an hour afterward.[150] The pertinent section of this document required that "all Indonesian leaders" line up on a main city boulevard at 6:00 p.m. that evening with their hands above their heads. They would then be interned. All others bearing arms were to surrender them similarly. If all requirements of the ultimatum were not fulfilled, the British would launch a full-scale attack on Surabaya begining at 6:00 a.m. the next morning.

There was no question of fulfilling the terms Mansergh laid down, which almost certainly were designed to be unacceptable. Soerjo and Doel Arnowo, among others, frantically attempted to reach Sukarno and Hatta by telephone (they were not in the capital, however, but in Yogyakarta), hoping to save the situation. They were not successful. Barricades went up all over the city, and sometime in the late afternoon of November 9 Sutomo urged the arek Surabaya to brace themselves for attack. "Our slogan," he said,

> remains the same: Independence or Death. And we know, brothers, that victory will be ours, because God is on the side of the righteous. You can believe that, brothers, God will protect us all. Allahuakbar! Allahuakbar! Allahuakbar![151]

At 9:00 in the evening Soerjo called for calm, waiting still for a message from Jakarta, and an hour later Doel Arnowo managed to speak with Subardjo, the minister of foreign affairs, who said that in the light of the government's failure to dissuade the British from carrying out their threat, it rested with the authorities in Surabaya to decide what should be done; if they decided to fight the British and defend the city, Jakarta would not fault them as it had done earlier.[152] At 11:00 p.m. Soerjo explained the situation over the government radio station. Shaking with emotion, he finished by echoing Sutomo's earlier speech. "Brothers," he began,

> . . . all of our efforts to negotiate have failed. In order to defend our sovereignty, we must stand firm and have the courage

to confront any situation. Repeatedly we have said that we believe it is better to be destroyed altogether than colonized again. Now, in confronting the English ultimatum, we will hold fast to that belief. We will stand firm, and refuse to accept the ultimatum.

When we face tomorrow and all that it may bring, let us hold tightly to the unity of the government, the people, the TKR, the police, and all the forces of the youth and the rakyat. Let us now ask the All-Powerful God for the internal strength and the blessing of the Almighty in our struggle. *Selamat berjuang!*[153]

■ Notes

1. Far too much emphasis has been placed on this event by both Dutch and Japanese, to say nothing of the British, who blamed Huijer for behaving stupidly. In retrospect, the arrangement seems less earthshaking, especially since it merely called official attention to the reality that Indonesians already exercised control over Surabaya, possessed nearly all Japanese arms, and could have overwhelmed the few remaining Japanese command posts any time they wished. Indeed, Huijer learned from Sudirman that there were plans to make this final move on the 3rd or 4th, information that may have convinced him to insert Allied interests at any point possible, regardless of the risk. (*Enquêtecommissie* 8A:597) As for Admiral Shibata, often accused of duplicity and of trying to prevent the establishment of Dutch or Allied rule, it should be remembered that he was open to severe criticism at home for turning over weapons to the enemy, a serious violation of military etiquette. In a 1971 interview, Shibata reflected that his underlying sympathy for the independence movement and his judgement that loss of life and equipment had to be prevented in order to conform with the spirit of the Allied orders were the inseparably intertwined factors behind his decision to hand over arms.

2. Stevens and Grevedamme:10–12.

3. This account based on the *Kaslan MS*:23

4. B. Anderson, using a 1962 interview with Doel Arnowo as his principal evidence, gives this event a rather different treatment, although his outline of what happened agrees generally with Bambang Kaslan's. B. Anderson (1972):155. Noting Doel's description of pemuda drinking blood from swords and thereby "imbibing the courage and bravery of the Japanese who had died at their hands," Anderson does not inform us that some of those watching and threatened by the blood-drinking individuals were pemuda, among them the

leader of the PRI, and does not describe their generally horrified response to the actions they witnessed.

5. Interview with Bambang Kaslan, 1971; *Kaslan MS*:23.

6. *Abdulgani MS*; interview with Sumarsono, 1980.

7. *Kaslan MS*:23-24.

8. The constitution appears in SR 10-23-45. All information and quotes in this paragraph are taken from this source.

9. The account in this and the following paragraph, except where cited otherwise, is taken from SR 10-11-45 and *Kaslan MS*:24-25.

10. The law invoked dated from the 1920s. SR 10-10-45 and 10-16-45.

11. On the searches; see Yoga:25-27; RvOIC 068665. On the boycott, see RvOIC 032388:3.

12. RvOIC 071004:3.

13. The text of the letter is presented in *Enquêtecommissie* 8A:599.

14. Schouten:123; SR 10-12-45.

15. See Kinoshita:106; RvOIC 032385:2; Nishimura (1962):33ff. RvOIC 032780:13 gives a particularly vivid account of Japanese being threatened by the inhabitants of long-embittered Kampung Keputeran.

16. Interview with Dr. Suwandhi, 1971.

17. The activity is described in a number of kampung interviews, and also is reflected in many accounts by Dutch residents who were present at the time.

18. SR 10-3-45.

19. SR 10-5-45 and 10-13-45.

20. SR 10-2-45. Here "upper class" was identified with the aristocratic Javenese honorific *ndoro*, and "lower class" with the Javanese *kere* and the Indonesian/Sudanese *marhaen*, the latter of which had been used by Sukarno so effectively in the prewar era.

21. Interview in 1971 with a kampung resident working in a factory at the time.

22. A careful check of *Soeara Rakjat* shows that in general the contemporary honorific *tuan* was applied to new priyayi figures, for example KNID member, while the more egalitarian *saudara* was reserved for some, but not all, pemuda leaders and lesser-knowns.

23. Kampung interviews, and interview with a former pemuda office worker who did such proselytizing, 1971.

24. The aliran concept is generally considered to have been fathered by Clifford Geertz, whose *Social History of an Indonesian Town* contains the fullest rendition of the idea. Basuki Gunawan has attempted to review the subsequent development of the study of aliran; Liddle has provided a largely critical appraisal. In these works, and in the literature in general, the aliran appears as a broad, vertical, socio-political stream essential for mass mobilization, Indonesian style. Golongan and their formation as described here for the period September and October 1945, however, present a somewhat different picture. It would be important to discover how closely the two phenom-

ena are related. Are golongan incipient aliran? Perhaps, but there is insufficient evidence with which to jump to that conclusion.

25. SR 10-6-1945, 10-9-45.

26. Interviews with participants in such events, and with an outside observer of them, 1971.

27. This account is based on descriptions given by kampung residents who seized a role in later fighting, contained in ARA APG 803b.

28. SR 10-6-45, 10-8-45.

29. Information used here and throughout the remainder of this paragraph is culled from the pages of SR 10-10-45, 10-22-45, 10-25-45, and 10-26-45.

30. Interview with Dr. Angka Nitisastro, who was a KNID member at the time, 1971.

31. SR 10-6-45.

32. What the newly shuffled executive committee agreed upon was intended, therefore, to be more representative than the earlier KNID, which merely had attempted to achieve a rough balance of points of view, not of groups and their outlooks. Members of the executive committee then were chosen because they seemed to represent gradually crystallizing golongan or *badan* (literally, "bodies") exercising or capable of exercising influence. The new committee, with each member's grouping, was listed as consisting of Golongan KNID: Dwidjosewojo, Bambang Suparto, Ruslan Abdulgani; Golongan PRI: Sumarsono; Golongan BBI [Barisan Buruh Indonesia, a government-connected labor organization]: Sjamsu Harya Udaya; Golongan Ekonomi: Soekardi; Golongan Polisi: Boediman, Moedjoko, Soeratmin, Jasin; Golongan TKR: Katamhadi, Muhammed, Moestopo, Atmadji; Golongan Masyumi: H. Ridwan, H. Abdul Hadi; Golongan Pertanian [agriculture]: Soedjoto, Ismoetiar. SR 10-11-45. It is highly unlikely that the latter four groups of representatives took a significant part in subsequent KNID meetings, but the bow in the direction of golonganized thinking may have served to bind some individuals more closely to Sudirman and government policies than might otherwise have been the case. This was particularly true of the TKR and Moestopo.

33. On 12 October, Radjamin Nasution issued a mayoral announcement that henceforth the following equivalents for Japanese municipal nomenclature would be used: tonarigumi: *rukun tetangga*; aza: *gabungan rukun tetangga*; ku: *lingkungan*; siku: *kewedanaan*. SR 10-16-45. Basically, the same system continues in use today.

34. This was the same Soerjo described above, 149–50. SR 10-13-45 contains a detailed account of his arrival in Surabaya.

35. RIPDJ:43–44; interviews with Sutadji and Doel Arnowo, who were present at the time, 1971–72.

36. See the personal histories given by the kampung men, between 23 and 35 of age, who joined or were encouraged to join the PRI, in ARA APG 803b.

37. Yoga:13; SR 10-13-45. The Dutch, who found their NICA currency boycotted in the marketplace from an early date, decided to make use of huge reserves of Japanese colonial notes rather than be limited to prewar Dutch notes. This policy not only angered Indonesians, who correctly saw in it an attempt to undermine the economy of the republic (not yet issuing its own currency), but the British, who did not like the idea of being paid in occupation currency. RvOIC 059277 and 059266. In some respects the Dutch decision to keep the Japanese money in circulation backfired, since in Surabaya a number of groups, in addition to the republican government itself, kept themselves financially afloat with the same currency, which they confiscated for their own use. RvOIC 059276:2 estimates that between 15 August and 10 October a total of f. 420,528,784.00 was taken from Japanese banks and currency depots. Sutomo noted in a 1973 interview that his group depended heavily on such funds, and continued to do so well into 1946, when the republican government in Yogyakarta sent him trunks full of Japanese occupation banknotes.

38. OBNIB I:146-148; ARA AAS 97b/I/20.

39. RvOIC 059385.

40 Interview with Jonosewojo, TKR commander at the time, in 1971. It is unclear whether pemuda made their request known beforehand to Sudirman and the KNID. Some Dutch reports indicate that their writers believed TKR troops took part in the roundup, but considering the trouble the TKR may have been experiencing at the time with the unauthorized use of uniforms and insignia, the truth of the matter is difficult to judge. SR 10-15-45.

41. RvOIC 030095:3.

42. The figure is given in Schouten:122. RvOIC 032385:2 notes that 800 others were placed in Bubutan Prison.

43. As there are no adequate Indonesian sources, the account presented here is drawn from Dutch eye-witness reports: Schouten:121ff; RvOIC 032385:3-5; RvOIC 068665; RvOIC 000387-44:4-6. Dutch participants, who might be expected to have felt that the crowds had not gathered spontaneously, almost universally imply that their impression was otherwise.

44. RvOIC 032388:3 indicates that about 40 were killed and 270 severely wounded. RvOIC 000387-44 notes, however, that of an eventual total of 5,000 prisoners collected at Kalisosok jail, 425 were wounded or sick, and that an unknown number were killed before reaching safety inside the prison.

45. The account given in this and the following paragraph is based almost entirely on Dutch sources. These must be used with great care, especially as they consist at least in part of police investigators' reports made several years after the events. In addition to the materials cited in note 43 above, the following have been examined: RvOIC 066724, 070890, and 070893-903, all of which are short investigative reports based on interviews carried out by the Dutch Investigative Service for Victims [of the Revolution], or ODO; Stevens and Grevedamme; RvOIC 02854 and 062073. There are no published Indonesian accounts, and the "Simpang Club murders" are rarely, if ever, discussed

among Surabayans today. M. Sapiya's generally complete and straightforward contemporary account, published in the pages of *Bakti*, breaks off exactly at this point. Two other accounts by principals Sajogia Hardjadinata ("Yoga") and Sutomo, mention little or nothing of the killings, and *Soeara Rakjat* is utterly silent on the subject. In a few cases interviews with contemporaries (but not participants) have been helpful in establishing some general points, but understandably all interviewees desired anonymity where this topic was concerned.

46. Interviews in Surabaya, 1971. The *Kaslan MS* lists the director of the section as Rustam Zain, secretary Jetty Zain, and aides Abidin, Deibel, and Boes Effendi. The Zains were brother and sister, children of the educator and writer Sutan Muhammed Zain. The Effendis were brothers.

47. A similar tribunal was set up on the premises of at least one PRI branch. It too started its activities coolly and "correctly."

48. Interviews with several persons who witnessed the events, 1971-72. Several Dutch accounts also indicate that this was the case, and the *Kaslan MS* implies the same thing.

49. The struggle in Semarang between Indonesians and Japanese troops began on 15 October and lasted 4 or 5 days. B. Anderson (1972): 146-48; RvOIC 058804 and 006762; *Sejarah pertempuran*.

50. *Abdulgani MS*. Sudirman apparently believed that the attack on the Japanese had been fomented by Sutomo, whom he summoned to the Resident's office and ordered to stop the slaughter. Interview with Sutomo in 1971. No other evidence is available to corroborate Sutomo's role.

51. *Abdulgani MS*. One reason for this was that the PRI leaders apparently refused to mention the Simpang Club killings or even acknowledge that they had occurred. Ruslan Abdulgani and others in his group did not understand how this was possible. The *Kaslan MS*, written in 1972 does not discuss the subject.

52. On 20 October (SR 10-23-45 says the 22nd) word was received by the KNID in a cable from Jakarta that the Allied landings could be expected on the 25th, and that the KNID should see to it that everything went smoothly and without opposition. *Abdulgani MS*.

53. Information in the remainder of this paragraph is drawn from SR 10-18-45 to 10-25-45.

54. SR 11-2-45.

55. SR 11-3-45.

56. SR 11-5-45 and 11-9-45.

57. SR 11-7-45.

58. Judging from the variety of PRI organizational changes announced in *Soeara Rakjat* between 18 October and 9 November, there probably was a struggle of ideas going on among top PRI leaders. It also may be that more highly educated leaders were being challenged by less-schooled youth from the kampung or, less likely, outside the city, but information is much too skimpy to suggest this as more than a possibility.

59. B. Anderson (1972):155–57 gives 13 October and the organizational name of Barisan Pemberontakan Republik Indonesia. Both are in error. The original clipping in SR 10-13-45 makes it clear that the group formed on 12 October and was announced the following day. The original name of the group, incidentally, was Pimpinan Pemberontakan Rakyat Indonesia (Leadership of the Indonesian People's Rebellion, PPRI), but this was changed to Barisan Pemberontakan Rakyat Indonesia on 29 October. RIPDT:916.

60. Biographical information on Sutomo in this and the following paragraphs is based on interviews with Sutomo in 1972, 1973, and 1978; Frederick (1978); Hambdy El Gumanti; and Frans M. Parera. Sutomo died in 1981.

61. Interview with Dr. Angka Nitisastro, 1971.

62. *Berita Yudha*, 4-3-71.

63. Sutomo (1951):42.

64. News of the regions was hard to come by in Jakarta. The main telephone lines between the capital and Surabaya were severed around 5 October, and even before that keeping up to date was difficult. Sutomo was welcomed as "someone from Surabaya," aside from his own still modest reputation.

65. *Sutomo MS*:32. Several sources, including B. Anderson (1972):156, and the *Kaslan MS*:25–26 say that Sutomo arrived back in Surabaya on 12 October. Sutomo's own accounts are not specific on the date, but there is reason to think that the return actually took place a day or so earlier.

66. The *Kaslan MS*:25 states that this advertisement appeared in *Soeara Rakjat*, but it does not seem to have been published there.

67. *Kaslan MS*:25–26.

68. There is a good deal of confusion over exactly who made up the original leadership of the BPRI. In some cases individuals not very close to Sutomo in 1945 have passively or actively acquired reputations for being charter members. Here the text of the original announcement, and Sutomo (1951): 59–63 have been followed. It is worth nothing that on different occasions Sutomo himself, orally and in writing, gave varying lists of names of persons included in his initial group. Interestingly, too, the collage of photographs of members published in *Soeara Rakjat* (reproduced in Frans M. Parera:48) is at variance with the list printed the same day and included in Sutomo (1951). The following biographical sketches are based on SR 10-13-45, and interviews with Sutomo in 1971 and 1973, as well as interviews with others who knew one or more of the individuals mentioned.

69. Sumarno was killed fighting the Allies near Surabaya in November 1945.

70. Asmanu died in a 1963 automobile accident.

71. In a 1972 interview, Sutomo indicated that Suluh Hangsono, not Amiadji, was the fourth original member. Both Sutomo (1951):61 and the *Sutomo MS*:39 contradict this, however, while the *Soeara Rakjat* article does not distinguish between the first four and the others. Since Amiadji lived in the same kampung as Sutomo did at the time, and seems more likely to have

known him earlier, he has been listed here and above as the final member of the initial group of four.

72. I have not been able to unravel the problematic appearance of one "Soedono" in the photograph mentioned in note 68 above. Is he really Sumarno? It is possible, but the same name appears nowhere else and because of the sequence in which the sources came to my attention, I was unable to ask Sutomo himself.

73. Sutomo (1951):80.

74. *Sutomo MS*:39. The newspaper announcement, understandably, waffled on this critical point.

75. Interview with a former PRI follower, 1971; Sutomo (1951):70.

76. Suluh Hangsono was killed on 21 July 1947 when Dutch forces attacked the barracks in which he was living. Barlan Setiadijaya:339.

77. Subedjo and Kandar, in fact, appear only on the BPRI lists prepared by Sutomo himself. Those made by others, whether BPRI followers or merely observers, omit the two men and supply other names in their stead. The two do not seem to have played important roles in events, and obviously have not been generally regarded as part of the core leadership.

78. Interview in 1972 with a former PRI follower.

79. Interviews in Surabaya, 1971–72. The opinion was not uncommon among KNID and TKR leaders at the time, judging from the recollections of several individuals who were there.

80. ARA AAS 97b/II/17:23; 97/XIX/27.

81. See, for example, B. Anderson (1972):156.

82. Sutomo (1951):63.

83. SR 10-15-45. There was some intermittent broadcasting done between 13 and 15 October. The official radio station, Radio Republik Indonesia (RRI) began broadcasting a regular program only a week earlier, on 7 October.

84. Information in this and the following paragraph is drawn, except where cited otherwise, from interviews with Sutomo in 1972, 1973, and 1978.

85. SR 10-19-45.

86. SR 11-5-45. The date of the conference would have been either 4 or 5 November.

87. Later, ceremonies of a similar nature were held at other specially chosen locales in Java, among them a place where Diponegoro is said to have meditated. ARA AAS 97b/II/17:24.

88. SR 10-24-45 and 10-27-45.

89. Kampung interviews, 1971.

90. Kampung interviews, 1971.

91. Interview with a pemuda participant, 1971.

92. It is hard to say when Sutomo began to be called Bung Tomo, but almost certainly after November–December 1945. The word *bung*, it is worth noting, was of Jakarta origin and was applied most frequently to daring activists with a populist flair of one sort or another. Curiously, Sutomo does not

seem to have ever been designated *cak*, which would be the arek Surabaya's equivalent for a comrade in arms or spirit. Doel Arnowo, for example, was known as Cak Doel, and Ruslan Abdulgani as Cak Rus. In later years the use of *bung* became cliche-ish and sometimes even a little laughable. Until his death, however, Bung Tomo always was given this title seriously, along with Mohammad Hatta and Sukarno. Sutomo's passing in 1981 brought that sort of unadulterated use of the term, and a whole generation, to a symbolic end.

93. This is vividly depicted in two literary pieces based on events in Surabaya in 1945. The first, inaccurate with respect to chronology but effective in getting across emotions and ideas among students and kampung folk, is Matu Mona's "Arek Soerobojo." The second, more ambitious as to style and more powerful in its portrayals, is Idrus's famous "Surabaya."

94. SR 10-23-45.

95. SR 10-25-45.

96. SR 10-24-45.

97. Several dozen major accounts, and innumerable minor ones, of events in Surabaya between 25 October and 10 November 1945 have been published. No attempt is made here to expand upon, collate, or repeat all the information contained in these works. Appropriate sections of the following publications however, have been consulted with particular care: Ruslan Abdulgani (1963) and (1974c); Doulton; J. H. B.; *Fakta*; Kirby; A. H. Nasution (1976) and (1979); Parrott (1970) and (1977); Nugroho Notosusanto (1985); Barlan Setiadijaya; and Wehl.

98. A ranking British officer well acquainted with the Surabaya situation, in a 1973 letter kindly made available to me by J. G. A. Parrott.

99. *Java Handbook.*

100. The only British account of this incident is contained in J. H. B.:76, but the story is repeated in many Indonesian sources, which attach considerable importance to it.

101. The exact number of troops apparently is not known. The Japanese expected an Allied force of 13,000 to land in East Java. RvOIC 006664:4.

102. J. H. B.:77.

103. Ruslan Abdulgani (1974c):26–27 gives the best view of the first formal meeting, which is not treated adequately in any British source.

104. This and all subsequent citations from texts of Allied-Indonesian agreements and Allied document are, unless noted otherwise, taken from RvOIC 058804:41ff, which contains complete translations of most of the basic texts. Occasionally spelling and translation have been altered slightly to conform with common usage or to correct obvious errors.

105. SR 10-26-45. *Fakta*:104 indicates that Indonesian officials understood the British also to be agreeing to recognize the Republic and to refuse aid the Dutch and the NICA.

106. Although many sources on all sides call these troops "Gurkhas," no units of that sort reached Surabaya until shortly before 10 November. Before that time there were only 2 units of Mahrattas and 1 of Rajputs.

107. SR 10-30-45.

108. Huijer only reached the capital, however, after a harrowing two-day passage from jail to harbor, sometimes disguised as a wounded Indian soldier. RvOIC 068665:18; *Enquêtecommissie* 8A:601.

109. *The Statesman* 12-4-45.

110. *The Fighting Cock* 10-19-45.

111. The complete text of one of the earlier pamphlets is given in the *Abdulgani MS*. It is likely that the item dropped over Surabaya was the same in all but a few respects.

112. SR 10-27-45.

113. Ruslan Abdulgani (1974c):30 relates that barely a half-hour after the pamphlets were dropped, Moestopo, Sudirman, and a handful of other government figures were in contact with Mallaby, who was shaken visibly by the news, which he apparently had not yet heard. The Indonesian leaders were incredulous that such a thing could happen, and never fully accepted Mallaby's denial of prior knowledge.

114. The significance of this moral aspect should not be underestimated. Virtually every Indonesian account highlights the feeling of betrayal by the British, who are depicted as lying to and trifling with Indonesian leaders. The feeling is seen as instrumental in pushing moderately inclined Indonesians to firmly anti-British positions. The British viewpoint differs. Doulton:250, for example, expresses the opinion that the pamphlets were of little true significance and merely "afforded the Indonesians a pretext" to do what they had intended all along. This is almost certainly not the case.

115. RvOIC 032368 gives a full account; also PRO WO203/2650d.

116. This account is based largely on RvOIC 071008, 071420, 066720, and 071224. Also Nederlands Gravendienst.

117. Doulton:253.

118. SR 10-30-45. The newspaper was not printed on 28 October, a Sunday, or on the 29th, due to heavy fighting in the area around the *Soeara Rakjat* office. The issue of the 30th was a one-page broadside, an emergency edition.

119. Wehl:55.

120. *Merdeka* 11-2-45.

121. SR 10-30-45.

122. No British works mention Dutch or British blackening their faces and donning uniforms to resemble—rather crudely, one must imagine— Mahratta corpsmen. Virtually every Indonesian source includes a reference to such practices, however, which have become enshrined in legend. Huijer does seem to have attempted something of the kind in his escape, and there were Dutch journalists and military who posed as Britishers, so that subterfuges of many sorts doubtless were frequently utilized.

123. Those present on the Indonesian side were: Soerjo, Sudirman, Doel Arnowo, Sungkono, Atmadji, Sumarsono, Ruslan Abdulgani, and others, in addition of course to Sukarno, Hatta, and Amir Sjarifuddin. On the British side were Hawthorn, Mallaby, Pugh, and other officers and aides. The only

published accounts of this meeting are contained in Doulton:259–61 and Ruslan Abdulgani (1974c):39ff.

124. Ruslan Abdulgani (1974c):40. Contact Bureau members on the Indonesian side were Sudirman, Doel Arnowo, Atmadji, Muhammed, Sungkono, Sujono, Kusnandar, Ruslan Abdulgani, and Kundan. On the British side were Mallaby, Pugh, Hodson, and Groom.

125. Some Indonesians in responsible positions believed at the time that Mallaby was the victim of gunfire from his own troops, and Doel Arnowo had such a version printed as an announcement from the Contact Bureau, clearly without the approval of the British members. RvOIC 056029 and SR 11-2-45 give the text. Parrott (1970) examines all available sources and concludes reasonably that Mallaby was shot by a single, unidentified Indonesian. British documents offer nothing additional, though one pertinent War Office file has been reclassified "secret" for undisclosed reasons and might one day reveal new details.

126. The most accurate figures appear to be those contained in PRO WO203/2650c, which lists 38 killed, 210 missing (and almost certainly killed), and 84 wounded between 25 and 28 October.

127. For the full text see *Fakta*:108–09 and *Merdeka* 11-1-45.

128. PRO WO203/2255e:1; *The Times* 10-15-45; PRO WO203/265b.

129. *The Daily Telegraph* 11-1-45; *The Fighting Cock* 10-31-45.

130. PRO WO203/4575; WO203/2255a. *The Statesman* 12-4-45 says 6,150, which is probably more accurate than the previous sources' 10,000.

131. It was discovered on 8 November that the expected 5th Division weaponry had not arrived, and help from the Navy was quickly called. Three heavily armed ships steamed into Surabaya on the 9th. PRO WO203/2650b:6.

132. B. Anderson (1972):164, drawing on Doulton.

133. Mohammad Hatta also mistakenly believed all Dutch to have been taken into Allied custody by 9 November. ARA AAS 101b/365-365.

134. RvOIC 061272:6–7.

135. *The Statesman* 11-1-45.

136. Ruslan Abdulgani (1974c):52.

137. See, for example, SR 10-31-45 and 11-3-45.

138. SR 11-6-45.

139. *Antara* 11-7-45; SR 11-2-45 and 11-4-45. At one point a local police commander requested British help with looters in the harbor area, and with situations which could endanger the evacuation program, but Mansergh refused. PRO WO203/2255b.

140. Kampung interviews, 1971–72.

141. SR 11-1-45.

142. SR 11-8-45.

143. Yoga:62. The KNID apparently took a firm stand against Jakarta's policy of releasing food supplies, even though East Java ended the occupation period with far larger stores of rice and other staples than either Central or West Java. The KNID refused to risk having these supplies fall into the

hands of the Dutch or the Allies. Jakarta thought this attitude foolish, as food was needed in other parts of Java. The Surabaya situation was behind the government's announcement of 24 October 1945. RIPDJ:126-127.

144. The full text is available in *Fakta*:109-110 and *Antara* 11-1-45.

145. Interview with Dr. Angka Nitisastro, 1971. The same sentiment is expressed, with tact, in many Indonesian publications.

146. SR 11-2-45.

147. This intent is made clear in PRO WO203/2650b:6.

148. The original texts of these letters are in PRO WO203/5570. Several are included in Ruslan Abdulgani (1974c):79ff. As Abdulgani points out, the November 7th letter handed to Soerjo's aides on that day originally had been dated November 3rd, which notation was crossed out in pencil and replaced with November 7th. The letter was prepared therefore before the November 4-5 deadline had been postponed.

149. Soerjo's own contemporary account of the sequence and flavor of events is included in Soemantro's article, written some years later.

150. RvOIC 064196 presents the original text, clearly made up well in advance, probably in accordance with some of the wording in Christison's earlier speech.

151. This excerpt is based on the reportedly transcribed version in Hambdy El Gumanti:59-61.

152. Ahmad Subardjo Djojoadisuryo:402-03.

153. "Selamat berjuang," literally "blessings on [good luck be with] you as you struggle," became a common revolutionary cry, but it had its roots in the prewar pergerakan. This version of Soerjo's speech is based on the slightly different renditions in Ruslan Abdulgani (1974c): 85-86 and A. H. Nasution (1979)II:379.

■ Epilogue

It does not matter whether one generation applauds the previous generation or hisses it—in either event, it carries the previous generation with itself.

José Ortega y Gasset, *Man and Crisis*

The battle for Surabaya, which began on 10 November 1945 and lasted for three terrifying weeks, proved far more desperate and destructive than either the Allies or Indonesians had imagined. The city was ravaged by constant shelling from warships positioned to the north and east; more than 500 bombs were dropped by Allied aircraft during the first three days alone.[1] Although the Allied command repeatedly announced that the 5th Indian Division was using "minimum force" and giving Indonesians every opportunity to avoid bloodshed,[2] the devastation was extraordinary. For the first time since the outbreak of the Pacific war, the city's electrical and water systems ceased to function, public transportation came to a halt, and food grew scarce. Allied guns tore enormous holes in business and residential districts, and Indonesian forces attempted to forestall the advance of Allied troops through the city by burning entire kampung areas. Although Indonesians frequently have been described in the European literature as fanatical and blind with fury, the Allies suffered from the same utter loss of control. When British-Indian troops and Dutch hangers-on reached the Kalisosok prison on 10 November, for example, they deliberately machine-gunned unarmed Indonesians amid blood-curdling cries of joy from Dutch prisoners; later some of the same Dutch rampaged in the nearby streets, looting stores for food and drink before the British could bring them under control.[3] Allied planes also were reported to have strafed the streams of evacuees that choked the road south to Sidoardjo.[4] Backed by superior firepower, the Allied forces sustained relatively minor losses, 14 killed and 59 wounded according to one official source.[5] On the Indonesian side, however, while the official body count was set by the same source at about 430, the real toll was estimated to run into thousands, many of them civilians; British military reports estimated 2,500 dead and 7,500 wounded.[6] As much as 90 percent of the Indonesian population left the city.[7] By 26 November, when British-Indian troops reached the Wonokromo Bridge, Surabaya lay empty and in ashes.

The significance of the conflict was not long in being recognized and has not since been in serious doubt. Technically an Allied victory, the battle nevertheless compelled the British to reconsider their position in Indonesia and to extricate themselves as quickly as possible.[8] In addition, the furious fighting brought the situation in the former Netherlands East Indies to the attention of the world, beginning the internationalization of Indonesia's struggle for independence. For Indonesians, especially in the longer term, Surabaya's heroic defense was enshrined in the public consciousness and invested with enormous emotional and symbolic power. Heroes' Day celebrates, on 10 November of each year, the collective memory of a "peoples' struggle" and of the principle of dedication to national independence.[9]

Yet in a number of respects the battle itself was a serious Indonesian defeat and an anticlimax to preceding events, especially those of mid- and late October. Nasution's analyses in particular, while acknowledging the emotional significance of the battle, point out that it was disorganized and dangerously wasteful of lives and equipment.[10] In every concrete way Surabaya was lost for the duration of the revolution. What is more, the struggle in November was not marked by the same participation on the part of the rakyat as often had taken place in the preceding month. The arek Surabaya emptied their kampung and evacuated the city, leaving the fighting to the TKR and its auxiliaries, and to several pemuda groups, which do not appear to have been exceptionally large.[11] A recent effort to highlight the three-week struggle following 10 November, portraying it as a culmination period and emphasizing its "higher values and intensity" as compared to earlier fighting,[12] is not especially convincing; in any case it offers little more than a shell-like military account. In an examination of the social history of the launching of the revolution, the battle for Surabaya is largely punctuation.

The degree to which the city was separated from the flow of its social development becomes clear in a brief sketch of its curiously stranded history after 1945. In this period, with the revolution raging around it, the municipality became a caricature of its former self, an enclave more precariously situated than the eighteenth century Dutch settlement on the banks of the Kali Mas. The British had considered abandoning Surabaya altogether even before the battle had ended,[13] and moved rapidly to surrender responsibility into Dutch hands. The hated NICA was replaced by an Allied Military Administration, Civil Affairs Branch (AMACAB),[14] but the change was cosmetic. By March 1946 the chief officers in this occupation government were Dutch rather than British; they included C. C. J. Maassen and F. W. T. Hunger, ex-internees who had been career colonial government officials in East Java during the 1930s. After May 1946 the defense of the Surabaya perimeter, approximately twelve miles around the city's center, was manned by a growing number of Dutch troops,[15] and by mid-1947 a hybrid variety of government had evolved under a Dutch commissioner (Regeeringscommissaris voor Bestuurs-aangelegenheden, Recomba). The latter position was held, after August 1947, by Ch. O. van der Plas, the former colonial governor of East Java. Despite a number of changes in nomenclature and position, the institutional framework remained the same until 1949.

It was a fragile existence at best.[16] Food sufficient even for the much reduced population was difficult to come by. As early as 8 December 1945 the AMACAB had to send representatives to attempt to barter for food along the battle lines.[17] In April 1946 six week's worth of food supplies remained in the city, and a year later, when half the wartime population of Indonesians had returned, the problem was even more severe because of late and meager shipments by sea.[18] During this desperate period, when most drinking water had to be brought in by ship, the death rate rose to an astonishing 91.9 per thousand. The municipal administration was swamped with paperwork and unable to count on the loyalty of Indonesians chosen as leaders in a revived precinct system.[19] Europeans lived in fear of Indonesians everywhere in the city, and huge numbers of "political prisoners" filled Surabaya's jails.[20]

Although a group of "new Dutch" spoke of disavowing the past, their views were at best naive and at worst, as even van der Plas took the trouble to note, pathetic. Every aspect of city life yielded examples of the restoration of prewar society. The Simpang Club and Oranje Hotel reverted to the exclusive, whites-only institutions they had been, and the Recomba settled into the same house he had occupied a decade earlier as governor.[21] Employers of coolie laborers joined forces to prevent wages from rising, and the pay scale for Indonesian employees of the colonial government was returned to that prevailing in March 1942. The impetus to put all the pieces back together again was so great that municipal workers, as late as November 1947, continued efforts to trace every one of the reportedly 2,072 Singer sewing machines in prewar Surabaya and return it to its rightful owner.

Dutch-occupied Surabaya was in the end unable to arrange an accommodation with the arek Surabaya, who reentered the city in large numbers beginning in early 1948, and sought to reoccupy former homes and search for employment.[22] The reigning atmosphere was grim and frightening to kampung families. Many said that the city seemed to be at war, unlike the countryside they had left; conditions reminded kampung dwellers of the worst of the Japanese occupation. Dutch police harassed ordinary people and habitually entered kampung to make searches and check on individual residents. Chinese, most of whom had not evacuated in 1945, took possession of homes in many kampung, seemingly with Dutch approval, and became the target of the anger of many returnees. When men sought employment at Dutch firms they had to submit to humiliating investigations, and even then they often were not hired. Kampung sentiment against those who worked directly for the Dutch grew rapidly, and many were pressured by kampung neighbors to resign. Colonial power and prerogative had long since ebbed, and efforts to revive what had been lost through military action and the formation of a so-called State of East Java (Negara Jawa Timur) came to nothing.[23] The city merely entered a kind of limbo, awaiting the outcome of the struggle for independence.

In this way the development of Surabayan society was cut loose from its urban setting. Despite this physical dislocation and the many new forces unleashed by the revolution outside of the city, the essential lines of social and intellectual change continued unbroken. In particular, new priyayi ascendancy was achieved and maintained in much the same terms as originally had been imagined, and the pemuda leadership continued true to the pergerakan foundations of its character; there were other continuities as well. In them lay the principal ingredients of social change during the later years of revolution. While a full treatment of the subject is well beyond the scope of this study, it is possible to trace out briefly the themes of major interest.

The most noticeable of the ongoing transitions concerned the new priyayi and the pangreh praja. The first few months of independence gave intellectuals only limited opportunity to pursue goals they had set long ago with respect to changing the elitist pangreh praja of colonial days. The pangreh praja, and other government servants as well, were given special attention because new priyayi leaders recognized their importance to the survival of the apparatus of state in the early revolutionary turmoil. Later, however, the new priyayi seem to have returned to earlier priorities and either accepted or searched insistently for "new" pangreh praja, that is, persons thought to be progressive, courageous, and capable of staying afloat in what everyone recognized as a sea of change. In many areas of East Java the entire character of the pangreh praja seems to have been altered over a period of four years, largely as a result of deliberate choice by new priyayi civilian and military leaders.[24]

This process was aided by several factors. One was the tendency of the older, professional pangreh praja either to be drawn into service with the Dutch in occupied regions, or to lose heart altogether and retire from service.[25] Vacated positions in the republic were filled with lower-ranking civil servants, who were newer to and less steeped in pangreh praja tradition, or with total newcomers from the ranks of school teachers, office workers, and the like.[26] In addition, the establishment of Dutch rule in large areas of East Java in mid-1947 made it necessary for the republican government to create a shadow administration in many regions, down to the lowest village level.[27] The manpower requirements of this double bureaucracy undoubtedly were sufficient to call a considerable number of new faces into the civil service, or into its equivalent under military supervision. Village- and district-level personnel replacements forced by popular threats or kidnappings also played a part in opening up the pangreh praja to change, but their role seems decidedly secondary.[29]

It is also true that the conditions of those years of exile and moving hurriedly from place to place had a powerful effect on the outlooks of civil servants, whatever their background, who took up or continued in pangreh praja positions.[29] The evacuation of Surabaya and the subsequent dislocation riveted the attention of civil servants on the problem of maintaining a semblance of order under trying conditions. Because of the threat of public displeasure and the need for active support from the people of small towns and villages, pangreh praja were forced to adopt a more flexible approach to their work; the physical and economic hardship shared with villagers, and the experience of being directly dependent on rural folk for survival, humbled a great many. For those with any kind of pergerakan background—and there were many of this sort—values earlier learned in the abstract were now tested against a new reality. Attitudes and circumstances infrequently combined in such a way as to produce surprising examples of social mobility. In the Surabaya Residency office a young man of kampung middle class origins started out in late 1945 as a typist, doing cooking and marketing on the side during the worst periods, and ended up as a district head; similarly another individual of even more modest background began as a courier and ended his career 25 years later as regent, a leap quite unheard of in either Dutch or Japanese times.[30] The transformation of the government services into new priyayi institutions, either by placing intellectuals in them or by "new priyayi-izing" middle class officials, may not have taken place precisely in the manner pergerakan thinkers originally imagined, but the results probably were not much different from what they had hoped for.

A problem of greater concern to the new priyayi than the reshaping of the pangreh praja was the threat of disintegrating institutional authority, the prospect of which appeared with the formation of the Indonesian People's Struggle Council (Dewan Perjuangan Rakyat Indonesia, DPRI) barely four days after the British attack on Surabaya began.[31] The DPRI was founded by the TKR, BPRI, PRI, and several other groups for the stated purpose of coordinating military efforts and acting as "the highest authority in the Surabaya region," but there is in fact considerable uncertainty about what the founders actually had in mind. In retrospect it seems likely that some leaders of the PRI, which after 10 November was a leading member of the highly politicized Socialist Youth of Indonesia (Pemuda Sosialis Indonesia, Pesindo) and often took that name, viewed the body as an incipient alternative to KNID government through which they might become politically powerful. The PRI leader Kusnander already had created a sensation by attempting to change the KNID's golonganized makeup through elections of an undefined sort, an idea which KNID members said they approved in the abstract but thought inappropriate for the moment; they also suspected Kusnandar's motives, and thought the DPRI could be another effort in the direction of securing additional powers for Pesindo.[32] For the most part, however, the DPRI seems to have been a reaction to types of disorder against which the KNID had limited powers to act. This included various examples of "undesirable incidents" such as murders of suspected spies by undisciplined pemuda and TKR officers, and what recently had come to be called the "disorder of the masses" (*kekacauan rakyat*), which were serious enough to have been met with force by both pemuda groups and TKR units.

The first chairman of the DPRI appears to have been Mohammad Mangoendiprodjo, who was an officer in the TKR; PRI leaders also were given prominent posts.[33] Soerjo, Sudirman, Doel Arnowo, and their colleagues appear to have viewed the DPRI has a threat to the unitary style of national government they had established, especially because it potentially joined political rivalries with those between civilian and military branches of the government. In June 1946, however, following republican elections in Kediri, Sudirman and Doel Arnowo established an East Java Defense Council (Dewan Pertahanan Jawa Timur, DPJT).[34] The announced purpose of this council was "to be the highest government body in the region," but it is clear that, whereas the DPRI had been a rather loose alliance of interests, the DPJT was designed as something firmer, within the bureaucratic framework laid down by the republican government. Aided by quarrelling within the DPRI—especially among the PRI, the BPRI, and a pemuda affiliate of the TKR known as the Students' Army (Tentara Republik Indonesia Pelajar, TRIP)—and a widespread impression that the DPRI had begun to oppose the legitimate government,[35] the DPJT enjoyed a modest success. The DPRI was disbanded a year to the day from its founding, as the BPRI and TKR pulled away from the PRI/Pesindo, whom they distrusted.[36] This event brought no long-term solution to the tensions surrounding it, which indeed worsened in the later revolution.[37] It did, however, indicate that the established group of new priyayi leaders were intent on defending their centralized, unitary state, and that the cleavages on this and other accounts were not simply those between pemuda and their elders.

Among Surabaya's pemuda, the intense and even fanatical fighting of November lapsed rapidly into confusion and paralysis. Only a few months after the British attacks, Ruslan Abdulgani felt compelled to write an article entitled "What are we fighting for?" that epitomized the search for significance going on among all groupings of youth at the time.[38] The sense became widespread that the spirit of struggle which had once drawn all Surabayans together was now dissipating. By September 1946 pemuda authors were deploring the tendency of so many of their colleagues to drop out of the struggle, returning to school or taking jobs when they could be found.[39] "Where are the pemuda of last year?" asked one particularly bitter article, "Why has Surabaya been forgotten?"[40] And on the anniversary of the great battle it was again asked what the purpose of the struggle had been, and how the "November spirit" could be brought to life once more."[41]

There was considerably more to this shifting pemuda outlook than simple nostalgia or frustration. As early as the first months of 1946 the pemuda relationship with the rakyat had begun to fall apart, altering the thrust of pemuda leaders' thinking and action. The spread of disorder and rampok in the wake of the mass evacuation from Surabaya, as well as the tendency of pemuda groups to fracture and move in directions of their own, forced pemuda leaders of all political types to look more carefully than before at the implications of their partnership with the masses. This was true in matters concerning the physical struggle against the Dutch and in the more abstract advocacy of "popular sovereignty." Among the first to ponder such points was Ruslan Abdulgani. In an academic piece that depended for much of its effectiveness on at least a passing knowledge of ancient Greece, he concluded that government of and by the people was praiseworthy as long as it operated in an orderly fashion.[42]

The opinions of Abdulgani, who by this time had established himself in the new priyayi republican government, were by no means isolated or merely reflective of new priyayi views. Pesindo writers made it clear that they had arrived at much the same judgment. Increasingly alarmed at the lack of order around them in the months after the battle for Surabaya, they expressed their new priorities as "independence, discipline, and popular sovereignty" in that order, and turned careful attention to the place of rakyatism in their thinking. PRI/Pesindo recruits were to have impressed upon them the importance of self-confidence, responsibility, discipline, and even such notions as "the value of time."[43] Kusnandar discussed at length the requirements for carrying on a proper government, emphasizing the need for education and the discipline to aim for clear goals. As it was clear that the rakyat were as yet incapable of these, he noted, it was dangerous to stir them up with propaganda; the outcome could never be certain and the results were not likely to be positive. It was up to "rational socialist" PRI/Pesindo leaders to attempt to awaken and change society, especially the masses, according to concepts originating in the thinking class.[44]

If these ideas were not so surprising coming from PRI leaders, who in 1945 had already experienced and cautiously expressed similar misgivings, that Sutomo and the BPRI should be thinking along the same line was a less expected and therefore telling development. The BPRI, after all, was widely supposed to embody the very soul of the physical revolution, a nearly mystical form of social union. But at the same time as they retained a sense of being in direct contact with the masses, BPRI leaders came to emphasize discipline and cool judg-

285

ment, utilizing a slogan that might have come straight out of the pergerakan: "Be forceful but calm!" (*giat tetapi diam*).[45] Even more vociferously than their Pesindo contemporaries, Sutomo and other BPRI leaders denounced the appearance of "social obstacles" such as egotism and opportunism in their own ranks as well as in government circles; in the same breath they avowed that the time for propagandizing had passed and implied strongly that the proper pemuda role was to understand and lead the rakyat in a disciplined fashion. Pains were taken to assure that the BPRI was appreciated not simply as a union of the masses, but of educated persons as well.[46] Several years later, with events and emotions still sharp in his memory, Sutomo reflected on paper that the primary social problem of the revolution was the struggle between educated and uneducated classes, a struggle in which he felt himself more or less caught in the middle.[47]

The pemuda vision that emerged from the early revolution, one of a unified society energized and supported by the rakyat, was never entirely surrendered. It survived as an ideal used to invoke the revolutionary spirit or to justify the demands it exacted. In a manner reminiscent of that of Surabaya's new priyayi when faced with the urban rakyat in the prewar period, Surabaya's pemuda in the early revolution pulled away from the masses yet remained attached to a variety of populism that had little to do with the way they believed social change actually occurred. The pemuda leadership that drew attention to the importance of the rakyat in the revolution, also underscored their own significance as protectors and leaders of the rakyat; while at pains to identify themselves as "from the rakyat and for the rakyat," none hesitated either to certify that they were also intellectuals.[48] In the final analysis these pemuda belonged more to the pergerakan tradition than to any other. In some cases this was plain to see, as the slogan of the TRIP, founded from students in Surabaya's highschool and often critical of the republican government during the early days of the revolution: "Of the rakyat, with the rakyat, and for the rakyat," a vintage message from Dr. Soetomo and the Parindra.[49] In many other cases the links were less obvious. Of singular importance, however, was the fact that pemuda leaders viewed themselves and their groups as the originators of change in society, and the proper models for that change; this was a perspective shared across political and other boundaries, as indeed it had been among prewar new priyayi.

After the electrifying days of late 1945 and early 1946, the gradual diffusion of youth—golongan, individuals, energies—may be seen as a natural development. As their organizational and emotional cohesion relaxed, and as both the civilian government and the military arm of the republic attempted to rationalize their respective spheres, pemuda sought out positions in the order they perceived coalescing around them. This did not represent a process of regolonganization, but a search for security or like minds. It left many pemuda, particularly those with good educational backgrounds, closer to new priyayi figures and activities than ever before.[50] Perhaps inevitably, there were those for whom the new opportunities of the revolution held little promise, but a substantial number of Surabaya's pemuda (including many who were not, in fact, so young) made their way in a variety of pursuits ranging from civilian to military, and took up positions on many different sides in the internal disputes of the republic. In doing so, they became part of a social transition already underway in the Dutch period. The revolution made it possible for this expansion of the new priyayi class to take place as rapidly and on the scale it eventually did, but its first stirrings and basic patterns are to be found in the society and culture of the previous decade.

In Surabaya in the early 1970s, both ex-pemuda and kampung residents looked back on the early revolution as a time of unity, when social distinctions did not matter and when differences between rich and poor were unimportant.[51] In the kampung view, however, this state of affairs did not last long; the upper classes soon began separating themselves from ordinary people and, in the popular perception, society began to return to its former outline. While some individuals were able to grasp the haphazard chance for advancement tossed up by revolutionary times and slip into the new priyayi stream, most arek Surabaya did not find this possible. Nevertheless, their typical realism led them to see that this course, too, was natural. There is no question but that the hope of social union, when held out, had been exciting, but it is also clear that its achievement was generally assessed as unlikely. What is more, the new priyayi ideal as a model for social change in the kampung world appears to have survived in much the same form as it took in the prewar era, touched with ambivalence and pointed humor, but powerful nonetheless.[52]

Unlike the average arek Surabaya, former pemuda who made the transition to the new priyayi world adopted in later years a romantic interpretation of the values of the revolution, a wistful appreciation of a special, moral time in their lives that has not been recaptured. This romanticism is remarkable to the historian, for it represents the survival of pergerakan rakyatism in a boldly renovated form, sealed in the blood of revolution. This brand of populism had—and still has—certain drawbacks, among them a lack of precise social imagination, but it was—and is—both vigorous and flexible. The very different world of Indonesia in the late 1980s scarcely can be understood without it.

■ Notes

1. PRO WO203 4575b–d.
2. See, for example, *The New York Times* 11-15-45.
3. RvO-IC 068665: 10-11.
4. *Merdeka* 11-21-45.
5. PRO WO203 2650c.
6. The British figure is found in PRO WO203 2650e. RvOIC 051177 gives a Dutch estimate of 8,000 Indonesian dead and 4,000 wounded. A. H. Nasution (1979) II:401 notes that for Chinese residents of Surabaya alone there were 1,000 dead and 5,000 wounded, with estimates for Indonesians being "tens of thousands dead and wounded." A *Sin Po* journalist on the spot was quoted in the Jakarta daily *Merdeka* of 12-5-45 as saying that local estimates were in the neighborhood of 1,100 Surabaya residents dead and 4,000 wounded. There does not appear to be any satisfactory way of deciding which figures reflect the truth.
7. ARA AAS 97b/VII/3.
8. Wehl:67; OBNIB II:307.
9. Typical examples are Ruslan Abdulgani (1963) and *Bhirawa* 11-8-69.
10. A. H. Nasution (1970) I:191–92; (1976):48–50.
11. See the figures, admittedly incomplete, presented in Nugroho Notosusanto (1985):235–38.
12. Nugroho Notosusanto (1985):v.
13. PRO WO203 2255d.
14. OBNIB III:311, 363, 408, 467, and 557 trace the development of AMACAB, officially founded in Surabaya on 2 December 1945.
15. ARA AAS 97b/I/23d.
16. Unless cited otherwise, the information used in this and the following paragraph comes from materials in ARA AAS 97b/I/23b and 97b/VII/28.
17. Thompson:59.
18. ARA MBZ IA/XIX/11:5–6.

19. Interviews in 1971 and 1972 with persons who were municipal employees at the time. Also ARA AAS 97b/XXII/17a.

20. Sillevis Smit:34–35; ARA APG 803b. *Aneta* 12-9-49 estimated that 3,000 political prisoners remained in Surabaya at that time. On the revival of the PID and the criticism of the British even in late 1945, see ARA AAS 97b/II/17c and ARA APG 803a.

21. ARA AAS 97b/III/15d–e.

22. According to ARA AAS 97b/X/29, 90 percent had returned by mid-1949. Kampung interviews in 1971–72 have shed much light on the attitudes and experiences of the arek Surabaya at the time, and are the bases of many of the remarks below.

23. Neither of these subjects has been studied in any detail, though original sources abound. For a general treatment see G. Kahin:378–82; Yong: 150–53; van Doorn and Hendrix:99–272; for an introduction to archival material, see ARA AAS 97b/V/61b, 97b/III/15a–c, 101b/938–39, and 101b/353.

24. Again, little has been written about this period, except from the point of view of guerrilla warfare, and there appear to be very few Indonesian documents touching on it. One of the more interesting, though incomplete, sources is a first-hand report on East Java contained in ARA APG 281.

25. On the dilemma facing pangreh praja, see ARA AAS 97b/VI/22e. Older pangreh praja became especially discouraged when they discovered that the Dutch not only searched for "new talent" among intellectuals (precisely as was happening on the Indonesian side), but treated civil servants with far less delicacy than before the war. Those even mildly suspected of wavering in their loyalty were given the sack, sometimes in publically humiliating ways. ARA AAS 97b/VI/22b, and 97b/I/35.

26. This section is based on interviews in 1971 with former middle-level pangreh praja, and also on ARA AAS 101b/210b and 97b/VI/22f.

27. One of the best reports on the republican shadow government in East Java is ARA AAS 101b/569b. For the role of the military in setting up administrations of this sort, see ARA AAS 97b/XI/23 and 101b/569c.

28. Unfortunately, available data does not permit a more precise accounting and it seems unlikely that more complete figures on this sort of removal of pangreh praja in East Java exist. The impression gained from Zijlmans:passim, a number of brief official reports on the subject, and interviews with former pangreh praja serving in East Java during the revolution, is that, especially in mid-1946 and in the last half of 1949, the removals were widespread at lower levels of the pangreh praja. These changes, however, were frequently the work of the republican military of the civilian government itself, and resulted in the placement of loyal new priyayi types in the positions.

29. Information in this paragraph, unless cited otherwise is taken from interviews in 1971–72 with former East Java pangreh praja, and "Riwayat hidup Radjamin Nasution."

30. Interviews in 1971–72 with individuals having these experiences.

31. On the DPRI see A. Moentallip; A. H. Nasution (1979) II:402–03; and Nogroho Notosusanto (1985):221–23.

32. *Abdulgani MS*; SR 11-5-45 and 11-8-45.

33. In PRI/Pesindo sources, Kusnander is often referred to as being in charge, but the information is not repeated anywhere else, and I have not been able to confirm it in interviews with persons who were there.

34. *Bakti* 9-9-46, 9-17-46, 9-22-46, 9-25/26-46. On the Kediri elections, see RIPDJ: 128-31.

35. Interview in 1972 with a ranking TKR officer at the time, and in 1973 with Sutomo.

36. *Bakti* 11-15-46.

37. In the course of the Madiun Affair of September 1948, PRI/Pesindo forces ended up doing pitched battle against Sutomo's BPRI, which in general upheld the republican government.

38. This article originally appeared in *Bakti* and is reprinted in Ruslan Abdulgani (1963):88–92.

39. *Bakti* 9-23-46.

40. *Bakti* 9-15-46.

41. *Bakti* 11-10-46.

42. *Bakti* 2-10-46.

43. *Keadilan* I,4 (5-25-46):3–7.

44. *Bakti* 2-17-46 and 9-7-46.

45. *Bakti* 3-10-46.

46. Radio speech cited in Overdijkink:116.

47. Sutomo (1952):37–39.

48. On this point, the PRI/Pesindo vehicle *Keadilan* was just as insistent as the TRIP organ *Patria*, as is evidenced in a comparison of articles running in mid-1946 and early 1947.

49. A. Radjab:30.

50. Sudirman and his staff worked hard to see to it that potential competitors were attracted whenever possible into working for the republican government. On efforts in this direction see *Bakti* 9-6-46. Especially in the area of spreading information and contacting the general population, pemuda proved to be of great use.

51. Material in this paragraph is drawn from kampung interviews, 1971–72.

52. At least this is the distinct impression I received in kampung interviews made in 1971–72 and 1978, and in watching ludruk performances in those years which concerned the social issues of the revolution.

■ Conclusion

Revolutions are not made; they come. A revolution is as natural a growth as an oak. It comes out of the past. Its foundations are laid far back.

Wendell Phillips, Speech of Jan. 8, 1852

The story of Surabaya's changing urban society and its role in the birth of the national revolution is distinctive in many respects. No other locale in the young Indonesian nation experienced the early revolution with quite the same intensity, and perhaps just as assuredly social developments elsewhere did not take place in quite the same fashion. The character of the arek Surabaya, and the nature of the social world of which they were a part, are such nearly indissoluble elements in this history that one may rightly question whether or not they obviate a wider application of its patterns to the Indonesian revolution as a whole. A satisfactory answer to this important question must remain for others to devise. This study, concerned with providing both the materials and interpretation for a different sort of local history than has been available for the period, must in conclusion content itself with drawing together several of the more important strands in the story and pointing out some of the historiographical issues they raise.

One of these strands concerns the nature of Indonesian nationalism, which in recent years has come under scholarly re-examination. The general result has been to throw nationalist unity and depth into question, and to point more insistently at the small nationalist elite's vulnerability to Dutch pressure and inability to communicate with the ordinary populace.[1] The view that nationalism of the classic Western sort was weak in colonial Indonesia is not beside the point, of course, and neither is the accompanying warning that the nationalist movement had little of the inevitable in its development. Clearly the efforts of a great variety of nationalists were subject to reversals and not entirely certain as to outcome. At the same time, however, an examination of the followers of the pergerakan in Surabaya suggests that it is possible to underestimate the strengths of at least a certain strain of nationalism, and to ignore many important aspects of its social setting. Surabaya's new priyayi comprised a lively and comparatively diverse class of leaders, unified not so much by precise political doctrine as by a more generalized view of the future, and by common outlooks on society and social change. While political parties were indeed weakened by the Dutch in the 1930s, the new priyayi and their ideas were not. Furthermore, in Surabaya the activities and ideas of intellectuals did receive an audience in other social groups, most notably those among the city's kampung population, where they appear to have had greater impact than existing scholarship allows. This is not to say that Surabaya's intellectuals had, by the mid-1930s, triumphed in their attempt to win the support of "ordinary people" and thus closed ranks with them; on the contrary, Surabaya's example indicates that the relationship remained ambivalent, even among the changing kampung middle class, and was strained in matters such as city government. Yet a certain commonality of interests is unmistakable, and the lines of communication between kampung folk and intellectuals were by no means completely closed.

Indeed, Surabaya's example shows us at least one urban colonial society that consisted of a great deal more than a tiny Westernized elite on the one hand and an undifferentiated mass of displaced rural villagers on the other. The arek Surabaya were part of a complex social world, the dynamics of which were hidden to outside observers but which nevertheless involved a lively interaction of ideas at all stops along the social scale. Kampung society was far from the limp oddity referred to in colonial reports, and kampung dwellers possessed clear ideas and inclinations of their own. The arek Surabaya had begun in the 1930s to seek an active role in their own affairs and were increasingly sensitive to the exercise of authority on their lives and particular urban environment. The subsequent emergence of the arek Surabaya in the crisis of the early revolution may with some justification be seen as part of an extended development rather than as a sudden or isolated occurrence. The rakyat—under self control as well as in unleashed fury—are crucial actors on the Surabaya stage, and are ultimately the source of the radicalism which inspires and frightens new priyayi and pemuda alike. Is it possible that in the birth of the revolution elsewhere the role of the rakyat, especially in relation to youth and intellectuals, was both greater and more terrible than accounts generally show? Whatever the answer, it is a question well worth asking.

Surabaya's experience during the Japanese occupation raises a number of questions about that period in the light of existing literature, nearly all of which is Jakarta-focused or meant to apply generally. The impression of a time of high drama and colorful change,[2] for example, fades in the Surabayan setting to a picture of grayer tones, intricate circumstances, and ambiguity. Here the Japanese design for a stable, productive New Order is clear, along with the goal of producing modernization in a comparatively orderly fashion; equally clear are the contradictions, due less to original intentions than to circumstances surrounding Japanese efforts to carry them out. Naive and ill-prepared as they were, the Japanese rulers ended up unsuccessful in their attempts to organize, mobilize, and administer Surabayans. Ironically, this urban society, which the Japanese tried to protect from the worst effects of occupation economic and labor policies, took greatest offense at them, reacting uncooperatively and in the end violently. If similar situations can be found in other Indonesian urban centers, it might occasion a recasting of some ideas of Japanese "success" and contribution to the birth of the revolution.

Especially for Surabaya's new priyayi, the occupation held out a confusing blend of change and continuity. Few were swept up into enthusiastic collaboration, but equally few could help noticing the opportunities which specific sorts of change under the Japanese afforded. These were, as it happened, precisely the opportunities the new priyayi had awaited: acquisition of real (if still limited) administrative power, increased (if still not full) freedom to proselytize their point of view in public, and greater (if not complete) control over key institutions such as schools, the civil service, and the media. It was not independence, to be sure, but it strengthened the real and psychological progress toward it that both the new priyayi and the rest of society appeared prepared to accept. At least in Surabaya, there is no mistaking the essential continuities in the Japanese occupation, continuities not merely of policy or administrative structure, but of ideas and social development. This is a picture at odds on important points with prevailing conclusions about the occupation of Indonesia as a whole, which rely on a portrayal of the period as marking a clear social break with the past and, uniquely among Southeast Asian nations, signaling the rise of a new generation of leaders.[3]

This brings us to the most celebrated of the historiographical topics in the study of the birth of the Indonesian revolution, the nature and role of the pemuda, who typically are shown emerging suddenly in the form of a new and dynamic social force, sharply at odds with the established order.[4] This picture is difficult to sustain, however, in the Surabayan setting and across the *tiga jaman*, the three periods of Dutch rule, Japanese occupation, and independence. Rather than a pemuda movement brought forth in response or reaction to the Japanese occupation, and rooted in the pesantren and asrama, we see a phenomenon heavily shaped by the prewar pergerakan, and founded upon a leadership of highly educated youth and a followership of both educated and kampung middle class youth. Given the degree of uncertainty in previous studies over exactly who the pemuda were, especially below the national level,[5] the detailed information available about the social and intellectual backgrounds of a good many Surabayan pemuda leaders and followers may be of particular significance. It suggests, for example, that at least as far as the launching of the revolution is concerned, the new priyayi and the pemuda operated more in concert than in conflict.

After all, the pemuda of Surabaya in late 1945 were figuratively— and very often literally—the children of the pergerakan and its leadership, a circumstance the Japanese occupation did not much alter. Differences did open up between youth and those with established positions in Surabaya, but the quarrel was over methods rather than direction. It was caused primarily by the changed role of intellectuals, who acted to safeguard the state which they stood on the verge of inheriting, and by the galvanizing effect of popular fury on the youth who saw it from close up. Surabaya's pemuda had a vested interest only in the nation as an idea, and most were inclined, to one degree or another, to be less cautious than their elders in reaction to crisis and in invoking the "will of the masses"; for the most part, however, they belonged squarely to the same intellectual world as their new priyayi teachers. This conclusion, furthermore, does not go unsupported in a brief consideration of pemuda activities in the Surabaya region immediately after 1945. Are Surabaya's pemuda unique in all this? Especially in light of Surabaya's reputation as the flashpoint of the physical revolution and in many ways the chief inspiration for pemuda everywhere, it seems unlikely, though a proper answer cannot be framed without examination of other localities from the perspective of social and intellectual backgrounds rather than politics.

Some scholars have written, not without a trace of bitterness, about the "failed social revolution" that seems to have accompanied Indonesia's struggle for independence, blaming a conservative new priyayi generation for the crushing of a radicalized and largely pemuda-led revolution.[6] Although chronologically the argument extends beyond the limits of this study, the example of Surabaya suggests two responses. First, it is difficult to speak confidently of a "pemuda revolution" in Surabaya, not only because the revolution clearly was brought into being by or with the new priyayi, but because there were practically from the beginning several varieties of pemuda revolution underway. They lacked political uniformity, operated very differently, and eventually came to blows, but they were fueled by much the same pemuda energies and style. To speak of a single pemuda revolution, or even a single pemuda movement, in Surabaya is to speak so vaguely that the all-important dynamics behind the birth of the revolution in at least that particular locale are thoroughly obscured.

Second, the social history of the making of the Indonesian revolution in Surabaya does not lend much encouragement to the notion that, even at the start, a substantial social revolution was under way. Change initiated largely from below and intent upon turning society upside down does not seem to have been a likelihood, much less the deliberate goal of any prominent group or class; given the structure of social and intellectual change established in the Dutch period and refined under Japanese rule—a structure to which new priyayi and pemuda of varying backgrounds were equally bound—there seems little reason to expect that such ideas would have been incorporated into the birth of the revolution by either group. What is more, specific experiences in the early days of the revolution probably did much to cause many new priyayi and pemuda in Surabaya to recoil sharply from the prospect of social change led by the masses. In this regard Surabaya provides at least a cautionary tale for those who would assess the social possibilities inherent in the Indonesian revolution from its inception.

Though it may appear to argue for a sudden and explosive kind of change, Surabaya in fact encourages a longer, transitional view of the launching of the Indonesian revolution. Through its example, the visions and heat which generated the revolution can be seen in the natural light of process in the broadest sense, throwing into relief durable social and intellectual patterns and helping to account realistically for aspects of both change and persistence. Perhaps this approach can free the Indonesian revolution as a whole from its unhappy and ahistorical fate of being considered a time apart from others, a phenomenon with only tenuous connections to the past and to the future.

■ Notes to the Conclusion

1. The latest example in this trend is the chapter by O'Malley in Fox, et. al.: 601-14.

2. B. Anderson (1966).

3. McCoy, introduction.

4. The classic example is B. Anderson (1972).

5. The question of precisely who the pemuda were is raised repeatedly in the literature—most recently in Wild and Carey (eds.): 156-62 and A. Kahin (ed.): *passim*—but the answers are not yet very satisfactory, due at least in part to the lack of good biographical data for the revolutionary period and Indonesan personalities in general.

6. Again, the best and most influential example is in B. Anderson (1972), but the same perspective is found in more recent works, such as Kreutzer's analysis of the Madiun Affair.

■ Bibliography

Abbreviations

AAS	Archief Algemene Secretarie
AFNEI	Allied Forces in the Netherlands East Indies
ALFSEA	Allied Land Forces in Southeast Asia
AKGJT	Archief Kantor Gubernor Jawa Timur (Surabaya)
APG	Archief Procureur Generaal
ARA	Algemeen Rijksarchief (The Hague)
BJERS	*Bewaking van den Japansche Expansie, Residentie Soerabaia*
BMHG	*Bijdragen en Mededelingen van het Historisch Genootschap te Utrecht.*
BKI	*Bijdragen van het Koninklijk Instituut voor Taal-, Land- en Volkenkunde*
ESS	*Encyclopedia of the social sciences*
EWvNI	*Economisch Weekblad voor Nederlandsch-Indië*
HvK	Hoofdvertegenwoordiger van de Kroon
JAS	*Journal of Asian Studies*
JSEAH	*Journal of Southeast Asian History*
JSEAS	*Journal of Southeast Asian Studies*
KT	*Koloniaal Tijdschrift*
MBZ	Ministerie voor Binnenlandse Zaken
Mr	Mailrapport
MvK	Ministerie van Koloniën
MvO	Memorie van Overgave
NEFIS	Netherlands Forces Intelligence Service
OBNIB	S. L. van der Wal (ed. and comp.) *Officiële bescheiden betreffende de Nederlands-Indonesische betrekkingen 1945-1950.*
ODO	Opsporingsdienst Overledenen
PA	*Pacific Affairs*
PG	Procureur General
PHR	*Pacific Historical Review*
PID	Politieke Inlichtingendienst
PPO	Politiek-politionele Overzicht

PRO   Public Record Office (London)
RIPDJ   Indonesia, Kementerian Penerangan. *Republik Indonesia: Propinsi Djawa Timur*
RvOIC   Rijksinstituut voor Oorlogsdocumentatie, Indische Collectie (Amsterdam)
TSSJ   *Toelichting op de 'Stadsvormingordonnantie Stadsgemeenten Java'*
TvNI   *Tijdschrift voor Nederlandsch-Indië*
TvP   *Tijdschrift voor Parapsychologie*
VBG   *Verhandelingen van het Bataviaasch Genootschap*
VN   *Vrij Nederland*
VS   *Verslag van den toestand der stadsgemeente Soerabaja*

Archival Sources

Introductory note: The Arsip Kantor Gubernor Jawa Timur (AKGJT) contains a treasure-trove of municipal documentation as well as a carefully preserved collection of prewar materials on colonial government. On the period during which Surabaya was occupied by the British and Dutch (1946–49), much unique material can be found here. The Algemeen Rijksarchief (ARA) in The Hague contains the largest collections of primary materials on the topics and periods examined in this book. For the years 1900–40 the archives of the Ministerie van Koloniën (MvK) abound in information on Surabaya, particularly in the form of Mailrapporten (Mr) and Memories van Overgave (MvO), indices to which are available. For the period 1940–49 the archival materials are much less easily accessible, though improved indices and subject guides exist. The principal collections are those of the Algemene Secretarie (AAS), the Procureur Generaal (APG), and the Ministerie voor Binnenlandsezaken (MBZ). Each is numbered or lettered in a distinctive series, and appropriate listing below should make it possible to locate the sources in question without difficulty. For the Japanese occupation, the chief lode of resources lies in the Rijksinstituut voor Oorlogsdocumentatie's Indisch Collectie (RvOIC). The documentation in this collection is better known than, for example, some sections of the archives mentioned above, but there are still quantities of untapped materials. The diaries preserved here, for example, have been ignored by scholars working on any subject other than Dutch prisoners of war, and even then they have been little utilized. The contents of the Public Record Office's War Office files on Java (most notably PRO WO203) are not extensive, but what exists is of considerable interest. One file devoted to the death of Brigadier Mallaby in Surabaya in 1945 was resealed in the early 1970s and will not be available to scholars for another half century.

AKGJT (1948a)		"Lapuran hatsil pembitjaraan dalam bagian tentang Rentjana Peraturan Hukum Tatanegara Negara Djawa Timur' beserta risalah jawaban dari lapuran tersebut."
AKGJT (1948b)		"Ontwerp: regeling staatsrechtelijke organisatie Djawa Timur."
AKDJT (1948c)		"Toelichting op de regeling staatsrechelijke organisatie Djawa Timur."
AKGJT (1949)		"Verzameling verordening Oost-Java, 1946–1949."
ARA AAS	97b/I/20a	Memorandum van der Plas. December 19, 1944.
ARA AAS	97b/I/20b	Codetelegram van der Plas to van Mook. September 29, 1945.
ARA AAS	97b/I/20c	Rapport van Straten. October 19, 1945.
ARA AAS	97b/I/23a	P. G. de Back, "Report on events in Soerabaja from 21st September to 27th October, 1945."
ARA AAS	97b/I/23b	Letter van der Plas to van Mook. October 31, 1945.
ARA AAS	97b/I/23c	Enquiry re actions of Captain Huijer, RNN, at Sourabaya," November 9, 1945.
ARA AAS	97b/I/23d	Brief outline of the military situation in the Netherlands East Indies as at [sic] 20th April, 1946."
ARA AAS	97b/I/35	Communication Kuiper to van Mook. October 17, 1947.
ARA AAS	97b/II/17a	NEFIS eerste periodiek verslag. December, 1945.
ARA AAS	97b/II/17b	Prawoto Soemodilogo, "Survey of the situation from [sic] Inramajoe from the economic side."
ARA AAS	97b/II/17c	Report X.
ARA AAS	97b/II/32	Letters on the Bornhaupt incident.
ARA AAS	97b/III/15a	Verslag inzake vergadering van de diensthoofden op 14-10-47 te Modjokerto.
ARA AAS	97b/III/15b	Rapport: vergadering op de kaboepaten op 9-10-47.
ARA AAS	97b/III/15c	Verslag inzake BPR op 11-10-47.

ARA AAS	97b/III/15d	Codetelegram.
ARA AAS	97b/III/15e	Telegram van der Wal to van Mook.
ARA AAS	97b/V/61a	Letter van der Plas to van Mook. January 9, 1948.
ARA AAS	97b/V/61b	Persatuan Rakjat Djawa Timur series.
ARA AAS	97b/V/61c	A. T. Baud, "Indrukken van de Oost-Java conferentie," November 19, 1948.
ARA AAS	97b/VI/22a	Recomba verslagen Midden- en Oost-Java. October 15–31, 1947.
ARA AAS	97b/VI/22b	Codetelegram Recomba OJ/Nedinreg. August 28, 1947.
ARA AAS	97b/VI/22c	Rapport: situatie in de desa Moenggoed-janti, 28 November 1948.
ARA AAS	97b/VI/22d	Codetelegram van Mook to van der Plas. October 14, 1947.
ARA AAS	97b/VI/22e	Rapport politie Oost-Java. September 10, 1947.
ARA AAS	97b/VI/22f	Verkiezingen regentschapraden.
ARA AAS	97b/VII/3	Letter van der Plas to van Mook. April 3, 1948.
ARA AAS	97b/VII/28	Verslag XVIII, Kantor voor Bevolkings-zaken, Surabaya. November 1947.
ARA AAS	97b/X/29	Letter van der Plas to HvK. August 18, 1949.
ARA AAS	97b/XI/23	Letter Kusumonegoro to HvK, September 30, 1949.
ARA AAS	97b/XIV/5a	Letters and memoranda on psychological warfare.
ARA AAS	97b/XIV/5b	Anti-Japanese activities in Java. December 10, 1944.
ARA AAS	97b/XV/15	Telegram Recomba OJ/Nedinreg. August 2, 1947.
ARA AAS	97b/XIX/27a	E. Brunsveld van Hulten, "Rapport over de Japansche invloeden op de merdeka-beweging."
ARA AAS	97b/XIX/27b	Adachi Hisayoshi, et. al., "Replies of [sic] questionnaire on the Sendenbu."
ARA AAS	97b/XXI/17	Eyre-Bachrach report. January 19, 1946.
ARA AAS	97b/XXII/17a	Letter van der Plas to Hoven, January 26, 1946.
ARA AAS	97b/XXII/17b	Letter van der Plas to Hoven, March 7, 1946.
ARA AAS	97b/XXII/45a	Verslag H. L. Pl. Nelissen.

ARA AAS	97b/XXII/45b	Verslag Hulscher.
ARA AAS	97b/XXII/45c	Verslag Jonas.
ARA AAS	97b/XXII/45d	Verslag van Kleef.
ARA AAS	97b/XXII/45e	Verslag Albert.
ARA AAS	97b/XXII/45f	Verslag Rothuizen
ARA AAS	97b/XXII/45g	Verslag Schansman
ARA AAS	97b/XXII/45h	Verslag Donleben, Holtz, en Broekman.
ARA AAS	97b/XXII/45i	Verslag Kuiper.
ARA AAS	97b/XXV/19a	Letter van der Plas to van Mook. November 16, 1945.
ARA AAS	97b/XXV/19b	"Suggestion." Undated and unsigned.
ARA AAS	101b/98	Opleiding van Indonesische officieren voor de federale troepen. S. H. Spoor. February 28, 1949.
ARA AAS	101b/164	Notulen hoofdpunten van bespreking tussen Kol. Scheffelaer en Kol. Sungkono op 4 November 1949.
ARA AAS	101b/165a	Note van der Plas. November 26, 1949.
ARA AAS	101b/165b	Rapport van der Plas. October 12, 1949.
ARA AAS	101b/165c	Rapport van der Plas. November 10, 1949.
ARA AAS	101b/200	Note van der Plas to HvK. August 22, 1949.
ARA AAS	101b/206a	Nota: meningen van voorstonden Indonesiërs uit TBA gebied in verband met het bestaan der Negara Djawa Timur. C. O. van der Plas. October 15, 1949.
ARA AAS	101b/206b	Note van der Plas to HvK. August 18, 1949.
ARA AAS	101b/206c	Note van der Plas to HvK. August 31, 1949.
ARA AAS	101b/206d	Korte analyse van de politiek toekomst van de Negara Djawa Timur. C. O. van der Plas. September 12, 1949.
ARA AAS	101b/210a	Beschouwingen over Raden Moestopo. July 8, 1947.
ARA AAS	101b/210b	Rapport algemeen politie Oost-Java to Recomba Oost-Java. February 17, 1948.
ARA AAS	101b/353	De achtergrond van Bondowoso. Undated.
ARA AAS	101b/365-7	Letter Moh. Hatta to Christison. November 9, 1945.
ARA AAS	101b/569a	Note van der Plas to Eysebaert. August 24, 1949.
ARA AAS	101b/569b	Uittreksel brief van de Regent van Malang. September 30, 1947.

ARA AAS	101b/569c	Telegrambrief van Liere to MBZ. September 19, 1949.
ARA AAS	101b/938-9	Laporan-laporan tentang daerah pendudukan Modjokerto serta perundingan-perundingan berdasarkan Linggadjati.
ARA APG	281	De regering der Repoeblik Indonesia. Dr. Moerdjani. April 24, 1948.
ARA APG	767a	Situatie rapport. Centraal Kantoor Recomba Oost-Java. December 17, 1948.
ARA APG	767b	Situatie rapport Djombang. January 18, 1949.
ARA APG	803a	F. Hulscher. "Geheime rapport algemeene politie Soerabaja, afdeeling recherche." December 10, 1946.
ARA APG	803b	Interneeringen Surabaja. November 1946 to February 1947.
ARA MBZ	IA/XV/9	Mr 699/APO secret. Afscheidswoord van het dagelijksch bestuur van de Parindra.
ARA MBZ	IA/XIX/11	Analyse en perspectieven inzake het Indonesiche vraagstuk. February 17, 1947.
ARA MBZ	Mr 31/1946	Untitled.
ARA MvK	Mr 139/1916	Letter from Director of Binnenlands Bestuur. December 20, 1915.
ARA MvK	Mr 557x/1926	Untitled.
ARA MvK	Mr 700x/1926	Untitled.
ARA MvK	Mr 727x/1926	Untitled.
ARA MvK	Mr 481x/1930	Verslag van de conferentie met de hoofden van Inlandsch Bestuur in de Provincie Oost-Java.
ARA MvK	Mr 29x/1932	PPO. November 1931.
ARA MvK	Mr 273x/1932	Indonesia Raya Congress.
ARA MvK	Mr 560x/1932	PID berichtgeving.
ARA MvK	Mr 125x/1933	Samenvoeging regentschappen Soerabaja en Sidoardjo.
ARA MvK	Mr 353x/1933	MvO Res. van Modjokerto, C. A. Schitzler.
ARA MvK	Mr 847x/1933	Memorandum van den afgetreden Gouverneur van Oost-Java. G. H. de Man.
ARA MvK	Mr 109x/1934	PPO June–July 1933.
ARA MvK	Mr 562x/1935	Notulen Regentsconferentie Oost-Java.
ARA MvK	Mr 569x/1935	PPO February–March 1935.
ARA MvK	Mr 1004/1935	MvO A. H. Moreau, Resident van Soerabaja.

ARA MvK	Mr 1239x/1935	PPO August–September 1935.
ARA MvK	Mr 343x/1936	PPO January–February 1936.
ARA MvK	Mr 602x/1936	Letter Director of Research Services to Governor-General. May 10, 1936.
ARA MvK	Mr 46x/1937	Rukun Tani in Oost-Java.
ARA MvK	Mr 893x/1937	BJERS 1, 1937.
ARA MvK	Mr 230x/1938	Letter Dir. Oost-Aziatische Zaken to Governor-General. March 9, 1938.
ARA MvK	Mr 795x/1938	Untitled.
ARA MvK	Mr 1044x/1939	Letter van der Plas to Governor-General. October 31, 1938.
ARA MvK	Mr 3x/1939	Circular from Procureur Generaal. December 19, 1938.
ARA MvK	Mr 4x/1939	Bemoeienis met inwendige politieke aangeledenheden van Ned.-Indië door Japanners.
ARA MvK	Mr 70x/1939	Oprichting Japansche jongelieden vereeniging te Soerabaja.
ARA MvK	Mr 143x/1939	Verkoop van Japansche oorlogsobligaties door Japansche jonglieden vereeniging.
ARA MvK	Mr 317x/1939	Untitled.
ARA MvK	Mr 432x/1939	PPO January 1939.
ARA MvK	Mr 1114x/1939	Untitled.
ARA MvK	Mr 1306x/1939	Rechten en plichten van plaatselijk overheid en bevolking in geval van vijandelijke bezetting.
ARA MvK	Mr 199x/1940	Verslag Hagenaar.
ARA MvK	Mr 383x/1940	Pers delict tegen *Pewarta Soerabaja*.
ARA MvK	Mr 559x/1940	BJERS 2, 1939.
ARA MvK	Mr 1108x/1940	Codetelegram Governor-General to Minister of Colonies. January 26, 1940.
PRO WO203 2255a		AFNEI interim sitrep. November 11, 1945.
PRO WO203 2255b		AFNEI OP report to November 3, 1945.
PRO WO203 2255c		AFNEI to ALFSEA, Special OP sitrep. November 4, 1945.
PRO WO203 2255d		Extract from notes on SAC meeting. December 2, 1945.
PRO WO203 2255e		Lloyd Carson report.
PRO WO203 2289		The Indonesian Republican Army Anonymous report.

PRO WO203 2650a		Report of proceedings. 30 October–22 November 1945.
PRO WO203 2650b		Report on proceedings of naval officer-in-charge, Sourabaya. 23 November–14 December 1945.
PRO WO203 2650c		Report of main HQ, 5th Indian division. November 14, 1945.
PRO WO203 2650d		Report on ambush of convoy carrying APWI women and children.
PRO WO203 2650e		Situation in Sourabaya on 16–17 November 1945.
PRO WO203 4575a		Emergency OTBPS. November 9, 1945. AFSEA to War Office.
PRO WO203 4575b		AFNEI Special OP Report.
PRO WO203 4575c		AFNEI to ALFSEA, November 13 [1945].
PRO WO203 4575d		AFNEI Report.
PRO WO203 5570		Letters Mansergh to Soerjo, Soerjo to Mansergh.
RvOIC	000387-31	Diary van Genderen
RvOIC	000387-32	Diary M. A. Cramer-Bakker
RvOIC	000387-42	Diary Egeter.
RvOIC	000387-44	Diary Dr. J. E. Quintus Bosz.
RvOIC	000387-53	Diary van den Bos.
RvOIC	000387-68	Diary Tjoa Han Yang. Unpaginated.
RvOIC	000664	Annex to Chart #1. Unpaginated.
RvOIC	002055	Process verbaal R. F. C. Smith.
RvOIC	002436	Rapport Bromet.
RvOIC	003309	Hoving report.
RvOIC	004684	Dringende waarschuwingen aan Nederlanders in Indië.
RvOIC	004685	Proclamatie aan het heele Indonesische volk.
RvOIC	004720	Ricardo report.
RvOIC	004980	Dagboek van de opbouw van de Nieuw Java. Unpaginated.
RvOIC	004981	Regeeringsvoorlichtingsdienst report on Indonesian newspapers during the Japanese occupation.
RvOIC	005140	Rapport Commisaris PID Hulscher.
RvOIC	005144	Rapport H. Tanner.
RvOIC	005148	Makloemat Soerbaja, 14-9-1945.

RvOIC	005197	16th Army headquarters. "Present status of Rangoon Instructions in practice." September 15, 1945. Unpaginated.
RvOIC	005192	Public peace intelligence bulletin, no. 5.
RvOIC	005309	Anonymous eyewitness report.
RvOIC	005315	Provisional proposals for reoccupation of Batavia. September 22, 1945.
RvOIC	005369	Group 2, directive 1, "Cumberland." September 15, 1945.
RvOIC	005374	Notes from a meeting aboard the "Cumberland." September 24, 1945.
RvOIC	005798	Beppan report on Putera.
RvOIC	006664	Report on the state of affairs in Java. September 27, 1945.
RvOIC	006762	Report on the Semarang incident.
RvOIC	006879	Interrogation of Mori Takeo.
RvOIC	006951	Interrogation of Shibata Yaichiro.
RvOIC	006958	Shibata report.
RvOIC	012614	Outline of the structure of the administration of Java.
RvOIC	012920	Verslag H. M. Juta.
RvOIC	015406	Verslag Moller.
RvOIC	015183	S. G. Noteboom. "Dagboek Maret-dagen."
RvOIC	015474	Verslag de Vries.
RvOIC	016341	Verslag Rompas.
RvOIC	020118	Short review of the economical [sic] situation. 1943.
RvOIC	020161	Wat wenschen de Indonesiers binnen het raam van de Tojo verklaring.
RvOIC	020254	HBS opstellingen.
RvOIC	028977	Verslag van den Berg.
RvOIC	029292	Houtkoop diary.
RvOIC	029521	Verslag du Mosch.
RvOIC	030905	Rapport A. C. H. Heringa.
RvOIC	032368	Oogetuige-verslag van het transport vrouwen.
RvOIC	032385	Report on happenings and conditions in Surabaya.
RvOIC	032508	Report of an Indonesian. October 11, 1943. Unpaginated.

BIBLIOGRAPHY

RvOIC	032780	Verslag E. Kijander.
RvOIC	032868	Trials of Malang kempeitai officers.
RvOIC	034101	Luchtbeschermingsdienst practice in Surabaya, 1941.
RvOIC	032388	Rapport E. H. W. van Stappershoef.
RvOIC	039357	Garis-garis besar tentang pengerahak romusha.
RvOIC	047309	Rapport J. H. Forch.
RvOIC	050497	Untitled.
RvOIC	050577	Verslag ten Cate-Lisse.
RvOIC	051163	Overzicht van de huideige voedsel situatie op Java.
RvOIC	051177	NEFIS rapporten over den toestanden en gebeurtenissen op Java na Japanse capitulatie.
RvOIC	058803	Table showing the principal events and incidents since the cessation of hostilities.
RvOIC	059385	Moh. Hatta. Opdracht aan de Residenten en Nationale Comites. October 14, 1945.
RvOIC	056029	Pengoemoeman dari Kontakt-Bureau Soerabaja. November 1, 1945.
RvOIC	058804	The independence movement immediately after the close of hostilities.
RvOIC	059266	Preliminary report on Japanese financial manipulations in the Netherlands East Indies. J. H. Sweeney. May 30, 1946.
RvOIC	059276	Japansche financiële manipulaties.
RvOIC	059277	The situation of currency circulation after the cessation of hostilities.
RvOIC	059381	Report of Maeda Tadashi.
RvOIC	059679	Prepared statement of K. A. de Weerd.
RvOIC	060750	Bijvoegsel rapport S. Malthes-Cornelius.
RvOIC	061272	NEFIS report S111/MJS.
RvOIC	062073	Kamp interview no. 80, H. S. van den Bos.
RvOIC	062511	Brief van Br. Faustinius.
RvOIC	062945	Dagboek Avis-Hulstijn.
RvOIC	062994	C. M. Pasteur-van Swieten. "De Japansche bezetting in Soerabaia en wat daarvan voorafgang."
RvOIC	064196	Fifth Indian Division operational instructions, n. 10.
RvOIC	064547	W. Keasberry. "Zoo een en ander."

RvOIC	066720	Kort verslag over de gebeurtenissen in Kampenmentstraat 210.
RvOIC	066724	Short investigative report.
RvOIC	066918	Verslag Wijting.
RvOIC	068665	Anonymous report on Surabaya in 1945.
RvOIC	069253	Priority system for Surabaya.
RvOIC	070851	Rapport inzaken het schema organisation of Republic Indonesia in Soerabaia [sic]. December 14, 1945.
RvOIC	070882	Untitled NEFIS document. November 23, 1945.
RvOIC	071004	Verklaring Pastoors.
RvOIC	071008	Untitled ODO report.
RvOIC	071038	Untitled ODO report.
RvOIC	071224	Untitled ODO report.
RvOIC	071264	Untitled ODO report.
RvOIC	071420	Verklaring S. M. E. Moorman.
RvOIC	072775	Diary Tan Eng Hie.
RvOIC	158781	Verslag Willinge-Sligsher.

Newspapers

Api
Asia Raya
Bakti
Bataviaasch Nieuwsblad
Berdjoeang (Surabaya)
Berdjoeang (Malang)
Berita Buana
Berita Yudha
Bok Tok
The Daily Telegraph
The Fighting Cock
Indische Courant
De Javabode
Javasche Courant
Kedaulatan Rakjat
Matahari
Menjala
Merdeka
Nieuwe Courant
Nieuwe Soerabajasche Courant
Pasoepati

Pewarta Perniagaan
Sawunggaling
Sin Tit Po
Sin Yit Po
Sinar Harapan
Sinar Matahari
Sinar Soerya Wirawan
Soeara Ansor
Soeara Asia
Soeara Indonesian Moeda
Soeara Oemoem
Soeara Parindra
Soeara Persatoean Bangsa Indonesia
Soeara Rakjat
Soeara Rakjat Indonesia
Soerabajasch Handelsblad
The Statesman
Swara Oemoem
Variasi
De Vrije Pers

Oral Sources

For this study over 100 persons were interviewed in the Netherlands, Japan, and Indonesia, resulting in more than 160 separate interview sessions and over 600 pages of typed notes. Interviews were not chosen "scientifically" or according to any statistical technique. Rather, individuals were sought who played major historical roles, were close to others who did, or who had extensive experience in times or places of interest to the research. In the case of kampung interviews, long-time residents of Kampung Peneleh, Plampitan, and Dinoyotangsi—neighborhoods with comparatively stable populations, located in either the central city or near the newer European areas of the 1930s—were more or less randomly contacted, the idea being to acquire a range of views on kampung life.

The format of interviews was not standardized, but generally followed lines suggested in a short autobiographical account requested of each person before the actual interview. Nearly all interviews were held in the interviewee's language. In Indonesia during 1971 and 1972, most interviews were recorded in writing by an assistant, Suparman, who subsequently typed these notes and checked them over with me for accuracy. Other Indonesian interviews in Indonesia, and those in the Netherlands, were entirely my responsibility. In Japan I was kindly aided by Kurasawa Aiko, who acted as translator as I took notes.

Using interviews as historical sources can be hazardous, especially when generalizations must be made or when the political atmosphere makes it unlikely that certain subjects can be discussed. On the first matter, interviews are depended upon here only when printed sources were unavailable or when an interviewee's personal experience clearly offered a superior guide to understanding an event or issue. Further, in such cases (with only a handful of exceptions, pointed out in the notes) only interviews offering first-hand knowledge are cited; where the object was to portray a general situation or circumstance, opinions from a number of interviewees on the same subject were brought together, and multiple interviews cited. On the second matter, it should be emphasized that nearly all the individuals with whom I spoke did so—or so it certainly appeared to me, and I tried to be sensitive on this point—freely and without hesitation. Even when potentially delicate or disturbing topics surfaced in an interview, the discussion almost always continued on course. The arek Surabaya were particularly frank and outspoken, for which I am grateful indeed. It is true, however, that on the topic of contemporary politics (which hardly concerned this study directly) nothing was asked and very little offered; and that on the topic of communism, whether contemporary or in the period of investigation, little was asked and, except in the case of several older political and military figures of some standing, almost nothing offered. As noted in the preface to this book, I am aware of the possible ramifications of this circumstance, but do not feel that the main points I wish to make are compromised by it. The effort here has been to look at the making of the Indonesian revolution in terms other than political or ideological, and the interviews deliberately touched infrequently on such matters, whether communist or otherwise.

When faced with scarce or patchy written sources, the contemporary historian is obliged to use oral materials, if and whenever they may be available. Like all sources, of course, interviews must be utilized with care lest they be overstepped or misinterpreted. I am aware of some of the pitfalls in this endeavor, and hope to have avoided pitching headlong into the more obvious and dangerous ones.

Other Manuscripts and Printed Materials

Abdulgani MS (1973) Unpublished autobiographical manuscript.

Abdulgani, Ruslan (1963). *Api revolusi tetap berkobar.* Jakarta: Depertemen Penerangan.

────── (1964). *Heroes' Day and the Indonesian revolution.* [Jakarta]: Prapantja.

────── (1972a). *Nationalism, revolution, and guided democracy in Indonesia.* Victoria: Monash University Centre for Southeast Asian Studies.

────── (1972b). "Sekelumit tjatatan pribadi dari gudang kenang-kenangan." In *Bung Hatta mengabdi pada tjita-tjita perdjoangan bangsa,* pp. 49-60.

────── (1974a). " 'Indonesia Muda' diantara tahun 1932-1937 dilihat dari kaca-mata Surabaya." In *Empatpuluhlima tahun Sumpah Pemuda.*

────── (1974b). "My Childhood World." Trans. William H. Frederick. *Indonesia* 17 (April 1974), pp. 13-136.

────── (1974c). *100 [i.e., Seratus] hari di Surabaya yang menggemparkan Indonesia.* Jakarta: Yayasan Idayu.

────── (1974d). *Almarhum Dr. Soetomo yang saja kenal.* Jakarta: Yayasan Idayu.

────── (1976). *Semangat dan jiwa kepahlawanan dalam peristiwa 10 November, 1945, untuk kelanjutan pembinaan bangsa.* Jakarta: n.p.

Abeyesekere, Susan (1972). "Partai Indonesia Raja, 1936-1942: A study in cooperative nationalism." JSEAS 3, 1 (March 1972), pp. 262-76.

────── (1973). "Relations between the Indonesian cooperating nationalists and the Dutch, 1935-1942." PhD Thesis, Monash University.

────── (1976). *One hand clapping: Indonesian nationalists and the Dutch, 1939-1942.* Victoria, Monash University Centre for Southeast Asian Studies.

Adams, Cindy (1965). *Sukarno: an autobiography.* New York: Bobbs Merrill.

Alatas, Syed Hussein (1977). *Intellectuals in developing societies.* London: Cass.

Alers, Henri (1956). *Om een rode of groene merdeka, tien jaren binnenlandse politiek Indonesia, 1943-1953.* Eindhoven: Vulkaan.

Almanak Soeara Asia (1942). Surabaya: *Soeara Asia.*

Anderson, Benedict R. O'G. (1961). *Some aspects of Indonesian politics under the Japanese occupation, 1944-1945.* Ithaca: Cornell Modern Indonesia Project.

_____ (1966). "Japan: 'The Light of Asia.' " In Silverstein, ed., pp. 13-50.

_____ (1972). *Java in a time of revolution*. Ithaca: Cornell University Press.

_____ (1979). "A time of darkness and a time of light: transposition in early Indonesian nationalist thought." In Reid and Marr, eds.(1979) pp. 219-48.

Anderson, David Charles (1976). "The military aspects of the Madiun affair." *Indonesia* 21 (April 1976), pp. 1-64.

Arnowo, Doel (1934). *Kamoes Marhaen*. Surabaya: n.p.

Arx, A. van (1949). *L'Evolution politique en Indonesia de 1900 à 1942*. Fribourg: Artigianella-Monza.

Asia Raya oentoek memperingati enam boelan balatentara Dai Nippon melindungi Indonesia (1942). Jakarta: *Asia Raya*.

Asmadi (1985). *Pelajar Pejuang*. Jakarta: Sinar Harapan.

Bartman, G. H. (1975). *Fotografiën van Soerabaja*. 's-Gravenhage: Thomas and Eras.

Baudet, H. and I. J. Brugmans, eds. (1961). *Balans van beleid: terugblik op de laatste halve eeuw van Nederlands Indië*. Assen, van Gorcum.

Het B. B. Congress 1938. Batavia: n.p.

Benda, Harry J. (1955). "The communist rebellions of 1926-1927." PHR 25, 2 (May 1955), pp. 139-52.

_____ (1958). *The crescent and the rising sun. Indonesian Islam under the Japanese occupation, 1942-1945*. The Hague: Van Hoeve.

_____ (1966). "The pattern of administrative reforms in the closing years of Dutch rule in Indonesia." JAS 25, 4 (August 1966), pp. 589-606.

_____ et. al., eds. (1965). *Japanese military administration in Indonesia: selected documents*. New Haven: Yale University Southeast Asian Studies.

_____ and Ruth T. McVey (1960). *The communist uprisings of 1926-1927 in Indonesia*. Ithaca: Cornell University Modern Indonesia Project.

Besturen overzee: herinneringen van oud-ambtenaars bij het binnenlands bestuur in Nederlands-Indië (1977). Franeker: Wever.

Bhirawa. Nomor chusus 10 Nopember (1969). Surabaya.

Blom, J. H. C. (1983). *De muiterij op De Zeven Provinciën*. Utrecht: HES.

Boeke, J. H., et. al. (1961). *Indonesian economics*. The Hague: van Hoeve.

Boekoe penoentoen Roekoen Tani Parindra (1938). Surabaya: n.p.

Brandes, J., trans. and ed. (1897). *Pararaton*. VBG 49, pt. 2.

Broeze, J. A. (1979). "The merchant fleet of Java, 1820-1850." *Archipel* 18, pp. 251-69.

Brugmans, I. J., et. al., eds. (1960). *Nederlands-Indië onder Japanse bezetting* 2nd ed. Franeker: Wever.

de Bruin, Rodney (1967). "Sense and nonsense in the Three-A Movement." Paper presented at the 27th International Congress of Orientalists, 1967.

_____ (1968). *De Seinendan in Indonesië*. Unpublished manuscript.

"Buah kongres jang kedua" (1941). *Terang Boelan* 3, 7 (July 1941), pp. 35-38.

Buiten de grenzen: sociologische opstellen aangeboden aan Prof. Dr. W. F. Wertheim (1971). Meppel: Boom.

Buitenweg, Hein [pseud. H. C. Meijer] (1964). *De laatste tempo doeloe.* The Hague: Servire.

———— (1966). *Soos en samenleving in tempo doeloe.* The Hague: Servire.

———— (1980). *Krokodillenstad.* Katwijk aan Zee: Servire.

Buku kenang-kenangan lima tahun Kota Besar Surabaja, 1950-1956 (1956). Surabaya: n.p.

Bung Hatta mengabdi pada tijita-tjita perdjoangan bangsa (1972). Jakarta: Panitia Peringatan Ulang Tahun Bung Hatta ke-70.

Bunga rampai perjuangan dan pengorbanan (1982). Jakarta: Markas Besar Legiun Veteran RI.

Burger, D. H. (1939). *De ontsluiting van Java's binnenland voor het wereld verkeer.* Wageningen: Veenman.

Cabaton, A. (1911). *Java, Sumatra, and the other islands of the Dutch East Indies.* London: Fisher Unwin.

de Casparis, J. G. (1958). *Airlangga.* Surabaya: Universitas Airlangga.

Chailly-Bert, J. (1900). *Java et ses habitants.* Paris: Armand Colin.

Chandra, A. M. (1968). "10 Nopember dan obor mental generasi muda." *Sinar Harapan* November 9, 1968.

Cobban, James L. (1970). "The city on Java: an essay in historical geography." PhD Thesis, University of California at Berkeley.

———— (1974). "Uncontrolled urban settlement: the kampong question in Semarang, 1905-1940." BKI 130, 5, pp. 403-27.

Cohen, S. (1926). "De Stadsgemeente-Ordonnantie." KT 15, pp. 499-515.

Colijn, H . (1928). *Koloniale vraagstukken van heden en morgen.* Amsterdam: De Standaard.

Come to Java (1920). 2nd ed. Weltevreden: Vereeniging Toursitenverkeer.

Congress Indonesia Raya ke-1 (1932). Surabaya: *Soeara Oemoem.*

Cool M. F. J. (1941). *Structuur-veranderingen in Nederlandsch-Indië in de laatse vijf-en-twintig jaar.* Rotterdam: n.p.

Dahm, Bernard (1970). *Sukarno and the struggle for Indonesian independence.* Ithaca: Cornell University Press.

30[i.e., Dertig]jaar Perhimpoenan Indonesia, 1908-1938 (1938). Leiden: n.p.

Djajadiningrat, Idrus Nasir (1958). *The beginnings of the Indonesian-Dutch negotiations and the Hoge Veluwe talks.* Ithaca: Cornell University Modern Indonesia Project.

Djawa Rengo Seinendan Honbu (1945). *Tjara mempeladjari kepandaian memakai takeyari.* Jakarta: n.p.

Amar, Djen (1953). *Bandung lautan api.* Bandung: Dhiwantara.

Djojoadisuryo, Ahmad Subardjo (1978). *Kesadaran nasional.* Jakarta: Gunung Agung.

Djojoningrat, Ajat (1954) *Tekad.* Fifth printing. Surabaya: n. p., 1954.

van Doorn, J. A. and W. J. Hendrix (1970). *Ontsporing van geweld.* Rotterdam: Universitaire Pers.

Doulton, A. J. F. (1951). *The fighting cock: being the history of the twenty-third Indian Division, 1942-1947.* Aldershot: Gale and Poulden.

Drooglever, P. J. (1980). *De Vaderlandse Club, 1929-1942*. Franeker: Wever.

Duparc, H. J. A. (1972). *Trams en tramlijnen: de elektrische stadstrams op Java*. Rotterdam: Wyt.

El Gumanti, Hambdy comp. (1983). *Selamat jalan Bung Tomo*. Jakarta: Aksara.

Eerste verslag van de Kampongsverbeteringscommissie (1939). Batavia: Landsdrukkerij.

Embree, E. R. (1934). *Island India goes to school*. Chicago: University of Chicago Press.

45 [i.e., Empatpuluhlima] tahun Sumpah Pemuda (1974). Jakarta: Yayasan Gedung-gedung Sejarah.

Encyclopaedie van Nederlandsch-Indië (1917-1939). 2nd ed. The Hague: M. Nijhoff.

Encyclopedia of the social sciences (1933). 1st ed. New York: MacMillan.

Enquêtecommissie regeringsbeleid 1940-1945. Militair beleid (1956). Vols. 8A, 8B, 8CI, 8CII. 's-Gravenhage: Staatsdrukkerij.

Ensiklopedi Umum (1973). Yogyakarta: Yayasan Kanesius.

von Faber, G. H. (1931). *Oud Soerabaia*. Surabaya: Gemeente Soerabaja.

———— (1936). *Nieuw Soerabaia*. Surabaya: van Ingen.

———— (1937). *Korte handeleiding voor de bezichting van het Provinciaal en Stedelijk Museum*. Surabaya: van Ingen.

———— (1953). *Er werd een stad geboren*. Surabaya: kolff.

Fakta dan dokumen-dokumen untuk menjusun buku 'Indonesia memasuki gelanggan international' (1958). Uncorrected interim edition. Jakarta: Kementerian Luar Negeri.

Fagg, Donald R. (1958). "Authority and social structure: a study in Javanese bureaucracy." PhD Thesis, Harvard University.

Fox, James J., et. al., eds. (1980). *Indonesia: Australian Perspectives*. Canberra: Australian National University.

Frederick, William H. (1978). "Indonesian Urban Society in Transition: Surabaya, 1926-1946." PhD Thesis, University of Hawaii.

———— (1982). "In Memoriam: Sutomo." *Indonesia* 33 (April 1982), pp. 127-28.

———— (1983). "Hidden Change in Late Colonial Urban Society in Indonesia." JSEAS 14, 2 (September 1983), pp. 154-71.

Frederick, William H. and John McGlynn, trans. (1983). *Reflections on rebellion: stories from the Indonesian upheavals of 1948 and 1965*. Athens: Ohio University Southeast Asian Studies.

Geertz, Clifford (1959). *The religion of Java*. Glencoe: The Free Press.

———— (1965). *The social history of an Indonesian Town*. Cambridge: MIT Press, 1965.

Gemeenteblad Soerabaja.

Geschiere, P. L. (1969) "De meningsvorming over het onderwijsprobleem in de Nederlands-Indische samenleving van de 20e eeuw; de controverse

'Westersch' of 'nationaal' onderwijs." *Bijdragen voor de geschiedenis der Nederlanden* 20, 1 (1968/1969), pp. 43-86.

van Geuns, M. (1911). *Soerabaja's strijd om een haven.* Surabaya: Soerabajasch Handelsblad.

de Graaf, H. J. (1941). "Soerabaja in de XVIII eeuw, van Koninkrijk tot Regentschap." *Djawa* 21,3 (May 1941), pp. 198-225.

——— (1949). *Geschiedenis van Indonesië.* The Hague: van Hoeve.

——— (1958). *De regering van Sultan Agung, vorst van Mataram 1613-1645.* The Hague: M. Nijhoff.

de Graaf, H. J. and Th. G. Th. Pigeaud (1974). *De eerste Moslimse vorstendommen op Java.* 's-Gravenhage: M. Nijhoff.

Gobée E. and C. Adriaanse, eds. (1965). *Ambtelijke adviezen van C. Snouck Hurgronje, 1889-1936.* 3 vols. 's-Gravenhage: M. Nijhoff.

Gonggrijp, G. (1927). "De belastingdruk op de inlandse bevolking en haar economise toestand." KT 16, pp. 159-69.

Goto Kenichi (1976). "Life and death of 'Abdul Rachman' (1906-1949): one aspect of Japanese-Indonesian relationships." *Indonesia* 22 (October 1976), pp. 57-68.

——— (1977). *Hi no umi no tsuyo; aru Ajia shugisha no ruten no kiketsu.* Tokyo: Jijitsu Shinsha.

Groeneveldt, W. P., trans. and comp. (1880). *Notes on the Malay Archipelago and Malacca, compiled from Chinese sources.* VBG 39, part 1.

Gunawan, Basuki (1971). "Aliran en sociale structuur." In *Buiten de grenzen:* 69-85.

Gunseikanbu (1943a). *Boekoe tentang minboku.* Jakarta: n.p.

Gunseikanbu (1943b). *Pemberitahoean tentang tjara mendjalankan* [*roekoen tetangga-tonarigumi*]. Jakarta: n.p.

——— (1944a). *Boekoe pengempoelan oendang-oendang* Jakarta: Balai Poestaka.

——— (1944b). *Boekoe petoendjoek praktek teknik bagi pemimpin seinendan.* Jakarta: n.p.

Hageman, J. (1858). "Bijdragen tot de kennis van de Residentie Soerabaja." TvNI 20, 2, pp. 86-104.

——— (1859). "Bijdragen tot de kennis van de Residentie Soerabaja." TvNI 21, 1, pp. 17-34, 105-28, and 129-64.

——— (1860). "Bijdragen tot de kennis van de Residentie Soerabaja." TvNI 22, 1, pp. 267-77.

Hamaguchi E. (1946). "De oorlog in Grooter Oost Asië en de zuikerindustrie in de zuidelijke gebieden." Trans. G. Rodenburg. EWvNI 12, 33 (October 26, 1946), p. 310.

Hanifa, Abu (1972). *Tales of a revolution.* Sydney: Angus and Robertson.

Hatta Mohammad (1952). *Verspreide geschriften.* Amsterdam: van der Peet.

——— (1953). *Kumpulan karangan.* Vol. I. Jakarta: Penerbitan dan Balai Buku Indonesia.

_____ (1971). *The Putera reports; problems in Japanese-Indonesian wartime cooperation.* Trans. and intro. by William H. Frederick. Ithaca: Cornell University Modern Indonesia Project.

Holt, Claire, et. al., eds. (1972). *Culture and politics in Indonesia.* Ithaca: Cornell University Press.

Idenburg, P. J. A. "Het Nederlandse antwoord op het Indonesische nationalisme." In Baudet and Brugmans, pp. 121–51.

Idrus (1948). *Dari Ave Maria ke Djalan Lain ke Roma.* Jakarta: Balai Pustaka.

_____ (1968). "Surabaya." Trans. Mrs. S. U. Nababan and Benedict Anderson. *Indonesia* 5 (April 1968), pp. 1–28.

"De ijsindustrie op Java tijdens de Japansche bezetting" (1946). EWvNI 12, 13 (October 12, 1946), pp. 289–90.

Ikhtisar keadaan politik Hindia-Belanda tahun 1839–1848 (1972). Jakarta: Arsip Nasional Republik Indonesia.

Indonesia, Kementerian Penerangan (1953). *Republik Indonesia: Propinsi Djawa Timur.* Malang: Paragon.

The Indonesian revolution. Conference papers (1986). Utrecht: Utrechtse Historische Cahiers 7, 2/3.

Ingleson, John (1981a). " 'Bound hand and food': railway workers and the 1923 strike in Java." *Indonesia* 31 (April 1981), pp. 53–88.

_____ (1981b). "Worker consciousness and labor unions in colonial Java." PA 54, 3 (Fall 1981), pp. 485–501.

_____ (1983). "Life and work in colonial cities: harbour workers in Java in the 1910s and 1920s." *Modern Asian Studies* 17, 3 (1983), pp. 455–76.

_____ (1986). *In search of justice: workers and unions in colonial Java, 1908–1926.* Singapore: Oxford University Press.

Irikura, James. comp. (1956). *Southeast Asia: selected annotated bibliography of Japanese publications.* New Haven: Yale University Southeast Asia Studies.

Iskandar, Nur Sutan (1937). *Naraka dunia.* Batavia: Balai Poestaka.

Issatriadi (1973). *Usaha pendekatan dalam mencari hari jadi Surabaya.* Mimeo. Surabaya: Team Penelitian Hari Jadi Surabaya.

J. H. B. (1946). "Sailor in Sourabaya." *Blackwood's Magazine* 260, 1570 (August 1946), pp. 73–84.

Jaarsma, S. (1936). *Grond voor der Nederlander.* 2nd printing. Surabaya: De Toekomst.

_____ (1938). *Empirebuilding door Nederlander middenstander.* 2nd printing. Surabaya: De Toekomst.

Jaarverslag Oost-Java.

Jacobs, Hans and Jan Roelands (1970). *Indisch ABC: een documentaire over historie en samenleving van Nederland-Indië-Indonesia.* Amsterdam: Arbeiderspers.

Japanese Military Administration in Indonesia (1963). Washington, D.C.: Joint Publications Research Service.

Jong, C. G. E. (1933). *De organisatie de politie in Nederlandsch-Indië.* Leiden: Luctor et Emergo.

Kahin, Audrey R., ed. (1985). *Regional dynamics of the Indonesian revolution.* Honolulu: University of Hawaii Press.

Kahin, George McT. (1952). *Nationalism and revolution in Indonesia.* Ithaca: Cornell University Press.

Kamadjaja (1964). *Zaman edan: suatu studi tentang buku Kalatida dari R. Ng. Ranggawarsita.* Yogyakarta: UIP.

Kan Po.

Kanahele, George S. (1967). "The Japanese occupation of Indonesia: prelude to independence." PhD Thesis, Cornell University.

———— (1977). *Nihon gunsei to Indonesia no dokuritsu.* Tokyo: Ho Shuppansha.

Kartodirdjo, Sartono (1972). "Agrarian redicalism on Java: its setting and development." In Holt, et. al., eds., pp. 71-125.

———— (1973). *Protest movements in rural Java.* Singapore: Oxford University Press.

———— (1974). "Bureaucracy and aristocracy. The Indonesian experience in the nineteenth century." *Archipel* 7, pp. 151-68.

Kaslan MS (1972). Unpublished autobiographical manuscript.

van Kempen, Th. W. (1926). "Over het kampungvraagstuk in de groote Indische stadsgemeenten." KT 16, pp. 441-53.

Kertapati, Sidik (1961). *Sekitar proklamasi 17 Agustus 1945.* 2nd ed. Jakarta: Pembaruan.

"Ketika warna biru bendera Belanda dirobek" (1981). *GEMA Angkatan 45* 44/50 (July 1980—January 1981), pp. 145-49.

Kerchman, F. W. M., comp. (1930). *25 jaren decentralisatie.* Weltevreden: Kolff.

Kinoshita Hajime (1961). *Marudeka.* Tokyo: Nagai Shuppansha.

Kirby, S. Woodburn (1969). *The war against Japan.* 5 vols. London: HMSO.

Kishi Koichi, et. al. (1959). *Indonesia ni okeru Nihon gunsei no kenkyu.* Tokyo: Waseda University Okuma Institute of Social Sciences.

Kreutzer, R. (1981). *The Madiun Affair: Hatta's betrayal of Indonesia's first social revolution.* Townsville: James Cook University Centre for South East Asian Studies.

Koentjaraningrat. *Javanese culture.* Singapore: Oxford University Press, 1985.

van Kol, H. (1903). *Uit onze koloniën.* Leiden: Sijthoff.

Konperensi Djawa Timor, Bondowoso 1948 (1948). Surabaya: Suprapto.

Korver, A. P. E. (1982). *Sarekat Islam, 1912-1916.* Amsterdam: Universiteit van Amsterdam, Historisch Seminarium.

Kurasawa Aiko (1986), "Japanese occupation and leadership changes in Javanese villages," in *The Indonesian revolution,* pp. 57-78.

Kuroda Hidetoshi (1952), *Gunsei.* Tokyo: Gakufushoin.

Laporan politik tahun 1837. Jakarta: Arsip Nasional Republik Indonesia.

Larson, George D. (1971). "Peta: the early origins of the Indonesian army." MA Thesis, University of Hawaii.

Leclerc, Jacques (1978). "La condition du parti: révolutionnaries Indonesiens à la recherche d'un identité (1928-1948)." *Cultures et Développment* 10, 1, p. 3-70.

Liddle, R. William (1977). *Cultural and class politics in New Order Indonesia*. Singapore: ISEAS.

Locher-Scholten, Elsbeth (1971). "De Stuw, tijdstekening en teken des tijds." TvG 84, 1, pp. 36-65.

_____ (1981). *Ethiek in fragmenten*. Utrecht: H and S.

Lombard, Denys (1976). "Sumbangan kepada sejarah kota-kota di Asia Tenggara." *Masjarakat Indonesia* 3, 1, pp. 51-69.

Long, Gavin (1963). *The final campaigns: Australia in the war of 1939-1945*. Canberra: Australian War Memorial.

Lucas, Anton, ed. (1986). *Local opposition and underground resistance to the Japanese in Java, 1942-1945*. Victoria: Monash University Centre of Southeast Asian Studies.

Ma Huan. *Yeng-yai sheng-lan, "The overall survey of the ocean's shores."* Trans. and ed. J. V. Mills. Cambridge: Cambridge University Press.

Malaka, Tan (1925). *Naar de Repoeblik Indonesia*. N.p.

Mangkupradja, Gatot (1968). "The Peta and my relations with the Japanese." *Indonesia* 5 (April 1968), pp. 105-34.

Mangoendiprodjo, H. R. Moehammad "Kisah pertempuran di Surabaya pada tanggal 30 Oktober dan 10 Nopember 1945." in *Bunga rampai*, pp. 262-75.

Marilah membela tanah air kita dengan darah dagining kita! (1944). Jakarta: Osamu 1602 Butai.

Marine-Sociëteit "Modderlust" 1867-1917 (1917). Amsterdam: van Heteren

McCoy, Alfred W., ed. (1980). *Southeast Asia under Japanese occupation*. New Haven: Yale University Southeast Asia Studies.

McVey, Ruth T. (1965). *The rise of Indonesian communism*. Ithaca: Cornell University Press.

Meijer, D. H. (1950). "Over het bendewezen op Java." *Indonesië* 3, pp. 178-89.

Meijer Ranneft, J. W. (1921). *De toemkomst ven het B. B.* Buitenzorg: Archipel.

Meilink-Roelofs, M. A. P. (1962). *Asian trade and European influence in the Indonesian archipelago between 1500 and about 1630*. The Hague: M. Nijhoff.

Memori serah jabatan 1921-1930, Jawa Timur dan Tanah Kerajaaan (1978). Jakarta: Arsip Nasional Republik Indonesia.

Milone, Pauline D. (1966). *Urban areas in Indonesia: administrative and census concepts*. Berkeley: University of California, Institute of International Studies.

Moentallip, A. (1946). "Dewan Perdjoeangan Rakjat Indonesia." *Bakti* 13 (8–17–46), pp. 18–19.

Moertono, Soemarsaid (1968). *State and statecraft in old Java: a study of the later Mataram period, 16th to 19th century.* Ithaca: Cornell University Modern Indonesia Project.

Moestopo (1960). *Sosialismus à la Indonesia.* Jakarta: n.p.

van Moll, J. F. A. C. (1905). "De onlusten in Sidoardjo." *Archief van de Java Suikerindustrie* 13, Bijblad 33, pp. 579–607.

Mona, Matu [pseud. Hasbullah Parinduri] (1947). "Arek Soerobojo." Loekisan Soeasana 1, 5 (December 1946–January 1947), pp. 1–48.

Muhaimin, Yahya A. "Politics, national businessmen and the Indonesian middle class." *Prisma*

Muljana, Slamet (1958). Runtuhnja keradjaan Hindu-Djawa dan timbulnja negaranegara Islam di Nusantara. Jakarta: Bhratara.

Mustoffa, Sumono, comp. (1986). *Sukarni dalam kenangan teman-temannya* Jakarta: Sinar Harapan, 1986.

Nagazumi Akira (1972). *The dawn of Indonesian nationalism.* Tokyo: Institute of Developing Economies.

Nakamura Mitsuo (1970). "General Imamura and the early period of Japanese occupation." *Indonesia* 10 (October 1970), pp. 1–26.

Nasution, A. H. (1970). *Tentara Nasional Indonesia.* 3 vols. 2nd ed. Jakarta: Seruling Masa.

―――― (1976). *10 Nopember 1945; Surabaya.* Bandung: Angkasa.

―――― (1979). *Sekitar perang kemerdekaan Indonesian.* 11 vols. Bandung: Angkasa.

De Nederlands Gravendienst (1950). *De gravenserie in Zuid-West Pacific.* Vol. 4. Bandung: n.p.

The Netherlands, Department van Defensie, Hoofdkwartier van de Generale Staf, Sectie Krijgsgeschiedenis (1961). *Nederlands Indië contra Japan.* Vol. 7, The Hague, Staatsdrukkerij.

Nishimura Kurazo (1962). *Surabaya no doran.* Yokohama: n.p.

―――― (1976). *Surabaya no shitai no kikan.* Tokyo: Eiko Shuppansha.

Nix, Thomas (1949). *Stedebouw in Indonesië en de stedebouwkundige vormgeving.* Bandung: n.p.

"Njala api 10 Nopember—mengenal orang dibalik lajar." (1968) Sinar Harapan November 9, 1968.

Noehadi (1968). "Poetera (Poetera Tenaga Rakjat) Maret 1943–Maret 1944." BA Thesis, Universitas Indonesia.

Notulen en gemeentebladen van de openbare vergaderingen van den Stadsgemeenteraad van Soerabaja.

Notosusanto, Nugroho (1979a). *The Peta army during the Japanese occupation of Indonesia.* Tokyo: Waseda University Press.

―――― (1979b). *Tentara Peta jaman pendudukan Jepang di Indonesia.* Jakarta: Gramedia.

―――― (ed.) (1985). *Pertempuran Surabaya.* Jakarta: Mutiara Sumber Widya.

Okano Shigezo (1942). *Nanyo no seikatsu kiroku*. Tokyo: Kinjo Shuppansha.

O'Malley, William J. (1980). "Second thoughts on Indonesian nationalism." In Fox et. al., pp. 601-14.

Onghokham (1968). "Runtuhnja Hindia Belanda." PhD Thesis, Universitas Indonesia.

――――― (1983). *Rakyat dan negara*. Jakarta: LP3ES and Sinar Harapan.

Orang Indonesia jang terkemoeka di Djawa (1944). Jakarta: Gunseikanbu.

van Oorschot, W. P. H. (1936). *De autonomie van de gemeente in Nederland en in Nederlandsch-Indië*. Utrecht: Oosthoek's Uitgevers.

Oost-Java gedenkboek; de 4e Infanterie-Brigade (1950). Tilburg: Bergmans.

Overdijkink, G. W. (1946). *Het Indonesische probleem: de feiten*. Vol. 2. 's-Gravenhage: M. Nijhoff.

Overzicht van de Inlandsche en Maleisch-Chineesche Pers.

Pakpahan, G. (1947). *1261 hari dibawah sinar matahari terbit*. Jakarta: n.p.

Parera Frans M.; comp. (1982). *Bung Tomo dari 10 Nopember 1945 ke Orde Baru*. Jakarta: Gramedia.

Parrott, J. G. A. (1970). "Who killed Brigadier Mallaby?" *Indonesia* 20 (April 1970), pp. 87-111.

――――― (1977). "The role of the 49th Indian Infantry Brigade in Surabaya, 25 October-10 November 1945." MA Thesis, Monash University.

Peacock, James L. (1967). "Anti-Dutch, anti-Moslem drama among Surabaya proletarians: a description of performances and responses." *Indonesia* 4 (October 1967), pp. 44-73.

――――― (1968). *Rites of modernization*. Chicago: University of Chicago Press.

Peraturan dasar persatuan pamong desa Indonesia (1959). Jakarta: PDI.

Petrus Blumberger, J. Th. (1931). *De nationalistische beweging in Nederlandsch-Indië. Haarlem: Tjeenk Willink*.

――――― (1935). *De communistische beweging in Nederlandsche-Indië*. Haarlem: Tjeenk-Willink.

Pigeaud, Th. G. Th. (1938). *Javaanse volksvertoningen*. Batavia: Volkslectuur.

――――― (1964). *Java in the Fourteenth Century*. 5 vols. The Hague: M. Nijhoff.

――――― (1970). *The literature of Java*. 3 vols. The Hague: M. Nijhoff.

Pires, Tomé (1944). *The Suma Oriental of Tomé Pires*. 2 vols. Ed. and trans. by A. Cortesao. London: Hakluyt Society.

van der Plas, Ch. O. (1938). "Opmerkingen over de desa in de inlandsche gemeente." In *Het B. B. Congress*, pp. 273-95.

Pluvier, Jan (1953). *Overzicht van de ontwikkeling der nationalistische beweging in Indonesië*. The Hague: van Hoeve.

Provincieblad Oost-Java.

Pugh, L. H. D. (1948). "Sourabaia—(NEI)—1945." *Journal of the Royal Artillery* 75, 4 (November 1948), pp. 320-49.

Quinn, George (1983). "The case of the invisible literature: power, scholarship, and contemporary Javanese writing." *Indonesia*: 35 (April 1983), pp. 1-36.

Raad Sinoman. Perhimpoenan pendoedoek kampoeng Dinojotangsi dan Darmoredjo (1933). Unpublished typescript.

Radjab, A. (1983) *TRIP dan perang kemerdekaan.* Surabaya: Kasnendra Suminar.

Raffles, Sir Stamford (1965). *History of Java.* Fascimile edition. 2 vols. London: Oxford University Press.

Rapport van het hoofd van het Kantor van Arbeid over de arbeidtoestanden in de metaal industrie te Soerabaja (1926) Weltevreden: LandsDrukkerij.

Rata, Abdul Wahid (1938). *Riwayat penghidoepan Dr. Soetomo dan perjoeangannja.* Medan: Sjarikat Tapanoeli.

Reid, Anthony J. S. (1974). *Indonesian national revolution.* Hawthorne, Victoria: Longmans.

———— (1975). "The Japanese occupation and rival Indonesian elites: northern Sumatra in 1942." JAS 35, 1 (November 1975), pp. 49-62.

———— (1979). *The blood of the people: revolution and the end of traditional rule in northern Sumatra.* London: Oxford University Press.

———— (1980). "The structure of cities in Southeast Asia, fifteenth to seventeenth centuries." JSEAS 9, 2 (August 1980), pp. 235-50.

Reid, Anthony J. S. and David Marr, eds. (1979). *Perceptions of the past in Southeast Asia.* Singapore: Heinemann.

Reid, Anthony J. S. and Akira Oki, eds. (1986). *The Japanese experience in Indonesia. Selected Memoirs of 1942-1945.* Athens: Ohio University Monographs in International Studies.

"Riwayat Dr. Mas Moerdjani" (1961). Unpublished typescript.

"Riwayat hidup R. A. Siti Soedari" (1954) Unpublished typescript.

"Riwayat hidup Radjamin Nasution" (1950). Unpublished typescript.

"De rijstpositie van Nederlands-Indië" (1946). EWvNI 12, 11 (May 25, 1946), pp. 81-85.

Ritsma, van Eck S. (1929). *Bezinning nopens Nederland's koloniale staatkunde.* Haarlem: Vragen des Tijds.

Rosidi, Ajip (1968). "A Japanese." Trans. by William H. Frederick. *Indonesia* 6 (October 1968). pp. 82-87.

Rodenburg, G. (1946) "Een Japansch oordeel over de Java rijstcultuur." EWvNI 12, 33 (October 26, 1946), p. 310.

Rothenbuhler, F. J. (1882). "Rapport van het staat en gesteldheid van het landschap Sourabaia." VBG 41, part 3.

Rouffaer, G. P. and J. W. Ijzerman, eds. (1929). *De eerste schipvaart der Nederlanders naar Oost-Indië.* 3 vols. 's-Gravenhage: M. Nijhoff.

Rutgers, H. C. (1928). *Wat ik op mijn Indische reis zag. Kampen: Kok.*

Said, Salim (1982). *Profil dunia film Indonesia.* Jakarta: Grafitipers.

Sam Karya Bhirawa Anoraga: sedjarah militer KODAM VIII/Bradwidjaja (1968). Malang: SEMDAN VIII/ Brawidjaja.

BIBLIOGRAPHY

Sapiya, M. (1946). "Pengalaman saja dalam revolusi." *Bakti* 17, pp. 16-18; 18, pp. 12-14; 19, pp. 16-17; 20, pp. 16-17; 21, pp. 12-14; 22, pp. 12-13.
———— (1960) *Sedjarah pemberontakan di Kapal Tudjuh.* Jakarta: n.p.
Sastroamidjojo, Ali (1974). *Tonggak-tonggak di perdjalananku.* Jakarta: Kinta.
Scherer, Savitri P. (1975). "Harmony and dissonance: early nationalist thought in Java." MA Thesis, Cornell University.
Schouten, C., comp. (1947). *RAPWI: genieskundig overzicht.* Mimeo, n.p.
Schrieke, B. (1957). *Indonesian sociological studies.* Vol. 2, Bandung: van Hoeve.
Sedjarah singkat perdjuangan bersendjata bangsa Indonesia (1964). Jakarta: Staf Angkatan Bersendjata.
Sejarah pertempuran lima hari (1977). Semarang: Suara Merdeka.
Setahun Negara Djawa Timur (1949). Surabaya: Djabatan Penerangan Negara Djawa Timur.
Setiadijaya, Barlan (1985). *Merdeka atau mati di Surabaya, 1945* Vol. 1. Jakarta: Widyaswara Kewiraan.
Shibata Yaichiro (1976). *Shibata shirei chokan no shuki.* Tokyo: n.p.
"Siapa sebenarnya pemuda yang merobek bendera rood wit blauw diatas Oranje Hotel?" (1975) BB November 12, 1974.
Sihombing, O. D. P. (1962). *Pemuda Indonesia menentang fasisme Jepang.* Jakarta: Sinar Djaya.
Sillevis Smit, J. H. (1946). *Met onze Mariniers naar Indië.* Amsterdam: ten Have.
Silverstein, Josef, ed. (1966), *Southeast Asia in World War II; four essays.* New Haven: Yale University, Southeast Asia Studies.
Sjarifuddin, Amir (1945). "Pengalaman saya dalam tahanan Djepang." *Merdeka,* 7 October 1945.
Sluimers, L. E. (1968). " 'Nieuwe Orde' op Java." BKI 124, 3, pp. 336-67.
———— (1971). "Enkele theoretische beschouwingen over de Japanse bezettingsperiode op Java." In *Buiten de grenzen,* pp. 240-66.
———— (1983). *The rice situation in Java and Madura during the Japanese era, 1942-1945.* Amsterdam: Universiteit van Amsterdam, Anthropologisch-Sociologisch Centrum.
Smail, John R. W. (1964) *Bandung in the early revolution.* Ithaca: Cornell University Modern Indonesia Project.
Soebagiyo I. N. (1977). *Sejarah pers di Indonesia.* Jakarta: Grafitipers.
Soedarsono (1974). "Gerakan kepanduan di Indonesia." In *Empatpuluhlima tahun,* pp. 269-76.
Soekadri, Heru (1977). *Dari Hujanggaluh ke Curabhaya.* Surabaja: IKIP Surabaya.
Soemantro (1961). "Sepuluh Nopember '45 di Surabaja." *Penelitian Sedjarah* 2, 4 (September 1961), pp. 2-6.
"Soerabaya mempertahankan Indonesia Merdeka" (1946). *Bakti* August 19-10, 1946.

Soeroso (1971a). "Hari djadi Kotamadya Surabaja—mengapa 1 April?" *Semeru* 9, 26 (July 1971), pp. 26–27.

—— (1971b). "Mengapa 1 April, 1906, Surabaja mendjadi Stadsgemeente?" *Gapura* 4, 3, pp. 6–8.

Soeryaningrat, Soewardi [Ki Hadjar Dewantara] (1913). "Als ik een Nederlander was." *De Expres,* July 19, 1913.

Soetedjo (1940). "Kemanoesiaan dan masjarakat." SP 5, 2, pp. 60–64; 3, pp. 93–96; 4, pp. 121–25.

Soetomo (1934). *Kenang-kenangan.* Surabaya: n.p.

—— (1937). *Poespita mantja negara.* Surabaya: Soeara Oemoem.

—— (1959). *Puspa rinontje.* 4th ed. Surabaya: Sumber Kemadjuan Rakjat.

—— (1987). *Toward a glorious Indonesia. Reiminiscences and Observations of Dr. Soetomo.* Edited, annotated and introduced by P. W. van der Veur. Athens: Ohio University Monographs in International Studies.

Soetomo, et. al. (1935). *Penoentoen oentoek mereka jang bersanggoep menghamba pada tanah air dan bangsa dengan azas dan dasar kebatinan P.B.I.* Mimeo. Batavia: n.p.

Soetrisno, Loekman "Changes in Indonesia's middle class." *Prisma*

Sosrodihardjo, Sudjito (1968). *Perobahan struktur masjarakat di Djawa.* Yogyakarta: Sekip.

van Sprang, Alfred (1946). *En Soekarno lacht . . . !.* 's-Gravenhage: van Hoeve.

Staatsblad van Nederlandsch-Indië.

Stadsvormingsordonnantie stadsgemeenten Java (1938). Batavia: Landsdrukkerij.

Statistische berichten der Gemeente Soerabaja 1927 (1928). Surabaya: Gemeente Soerabaja.

Statistische zakboekje voor Nederlandscsh Indië, 1939. Batavia: Kolff.

Stevens, J. A. and Ben Grevedamme (1947). *Vrij.* Deventer: n.p.

Stromquist, Sheldon (1967). "The communist uprisings of 1926–1927 in Indonesia: a reinterpretation." JSEAH 8, 2 (September 1967), pp. 189–200.

Suhadi (1970). "Baru sekarang diketahui pelaku-pelaku jang mengibarkan merahputih." *Liberty* 897 (November 14, 1970), pp. 53–55.

Sukarno (1975). *Indonesia accuses!* Trans. Roger Paget. Kuala Lumpur: Oxford University Press.

Supardi, Imam (1951). *Dr. Soetomo, riwayat hidup dan perdjuangannja.* Jakarta: Djambatan.

Surabaja baru (1956). Surabaya: n.p.

Sutherland, Heather (1973). "Notes on Java's Regent families, part 1." *Indonesia* 16 (October 1973), pp. 113–48.

—— (1974). "Notes on Java's Regent families, part 2." *Indonesia* 17 (April 1974), pp. 1–42.

—— (1975). "The priyayi." *Indonesia* 19 (April 1975), pp. 57–78.

—— (1979). *The making of a bureaucratic elite.* Singapore: Heinemann.

Sutjiantiningsih (1975). *Gubernor Suryo*. Jakarta: DP&K, Proyek Biografi Pahlawan Nasional.

Sutomo (1946). *Kepada bangsakoe*. N.p.

——— (1950). *Kenangan bahagia*. Yogyakarta: Balapan.

——— (1951). *10 Nopember*. Jakarta: Balapan.

——— (1952). *Kemana bekas pedjuang bersendjata?* Jakarta: Balapan.

Sutomo MS. Untitled and undated manuscript. Microfilm #903, Echols Collection, Cornell University Library.

Sutter, John O. (1959). *Indonesianisasi: politics in a changing economy, 1940-1955*. 3 vols. Ithaca: Cornell University Modern Indonesia Project.

Takatu A. (1944). *Dari sekolah ke medan perang*. Jakarta: Poesat Keboedajaan.

Takeda Shigesaburo, ed. (1958). *Djagatara kanra ran-in jidai hojin no Asiato*. Nagasaki: n.p.

Tantri, K'tut [pseud.] (1960). *Revolt in paradise*. London: Heinemann.

Taylor, Jean S. (1968). "Some Indonesian perceptions of the revolution. A study in Indonesian historiography." MA Thesis, University of Melbourne.

Thomas, David A. (1969). *The battle of the Java Sea*. London: Deutsch, Stein and Day.

Thompson, John (1946). *Hubbub in Java*. Sydney: Currawong.

Thomson, Eliza (1965). *Setengah mati (Half dood)*. Amsterdam: van Ditmar.

Tichelman, Fritjof (1970). "De opkomst en neergang van de NSB in Indonesia." *VN* May 2, 1970, p. 23; May 16, 1970, pp. 21 and 23.

——— (1980). *The social evolution of Indonesia: the Asiatic mode of production and its legacy*. The Hague: M. Nijhoff.

Tillema, H. F. (1915-1916). *Kromoblanda*. 2 vols. Semarang: n.p.

Timur, Soenarto (1973). *Mythos Cura-bhaya*. Mimeo. Surabaya: Kotamadya Surabaya.

Toer, Pramoedya Ananta (1980a). *Bumi manusia*. Jakarta: Hasta Mitra.

——— (1980b). *Anak semua bangsa*. Jakarta: Hasta Mitra.

Vanickova, E. (1965). "A study of the Javanese ketoprak." *Archiv Orientalni* 33, pp. 397-450.

Van Niel, Robert (1960). *The emergence of the modern Indonesian elite*. The Hague: van Hoeve.

Carla Vermeer-Van Berkum (1980). *Kon ik maar een gewoon meisje zijn*. Amsterdam: Elsevier.

Verordeningen Gemeente Soerabaja (1934). 4 vols. Surabaya: Gemeente Soerabaja.

Verslag omtrent de koeliemoeilijkheden in de haven van Soerabaja ged. Aug./Sept. 1921 (1922). Surabaya: De Handelsvereeniging.

Verslag van der toestand der stadsgemeente Soerabaja. Annual.

Veth, B. (1900). *Het leven in Nederlandsch-Indië*. Amsterdam: van Kempen.

Veth, P. J. (1882). *Java, Geographisch, ethnologisch, historisch*. 3 vols. Haarlem: Bohn.

van der Veur, Paul W. (1981). *Dr. Soetomo: pandangan dan cita-cita untuk bangsanya.* Surabaya: Universitas Airlangga.

de Vries, H. M. (1928). *The importance of Java, seen from the air.* Batavia: Kolff.

de Waal. W. F. (1940). *Indisch of Rijksburgerschap?* Surabaya: E. Fuhri.

van der Wal. S. L. (1968a). "De Nationaal-Socialistische Beweging in Nederlands-Indië." BMHG 82, pp. 35-58

―――― (1968b). *Het Onderwijsbeleid in Nederlands-Indië.* Groningen: J. B. Wolters.

van der Wal, S. L., ed. and comp. (1979-). *Officiële bescheiden betreffende de Nederlands-Indonesische betrekkingen 1945-1950.* 13 vols. 's-Gravenhage: M. Nijhoff.

Wawardi, R. (195?). "Perhimpunan Rukun Tani." Undated, unpublished typescript.

―――― (1971a). "Sedjarah hidup dan perdjuangan almarhum Dr. Soetomo." Unpublished typescript.

―――― (1971b). "Sikap bangsa Indonesia terhadap Jepang sebelum Perang Dunia ke-II." Unpublished typescript.

Wehl, David (1948). *The birth of Indonesia.* London: Allen and Unwin.

Wertheim, Willem F. (1955). "Changes in Indonesia's social stratification." PA 28, 1, pp. 41-52.

―――― (1956). *"Indonesian society in transition."* 2nd ed. Bandung: Semur Bandung.

Wertheim, Willem F., et. al., eds. (1958). *The Indonesian town.* The Hague: van Hoeve.

Wertheim, Willem F., and the Siauw Giap (1962). "Social change in Java, 1900-1930." PA 35, 3, pp. 223-47.

Wild, Colin and Peter Carey, eds. (1986). *Gelora api revolusi; sebuah antologi sejarah.* Jakarta: Gramedia.

Wijnmaalen, H. J. (1977). "Bestuursambtenaar in Oost-Java, 1926-1932." In *Besturen overzee,* pp. 176-98.

Wirjopranoto, Sukardjo (1938). *Juni 1938―Kongres Bahasa Indonesia di Soerakarta-Hadiningrat; Juli 1938―Fractie National Volksraad mempergoenakan bahasa Indonesia dalam pemandangan oemoem.* Mimeo. Malang: Dr. Seotomo Foods.

Wirjosuparto, Sutjipto (1958). *Apa sebabnja Kediri dan daerah sekitarnja tampil kemuka dalam sedjarah?* Malang: Kongres Ilmu Pengetahuan Nasional.

Wiselius, J. A. B. (1872). "Djajabaja, zijn leven en profitieën." BKI 8, pp. 172-217.

Woestoff, P. F. (1915). *De Indische Decentralisatie-Wetgeving.* Leiden: n.p.

Woodside, Alexander (1971). "The development of social organizations in Vietnamese cities in the late colonial period." PA 44, 1, pp. 39-64.

Wormser, C. W., comp. (1943). *Zo leven wij in Indië.* 3rd printing. Deventer: van Hoeve.

van Wulfften-Palthé, P. M. (1950). *Over het bendewezen op Java*. Amsterdam: Rossen.

Yoga [pseud. Sajogia Hardjadinata] (1958). *Surabaja berdjuang*. 2nd ed. Surabaya: Fadjar.

Yong Mun Cheong (1982). *H. J. van Mook and Indonesian independence*. The Hague: M. Nijhoff.

Zijlmans, G. C. (1985). *Eindstrijd en ondergang van de Indische bestuursdienst*. Amsterdam: De Bataafsce Leeuw.

Zorab, G. (1946). "De zoogenaamde voorspellingen van Djojobojo, den Javansche Nostradamus." TvP 14, pp. 146–53.

■ Index

Abas, 222n.63

Abdoelkarim, H. [H. Abdulkarim], 221n.39.

Abdulgani, Ruslan, x, 43, 56, 57, 79n.112, 94, 164 ff., 172n.12, 180n.140, 183, 192, 198, 203, 204, 208, 221n.39, 229n.165, 231, 242, 243, 245, 257, 269n.32, 271n.51, 274n.92, 275n.123, 276n.124, 284; activities in early occupation, 160; family history, 26 ff.; pemuda populism and, 285.

Abdullah, 248.

Abdulrachim, 124n.101.

Action Committee, 198, 199.

Advisory councils, formed by Japanese, 140-141.

Air raid: practice, 117-118; shelters, 82, 119.

Al Kasjaf wal Fadjrie, 79n.103.

Al Irsyad, 14, 77n.78, 79n.103.

Alaydroes [Alaydrus], 221n.39.

Algemeene Studieclub, 79n.103.

Ali, Jamal, 164.

Ali, Mohammed, 75n.39, 130n.174.

Aliran, 235; concept of, 268n.24. See also, *golongan*.

AMACAB, 280.

Ambonese, 13, 211, 242.

Amiadji [Amiaji], 169, 248, 249, 272n.71.

Amin, Hasjim [Hasyim Amin], 208-210, 224n.89.

Angkatan Muda, 164-165, 179n.126, 198.

Angkatan Muda Committee, 165, 166, 167, 168, 169, 180n.140, 189, 198, 199, 203, 204, 229n.165, 242.

Angkatan Pemuda Indonesia, 211.

Angkatan Tua Indonesia, 253.

Ansor, 74n.22.

Arek Surabaya: attitudes toward: foreigners, 17, 32n.72, Japanese occupation, 118, ludruk, 65-66, intellectuals, 57, 60-62, 168, Japanese administration, 110-112, new *priyayi*, 36, 57, 60, 148, religion, 15, returning Dutch, 197, 281, taxes, 10; *becak* and, 111; BPRI and, 253; defined, 1, 6-7, 28n4, 29n.24, 30n.28; economic values of, 32n.69, 111, 113; Eurasians and, 20, 22, 26, 210; humor of, 48; Japanese and, 211-212; Japanese propaganda and, 138-139; Japanese view of, 90, 93, 103, 109, 118; *keibodan* and, 116-118; *kempeitai* and, 100; municipality and, 3-4, 10-11, 75n.44, 82-83; resistance to Allied forces, 265; revolution and, 287, 291-292; rice supply of in wartime, 101-102; *romusha* and, 104-105, 142; *segan*, feeling of, 22; *seinendan* and, 157; violence and, 233-234, 260, 261.

Arnowo, Doel [Dul Arnowo], 55, 69, 75n.42, 123n.92, 123n.94, 141, 168, 174n.31, 179n.125, 188, 189, 190, 191, 193, 199, 203, 205, 206,

propaganda and, 174n.27; Putera and, 136–138; *rampok* and, 87; scouting and, 67–68; *seinendan* and, 158–160; Three A and, 134–5; urban populace and, 292; violence and, 265; youth and, 67–68, 149 ff. *See also,* new *priyayi.*

Internment: Europeans by Japanese, 91; Europeans emerge from, 193–194; Dutch by Indonesians, 162, 239–240; Indonesians by British, 266.

Internatio Square, 263, 264.

Isbandi, 48.

ISI, 178n.70.

Ismoetiar [Ismutiar], 145, 173n.12, 269n.32.

Jago, 251.

Jakarta, 111, 117, 125n.114, 127n.134, 134, 140, 149, 153, 163, 164, 169, 170, 172n.10, 182, 183, 186, 187, 188, 190, 198, 202, 206, 207, 233, 237, 239, 246, 247, 254, 256, 258, 259, 263, 265, 266, 272n.64.

Jaman edan, 134.

Japanese: between Allies and Indonesians, 201; currency, 270n.37; disarmed, 257; Dutch and, 89, 91, 195–196, 123n.89; Dutch fear of, 84; expansionism of, 85; in Hokokai, 142; in prewar colony, 84–85; Indonesians and, 83, 92–93, intellectuals and, 85, 133; interned by Dutch, 85; interned by Indonesians, 216, 218; kampung folk and, 211; language: influence on Indonesian language, 173n.17, 176n.61, in schools, 107, 129n.168, lectures to *pangreh praja* in, 143; taught to: municipal employees, 99, *becak* drivers, 112; legal status of, prewar, 84;

ludruk and, 110; new *priyayi* and, 94; occupation: administration, 96 ff., continuities of, 293, failure of, 293, nature and evaluation, 293; peacekeepers at end of war, 184; police: 125–126n.125, cruelties of, 126n.129; policies, cultural, 105 ff.; prewar propaganda, 84; racism and, 105; revolution, role in the birth of, 293; role as liberator and ruler, 97; slaughter of, 231, 242; views of: intellectuals, 93, Indonesians, 85, 91, 97, 106, 118, 123n.89, 133, 201; productivity, 101; *becak* drivers, 112–113; *pangreh preja,* 95–96, 143; youth and, 149 ff., 161.

Jasin, Moh. [Moh. Yasin], 212, 269n.32.

Java War, 244.

Javaansche Padvinders Organisatie, 68.

Javanese Scouting Organization, 68.

Jawa Hokokai, *see* Hokokai.

Jawa Minshu Soryoku Kisshu Undo, *see* Putera.

Jombang, 110, 252.

Jong Java Padvinderij, 79n.103.

Jong Islamieten Bond, 79n.103.

Jong Java, 79n.103.

Jong Indonesische Padvinders Organisatie, 79n.103.

Jonosewojo [Yonosewoyo], 191, 239.

Journalism, 46–51, 75n.44, 138, 169, 245.

Joyoboyo prophecy, 27, 33n.76; among Dutch, 86.

Kalimantan, 196, 208.

Kalisosok prison, 240, 270n.44, 278.

Kamoes Marhaen, 50.

Kamoes Pergerakan, 76n.45.